John L. Mackay's Mentor commentary on Hosea is a rare thing: a commentary that is both scholarly and readable. The engagement with the text is thorough without ever getting over-complicated while the prose is consistently clear and vibrant. Even though all the questions you want addressed are addressed, you never feel like you are losing sight of the big picture. Hosea's message of God's deep love for his people and his covenantal commitment to them shine through. Meanwhile the regular reflection sections point in the direction of contemporary application. Preachers will find it a valuable guide to preaching Hosea.

TIM CHESTER,
The Porterbrook Network and The Crowded House Sheffield

A divine tragedy played on a human stage, Hosea portrays the heart of God like no other Old Testament prophet and Mackay exposes it brilliantly. Whether unveiling the richness of the historical record, the prophet's exalted Hebrew prose, or the anguish of a jilted lover, this commentary successfully maps the intersection of human faithlessness and God's relentless grace. Connecting the text to its contemporary setting and highlighting its prophetic function within the story of God's redemption of His people, within these pages one discovers a comprehensive treatment that every student who desires to understand Hosea and every preacher who aspires to explain it will be wise to consult.

HERSHAEL W. YORK,
Associate Dean, School of Theology,Victor & Louise Lester Professor of Preaching
The Southern Baptist Theological Seminary, Louisville, Kentucky

This is a remarkable commentary on a remarkable book of the Bible. Hosea had a difficult message to bring to a faithless people, and God made the prophet's own life a visual illustration of his message. In this commentary, full of characteristic attention to the original language, historical context and theological themes of the Book of Hosea, Professor Mackay makes the prophet speak afresh to us. Of help to all serious readers of the Bible, this book brings out the timeless significance of the ancient prophet, and is a welcome addition to the literature on Hosea.

IAIN D. CAMPBELL,
Minister of Point Free Church, Isle of Lewis.

This commentary is vintage Mackay! It combines first rate scholarship with warm evangelical exposition. It is clear, concise, well researched, and written from a pastoral and practical perspective. Professor Mackay is no ivory tower academician; that much is sure. He is engaging and undeniably relevant, and he quite obviously loves the very Scriptures that he seeks to expound. Every pastor and student of the Bible will want to get a copy of this valuable resource. No library should be without it.

Guy M. Richard,
Minister, First Presbyterian Church, Gulfport, Mississippi

Hosea

A Mentor Commentary

John L. Mackay

MENTOR

John L Mackay is Professor of Old Testament at Free Church College Edinburgh. He is an internationally respected Old Testament Scholar who has written several Old Testament commentaries including Focus on the Bible commentaries on *Jonah, Micah, Nahum, Habbakuk & Zephaniah*(ISBN 978-1-84550-345-1) and, *Haggai, Zechariah & Malachi* (ISBN 978-1-85792-067-3) and Mentor commentaries on *Exodus* (ISBN 978-1-85792-6419), *Lamentations* (ISBN 978-1-84550-363-5) and two volumes on *Jeremiah* (Vol. 1 ISBN 978-1-857910-9379, Vol. 2 ISBN 978-1-85792-938-6),

Unless otherwise stated, all biblical quotations are the author's own translations.

ISBN 978-1-84550-634-6

10 9 8 7 6 5 4 3 2 1

Published in 2012
in the
Mentor Imprint
by
Christian Focus Publications,
Geanies House, Fearn, Tain,
Ross-shire, IV20 1TW, Great Britain

www.christianfocus.com

Cover Design by Daniel Van Straaten

Printed and Bound by MPG, Cornwall

INTRODUCTION

1. The Prophets of Israel 8
2. The End of the Northern Kingdom 10
3. The Prophet and His Ministry 18
4. Composition and Style 21
5. Theological Themes 28

COMMENTARY

I. A Broken Marriage (1:1–3:5) 41
II. Waiting for Repentance (4:1–6:3) 123
III. The Forgetful People (6:4–11:11) 187
IV. The Final Resolution (11:12–14:9) 313

Abbreviations 376
Works Cited 378
Subject Index 384
Scripture Index 389
Index of Hebrew Words 394

Introduction

Hosea is a book about divine love confronting human perfidy and failure. The prophet was sent to minister to a spiritually hardened and deviant people who had turned their backs upon God. But the gracious wonder displayed in the book is that the LORD had not reciprocated the attitude and action of the people by abandoning those who had abandoned him. The enduring and reclaiming power of his love is reported in terms of two stories which mirror each other. One narrative (found in chapters 1 and 3) records how the LORD ordained Hosea's marriage to reflect his own relationship with Israel. We learn that when, some time later, the prophet's wife left him, he was directed to take steps to bring her back. So Hosea himself experienced the hurt of having an unfaithful spouse. Consequently, when he spoke to the nation, it was not in detached, abstract terms, but with the warmth and insight of one who knew the anguish of a sore heart and the difficulty of reclaiming one who had wilfully gone astray.

The major emphasis of the book, however, is on the second story which it records, that of the LORD's dealings with his unfaithful people. They had been attracted by material wealth and by the pagan culture and religion of surrounding peoples. One task Hosea had to perform was to alert them to the gravity of their misconduct, and to plead with them to return in repentance. If this was not forthcoming, it was inevitable that God would act against them in judgement, and what that would involve is graphically spelled out as an inducement to renewed commitment—a change of heart which did not occur in Hosea's day.

Yet the penalties God would impose on the people's transgression and obstinacy are not the end of the story because the LORD is not fickle as they are. His is a committed love. Despite their sin the LORD refused to abandon them utterly. 'How can I give you up?' (11:8). On the other hand he did not resort to a weak love which accepts a compromise in the face of intransigent and misguided behaviour. 'I will care for him' (14:8) is the pledge of a love that will work through lengthy and painful discipline to achieve the spiritual change which is required to restore harmonious relationships and usher in an age of eternal satisfaction (1:10-11; 2:23; 14:3-8).

In this Introduction further details are provided regarding the background to the situation which existed in the northern kingdom of Israel and how Hosea functioned as a prophet there. Some readers may wish to begin immediately with the exposition itself. If this is done, opportunity should be taken at a later stage to return to the Introduction because it provides greater depth regarding various matters which recur throughout the prophecy.

1. The Prophets of Israel

The division of the Davidic kingdom on the death of Solomon in 931 B.C. was not just a matter of politics. It impinged directly on the religious life of the ten northern tribes which comprised the newly formed kingdom of Israel. To differentiate his regime from that in Judah and to divert his citizens from going south to the Jerusalem Temple to worship, the king of the new state, Jeroboam I, instituted various changes in the cult of the north. He erected two shrines close to the borders of his realm, at Dan in the north and at Bethel in the south, and provided each with a golden bull-calf (cf. comments on 8:5). He changed the dates of the religious festivals (1 Kgs. 12:33) and instituted a new priesthood (1 Kgs. 12:21; 13:33-34). These innovations were in defiance of the ordinances of the Mosaic covenant even though the king and people still professed to worship the LORD. But the official religion of the north had become syncretistic, an amalgam of genuinely Israelite practices with those of Canaan. This exposure of the northern tribes to pagan influences led to the history of the kingdom of Israel being a record of persistent backsliding and rebellion against the LORD.

The LORD did not, however, abandon the people of the north. He used prophets as his messengers. Through their ministry God continued to remonstrate with the Israelites regarding their misconduct. Initially reform of the situation in the north was sought by means of prophets communicating with the king (cf. 1 Kgs. 13:1-10; 14:1-18), but increasing royal unresponsiveness led to the LORD directing his messengers to address the people directly.

This change is particularly evident after 860 B.C. when Elijah dramatically intervened in the affairs of the north. Kings of the Omride dynasty (885–841 B.C.) grasped every opportunity to promote Israel as an international power, and they did succeed in large measure in bringing military and economic success to their realm. But this was achieved through alliance with the Phoenicians of Tyre, which introduced an even greater religious peril for Israel—not merely the syncretism of Jeroboam I, but outright devotion to Baal, the god of the Canaanites (cf. comments on 2:5). Elijah was called on to oppose their policies, and the contest on Mount Carmel between Baalism and true devotion to Yahweh marks a major transition in the prophetic movement. Although the king and his court were present, the basic appeal was from the prophet to the people over the head of the king. 'Elijah came near to all the people and said, "How long will you go limping [possibly, hovering] between two opinions? If the LORD is God, follow him; but if Baal, follow him" ' (1 Kgs. 18:21). On that occasion the people did eventually respond positively, but the next dynasty—that of Jehu, which lasted from 841 to 753 B.C.—did not revert to true Yahwism but to the syncretistic practices of Jeroboam I (2 Kgs. 10:31). So when Hosea began his ministry in the closing years of Jehu's dynasty, he had to face a land which was muddled as to its religion. Their state-sponsored religion claimed its allegiance lay with the LORD, but its practice revealed otherwise. Furthermore the situation was not static. There was a continuing drift into open conformity with heathen ways and thought.

Before leaving the era of Elijah and Elisha, it is of some significance to note that we have no Prophecy of Elijah or Prophecy of Elisha in the way in which we have the Prophecy of Hosea or the Prophecy of Isaiah. The earlier ninth-century prophets left no direct written records. The messages they were divinely commissioned to announce were for the most part intended for individuals and specific situations, and they were delivered with a view to effecting an immediate change of behaviour. Because the later prophets addressed the people as a whole, it was fitting that there be a written, public record of their message so that it could become more widely known at a time when the general population was becoming increasingly literate (Scanlin 1978).

Furthermore, by the eighth century the nation had progressed further down the road to apostasy, and judgement drew inexorably closer. The message given to those prophets looked beyond the impending catastrophe to the restoration which the LORD would effect. Increasingly this involved the One to come, who would succeed where previous kings had failed. As the prophets' message moved on from challenging the contemporary generation to covenant loyalty to setting out how the LORD would provide for the faithful remnant after judgement, so too it became more important that the prophetic message be preserved in writing for future generations. This would enable them to discern the LORD's hand at work. Earlier warnings had not been idle threats, but had been enacted with all their dire consequences. Even so, that opened a door of hope that God would fulfil his promises made through the prophets, and bring lasting blessing to the nation.

2. The End of the Northern Kingdom

There is no explicit statement regarding the starting or concluding dates of Hosea's ministry. However, his initial message recorded in 1:2-5 implies that the dynasty of Jehu was still ruling in Israel, and this agrees with the mention of Jeroboam II in 1:1. Dates for the reigns of kings of Israel and Judah remain a source of controversy, but since the work of Edwin R. Thiele has proved robust and largely consonant with Scripture, a slightly modified version of his scheme of dating is adopted here.[1] On this basis Hosea's ministry may be taken to begin no later than 755 B.C., several years before Jeroboam's death.

As for determining when Hosea's ministry ended, it may be that the Shalman he mentions in 10:14 is Shalmaneser V (727-722 B.C.) in whose reign Samaria fell. Also, the description in 12:1 fits in well with the diplomatic intrigues of the troubled reign of Hoshea (732-723 B.C.). Now, though the fall of Samaria and the exile of the people are certainly foretold in the prophecy, there is no clear indication of their occurrence; so the book does not require that Hosea was alive to witness the collapse of the city. Consequently, the prophecy may well have reached its present form before 722 B.C. Scenarios envisaged by earlier commentators (as far back as the patristic period) presented the prophet as escaping to Judah and there writing up his memoirs, but this probably derived from the mention of Hezekiah in 1:1 and the assumption that this pointed to Hosea being alive after Hezekiah's accession in 715 B.C. However, suasive evidence exists for a co-regency between Hezekiah and his father beginning in 729 B.C., and on that basis it is more plausible to accept that Hosea's ministry ended in the early part of Hezekiah's reign (when he was co-regent, that is, a junior partner with his father) and before the fall of Samaria (McFall 1991:33–34).

The foregoing discussion clearly indicates the impossibility facing us in establishing with any great degree of confidence precise dates for the beginning or the conclusion of Hosea's ministry. Similar uncertainty exists regarding the date and setting of particular passages in the prophecy. However, the absence of clear chronological data ought not to be misunderstood. It is not the case that what Hosea had to say was so general in its significance that the circumstances of his times are irrelevant or subsidiary in interpreting the text. Far from it. Hosea's message was directly linked to the conditions current in his day and to incidents which occurred then. But specific information about what

1. Thiele 1983, with later corrections and amplification from McFall 1991.

was happening was already available to his contemporaries; the prophet did not need to provide them with further facts in that connection. What he could, and must, do was to relay the divine evaluation of those trends and events.

To understand the prophet's original message and to apply it to our own or later periods it is advantageous to build up as complete a picture as we can of the background against which his words were uttered. Our inability to tie every reference down precisely does not detract from the value of being aware of the general circumstances which prevailed. To achieve this it is helpful to consider Hosea's ministry as occurring during three, somewhat overlapping, phases in the period leading up to the demise of the northern kingdom.

(a) A Period of Prosperity

When Hosea was called to be a prophet towards the end of the reign of Jeroboam II, the northern kingdom had enjoyed a time of great economic prosperity with its political influence in the region coming close to Solomonic levels. This blessing had been divinely promised through the prophet Jonah. In 2 Kings 14:25 we read of Jeroboam that 'he restored the border of Israel from Lebo-Hamath as far as the Sea of the Arabah, according to the word of the LORD, the God of Israel, which he spoke by his servant Jonah the son of Amittai, the prophet, who was from Gath-Hepher.' His zone of influence thus stretched from central Aram (Syria) to the Dead Sea. The absence of external aggression and the consequent relief from paying tribute to foreign powers left Israel free to enjoy the surplus generated by its agricultural fertility (2:5, 8; 12:8; Amos 3:15; 5:11) as well as to receive tribute paid to it by neighbouring peoples and to profit from the international trade routes which crossed its territory. However, Israel's affluence did not induce grateful loyalty to the LORD. Instead it accelerated the trend to Baal worship (2:11, 13; 4:11, 13; 8:13; Amos 2:7-8; 4:4; 5:21-24), and this was accompanied by a false sense of security based on military prestige (cf. 5:5) and national defences (cf. 8:14).

One of the positive features of this period was the relatively good relations which obtained with the smaller, southern kingdom of Judah under its ruler Uzziah. There too the people were enjoying a time of prosperity and security.

When Hosea began his prophetic ministry, we must therefore envisage him as raising an unpopular voice of criticism. To speak of impending disaster and judgement in a period of expansion and affluence was to run contrary to the mood of the times, particularly among the elite and influential in the land ('Surely I have become rich', 12:8). They were enjoying the wealth and prestige of the expanded kingdom, and would not have responded favourably to having their complacent attitudes challenged.

Now Hosea was not alone in providing a critique of the situation in the northern kingdom of Israel. Some years earlier, the LORD had sent the prophet Amos from the southern kingdom of Judah to warn the north of the error of their ways. Amos particularly focused on the injustice and social irresponsibility of the rulers of the north, whereas Hosea's principal concern was to trace their unrighteous and oppressive acts back to their religious faithlessness.

Despite the social and political unrest which was going to come upon the north, at root their problem was one of religion. Economic progress had boosted the self-confidence of the nation's leaders, and they had become greedy and self-indulgent. Consequently they had turned their backs on the LORD, an attitude which had aroused his anger against them. Economic success and social prestige were coupled with poverty and injustice in the land, contrary to the demands of the covenant. The gap between rich and poor had become ominously wide, with the poor being reduced to the status of forced labourers/slaves, and the upper classes adopting an increasingly lavish lifestyle. The rich were prepared to use their new found wealth ruthlessly, to corrupt the verdicts of the lawcourts: 'they sell the righteous for silver and the needy for a pair of sandals' (Amos 2:6); 'you who turn justice to wormwood and cast down righteousness to the earth' (Amos 5:7); 'you trample on the poor ... you take a bribe and turn aside the needy in the gate' (Amos 5:11-12). Israel's politicians hoped to chart a way of maintaining the nation's prestige through a series of alliances with foreign powers, but that was a doomed policy because it was an expression of self-reliant rebellion against Yahweh.

(b) A Period of Internal Unrest.

While Jeroboam lived he provided sufficiently strong leadership to maintain the political coherence of his kingdom. But when he died in 753 B.C.,[2] there was no robust succession strategy and Israel collapsed internally into factionalism and feuding.

2. Different chronologies place the event a few years before or a few years after the middle of the century, largely because of difficulties which exist as regards the dating of Pekah's kingship.

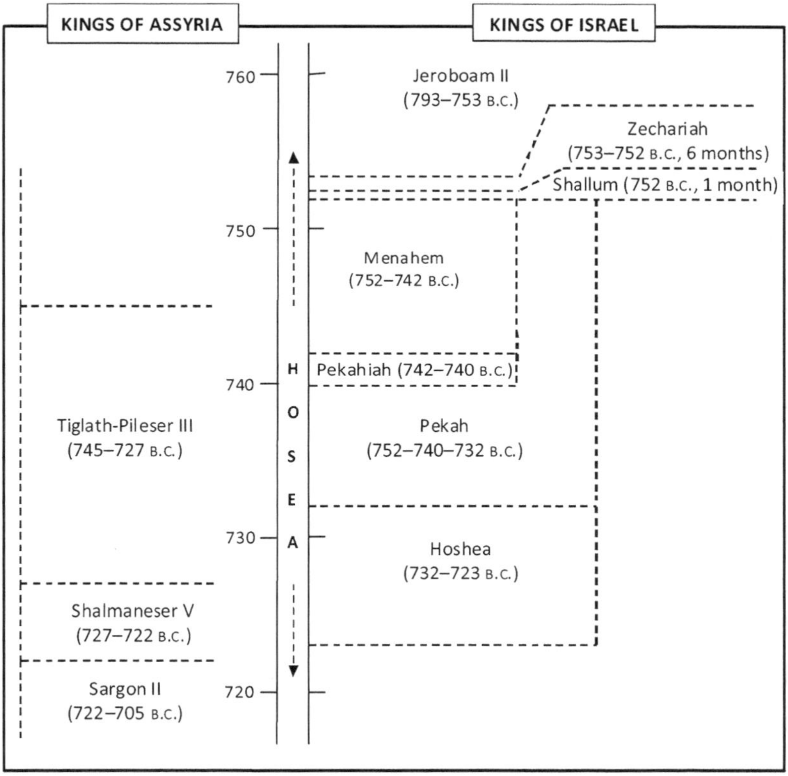

Indeed six kings ruled the nation in the thirty years before it was eliminated—Zechariah, Shallum, Menahem, Pekahiah, Pekah, Hoshea. But they were unworthy of the designation 'king', and the introductory verse of the prophecy passes over them in silence (1:1). Most of these rulers were opportunistic murderers who did not shrink from assassination as a political weapon, slaying their predecessors to gain the throne. No matter how much they engaged in self-promotion by surrounding themselves with the trappings of kingship, they contributed nothing to the well-being of the land. Instead their actions weakened it before its enemies, and hastened its fall. For people who had grown up during the forty-year reign of Jeroboam, such a rapid sequence of regime change would have been especially unsettling and destabilising.

Jeroboam II was succeeded by his son Zechariah, but he ruled for only six months. His death marked the end of a dynasty which had held power in the northern kingdom of Israel from the time of Jehu's violent revolt about ninety years earlier (2 Kgs. 9–10). Shallum, Zechariah's murderer, reigned for only one month before he himself was killed by Menahem, who then seized the throne (2 Kgs. 15:14). There had thus been four kings within a twelve-month period. As yet the land was not facing any external challenge. The instability it was exhibiting was generated by internal tensions and corruption.

Throughout his ten-year reign Menahem continued the aberrant religious policy which typified the north (2 Kgs. 15:18). On his death in 742 B.C. there was another unsettled period. Though he was succeeded by his son Pekahiah, after a short reign he too was murdered, in the autumn of 740 B.C. or the spring of 739 B.C. His assassin Pekah had maintained a regime in Gilead, east of the river Jordan, which had rivalled that of Menahem in Samaria.[3] It is this phenomenon which explains the figure of 25 years given for his reign in 2 Kings 15:27. (Over the land as a whole he reigned only for eight years.) It may well be the constant threat from Pekah that induced Menahem in the 740s to submit to Assyria and to pay the emperor 'a thousand talents of silver, that his hand might be with him to strengthen control of the kingdom in his hand' (2 Kgs. 15:19)—though no doubt the strength of Assyrian aggression had its part to play as well. At any rate it would seem that on Menahem's death Pekah entered into some arrangement with Pekahiah, becoming his second in command (2 Kgs. 15:25). But the alliance did not last, and soon Pekah seized the throne in Samaria and pursued anti-Assyrian policies in line with those of Aram (Syria) with whom he had been on close terms for some years.[4]

Pekah's rule over the whole kingdom lasted for eight years until he himself fell victim to a conspiracy which put Hoshea the son of Elah on the throne in 732 B.C. The name of Hoshea, the last of the kings of Israel, is actually identical to that of the prophet. The difference in spelling is one which has become accepted in English to distinguish the two individuals. The name means 'salvation' (cf. 1:1)—something which this king singularly failed to provide for his people (13:10). The details are unclear as to why Hoshea revolted against the Assyrians;

---

3. It was Edwin Thiele who promoted the thesis that, after the death of Shallum, Menahem and Pekah established rival kingdoms in the west (Ephraim, centred on Samaria) and in the east (Gilead) respectively. While many scholars remain unwilling to accept this proposal, it does have the merit of harmonising the Scriptural data for these reigns. See Young, R. C. 2005.

4. It may even be the case that Pekah deliberately took a throne name modelled on that of Pekahiah. Certainly Isaiah prefers to dismiss him as 'the son of Remaliah' (Isa. 7:4, 5), an upstart with no pedigree.

possibly it was stimulated by Egyptian intrigue. When Hoshea withheld tribute, the Assyrians reacted violently against the troublesome nation and Hoshea was taken prisoner.

Various dates are given for the fall of Samaria, including 722 B.C. and 721 B.C., and more recently 723 B.C (Young, R. C. 2004). This has arisen, not only through the confusing chronologies used by the scribes in Judah during this period, but also because of the claims made by the Assyrian emperor Sargon II (722-705 B.C.) who came to the throne in late December 722 B.C. or early January 721 B.C. Sargon asserted that Samaria had been captured in the first year of his reign, but this is increasingly assessed as late political spin in the Assyrian annals. Rather the city fell towards the end of his predecessor's reign, though there may well have been continuing mopping up operations in the northern kingdom, which by then had been incorporated into the Assyrian empire as the province of Samirina. In Sargon's second full year on the Assyrian throne (720/719 B.C.) there was a rebellion organised by the northern Aramean city of Hamath, but involving to some extent Damascus, Gaza, Egypt and other peoples, including some remaining resistance fighters in Israel. This also may have fostered the perception that Sargon was involved in the capture of the city.

(c) A Period of External Aggression Ending in Collapse

Mention has already been made of the Assyrians, and their expansionist policies were undoubtedly the dominant feature in the international political scene during most of Hosea's ministry. For the first fifty years of the eighth century B.C. Assyria had been preoccupied with the security of her homeland, particularly in the face of pressure from the mountain peoples of Urartu to her north and Media to her east. This northward focus of her policy made possible Jeroboam's largely unopposed expansion of his zone of influence which led to Israel's heightened economic prosperity. Also, at a more local level, there was the weakness of the Arameans of Damascus after the mauling they had received around 796 B.C. at the hands of the Assyrians under Adad-Nirari III (811-784 B.C.). Any military might the Arameans possessed after those reverses was spent fighting one another, with conflict especially existing between the city-states of Hamath and Damascus. It was possible for Israel (and also to a lesser extent, Judah) to fill the power vacuum in the area.

But, after an extended period of internal dissension and weakness, the fortunes of the Assyrian empire were revived when Tiglath-Pileser III usurped the throne in 745 B.C. He was also known as Pul

(2 Kgs. 15:19; 1 Chron. 5:26), a throne name which he assumed when he later took over direct rule of Babylon. His policies were well conceived and ruthlessly implemented. He organised the Assyrian army into an even more effective military machine than previously. Its equipment and logistics were far in excess of anything its opponents could muster, and Tiglath-Pileser himself provided the carefully thought-out strategy that could deploy it to maximum effect. Furthermore, military conquest was accompanied by efficient administration of the empire. An army may overthrow a nation; it takes a bureaucracy to grind it into extinction. Assyrian ideology suppressed local cultural and ethnic distinctives throughout the provinces of the empire (it was nothing like as intrusive as regards vassal states; for the distinction, see below). Instead it promoted loyalty to the gods of Assyria and the emperor as their representative.

Tiglath-Pileser's numerous and successful military campaigns probably started as attempts to disrupt the trade of Assyria's northern neighbour Urartu with Aram, but as his victories gave him the upper hand he developed an elaborate policy of extending Assyrian control as far as possible. Local rulers who were unwilling to accept, or to remain loyal to, the treaty conditions imposed by the Assyrians were ruthlessly suppressed. The Assyrians had long been interested in controlling Syria-Palestine not just because of its indigenous resources (the timber of Lebanon always looked attractive from treeless Mesopotamia) but also because of the trade routes which traversed the area, and because of the prize that lay beyond—Egypt.

Tiglath-Pileser first moved into the area of Syria-Palestine in 743 B.C. Northern Syria and the central area around Hamath were turned into Assyrian provinces, but further south it suited Tiglath-Pileser at this time to avoid outright annexation of territory. A number of local rulers, including Menahem of Samaria and Rezin of Damascus,[5] were permitted to continue to rule on condition that they paid tribute. This marked the first stage in Assyrian policy for extending control over an area. A kingdom became a tributary/vassal state which was allowed to retain its traditional ruler and nominal independence, but had to contribute substantial sums to the coffers of the empire.

As far as Israel is concerned, we know from the Old Testament (2 Kgs. 15:19-20) and from Tiglath-Pileser's own annals that

---

5. An Assyrian text of this period mentions an Azriyau of Yaudi as paying tribute. The identification of this figure as Uzziah (Azariah) of Judah has been challenged, and the reference has not been positively established.

Menahem paid tribute to Assyria (*ANET* 283), perhaps in a misguided attempt to strengthen his internal position (cf. section (b) above).[6] It is of some interest to note as regards the depleted resources of the nation that 60,000 land owners were forced to contribute to the tribute imposed on the land (2 Kgs. 15:20), and that later Sargon records that 27,290 were deported from Samaria and the hill country surrounding it in the final conquest of the land (*ANET* 285).

In Israel Pekah assassinated Menahem's son and successor, and seized the throne in late 740 B.C. (2 Kgs. 15:25). For some time before that Pekah had controlled territory east of the Jordan, and had been on friendly terms with Rezin of Damascus. Indeed many suppose that he was a client of Rezin and reliant on him for support. Together they formed what is known as the Syro-Ephraimite alliance, and began to harass Judah (cf. 2 Kgs. 15:37) as Rezin sought to expand southwards (cf. 2 Kgs. 16:5-6). These expansionist policies came to a sudden halt when Tiglath-Pileser returned to the area in 734 B.C. He first moved down the coastal plain to attack the Philistines in the south-west, probably as a warning to the Egyptians not to interfere. Around this juncture the Syro-Ephraimite war took place, perhaps because Rezin and Pekah, having failed to win the support of Judah against Assyria, decided not to risk a possible attack from the rear and marched south to depose Ahaz, king of Judah, and install a sympathetic regime in Jerusalem (cf. Isa. 7). Ahaz appealed for help to Tiglath-Pileser, and by paying him tribute accepted the first stage of Assyrian overlordship (2 Kgs. 16:8).[7]

The Assyrians then directed their attention to Aram and Israel—they would in all likelihood have done this quite apart from Ahaz's plea for protection. In 733 B.C. most of the northern kingdom was brought totally under Assyrian vassalage with the annexation of Gilead, Galilee and Naphtali (2 Kgs. 15:29; *ANET* 283-284). This represented the third stage of domination in which a territory was reduced to a province of the Assyrian Empire under an Assyrian governor. All Galilee and the plain of Jezreel became the province of Megiddo; the coastal plain

6. The date of Menahem's payment of tribute is often given as 738 B.C., but this figure reflects a variety of chronological assumptions. On Thiele's dating Menahem died in 742 B.C., and this payment seems to have occurred in the year before his death.

7. Though Judah became a vassal state of Assyria, it was never reduced to being a province of the empire. Its national identity and religious institutions were thus preserved from direct Assyrian interference, something which was not true in the case of the northern kingdom.

south of Carmel became the province of Dor; and Transjordan became the province of Gilead. Many of the population, particularly the upper classes, were deported. The kingdom of Israel was reduced it to an area of about one-third of its former size, becoming just an enclave centred on Samaria and including the surrounding hill country of Ephraim.

In the following year (732 B.C.) the Assyrians completed their conquest of Aram by overthrowing Damascus, killing Rezin and deporting the other leaders to Qir (2 Kgs. 16:9). At the same time, in Samaria Pekah was assassinated by Hoshea, and Tiglath-Pileser was pleased to acknowledge Hoshea as his vassal, again on payment of substantial tribute (2 Kgs. 15:30; *ANET* 283-4). The rump of the kingdom thus stuttered on for a further decade with its status at the second stage in Assyrian domination of an area: regime change with a new indigenous ruler but with a diminished realm.

However, Hoshea's loyalty to Assyria was fragile. Though for a time he paid tribute to Shalmaneser V (727-722 B.C.), Tiglath-Pileser's son and successor (2 Kgs. 17:3), Hoshea engaged in political intrigue to secure Egyptian help (cf. 12:1) and withheld his annual tribute from Assyria (2 Kgs. 17:4). The Assyrians imprisoned him for his rebellion, and Shalmaneser besieged Samaria for three years before taking it (2 Kgs. 17:5; 18:9-10). See *(b)* above for a discussion of precisely when the city fell. The remainder of the land was then also subjected to the third and final stage of Assyrian conquest. It no longer had a native ruler. Its inhabitants were deported to Mesopotamia (2 Kgs. 17:6) and peoples of other nationalities were settled in the territory (2 Kgs. 17:24) which had now become the Assyrian province of Samirina.

3. The Prophet and His Ministry

Little biographical information has been preserved about Hosea. Like his contemporary, Amos, Hosea was a prophet to the northern kingdom of Israel. However, Amos was himself a southerner who hailed from Tekoa in the highlands of Judah and who returned there after a seemingly brief ministry in the north (Amos 1:1; 7:14-15). Such indications as exist point to Hosea as being a northerner and his ministry as one which extended for at least thirty difficult years during challenging and disastrous times for Israel.

His father's name is recorded as the otherwise unknown Beeri (1:1). By identifying him with the similarly named Reubenite chief Beerah who was deported by Tiglath-Pileser Rabbinic tradition considered Hosea to have come from the tribe of Reuben. The connection is precarious and without substance.

Davies (1993:14) argues that Hosea may have been a native of the city of Samaria on the grounds that it might have been thought necessary to mention a prophet's origins only if he did not come from the capital. Again this is mere conjecture, though the conclusion has a measure of plausibility. Certainly Hosea was well versed in the Scriptures, had a grasp of the political affairs in the nation, and was adept in his use of language. These features are consistent with him being a well-educated citizen of Samaria, but that still falls far short of proof.

Hosea's occupation is unknown. R. K. Harrison (1969:859) mentions—and dismisses—suggestions that he was a baker (inferred from the detail given in 7:4-8) or a farmer (inferred from his numerous agricultural comparisons). Equally, proposals that he was from a priestly family lack corroboration.

Somewhat more firmly based inferences may be drawn from the mention of 'our king' in reference to the king of Israel in 7:5. While the words may be an ironic citation of the speech of others, it is quite likely that they reflect the prophet's own origins and loyalties. Elsewhere also his focus is firmly on the north. He is silent about Jerusalem and other cities in the southern kingdom of Judah, and the royal line of David is referred to only once (3:5). The many contemporary place names mentioned by Hosea are, with one exception, all in the north or east: Jezreel, Gilgal, Bethel, Mizpah, Tabor, Shittim, Gibeah, Ramah, Gilead, Shechem, Samaria, Baal-Peor, Beth-Arbel. The only exception is the valley of Achor (2:15) which lay on the border between Judah and Benjamin (Josh. 15:7), and so it was technically within the area of the southern kingdom.

Furthermore Hosea's northern orientation is also evident in the fact that he mentions Ephraim 37 times and Israel 44 times, whereas the name of Judah occurs only 15 times. Though critical scholars are prone to see many, if not all, of these references to Judah as insertions of later southern scribes, they probably do testify to Hosea's awareness of affairs in the south and concern for the outworking of the covenant promises (see Garrett 1993:3), but he devoted himself to his immediate mission and duty in relation to the north.

The one area of the prophet's life to which we seem to have greater access is his marriage to Gomer (chapters 1 and 3), though here too details are elusive. His prophetic ministry probably started when he was about twenty years old (an age by which most young men would already have been married). His call took the form of a divine directive that he marry 'a wife of whoredoms', a term which has been variously analysed (cf. 1:2). Their three children were given symbolic names,

Jezreel, Lo-Ruchama, and Lo-Ammi (1:4, 6, 9), and it is evident that his marriage and the names of his children formed the basis of the message he conveyed to Israel in the early years of his ministry.

Furthermore, although Hosea does not record for us the sequence of events, his marriage apparently broke down through the desertion of his wife whom he had to reclaim from another man (3:1-2). Because of his personal experience during the turbulent years of the disintegration of his marriage Hosea was able to empathise with the LORD's attitude towards Israel. God could lovingly confront the wrong which was in the land and yet entertain hope for good beyond the impending disaster. In the absence of repentance it was inevitable that judgement would ensue, but judgement would not be the last word on the Israel's situation because of the LORD's constant adherence to the covenant commitment he had entered into.

Hosea was so taken up with the situation of his own nation that he does not record any oracles concerning the affairs of other lands in a way similar to Amos or Isaiah. Like Amos, Hosea was aware of the socio-economic problems which stemmed from Israel's desertion of covenant standards (cf. 4:1-2), but the focus of his critique was on the underlying spiritual insensitivity and contrariness of the community. The people failed to appreciate the love which God had lavished on them, and they misappropriated his gifts to them (2:8). Blinded by a spirit of infatuation into indulging in Canaanite debauchery (4:12; 5:4), they drew doom down on themselves (7:13; 9:9; 13:6, 16). Yet—despite all their provocation and waywardness—the LORD was, through judgement, preparing for their return (2:14; 11:8-9; 14:4).

The LORD called Hosea to a difficult and challenging ministry in which he had to stand against the prevalent outlook of his fellow countrymen. It is never easy or popular to oppose the consensus of one's day. However, it is probably wrong to view Hosea as a totally isolated figure. Shortly before Hosea, Amos had exercised a brief prophetic ministry in the north, until he was ordered to leave the country through official opposition (Amos 7:10-17), which might well have been because his message was endorsed by some in the community. After all, a century earlier in the history of the northern kingdom Elijah had thought himself utterly isolated, yet the LORD had then revealed that there were 7000 who had not succumbed to the pressures of Baal worship (1 Kgs. 19:18). A similar remnant no doubt continued to resist the inroads of Baal worship and maintained their loyalty to the LORD in Amos's and Hosea's day. To some extent they would have formed a group ready to give a congenial reception to the prophet's message.

The perception that Hosea need not have been a solitary voice of protest and warning is heightened by archaeological evidence. It has made clear the extent to which Jerusalem expanded in Hezekiah's reign to accommodate an influx of refugees from the north. Amongst those who had opted to flee south (rather than to areas such as Edom or Moab, or indeed to Egypt) would be those sympathetic to the religious outlook of the south. It may well be that we should envisage that among these refugees were some who treasured Hosea's ministry and brought the record of it south with them. Equally it is possible to trace Hosea's influence on later prophet's such as Jeremiah, which points to the extent Hosea's ministry continued to be appreciated.

4. Composition and Style

(a) The Minor Prophets

The last twelve books of the Old Testament in English bibles are commonly known as the Minor Prophets. That designation is not intended to belittle the significance of the message they convey or of the impact of the ministries described; rather it has arisen from the size of the books left by these prophets. Even when combined, they are not as large as one of the three major prophets: Isaiah, Jeremiah and Ezekiel. In the Hebrew canon the records of minor prophets are referred to as the Book of the Twelve, probably because their shorter works could be contained in one scroll, which would sit comfortably alongside those of the three major prophets.

First place among the Twelve was given to Hosea. This was certainly not because he was the earliest of the prophets in the Book of the Twelve. The ministries of Jonah and Amos preceded his, and there are scholars who would argue that those of Obadiah and of Joel did so also. As regards the traditional presentation of the canon of Scripture, what is normative—because it is a matter of divine inspiration—is the content of the books. The order in which they are gathered is generally understood to be a matter of human convenience rather than divine imposition.

Even so, it is not without interest to ask why the early scribes arranged these books in the way that they did. One piece of evidence is to be found in the Septuagint (LXX), the Greek translation of the Old Testament made in the century following 250 B.C. There the first six books of the Twelve are found in the order: Hosea, Amos, Micah, Joel, Obadiah, Jonah. This presumably reflects the traditions to be found in Alexandria when the Septuagint was translated. The later arrangement of the contents of the Twelve which is found in Jewish manuscripts, while retaining an overall historical progression, was also influenced by considerations of the length of the books and of their content. The fact that Hosea is placed first among this early group of six prophets is probably just a matter of size—his writings are the most substantial apart from those of the later Zechariah.

(b) One Author or Many?

Much modern scholarship is sceptical about the extent to which the prophecy of Hosea in its present form can be directly related to a prophet who lived and ministered during the closing years of the northern kingdom. Instead it is argued that there was a process of composition, which began with refugees from Israel taking south with them a variety of notes and recollections of Hosea's ministry. Later groups of scribes in Judah, looking back on the ministry of the northern prophet, collected and adjusted this material, perhaps in the aftermath of the withdrawal of the Assyrian army in 701 B.C., or possibly at an even later period. Earlier critics excised many texts as late additions on the basis of their perception that the prophets originally only spoke messages of doom and positive passages were subsequently added to give balance to their work (e.g., Harper 1905:cliii). Others have argued that the references to Judah in the book were contributed by later Judahite redactors because the work of the prophet was originally concerned only with the north. On this approach the literary structure of the book does not derive from Hosea himself, and the primary audience of the completed text is the Judahite circle for whom those scribes wrote.

However, there is no conclusive evidence to support current models for analysing the prophecy as an agglomeration of texts, variously contributed. We do not know when or how the book was composed. The text is not interspersed with historical annotations, such as those found in Ezekiel or Haggai, nor does it contain allusions which can be readily identified with events known from other sources. Consequently it is impossible to pinpoint detailed scenarios as background for the prophecies. Even so, there is no compelling reason to abandon the traditional hypothesis, derived from 1:1, that both the contents of the book and its literary structure originate with the prophet himself, and that there is an overall historical progression from earlier to later material. This provides a coherent and sensitive basis for analysing the prophecy.

(c) Transmission of the Text

The text of Hosea originated in some form or other in the northern kingdom, and was subsequently brought south to Judah where scribes repeatedly copied it over the centuries. Andersen and Freedman who contributed a major and lengthy commentary on Hosea to the Anchor Bible series remarked that Hosea competes with Job for the distinction of containing more unintelligible passages than any other book of the Hebrew Bible (1980:66). Their verdict reflects the state of the Hebrew text (MT) bequeathed to us by the Massoretes, Jewish scholars active from the seventh to the tenth centuries A.D. It is especially true as regards chapters 4–14 that in quite a number of places it is difficult to understand the Hebrew text in its present form. Some of these conundrums may have been present from the start because Hosea's style is frequently elliptical and obscure. In other places it may be that southern scribes struggled to understand Hosea's northern diction and grammar. Their deliberate attempts to transmit a meaningful text may have introduced problems which were not originally present, quite apart from the accidental corruptions which were inherent in the process of copying manuscripts over such a long period of time.

Some help in resolving textual difficulties may be obtained from various early translations and sources: the Greek Septuagint (LXX, from the 3rd century B.C. onwards), the Aramaic Targums (5th century A.D., but reflecting earlier Jewish traditions), the Syriac Peshitta (possibly from 2nd century A.D. onwards), and the Latin Vulgate (4th century A.D.). The pre-Massoretic Hebrew text consisted only of consonants to which the reader had to supply the vowels to reconstitute the text. These versions in other languages record how their translators read the text (consonants and vowels), and they all predate the current vocalised (with vowels added) Massoretic text. They can therefore yield insights into the Hebrew text which the translators had before them as they worked, and into the meaning they assigned to that text. In the vast majority of passages the Septuagint supports the reading of the Massoretic Text.

Not only did the Massoretes add vowels to what had previously been a consonantal text, they also indicated the equivalent of what we would now consider to be sentences and paragraphs. The existence of these paragraph markers helps us to understand how the Massoretes analysed the structure of the text. Our chapters and verses are of much later origin, but generally the verses reflect the Massoretic sentence structure. There are three places where the versification of the English text differs from that of the Massoretic Text.

1:10-11 (MT 2:1-2) and 2:1-23 (MT 2:3-25)
11:12 (MT 12:1) and 12:1-14 (MT 12:2-15)
13:16 (MT 14:1) and 14:1-9 (MT 14:2-10).

These variations are liable to cause confusion when reference is made to works based on the Hebrew text. In this commentary the Massoretic verse numbers are not used.

In trying to understand the text of Hosea, translators emend the text in varying degrees. In this commentary the viewpoint is adopted that if sense can be made of the existing Hebrew text, it would require overwhelming evidence (and not merely a scholarly predilection to bolster a pet theory) to warrant making any change. The somewhat wooden rendering presented here stays as close to the Massoretic Text as the English language and common sense will reasonably permit. Where words are present in the translation because of the requirements of English language and style, these are marked with underbrackets. These features are designed to help those unfamiliar with Hebrew to follow as much of the discussion as possible, and also to permit a connection to be made easily between the comments and whatever modern translation the reader prefers to use.

It is also of significance to note that Hosea is cited in a number of places in the New Testament, and no understanding of the prophet's message is complete until it is related to the subsequent biblical exposition of it. The passages quoted are: 1:10 in Rom. 9:26; 2:23 in Rom. 9:25; 6:6 in Matt. 9:13; 12:7; 10:8 in Luke 23:30; 11:1 in Matt. 2:15; and 13:14 in 1 Cor. 15:55.

(d) Structured or Disjointed?

After consideration of the text of Hosea, it is convenient to examine its literary characteristics. If one assesses the book on the hypothesis that many hands contributed to its present form, then it is easy to endorse the verdict of Jerome that Hosea's style is *commaticus*,[8] that is, disjointed and written in small units which do not have discernible structural links to bind the material into a tightly worked composition. Commentators generally accept that because chapters 1–3 are focused on the prophet's marriage they possess thematic coherence and so form a distinguishable unit. A similar consensus does not prevail as regards

8. Jerome, 'Praefatio S. Hieronymi in Duodecim Prophetas', in *Divinae Bibliotheca Pars Prima. Hieronymi Opera* 9, cols.1013-16.

assessments of chapters 4–14, where scholarly analysis has distinguished between fourteen and thirty largely independent sections.[9]

However, given the skill with which Hosea manipulates words (see *(f)* below), it is improbable that he gave little thought to the overall structure of his prophecy. Some idea of the way he ordered the record of his message may be achieved by examining the structure of the biographical material in chapters 1–3 which, it is accepted, form a literary unit. Within these chapters it is possible to detect an envelope, or chiastic, structure, a literary device common throughout the ancient Near East. In it the outer sections (1:2–2:1; 3:1-5) have a similar theme, in this case, the presentation of information regarding the prophet's own marriage, and they bracket the central section (2:2-23), where the focus switches to the LORD's relationship with Israel. As was customary in chiastically structured material (which may contain more than three sections) it is here in the central section that the principal thematic focus lies.

Furthermore, the chiastic pattern is not the only structure evident in the first division of the book. Within each section there is a progression from a message of condemnation and judgement (1:2-9; 2:2-13; 3:1) to one of restoration and blessing (1:10–2:1; 2:14-23; 3:2-5). Wyrtzen has ably argued that the form of the prophet's presentation reinforces his core message: 'an intensely personal divine restorative confrontation with Israel' (1984:315). Recognising how suitably this structure accords with the theme of the book provides a valuable aid to understanding how various parts of Hosea's material are connected. Also in that it evidences one editorial hand at work (and who better for that role than Hosea himself?) in ordering the material in the book, the structural analysis undermines critical attempts to reorder the material in the prophecy and assign a late date to some passages, such as those holding out the prospect of future restoration.

Moving on from chapters 1–3, a similar literary progression from messages of condemnation to those of blessing may then be employed to analyse the structure of the remainder of the book. The positive

9. 'The Book of Hosea does not display a sophisticated macrostructure; it appears to be a loose anthology of speeches rather than a tightly structured collection' (Chisholm 2002:336). 'The second section, chs. 4–14, lacks the clear plan of the first. Here the collector is working simply to arrange the rest of the material available to him and he is using common themes and catchwords to organize it' (Mays 1969:15), and indeed Mays provides no structured outline for the book, simply listing 37 sections.

material of divine promise found in 11:10-11 and 14:4-8 functions to close divisions of the prophecy. The formula 'declares the LORD', though common in prophetic speech, is used sparingly by Hosea (cf. 2:13), and so its occurrence in 11:11 is also a significant marker of a break in the material at that juncture. However, the interpretation of 6:1-3 is more controversial. Detecting in that passage a positive, though unrealised, declaration suggests that after the accepted initial division consisting of chapters 1—3, three further blocks of material may be identified (4:1–6:3; 6:4–11:11; 11:12–14:9), each of which begins with exposure of the people's transgression and warning of impending judgement, but then goes on to provide a concluding glimpse of the further outworking of the LORD's purpose in salvation.

(e) Prose or Poetry?

Old Testament prophets employed, to a greater or lesser extent, the conventions of Semitic poetry to shape their message. It is not entirely clear why they did so. Possibly two factors were at work. A poetic presentation may have accorded a dignity to their speech which reflected the divine origin of their message. Rather than conveying an impression of contrivance or artificiality which some associate with poetic expression, the use of poetry was regarded as indicative of measured, elevated speech. Another consideration is that of memorability. Although the culture of Hosea's day habitually used permanent written documents to transmit important records to posterity, most contemporary communication was oral. A structured form of speech would lend itself to more accurate dissemination of a message.

The principal technique employed by Semitic poets is that of carefully balanced thought (*parallelism*) in which the second part of a poetic unit re-expresses the thought of the first part often in synonymous terms, or with some significant variation. Hosea exhibits a marked preference for synonymous parallelism, generally expressed in a two-part unit, though three-part units do occur, generally to begin or conclude a passage (Wolff 1974:xxiv). The translation follows the convention of representing each Hebrew poetic unit with two or three lines of poetry, as appropriate, with the second and third lines indented. It is not always proved possible to preserve the word order of the original to the extent that the line divisions of the translation match the Hebrew structure, though this has been attempted wherever practicable.

Since there is no clear dividing line between poetry and impassioned prose—and the prophets used both—views differ as to which category some passages should be assigned. This particularly affects chapters 1–3 of Hosea. Translations are generally agreed that the central section (2:2-22) is written in poetry, though the REB presents 2:18-22 as prose, while the RSV, NRSV, ESV take 2:16-20 as prose. However, there are more significant divergences as regards the language of the first and last sections. Because chapters 1 and 3 are formally identified as being predominantly narrative, it is felt that they are appropriately presented as prose. With the exception of the REB which sets out the speeches of chapter 3 as poetry, translators prefer to identify them as prose. The framework of chapter 1 is generally presented as prose, and the NRSV, ESV and NIV maintain this throughout, whereas other translations identify poetry in the speeches, totally so in HCSB, NKJV, partly so in REB and NASB.

Are these presentational differences of significance? Some early critics were inclined to treat poetic passages as genuine and prose passages as later redactional insertions. Others consider the narrative of chapters 1 and 3 to require a prose presentation whereas the divine injunctions of chapter 2 are more suitably cast in poetry. Identification of the precise point in the spectrum at which prose becomes poetry is so subjective that it seems inappropriate to mark the prophetic and divine speeches in these chapters as if there was some fundamental difference between them, and all have been presented as poetry. This viewpoint is supported by a number of scholars. For instance, 'The literary form of this section [3:1-4] is distinctly poetic. In no portion of the book is the parallelism more marked, or more perfect' (Harper 1905:215).

(f) Metaphorical Language

Hosea is a master wordsmith, and the LORD employed his aptitude in this regard to ensure that his message was presented to Israel in an attention-grabbing and memorable garb, which was all the more needed because of the spiritual obtuseness of those addressed. The prophet employs many rhetorical devices to achieve his ends, including startling juxtaposition of thought (e.g., 1:10; 3:1; 4:1; 6:4), repetition of key words and concepts, rhetorical questions (e.g., 2:2; 6:4) homophony (a play on similarly sounding, but not identical, words; e.g., 4:16; 8:9; 9:15), citation of proverbs (e.g., 4:11, 14) and employment of other modes of wisdom speech (e.g., 14:9), as well as less common devices such as pseudo-sorites (e.g., 8:7).

Hosea's favourite technique is to employ metaphor and simile to arrest attention and induce thought, and he does this to a greater extent than other Scriptural authors. At times Hosea takes a metaphor and develops it in detail (the adulterous wife, 2:2-13; or God as the loving parent, 11:1-4); at other times there is a kaleidoscopic effect in which one striking image is quickly replaced by another (5:11-15; 7:4-12; 13:3, 15; 14:5-7). To ascertain the point of a comparison which the prophet was making drew the hearer into looking at the world from the prophet's perspective—which is, of course, that of God—and so broke down the preconceptions they had adopted from the pagan presuppositions of surrounding culture. Use of metaphorical language also induced the prophet's audience to approach their own conduct and prospects from a new angle, and possibly to develop a less complacent attitude towards themselves.

Undoubtedly Hosea's most provocative comparisons are those he employs for the LORD and for Israel.[10] The LORD is pictured as a husband (2:2), a father (11:1-4), a doctor (6:1; 7:1; 11:3; 14:4), a shepherd (4:16; 13:6), a fowler (7:12). There are also unusual and more disturbing metaphors for God: a lion (5:14; 13:7), a leopard (13:7), a bear (13:8), dew (14:5), an evergreen cypress (14:8), a moth (5:12), decay (5:12). On the other hand, Israel appears as a wife (2:2-13, 19-20), a son (11:1-4), a sick person (5:13; 6:1; 7:1; 14:4), a flock (4:16; 13:6), a dove (7:11), a flock of birds (7:12; 9:11; 11:11)—these being largely counterparts to the descriptions of the LORD. Israel is also compared to a trained (10:11) as well as a stubborn heifer (4:16), a grapevine (10:1; 14:7), its grapes (9:10) and the wine of Lebanon (14:5), the forest of Lebanon (14:5, 6), an olive tree (14:6), a mother in labour as well as an unborn son (13:13). Israel is like a half-baked loaf (7:8), a slack bow (7:16), a morning cloud and early dew (6:4; 13:3), a shrivelled plant (9:16), chaff blown by the wind (13:3), smoke from an opening (13:3). This variety of images would hold the attention of an audience no matter how blasé they had become about religion.

5. Theological Themes

Like the other prophets, Hosea was no theological innovator. There can be no doubt that his message was vividly and dramatically presented, but his aim was not to introduce new concepts or teaching into Israel's faith. His goal was rather to rid the people of the corrupt notions they had adopted from Canaanite thought and to set up a robust covenant faith once more. The covenant drew its expression from

10. The following list draws on that provided by Wolff (1974:xxiv) with the translations conformed to those found in this commentary.

international treaties by which an emperor of the ancient Near East dictated the terms on which he incorporated a subordinate nation into his realm or under his protection. To continue to enjoy the emperor's favour a subordinate or vassal had to observe the terms of the covenant in perpetuity. Similarly, at Sinai the LORD as the King of Israel constituted the nation as his own special possession (Exod. 19:5-9) and set before them the terms on which their relationship was to structured, terms to which they were thereafter required to adhere if harmony was to be preserved between the covenant partners. So covenant is essentially about relationships, the interpersonal bond which the LORD has sovereignly inaugurated between himself and the people he has chosen. As the LORD's covenant spokesmen the prophets were therefore re-presenting what the LORD demanded of the people, and also what he had undertaken to do for them. The relationship was two-sided, and the divinely stated obligations applied to both parties.

Hosea only explicitly mentions the LORD's covenant on three occasions (2:18; 6:7; 8:1), but the reality of Sinai permeates his whole work. There is, for instance, his preference for the name, the LORD, over against God to describe the deity (see on 1:7). The LORD is the covenant name of God (see on 1:9), and it is also a personal name, a feature which is unfortunately obscured by the rendering conventionally employed in English translations and which is hardly bettered by the virtual transliteration involved by representing it as Yahweh. However, translational inadequacies should not be permitted to obscure the personal dimension of the name, and the overtones of familiarity and intimacy involved in its use. He is the one who recalls his people to himself by employing the covenant formula, 'I am the LORD your God from the land of Egypt' (12:9; 13:4). He instituted the relationship and determined its structure, and these terms were recorded in the Scriptures possessed by the nation.

It is a mark of the covenant orientation of Hosea's thought that his message is permeated with Scriptural references. The evaluation of critical scholarship diverges at this point because it favours a date centuries after Hosea for the finalisation of the Old Testament scriptures in the form they have come down to us. Instead critical reconstructions prefer to talk about the oral traditions to which Hosea had access, but which were not yet written down. But there is no need to set aside the view that, though the people had to be taught orally by the priests, and though they also acquired knowledge handed down in the family circle, the nation possessed a written record of divine revelation. This had been at the heart of the worship since Moses placed the Decalogue in the ark (Exod. 26:16; 40:20), and the Book of the Law had been put there also (Deut. 31:26). The growing body of canonical material continued to present a fixed reference point for their national life. It is evident that Hosea himself was intimately acquainted with the five books of Moses, as well as later records. Even more significant is the fact that he unhesitatingly assumed that those whom he addressed were also familiar with these divinely inspired writings, and he uses this in two important ways: to stress the significance of divine law for the nation; and to remind them of the lessons their history taught them.

(a) The Divine Law

The covenant sets the agenda for Hosea's ministry. Just as there were two parties to the covenant, the LORD and Israel, so the prophet's message has two principal themes: the LORD's attitude towards Israel, and Israel's attitude towards the LORD. Considering the latter in the first instance, Hosea is at pains to point out how far Israel's conduct diverged from what it ought to have been.

There was no doubt as to the ideal Israel should have observed. When the LORD chose the people as his own, he made very clear to them that obedience to his voice and adherence to his covenant were necessary for them to fulfil their destiny (Exod. 19:5-6). This was not expressed simply in general terms, with the people left to work out for themselves the details of how they could properly conduct their lives. As well as the general injunctions of the Decalogue (Exod. 20:1-17; Deut. 5:6-21), there were the many specific regulations found throughout the Pentateuch. These did not constitute life-style options or prudent advice which they could adopt as they thought fit; they were commands, non-negotiable requirements which the covenant Overlord demanded that his people obey. Moreover, as that which was written (8:12), these divine laws were permanently preserved and accessible to the nation as a whole. They could not plead ignorance of their heritage.

But 'Israel has forgotten his Maker' (8:14) and treated the precepts of his law as 'something strange' or alien (8:12). They forgot his law (4:6). Like Adam (6:7) they transgressed the covenant (8:1), not only in their overall loyalty to the LORD, but also in specific breaches of his law (4:1-2). They are therefore condemned for their sin and iniquity, and the corruption of their conduct will lead to divine punishment (9:9).

This should have come as no surprise to Israel for the terms of the covenant had always been starkly clear. Being the covenant people of the LORD was no feather-bedded existence. Moses set before Israel the choice of 'life and death, blessing and curse' and urged them to 'choose life' (Deut. 30:19) by displaying obedience to the LORD's commands. There are perils, as well as potential, in great spiritual privilege, for 'everyone to whom much was given, of him much will be required' (Luke 12:48). If the terms of the covenant were adhered to, there would be enjoyment of great blessing. But the dark side to the covenant meant that if its terms were set aside, then the curse of the broken covenant would be activated.

Stuart (1987:xxxi-xli), drawing principally on Leviticus 26 and Deuteronomy 28–32, has calculated that, while there are ten different types of covenant blessing, there were twenty-seven different modes in which the covenant curse might be imposed. Hosea draws extensively and repeatedly on the penalties threatened for disobedience. The LORD's chastisement and correction will come upon the disobedient (5:2b, 9a compared to Lev. 26:18, 28). Stumbling will occur in a context of divine imposition of defeat (4:5; 5:5b compared to Lev. 26:37). The sword which executes vengeance for the covenant will destroy (11:6; 13:16 compared to Lev. 26:25, 33; Deut. 32:24). Wild animals will ravage (2:12c; 5:14; 13:7-8 compared to Lev. 26:22; Deut. 32:24). Their food will not satisfy them (4:10 compared to Lev. 26:26) and their crops will fail (2:9; 9:2 compared to Lev. 26:20, 26; Deut. 28:28-40). There will be barrenness of the womb (9:11, 14, 16 compared to Deut. 28:18), and their population will diminish (9:13, 16 compared to Deut. 28:62). The enemy will come like a vulture (8:1 compared to Deut. 28:49), will pursue them (8:3 compared to Lev. 26:36), and the nation will wander throughout the lands (9:17 compared to Deut. 28:41, 64).

Perhaps being reminded of the horrors which would be experienced in the land when the LORD acted against it would alert the people to the danger they were in, and stir them into appropriate action before it was too late.

(b) The Importance of History

Another consequence of Hosea's covenant orientation is the place he accords the data of history when presenting his prophetic message. This stems from the fact that the LORD as the God of covenant did not just set standards for his people, but also committed himself to monitor their situation and intervene should anything go amiss. God is not some distant and disinterested deity. He is the God of history, actively controlling what occurs. He was not just 'the LORD your God' but had been so 'from the land of Egypt' (12:9; 13:4; cf. 12:13). 'I am the

LORD your God, who brought you out of the land of Egypt, out of the house of slavery' (Exod. 20:2) set out the historical fact which established his right to rule over them and also the grand motive for their loyal devotion to the God of their salvation.

There are many other passages in which Hosea utilises his knowledge of the narratives about the Exodus and Israel's subsequent wanderings in the wilderness (2:3, 14-15; 11:1; 12:9, 13; 13:5). He uses 'Egypt' as a summary description of the oppression from which they had escaped (8:13; 9:3; 11:5). Drawing on the account of Numbers 25:1-5 of what happened at Baal-Peor, he shows how early Israel's propensity to engage in pagan worship manifested itself (9:10). This is no mere antiquarianism. All pointed to the permanent claim the LORD had on their allegiance. They had been chosen by him, and had been cared for from the very start. The LORD was truly Israel's 'first husband' (2:7) and that fact was something from which they could never escape.

Moreover the scope of Hosea's familiarity with existing Scripture was not confined to the forty years of deliverance and wilderness wanderings. He displays knowledge of the creation narrative in the way he describes the animals in 2:18. 'The reference to the series of animals in Hos. 2:18, following the creation order, is a return to the harmony that existed in creation' (Rooker 1993:52). A similar allusion is found in 4:3, and in both passages there are probably also echoes of the Genesis flood narrative.

Hosea has no hesitation in reminding his hearers of the impact of Adam's conduct (6:7), and also shows in 1:10 familiarity with the terms of the Abrahamic covenant (Gen. 22:17). His most extensive employment of Genesis is found, however, in the lessons he draws from the story of the patriarch Jacob (12:3-4, 12). Incidentally he does so in a way which again presupposes intimate acquaintance with it in its canonical form on the part of his hearers.

From later parts of the Old Testament Hosea makes mention of the valley of Achor (Josh. 7:26). He also refers to 'the days of Gibeah' (9:9; 10:9) alluding to the tragic and depraved incidents recorded at the end of the book of Judges. The use of Jezreel in 1:4-5 to recall events which are described in 2 Kings 9:14-37 is another instance of Hosea's employment of acknowledged facts to provide a starting point for interacting with his audience. There is a call to remember the LORD's past goodness, but also their own past faithlessness. Israel still retained a pride in her history as it had been filtered through her present perceptions. Rehearsal of her previous national failures and of the speed with which she had abandoned her covenant loyalty were intended to prick the bubble of her arrogant self-confidence (cf. 13:6) and to cause her to reappraise her conduct.

(c) Spiritual Infidelity

The most serious allegation which Hosea presents against Israel's conduct is breach of the first two commandments by worshipping other gods (cf. 3:1; Exod. 20:3) and the use of idols (cf. 8:5-6; Exod. 20:4). Israel had not needed foreign nations to encourage her in this respect (cf. the golden calf of Exod. 32:1-10), but exposure to the allure of other gods was intensified once the people had settled in Canaan and encountered the Baal worship which had been prevalent there for centuries before Israel went down to Egypt, never mind returned from it.

The Canaanite cult practised a nature religion which had no moral content but focused on climatic and agricultural cycles. Baal was pre-eminently the god of fertility, who sent the rain at the appropriate time and so ensured a fruitful harvest. The agriculture-oriented communities of Canaan were therefore at pains to appease him and to ensure that he was well disposed towards them. As the god who gave and sustained life, his worship was frequently associated with sacred prostitution (cf. 4:14) which, as a form of sympathetic magic, was viewed as reminding Baal (the word means husband as well as master, cf. 2:16-17) of his capacity to make the earth fertile. Such lewd and sensuous worship was a snare to the baser side of the Israelites' nature. Furthermore, coming out of the wilderness as mainly keepers of cattle and sheep, in settling down to fixed agriculture in Canaan, they had the task of distinguishing the technology of such farming (e.g. the maintenance of terraces on hill sides) from the cultural and religious practices in which it was embedded. Their Canaanite neighbours would have argued that a successful harvest depended on appropriate agricultural techniques *and* worshipping the god of the land in the accepted manner. Such a mindset was embedded in the culture of the ancient Near East, and so Israel had been well warned against conforming to Canaanite beliefs and practices before they had entered the land (Lev. 18:24-30; Deut. 7:1-5).

Nevertheless Israel repeatedly succumbed to the pressure to participate in Baal worship. It was the northern kingdom which led the way in this regard. With its repudiation of Jerusalem and the worship at the Temple there, it was open to assimilating religious ideas from elsewhere. Throughout much of the history of the north the prevalent form of religion was syncretistic, which is to be distinguished from the programme of outright and intolerant Baalisation promoted by Ahab under the influence of his Phoenician queen Jezebel. Syncretism represented the politically correct outlook of the day in which everything was permitted except exclusive loyalty to the LORD. It was not that they utterly repudiated the LORD; Israel would claim to worship him (8:2). Admittedly there were bull calves at Dan and Bethel, but could they not quote the precedent of Aaron in that regard, and were they not using these images to worship the LORD?

Syncretism, however, though less blatant in its approach, just as surely corrupted Israel's loyalty to the LORD as Jezebel had sought to. This was not just because the use of material images had been forbidden. There was also the depraving effect on Israel's conception of the LORD from the repeated association of him with a physical object. Their perception of the distinction between Creator and creature was blurred, and from there it was easy to lose sight of the uniqueness of the LORD. That uniqueness was a major predisposing factor in the employment of covenant as the dominant metaphor in Israelite religion. The overlords of the ancient world would not permit their subject peoples to have dealings with any political rival. Such infringement of their majesty and sovereign rights was outright treachery and speedily punished. Similarly because the LORD was unique ('There is no other besides him', Deut. 4:35), he demanded the exclusive loyalty and permanent affection of his people, anything less failed to appreciate who he is. That was why covenant never caught on as a religious metaphor in surrounding polytheistic cultures. Their worldview was such that there were many gods who could claim the worship and service of those who inhabited their territories.

When Israel adopted that mode of thought, its credibility as the covenant partner of the LORD was in tatters. Hosea, however, goes beyond the infringement of the rights of the LORD as covenant King to explore the implications of the LORD as the marriage partner of Israel. Though this conception lies behind many early expressions of Israel's faith (see on 1:2), its use had not been developed to the same extent as the metaphor of kingship, probably because it was liable to be misunderstood in Canaanite terms, that is, in a crassly physical fashion, with the worshippers being in some sense divinised and the transcendence of God compromised. Deployment of the metaphor was probably also inhibited by the toleration of polygamy, awareness of which would detract from perception of the uniqueness of the bond the LORD instituted with his people. Hosea is, however, led to highlight the language of husband, wife, marriage and betrothal because it inescapably presents the personal dimension of the relationship. Covenant infidelity was not just breach of solemn obligations to a distant king; it was gross ingratitude and personal injury to a spouse. Hosea's use of the terms 'whoredom' and 'adultery' emphasises the abhorrent nature of Israel's betrayal and the pain they caused the LORD.[11]

(d) The LORD's Commitment

There were two parties to the covenant, and Hosea's presentation would be woefully incomplete if it ignored the LORD's role in the relationship. It is always evident that it was the initiative of divine love which had given Israel their unique status. 'When Israel was a youth, I loved him' (11:1) sets before us the fundamental, constitutive act of God's grace. That act is inexplicable in that we are never informed of any motive for the existence and exercise of divine love. 'I will be gracious to whom I will be gracious, and I will show compassion to whom I will show compassion' (Exod. 33:19), and beyond that brilliant screen of divine benevolence human vision cannot penetrate. No more can be said than that God's love exists because of his initiative: he first loved us (cf. 1 John 4:10).

Divine election of the people was not just a matter of the initial bestowal of love; it was also manifest in ongoing care and protection. The LORD ordered the circumstances of the nation, dealing gently with them in their youth (11:3) and continuing to draw them to himself 'with bands of love' (11:4). At the time of the Exodus he had brought them out of Egypt by Moses (12:13), and had provided for them as they travelled though the wilderness (13:5). He had then given them his own land as their residence (9:3), where he continued to lavish his bounty on Israel (2:8). When the nation was unresponsive to his goodness and transgressed the covenant, the LORD dealt with them in longsuffering, sending them prophetic warnings about their conduct (12:10).

Now through Hosea the LORD was issuing his final notice to the people. The punishment for their misconduct could be withheld no longer. The LORD was not imposing this penalty lightly, but with a heavy heart. In the emotional intensity of 11:8-9 we are given a glimpse of the tension caused by divine love reacting to human sin.

11. Bergen (1993:41) lists twenty-one explicit references to Israel's or Judah's infidelity to the LORD, 1:2; 2:5, 8, 13:4:1, 10, 12; 5:4, 7; 7:10, 13, 15, 16; 9:7, 17; 10:3; 11:2, 7, 12; 13:6, 9.

Furthermore, Hosea shows that the intervention of divine love is supported, not (as might be expected) opposed, by divine holiness. He is the Holy One (11:9) who is different from his creation and exalted in purity above it in its fallenness. Yet he does not hold himself aloof from the plight of humanity, nor is he indifferent to the suffering which their sin has brought in its train. His love refused to be quenched by rejection and his commitment cannot be diverted by his people's intransigence.

Judgement was inevitable, but its imposition was tempered and channelled by the action of reclaiming love. The people were unable to remedy their own situation, but, though judgement could not be averted, the LORD was going to use it to bring into existence a new situation where idol worship would be purged from their midst, and the people would yearn for a restored relationship with the LORD. He would act as the healer who would remedy the spiritual apostasy of the people (14:4) and reinstate them in his favour.

(e) The Nature of Hosea's Marriage

The nature of Hosea's marriage has been the occasion of much controversy. It is useful to distinguish two broad areas of inquiry: the nature of the events recounted in chapters 1–3, and the character of Gomer. The latter issue will be taken up in the discussion of 1:2; for the moment attention is focused on what kind of account Hosea presents.

At one level differences over the nature of the events recorded do not affect the teaching of these chapters.[12] The focus is on the LORD's love for Israel, and his determination to display that love despite her misconduct (3:1), but the command to marry someone who was sexually promiscuous, probably a prostitute, has left many uneasy.

While there were always those who argued for the historicity of Hosea's marriage, over the centuries many interpreters have considered the LORD's command that he marry a 'wife of whoredoms' (1:2) raises so many issues of moral propriety that some ameliorating interpretation

---

12. 'If we adopt the realistic view of chapters 1–3, we shall have to assume that the prophet was by special grace enabled to live on a higher plane of love towards his wife than the average Israelite of that time [cp. Jer. 3.1]. If on the contrary we choose the allegorical interpretation, we must say that, at least in his understanding and vision of the matter, he was led by the Spirit to frame a conception of the divine-marriage-love towards Israel, far transcending, not only his own, but every ordinary experience known to him. The dispute between allegorists and realists is interesting, but doctrinally the points of arrival on each view coincide' (Vos 1975:261).

of it ought to be sought. How could the LORD who forbad his priests to marry a prostitute (Lev. 21:7, 14) demean his prophet by requiring that he do so? Calvin's comment in this connection has often been cited. 'And yet it seems not consistent with reason, that the Lord should thus gratuitously render his prophet contemptible; for how could he expect to be received on coming abroad before the public, after having brought on himself such a disgrace? If he had married a wife such as is here described, he ought to have concealed himself for life rather than to undertake the prophetic office' (Calvin 1986:44). Furthermore, such a union would seem to involve a clear violation of the standards of the covenant (Exod. 20:14), and in the Old Testament adultery is repeatedly condemned (2 Sam. 11:1-5; Prov. 2:16-19), and severely punished (Lev. 20:10; Deut. 22:23-24). How could the LORD have ordered his prophet to enter into such a compromised relationship? How could a prophet who inveighed against sexual immorality have been ordered to get involved in such a scandalous liaison?

In the nineteenth century Patrick Fairbairn, who played an influential role in the development of the modern conservative approach to prophecy, went so far as to argue that all prophetic actions were symbolic unless they are explicitly designated as real (1964:116–120). He therefore considered the story of the marriage to have been merely visionary. The renowned conservative theologian, Edward J. Young, is known to have changed his views on the matter. In his *Introduction to the Old Testament*, first published in 1949, he wrote: 'In company with many biblical students, the present writer has become more and more convinced that the whole episode has a symbolical significance. The entire message was revealed to the prophet, and the prophet related this revelation to the people. ... This symbolical interpretation, of course, is not without difficulty, but it seems to be correct' (1984:253). However, speaking over a decade later, he acknowledged that his viewpoint had swung in the other direction. 'Now it just so happens that most of the Conservatives adopt that view that it occurred in vision. I have held to that view, but right now I want to say frankly I am not so sure that that is right. Despite all the objections that may be raised against the literal view, it may be that that is intended' (Young, E. J. 1965:65).

There are, however, many passages where a prophet is divinely directed to engage in some surprising activity. Isaiah walked round Jerusalem for three years naked and barefoot (Isa. 20:2-3). Jeremiah hid his underwear near a stream until it had rotted (Jer. 13:1-7), and he also smashed a clay jar (Jer. 19:10). As for Ezekiel, his activities have attracted much adverse comment (cf. Ezek. 4–5). But these were all symbolic actions which vividly embodied the message to be delivered by the prophet. They were designed to attract the attention of those to whom they were originally addressed and bring graphically home to them the enormity of their conduct and the danger of the situation. Allegory or vision might have conveyed the same message, but the imagined or contrived element in such techniques would have lessened their impact.

Hosea's marriage is not a fictional narrative, crafted to tell a story, but an account of real-life incidents, as factual as Israel's misconduct itself. The context does not indicate that Gomer and her children are anything other than historical figures, and it is far from clear that presupposing a visionary or allegorical basis for the passage circumvents the perceived moral problem. Is a divine command in a vision or in an illustration to be assessed on a different basis from one that pertains to ordinary living? Moreover, it soon becomes clear that Hosea was not being asked to do anything in respect of Gomer which was other than what the LORD himself has done with respect to Israel. And that is where the whole emphasis lies. Through Hosea's marriage, the LORD was pleading with his people to recognise how they have spoiled their relationship with him and to take appropriate action.

Marriage was divinely intended to institute an exclusive and permanent bond between a man and a woman (Gen. 2:24), and so it also is a covenant relationship (Prov. 2:17; Ezek. 16:8; Mal. 2:14; cf. *5(c)* above). In this way the circumstances of Hosea's marriage vividly illustrated the LORD's own relationship with Israel. In place of the intimate and harmonious fellowship which should have existed between the partners to the bond, unfaithfulness had arisen. Marital infidelity, which is what Hosea's wife Gomer is ultimately accused of (3:1), is likened to Israel's apostasy when they adopted Canaanite ideas of worship and set Yahweh on a par with Canaanite gods. The people's thoughtless behaviour had ruptured the covenant/marriage bond, and such a situation could not be allowed to continue. The LORD would punish their disobedience, and yet this would be done in love. He would not desert his commitment and, through corrective discipline, would bring Israel to repentance and reinstate them in enjoyment of his favour.

(f) The Restoration of Israel

It is clear from chapter 3 that Hosea was aware of the LORD's intention to treat Israel in a way parallel to that which the prophet himself was instructed to impose on Gomer. First of all there would be a period of isolation and deprivation during which Israel would be induced to abandon her infatuation with pagan worship and return in fidelity to the LORD (3:4). This was in measure achieved through the conquest of the land by the Assyrians and the subsequent deportation of the people. As a political entity, the northern kingdom was wiped from the map.

Later in the prophecy Hosea reveals that he is also aware of a similar destiny awaiting Judah. The southern kingdom will too become the subject of a divine complaint (12:2), cause the LORD perplexity by her conduct (6:4), stumble (5:5), be ravaged by the LORD's judgements (5:14), and be cut down in the divine harvest (6:10). Furthermore the prophet had also been informed that the timescale of events involving Judah was not identical to that for Israel because Judah was for a while to experience divine relief (1:7). However, when the time for restoration came, remnants from north and south would both be involved in it (1:11).

The passages in which the visions granted to Hosea stretch beyond a time of impending judgement to the restoration of God's people remain a source of difficulty for interpreters. One approach is to say that these promises of future prosperity were conditioned on the people responding appropriately to the message delivered to them, and that when repentance was not forthcoming, the promises lapsed. We are therefore not to attach any continuing significance to them. That, however, is to negate the message which Hosea presents. Although judgement is justly inflicted on the errant people, their disobedience will not be permitted to nullify the purposes of God. He will summon them and they will come (11:10-11).

At a certain level the promises of restoration were fulfilled when the exiles returned to Judah after the Babylonian exile. 'In Jerusalem there dwelled some of the sons of Judah and some of the sons of Benjamin and some of the sons of Ephraim and Manasseh' (1 Chron. 9:3), so that there were returnees from the north as well as from the south in the restored city. But the reality of life in the Persian province of Yehud hardly matched up to the scope and grandeur of the pledges God had given regarding the restoration of the people. There had to be more.

As with all the promises of Scripture that 'more' is to be found in Christ. Apart from him the purposes of God never reach their consummation. The question which remains is how that conclusion will be realised. There are those who support the view that the Old Testament predictions of restoration to the land and subsequent growth in numbers (found in Hosea in 1:10-11; 11:10-11) still await literal fulfilment in time to come for ethnic Israel. But when Paul examined the question of what the future holds for those who are blood descendants of Abraham he did not talk in terms of a restored land or city and of extensive population growth, though he did disclose that a grand destiny is still reserved for them (Rom. 11:26). Even though with the accession of the Gentiles into the Christian church it might have seemed that the Jews no longer had a place within God's purposes (and that impression would be reinforced by the devastating overthrow of Jerusalem in A.D. 70), God has not given up on his ancient people. Paul asserts this in terms of two illustrative figures: the lump of dough (Rom. 11:16), and the olive tree (Rom. 11:17-21). Each figure embodies a single entity: *one* lump of dough, *one* olive tree. Incorporation into that single entity, the church of Jesus Christ, into which entry is achieved only by faith in the one Saviour, is the prospect held out by the apostle for his kinsmen according to the flesh, as also for Gentile believers who are no longer 'alienated from the commonwealth of Israel' but participate fully and equally in the 'covenants of promise' (Eph. 2:12). That vision is in harmony with the statements of Christ himself: 'I have other sheep that are not of this fold. I must bring them also, and they will listen to my voice. So there will be one flock, one shepherd' (John 10:16). Which is, of course, in alignment with Hosea's vision of 'one head' for the reunited people (1:11) restored under the Davidic Messiah (3:5).

The visions granted to a prophet like Hosea were presented in terms of the reality of God's people as it was known and visible in his time. The outward symbols of God's truth for Old Testament times are now fulfilled in other ways which preserve and enhance the truth they have always conveyed. No longer is worship confined to the Jerusalem Temple. The Temple is now realised wherever the people of God gather to worship: the Lord is in their midst. No longer is the church of God localised in terms of one geo-political entity. The shadows of the past, the elementary instruction suited to the age before Christ, are indeed no longer applicable, but the underlying truths are fulfilled—and more so. Both Jew and Gentile are united in the one church of Christ where there is displayed the depths of the riches and wisdom and knowledge of God in salvation (Rom. 11:33). The dividing wall of hostility (Eph. 2:14), having been broken down by Christ, is not going to be re-erected in some future period of nationally exclusive blessing.

I. A Broken Marriage

(1:1–3:5)

OUTLINE

A. The Prophet's Family (1:1–2:1)

1. Introduction (1:1)
2. Gomer (1:2-3)
3. Jezreel: Blessing Reversed (1:4-5)
4. Lo-Ruchama: Compassion Withdrawn (1:6-7)
5. Lo-Ammi: Estrangement Complete (1:8-9)
6. Restoration (1:10–2:1)

B. The LORD and Israel (2:2-23)

1. Israel's Disgraceful Behaviour (2:2-13)
2. Love's Initiative (2:14-23)

C. Reclaiming Love (3:1-5)

1. The Restoration of Hosea's Wife (3:1-3)
2. The Restoration of Israel (3:4-5)

Hosea's account of his prophetic ministry begins with his marriage. The prophet relates how God commanded him to marry a woman of doubtful character (1:2), and how children were born and given symbolic names (1:3-8). Later he reveals that their family life broke down because of his wife's unfaithfulness (3:1), but even then, in accordance with divine instructions, he reclaimed his wife and took steps to restore their relationship (3:2-3). Beyond that skeletal outline Hosea is reticent about what must have been a painful and turbulent experience. Such silence has opened the door for much speculation—which has inevitably proved inconclusive. However, there is no doubt that both at the level of God's intention in arranging the marriage and at the level of Hosea's rationale for beginning his prophetic memoirs in this way, his marriage to Gomer served a useful purpose: it engaged the attention of his contemporaries, and of succeeding generations as well.

Still, though our interest is naturally stimulated by the prophet's unusual marital circumstances, we ought not to be diverted from the substance of his message. Moreover, Hosea goes out of his way to direct the reader's focus away from himself. That seems to be why the early chapters of the book provide such scant personal information. Indeed, after the first few verses Hosea does not again mention either himself or Gomer by name. For it is not the messenger or his family history which are of primary importance. Hosea's relationship with Gomer was designed to reflect that between the LORD and his people, Israel. Guided by the Holy Spirit, the prophet gives just enough details of his own domestic tragedy to illumine the main story, but not to replace it. What is of paramount significance is the LORD's evaluation of the bond between himself and his people. They had sinned gravely and persistently, and consequently dire judgement was looming over the nation. In the ultimate analysis the marriage which has broken down is not that between Hosea and Gomer, but that between the LORD and Israel. However, despite all that had gone wrong, the prophet's vision is repeatedly brought back to the restoration which will be achieved because of the committed love of the LORD who will not let his people go. His resolve establishes and proclaims the final verdict on their destiny, which is sovereignly and irrevocably determined by his grace and compassion.

Hosea gives literary expression to the centrality of the LORD's relationship with Israel in the way he arranges the material in this division of the book. Chapters 1–3 have a simple three-part chiastic (cross-over or envelope) structure in which the two outer sections, A (1:1–2:1) and

C (3:1-5), provide a mixture of information about Hosea's personal circumstances and the message the LORD wished to convey through them. However, in the central section, B (2:2-23), the details of Hosea's marriage fade almost completely into the background, and the dominant theme is the relationship between the LORD and his covenant people. Furthermore, each of these three sections possesses a similar internal arrangement. Three times there is a movement from the sinful behaviour of the people and the judgement that is going to come on them (1:2-9; 2:2-13; 3:1) to the divine initiative of love which, despite Israel's spiritual wandering, will effect their restoration (1:10–2:1; 2:14-23; 3:2-5). So it is clear that the overriding purpose of this division of the book is not to acquaint us with particulars of Hosea's life, but to bring out the way in which the LORD was prepared to redeem his people despite their rebellion.

As regards the date of composition of these chapters, it is evident that what is recorded here was put into its present form some time after the events which are described actually took place. 'Beginning' (1:2) indicates that subsequent communications from the LORD to Hosea were known about when that verse was written. It is not possible to give a definitive answer to the question of who was responsible for bringing Hosea's memoirs into their present form. Trends in modern scholarship favour redactors or groups of redactors at various dates. There is, however, nothing in the text to rule out the simpler hypothesis that it was the prophet himself who set out the record of his life and ministry in the form in which we now have it.

The messages of chapters 1–3 reflect a period of national prosperity in the northern kingdom of Israel, which fits in well with what we know about the closing years of Jeroboam's reign. Since the events recorded here require at least five years, but more probably as long as ten years, the record would cover what occurred between the mid 750s and mid 740s B.C., that is, between the closing years of Jeroboam's reign and the resurgence of Assyria under Tiglath-Pileser (see *Introduction*, pg. 15).

A. The Prophet's Family (1:1–2:1)

After an initial heading (1:1), we are introduced to Hosea's wife and children. Their family history embodies the message of the entire book, and indeed of the history of the northern kingdom of Israel. By designating a wife of questionable character for Hosea, the LORD used the prophet to give a vivid illustration of the unfaithfulness of the people to himself (1:2). The names of the prophet's three children presage the judgement which is inevitably coming upon the land (1:4-9). Yet, when all seems headed for an irretrievable disaster, a message of hope and salvation suddenly intrudes into the ominous scene (1:10–2:1). This change does not originate in any recovery which Hosea and his family manage to bring about, or in what the nation contrives to achieve. The dominant lesson of this section is that of the controlling purpose of the LORD, who will sovereignly reclaim and restore his people. The great reversal is the product of restoring grace.

There is no reason to doubt that the third person account of this section goes back to the prophet himself. In its present form it comes from a period subsequent to the events described (cf. 1:2), but it is probable that Hosea himself kept records of his ministry from its early days. For a discussion of the historical nature of the account, see *Introduction* pg. 36, and the decision to set out certain verses in this section as poetry is argued for in *Introduction*, pg. 26.

(1) Introduction (1:1)

1:1 The word of the LORD which came to Hosea, son of Beeri, in the days of Uzziah, Jotham, Ahaz ⌞and⌟ Hezekiah, kings of Judah, and in the days of Jeroboam, son of Joash, king of Israel.

This verse brings to the attention of the reader factors which are of importance for understanding the book correctly: the document which follows is the record of a prophetic ministry, and its significance requires that it be interpreted against the background of the prophet's own times.

Hosea differs from Isaiah (Isa. 1:1), Ezekiel (Ezek. 1:1) or even his contemporary Amos (Amos 1:1), by not mentioning an initial visionary experience. He simply speaks of ***the word of the LORD*** (cf. Jer. 1:2; Mic. 1:1), which refers to the content of what he, as a spokesman for the LORD, had been commissioned to proclaim. Though Hosea delivered various messages over a number of years, his ministry was integrally related and constituted one co-ordinated declaration from the LORD. The word ***came*** refers to that which originated outwith Hosea himself and was divinely disclosed to the prophet's inner consciousness. So what follows is not human analysis or social commentary emanating from an individual pondering the destiny of his nation; rather this is the declaration of a prophet whose message has been directly revealed to him by God.

The prophet's own name, Hosea, is a shortened form of Hoshaiah (cf. Neh. 12:32; Jer. 42:1; 43:2), which means 'the LORD has saved' or

'LORD, save!' Its significance is therefore close to that of the name Joshua ('the LORD has saved'), and indeed Hoshea had been Joshua's name until Moses changed it (Num. 13:16). ***Son of Beeri*** (literally 'my spring' or 'my well') indicates his descent, but neither the identity of his father nor the interpretation of his name are of relevance for understanding the book. Beeri is attested as a name in Genesis 26:34, and also in extra-Biblical sources.[1] The patronymic serves to distinguish the prophet from others with the same name, particularly Hoshea the last king of Israel (2 Kgs. 15:30; see *Introduction*, pg. 18). We are not told anything of the prophet's background, but he was evidently a northerner himself (see *Introduction*, pg. 19).

In the days of is equivalent to 'during the reign of', and the names of the kings indicate the historical context of Hosea's ministry, stretching from before Jeroboam's death in 753 B.C. until after Hezekiah's accession in 729 B.C. The list begins by recording four ***kings of Judah*** (for further details regarding them, see *Introduction*, pg. 13). This sequence corresponds to that found in Isaiah 1:1, though the latter prophet was called at the end of Uzziah's reign around 739 B.C. (Isa. 6:1) and outlived Hosea by many years. Furthermore, the kings of Judah are mentioned first, a feature which may reflect a measure of approbation extended by Hosea to the southern monarchs, and his expectation that salvation would come through the house of David (cf. 3:5). Also Jeroboam is the only Israelite king named, and this may be a way of expressing doubts as to the legitimacy of his successors (cf. 8:4), though that would scarcely apply to Zechariah, Jeroboam's son and heir. More probably the others are passed over as non-entities who scarcely merited the title of king, especially since so many of them assassinated their predecessor to gain the throne. For further information regarding Hosea's views of kingship, see on 1:11; 3:5; and 7:3-7, and for his interest in Judah, see on 1:7.

Critical scholars have argued that this introductory verse was added later by the scribes who preserved Hosea's oracles after the overthrow of the northern kingdom. As their intended audience was in the south, the scribes added information which was of relevance to them. While this might account for the kings of Judah being listed first, it is still probable that the arrangement derives from Hosea himself. His

1. A Jewish tradition identifies Beeri with 'Beerah', the Reubenite leader who was deported by Tiglath-Pileser (1 Chron. 5 6). That would imply that Hosea was a northerner from the tribe of Reuben, but there is nothing to substantiate this speculation.

knowledge of the history of the covenant people and his commitment to the faith revealed through Moses is consonant with an acceptance of the southern line of kings as the true successors of David and as those through whom the LORD would realise the commitments he had made in the Davidic covenant. This outlook is reinforced by the fact that the final kings of Israel are passed over in silence (cf. Harrison 1969:860).

Jeroboam, however, could not be disregarded. He is here designated ***son of Joash*** (also known as Jehoash, cf. American editions of NIV, NLT), to distinguish him from Jeroboam I, the first king of the breakaway northern kingdom, who was 'son of Nebat' (1 Kgs. 12:2). Jeroboam II was a significant figure in the history of the north, and under him Israel was a considerable local power. Territory was regained (2 Kgs. 14:25) and the land enjoyed security and economic prosperity. But it was affluence accompanied by religious apostasy, and that scenario provides the background for the initial period of Hosea's ministry during the closing years of Jeroboam's reign. After his death the land lurched into internal chaos in a series of short reigns during which no monarch of any great significance arose, certainly none who could effectively combat the dangers facing the land. Throughout these troubled times for the northern kingdom Hosea's ministry provided the LORD's commentary and his call for repentance as the way to avert further disaster.

REFLECTION

- When Paul brought out the significance of events which occurred long before Hosea's time, he wrote, 'Now these things took place as examples for us so that we might not desire evil things as they too desired' (1 Cor. 10:6), and the same style of interpretation applies here also. The word of the LORD was not expressed in generalised theological observations, but in a form which directly related to the specific historical context of the prophet's day. The preservation of that message for centuries long after that time indicates that embedded in it are truths of lasting significance. It is to that point that the epilogue to the book returns (14:9). The reader is challenged to discern how God has worked in past situations and to apply to the varying circumstances of later ages the lessons taught by the inspired record of earlier events. This approach is valid because of the unchanging character of God, and the teaching it provides is needed because of the enduring sinfulness of humanity.

(2) Gomer (1:2-3)

Prior to Hosea's ministry there had been no extended exploration of marriage as a metaphor for the LORD's relationship with Israel, and so there had been no explicit identification of him as the husband of his people. However, indications were given that it was an appropriate analogy, so that Hosea's presentation is not wholly innovative.[2] For instance, an expression such as 'commit whoredom after their gods' (Exod. 34:15) in connection with the spiritual unfaithfulness of the people derives its force from the acceptance of an underlying resemblance between the covenant bond and marriage. The Scriptural norm for marriage is presented in Genesis 2:23-24 as a union which takes priority over other human relationships, even those that exist naturally and have their own proper basis ('Therefore a man shall leave his father and mother'), and which entails an exclusive, permanent commitment ('the man shall … hold fast to his wife'). Breaches of this bond were not tolerated ('You shall not commit adultery', Exod. 20:14). Similarly the LORD wished to forge a union with his people in which they would treat all other allegiances as secondary to the one which they had with him. So he required them to renounce every spiritual connection which was inconsistent with his primary, unique, perpetual rights over them. Just as the metaphor of covenant reflected the international treaties of the ancient world and demanded Israel's undivided allegiance to the LORD as their sovereign King, so the metaphor of marriage added a dimension of intimacy to the description of the covenant bond, emphasising that the LORD was jealous of his relationship with his people and not prepared to share their devotion with a third party (Deut. 32:21). The union between God and Israel created by this bond intensified the sense of betrayal involved in their infidelity; it was not simply breach of a contract, but treachery which caused personal hurt.

1:2 The beginning of ⌞what⌟ the LORD spoke through Hosea.

And the LORD said to Hosea,
'Go, take for yourself a wife of whoredoms
and children of whoredoms,
for the land is committing great whoredom
⌞departing⌟ from the LORD.'

2. A thorough exploration of these earlier passages is provided by Ortlund 1996:15–45.

Instead of being treated as an introductory temporal clause ('When the LORD first spoke …', ESV), ***the beginning of what the LORD spoke***[3] ***through Hosea*** is to be taken as a subtitle covering 1:2b–2:1. It is unlikely that it covers the whole division of the book to the end of chapter 3, because there is every reason to suppose that, during the period in which the events of the first three chapters occurred, Hosea engaged in other ministry which may now be incorporated in subsequent chapters. Rather this expression indicates that Hosea's call to be a prophet took the form of a divine command to get married, after which the LORD communicated with his appointed messenger on various occasions. Hosea was evidently unmarried when he received this command, and it would be in accordance with prevailing social practice to envisage him as around twenty years old.

The terse record does not seek to inform about the precise circumstances of the prophet or of the community when this message was delivered. What mattered was that the LORD was going to speak to his errant people, and they had to grapple with the challenge his message brought to their personal and national conduct. Furthermore, if this record was finally prepared by Hosea for transmission to the southern kingdom and preservation there, then it would confront Judah also regarding their attitude towards the LORD and how he would deal with them.

It is significant to note that 'the LORD spoke *through* Hosea', not 'to' him or 'about' him. While the preposition may be used to indicate action shared 'with' another, the idiom 'to speak in/by means of' (*dibber bə*) designates Hosea as the channel through whom the LORD communicated with others. The same expression is employed in Aaron and Miriam's indignant questions, 'Is it only with/through Moses that the LORD has spoken? Has he not also spoken with/through us?' (Num. 12:2; cf. 1 Kgs. 22:28). Hosea's marriage and the names he gave children were not primarily personal, family matters, but were

---

3. Literally, the expression is 'beginning of the LORD spoke'. While this combination of a noun in the construct followed by a finite verb is unusual, it is attested elsewhere (e.g. Exod. 6:28; 1 Sam. 25:15; Isa. 29:1; cf. GKC §130d). The LXX rendering 'beginning of the word of the Lord' represents an attempt to express this thought in Greek. The repetition of both 'the LORD' and 'Hosea' makes it more likely that the expression is a heading to the section, standing grammatically separate, rather than a subordinate clause introducing what follows, 'When the LORD began to speak to Hosea' (cf. NRSV, ESV).

intended as a means of addressing the community as a whole. The subtitle thus emphasises the divine legitimation of Hosea's startling conduct, and therefore of his ministry—something which was doubtless needed in the light of the instructions given to him.

There then follows the first of four divine injunctions (cf. 1:4, 6, 9), each of which is implemented by the prophet and each of which is accompanied by an explanation which points out its significance for the entire nation.

Go, take for yourself a wife/'woman' is a formula for marriage, as in Genesis 4:19, 'And Lamech took for himself two wives/women' (cf. Gen. 6:2; 11:29; 24:67; Exod. 6:20). Indeed 'take' on its own may be used of choosing a bride (cf. Gen. 24:3; Exod. 34:16; Lev. 21:13). So it is clear that Hosea is commanded to get married.

What causes considerable difficulty is the description which is given of his bride, 'a woman of *zənûnîm*', an uncommon plural form for which many translations have been proposed: whoredoms, harlotries, prostitutions, promiscuities, fornications, unfaithfulnesses. It is an ugly, abrasive, accusing term which should not be narrowed or toned down. Its pejorative and condemnatory connotations are clearly evident when it is used along with 'sorceries' to describe the conduct of the notorious Israelite queen Jezebel (2 Kgs. 9:22). The associated verb *zānâ* nearly always has a feminine subject and denotes engaging in illicit sexual behaviour outside the bond of marriage. It usually involved receipt of payment of some sort, and it always attracted social disapproval and opprobrium. Terms derived from the same root are also used metaphorically in connection with other types of unfaithful behaviour, particularly violation by Israel of the covenant bond with the LORD (cf. Lev. 20:6; Deut. 31:16; Judg. 2:17). Many views have been advanced as to the precise significance of the expression 'a woman of *zənûnîm*' as applied to Gomer.[4]

One way of approaching the matter is to observe what Hosea does not say. Some commentators have supposed that Gomer is described as a woman whose sexually immoral behaviour was connected with the Canaanite fertility cult. However, there is a specific Hebrew word for a 'cult prostitute', which Hosea does in fact employ in 4:14. Hence his avoidance of the term in connection with Gomer may be taken as a fairly conclusive indicator that her misconduct lay elsewhere. Nor is

4. For a survey of theories up to that point, see the comprehensive treatment of Rowley 1963. An evaluation of later literature is provided by Kelle 2009.

Gomer's whoredom to be viewed as merely involvement in Baal worship in general. Undoubtedly that was common in Hosea's day; it is after all the charge which is brought against the people as a whole (cf. 4:12, 15, 18; 9:1). However, if no more was meant than that Gomer was a typical Israelite woman of her day, 'then the drama and anguish of these chapters would be incomprehensible' (Anderson 1975:427). That Gomer was a child of her own generation who may have participated in the religious aberrations and unfaithfulness of the north is beside the point. Rather than assuming that this is an instance where actual practice and metaphorical usage overlap, it is preferable to take the comparison as being between Gomer's *marital* unfaithfulness to Hosea and Israel's *religious* infidelity to the LORD.

Furthermore, at this juncture Hosea does not use the narrower terms 'adultery' or 'adulteress'. In the Old Testament 'adultery' refers to voluntary sexual relations between a *married* woman and any male other than her husband. That is how Hosea uses the term in 4:13 and 4:14, where it is 'your daughters-in-law', that is married women, who commit adultery. An allegation of adultery would be inappropriate when Gomer is as yet unmarried, but it is made at a later stage (3:1).

Somewhat surprising is the fact that here and elsewhere Hosea does not apply to Gomer the usual term for a 'prostitute' (*zônâ*), which is derived from the root under discussion (e.g., *ʾiššâ zônâ*, 'a woman, a prostitute', Lev. 21:7-14). So Gomer is not directly described as someone who earned a living by soliciting sex for financial compensation. Instead, the plural of an associated noun is employed. While this may simply be a synonymous expression, it is highly probable that a specific emphasis is intended. The plural of a noun may convey the notion of repeated action of a certain sort, or it may be a plural of abstraction describing the character of an individual.[5] Similar phrases, such as 'man of bloods' (2 Sam. 16:7) and 'woman of contentions' (Prov. 21:9; 25:24; 27:15), are found elsewhere in the Old Testament, but it is doubtful if they ever portray an individual's make-up apart from the external actions to which it gives rise. Significantly, Hosea uses the phrase 'a spirit of whoredoms' in 4:12 and 5:4 to specify an inner propensity to unfaithfulness which manifests itself in observable

---

5. The expression *ʾiššâ zənûnîm* is identified as a plural describing a repeated series of actions or a habitual behaviour, *IBHS* §7.4.2c. However, they also note the use of the plural to express an abstract quality where the plural 'may have originally signified the diverse concrete manifestations of a quality or state' (§7.4.2a).

behaviour. So it is probable that Gomer is presented as someone who, while not necessarily a professional prostitute, is notorious for her promiscuous behaviour.

The question then arises as to when this character trait first manifested itself in Gomer's conduct. Often through a desire to mitigate perceived ethical problems, commentators have proposed that this description of Gomer expresses Hosea's retrospective evaluation of her. Gomer was chaste when Hosea married her, and it was only afterwards that he learned the truth regarding her. However, such a proleptic usage seems to be an expedient adopted without any feature of the text providing a peg on which to hang it. It is not stated that the LORD directed Hosea to Gomer personally; rather he gave the prophet a general description of the sort of woman whom he was to marry and left the individual choice to the prophet himself. Since Hosea was not to engage in psychoanalysis, Gomer's inner disposition must already have been evident in her conduct. Furthermore, Hosea's marriage was an instance of prophetic symbolism, designed to speak to his contemporaries (see *Introduction*, pg. 36). For them to be aware of its full significance, Gomer's behaviour must have been scandalous from the outset.

It may be objected, however, that this conclusion mars the parallel between Hosea's marriage and the LORD's union with Israel because when Hosea looks back on the early history of the people he detects an initial stage of positive relationship (2:14-15; 9:10; 10:1, 11), as later Jeremiah would also (Jer. 2:2). Nonetheless, it was always acknowledged that Israel had an idolatrous past, both before Abraham left Ur, and while in Egypt. Joshua's words are well known: 'Remove the gods which your fathers served beyond the River ⌞Euphrates⌟ and in Egypt, and serve the LORD' (Josh. 24:14). Although the incident of the Golden Calf in Exodus 32 reveals how shallow Israel's commitment was, it is argued that there was a short-lived period of promise and potential when the people pledged themselves to the LORD (cf. Exod. 24:3, 7). Even so, the main focus of the present passage is that because of Israel's unfaithfulness the relationship had not progressed as it should have done. Consequently the prophet's situation reflected that of the LORD with respect to Israel, for he had entered into a covenant bond with the people knowing full well the stresses and strains the relationship would come under due to their character, and Hosea likewise knew that Gomer's misconduct would parallel that of Israel. When anyone would challenge the prophet as to his choice of wife, he could readily respond that they were looking in a mirror at their own relation to the LORD—and this would be facilitated by the earlier religious use of 'commit whoredom'. Gomer's wandering looks and corrupt behaviour—fickle in relationships, unstable in commitments, of changeable and capricious personality—were a living embodiment of Israel's infidelity in their relationship with the LORD.

Gomer's children are described as ***children of whoredoms***, which in itself may describe them as being born through their mother's misconduct, though this is not true of the first son (1:3), and need not be so of the other two children (1:6, 8). Indeed, because there is only one verb used, this phrase has even been taken to refer to children already born as a result of promiscuous behaviour prior to her marriage whom Hosea was to adopt (McComiskey 1992:15–16), but it is more probable that there is here an instance of a figure of speech known as zeugma. In this compressed mode of expression one verb governs two objects, but in somewhat different senses. Hosea is commanded to take/get a wife and so in a somewhat different sense to get a family. Furthermore, it is predicted that the children will inherit character traits from their mother, whose conduct will adversely impact their own.

For introduces the second, more significant part of the verse. The prophet is to engage in such unusual behaviour to alert his contemporaries to their violation of the terms of their covenant with the LORD. This shows that from the outset Gomer and her children were divinely designated as having symbolic significance for the nation. ***The land*** may well be a designation of both the northern and the southern kingdoms; it functions as a metonymy for the people associated with the land who, taken collectively, occupy the land as recipients of the LORD's favour and his covenant blessing (cf. 9:3). ***Committing great whoredom*** (an infinitive absolute preceding a finite verb) is an emphatic expression denoting how completely the people despised their privileged relationship with the LORD and acted with gross promiscuity (cf. Exod. 34:15-16 where the root *zānâ* occurs three times in connection with improper attraction to Canaanite gods in conjunction with the term 'after'). ***⌊Departing⌋ from the LORD*** (literally, 'from after the LORD'; cf. 2:5; Num. 14:43; Deut. 7:4; Josh. 22:16[6]) indicates a repudiation of his authority and leadership.[7] Here the focus is not on

6. Hebrew style frequently permits such an ellipsis of a verb of motion if it can be readily inferred from the context (GKC §119ee-gg; *IBHS* §11.4.3d). Hosea also uses this construction in 2:17, 20; 3:5; 12:7.

7. Third person references to the LORD within direct speech are permissible in Hebrew idiom (cf. 1:7, 3:1; Zeph. 1:5, 6).

the deities whom the people take as the objects of their misplaced devotion, but on the sheer folly of the national malaise in which they rebelled against the LORD, their covenant benefactor, and put their trust elsewhere.

The explanation given here no doubt also eased the considerable personal challenge for the prophet in responding to the instructions given to him. The focus of the book is not on what obedience cost Hosea, and he is silent as to any questions he may have had. Even so, the strangeness of his call would have been mitigated when he was told how the pattern of his life would function in conveying the LORD's message to the people. It also provided him with an answer if any of his contemporaries mocked him regarding his choice of wife.

1:3 So he went and took Gomer, daughter of Diblayim; and she conceived and bore to him a son.

In ***he went and took***, the repetition of the verbs 'go' and 'take' from the divine directions of 1:2 indicates that Hosea did exactly what the LORD had commanded. There is no hint of demurral or delay. ***Took*** in this verse is not accompanied by the word 'woman'/'wife', but the thought is carried over from the previous verse and is used to report a legitimate marriage. Gomer is assigned a totally passive role in the matter as was Israel in the LORD's election of them.

Various attempts have been made to ascertain the meaning of the names ***Gomer*** and ***Diblayim***, but no conclusive results have been obtained. Gomer occurs as a male name in Genesis 10:2, and it may be related to a fuller form, Gemariah ('the LORD has accomplished', Jer. 29:3; 36:10). However, the opacity of these names in contrast to those subsequently given to the children strongly indicates that here Gomer is a real person who had that name before Hosea married her, and that Diblayim is the name of her father, and not a place name (such as Diblathayim in Moab, cf. Num. 33:46; Jer. 48:22). It then follows that the ***son*** mentioned is also a real person. It is significant that ***to him*** is explicitly present to indicate that Hosea was his father.[8] Opinions differ as to what weight is to be attached to its omission as regards the subsequent children; it may simply arise from the compressed nature of the account.

8. It is noted by Harper (1905:206) that 'to him' is omitted in some Hebrew and Greek manuscripts, and also in Arabic. This phenomenon, however, is easily explained as assimilation to the form of the subsequent verses (1:6, 8). Nonetheless Laetsch takes the view that the child was indeed illegitimate (Laetsch 1956:20).

REFLECTION

- The language of whoredom and prostitution emphasises the ugly and repulsive nature of religious infidelity as well as how it intrudes into and disrupts the unsullied relationship which the people of God should have with him. Paul desired that those who benefited from his ministry should exhibit 'sincere and pure devotion to Christ' (2 Cor. 11:3) in accordance with Christ's own aim to 'present the church to himself in splendour, without spot or wrinkle or any such thing, that she might be holy and blameless' (Eph. 5:27) and so ready to fulfil her role as the bride of the Lamb (Rev. 19:7). Whatever does not accord with that outcome is to be spurned, and whatever sinful blemish already exists needs to be cleansed 'by the washing with water through the word' (Eph. 5:26). Since the ultimate purpose of Christ is to present his people pure and blameless in his heavenly kingdom, that same outcome should be accorded the highest priority now.
- 'Children of whoredoms' (1:2) points to the spiritual legacy which is transmitted by parents to their children. While each generation is influenced for better or worse by the preceding, its impact is most intensely felt within the family circle (cf. Exod. 20:5-6). It is not merely a matter of profligate parents being unable to bequeath a material inheritance to their children. The ultimate deprivation is that experienced by those who do not receive the teaching of the family circle from parents who fear the LORD (cf. Deut. 4:9-10; 6:7).

(3) Jezreel: Blessing Reversed (1:4-5)

Giving a prophet's children symbolically significant names also occurred later in the eighth century B.C. with Isaiah's two sons, Shear-jashub ('A remnant will return', Isa. 7:3) and Maher-shalal-hash-baz ('Speeding is booty; hastening is plunder', Isa. 8:3). These names were not intended to convey information about the personality of the individuals involved. The children were rather instruments used by God to stir the interest of the people and convey his challenge to them as to their conduct and the legacy they were bequeathing to subsequent generations.

1:4 And the LORD said to him,
'Call his name Jezreel,
for yet a little while
and I will appoint the bloodshed of Jezreel
upon the house of Jehu,
and I will cause to cease the kingdom of the house of Israel.'

The narrative is terse, wasting no time in background details before proceeding to the second divine injunction, which would naturally have come shortly after Hosea's son had been born. ***Call*** is a masculine singular imperative addressed to the prophet. ***Jezreel*** ('May God sow'/'make fruitful'; cf. 2:21-23) could be used as a personal name (1 Chron. 4:3),[9] but it principally described a town which was situated in a valley of the same name in the northern tribal territory of Issachar (Josh. 17:16), and which in the time of Ahab became the winter capital of the Israelite kings. In itself the name originally possessed very positive associations (cf. 1:11; 2:22) because this area was at the heart of the agricultural prosperity of the northern kingdom, and the valley also formed part of a major international trade route from Egypt to Damascus and thence to Mesopotamia. Moreover, since Jezreel (*yizrəʿeʾl*) is similar in sound to Israel (*yiśrāʾēl*), it is easy to connect the two, and so there is an obvious hint that the fortunes of Jezreel set a precedent for those of the northern kingdom as a whole. In this verse the original significance of Jezreel is reversed to make it a symbol of the besetting sin of the current regime in Israel which was ruthlessly committed to advancing its own interests in any way which came to hand.

For introduces the reason for the LORD's choice of this name, which focuses on its negative associations, rescinding the thought of the land where the LORD has sown abundantly, and pointing to the judgement which would come upon the sin of the people. ***Yet a little while*** indicates that it would not be long before circumstances changed (cf. Isa. 10:25; 29:17; Jer. 51:33; Hag. 2:6). What is in view here is divine intervention to reverse the prosperity currently enjoyed by Israel and to impose on them the punishment they deserved. It may well be that it links the time it would take the child to grow and the period which will elapse before the prophecy is fulfilled. This would locate the beginning of Hosea's ministry in the closing years of the reign of Jeroboam II, after whose death the fortunes of the land plummeted, starting with the assassination of Zechariah, Jeroboam's son and successor, just six months into his reign (2 Kgs. 15:10).

I will appoint employs one of the more versatile roots in the Hebrew language (*pāqad*), which basically indicates the attention a superior

9. This seems to be overlooked by Macintosh: 'The name is not elsewhere attested as a personal name and ... we may conclude that Jezreel and other such symbolic names were literary and contrived rather than actual names in daily use' (1997:15).

gives to the situation or action of an inferior. The traditional rendering 'to visit' is not intended to picture a cosy, fire-side chat, but an inspection which may involve conducting a census, imposing taxation, appointing to a post, mustering troops, extending protection, or rewarding the diligent as well as penalising the offending (cf. 2:13; 4:9, 14; 8:13; 9:9; 12:2). The precise nuance of the verb depends on its context.

Mention is made here of ***the bloodshed of Jezreel***, literally 'the bloods of Jezreel', with the plural term probably indicating blood violently shed (cf. 4:2; Gen. 4:10, 11; Ps. 5:6; 9:12). This was something which happened regularly in the valley of Jezreel, which as a major trade route had strategic significance and was the location of many battles. 'Bloods' may also convey the notion of 'blood-guilt' arising from death of the innocent (12:14; Exod. 22:1; 2 Sam. 21:1). The further connection with ***the house of Jehu*** points to what took place in Jezreel when Jehu ousted the dynasty of Omri by killing Joram, piling the heads of Ahab's seventy sons at the city gates, and massacring Ahab's followers (2 Kgs. 9:21–10:10).

Traditionally the idiom 'to bring to account *something* upon *someone*' has been taken to indicate that the LORD will bring retribution on those who have transgressed, matching the punishment to the offence. However, while such an approach to the expression fits elsewhere, it does not seem appropriate in this instance (cf. also 'I will appoint upon them four kinds ⌊of punishment⌋', Jer. 15:3). The account in 2 Kings 10 does not indicate that Jehu's action had been viewed unfavourably by the LORD, even though he may have gone further than was warranted. Rather, the coup had been initiated with the LORD's blessing as conveyed through Elisha (2 Kgs. 9:1-10), and earned the LORD's commendation: 'And the LORD said to Jehu, "Because you have done well in carrying out what is right in my eyes—according to all that was in my heart you have done to the house of Ahab—your sons of the fourth generation shall sit on the throne of Israel" ' (2 Kgs. 10:30). Hosea is not predicting that Jehu's dynasty will end because of the way in which they had seized power, but because of what they proceeded to do with that power.

The idiom of 'to bring to account something upon someone' is here used in the sense of the LORD imposing on the house of Jehu an end like that which they had been instrumental in bringing upon the previous regime. 'The prophet's words are ironic. Jehu's dynasty came to power by virtue of a bloody coup at Jezreel. It was to meet its demise in a hauntingly similar way' (McComiskey 1993:101).[10] Why? The dynasty had not learned the lesson of the overthrow of Ahab. Instead Jehu sponsored the syncretistic worship which had been promoted by earlier kings of the north (2 Kgs. 10:29, 31), and this practice was continued by successive members of the dynasty, who were condemned for it: Jehu (2 Kgs. 10:30-31), Jehoahaz (2 Kgs. 13:2), Jehoash (2 Kgs. 13:11), Jeroboam (2 Kings 14:24). The same verdict was divinely pronounced upon the six month king, Zechariah (2 Kgs. 15:9). Their compromised loyalty to the LORD would result in their overthrow with violence which would match that originally exhibited by Jehu.

Indeed, when the LORD reviewed the state of the northern kingdom, the scope of his verdict would extend beyond the dynasty of Jehu. ***I will cause to cease the kingdom of the house of Israel*** does not simply restate the judicial sentence of the previous line. 'House of Israel' includes more than the current dynasty. The term first occurs in Exodus 16:31 in reference to the whole of the covenant people (cf. Exod. 40:38; Lev. 10:6; 17:10), though later it may be used of the northern kingdom on its own (cf. 1 Kgs. 12:21; 20:31; Amos 5:1, 3, 4; 6:1, 14; 9:9). Combined here with 'kingdom'/'royal dominion' it points to the end of the independent existence of the state.[11] Bereft of its king, it will no longer exist as a political entity. Possibly this evokes the sentence implicit in the negative reading of Jezreel, 'the LORD sows'. In view is not the scattering of seed for a good harvest, but the scattering of the people before their enemies, culminating in the judgement of

10. Indeed, McComiskey goes further by suggesting that it was near Jezreel that Jehu's dynasty was ended. Some Greek manuscripts read that Zechariah's assassination took place 'at Ibleam' (*bəyiblə'am*) a town in the Valley of Jezreel (cf. GNB, ESV), rather than 'before people'/'in public' (*qābāl* [an Aramaic term] *'am*) as in the MT of 2 Kgs. 15:10. Other LXX manuscripts read a place name also, and specification of the place of assassination would fit in with the pattern found in 2 Kgs. 15:8-30 (McComiskey 1992:21).

11. An alternative explanation of the phrase is that it refers to the 'extended kingdom of Israel'. Its cessation would particularly involve the loss of territory in Galilee and Trans-jordan which had been regained by Jeroboam II. This might be associated with the resurgence of Aram (Syria) under Rezin (Irvine 1995:502). Equally, it might point to the division of the northern kingdom between Menahem and Pekah as envisaged in Thiele's reconstruction (see *Introduction*, pg. 14).

deportation from the land. In Zechariah 10:9 'I will sow them among the peoples' may refer to the dispersion at and after the exile.

1:5 'And it will happen on that day
that I will break the bow of Israel
in the valley of Jezreel.'

On that day extends beyond Zechariah's death, which marked the extinction of Jehu's dynasty, to include the aftermath of his overthrow. While 'that day' does refer to a period when the LORD makes his control of human history obvious, it is improbable that the phrase here has explicit eschatological overtones connected with an inbreaking of the final day of the LORD.

The ***bow*** was the typical weapon of warfare (cf. 1:7; 2:18; Ps. 46:9; 76:3; Jer. 49:35; 51:56; Zech. 9:10; 10:4). When it is broken, all Israel's military might will be devastated. Though the nation relied on military strength and strategic alliances for preservation, when the LORD imposed his judgement on them, the futility of their efforts would be completely exposed. It took around thirty years for the implications of the child's name to be fully realised, but the fall of Samaria and the removal of the people showed that it had been no idle threat.

In the valley of Jezreel brackets verses 4 and 5 together with the repetition of Jezreel in an inclusive pattern. The valley was the eastern part of what was also known as the plain of Esdraelon (the Greek form of the name Jezreel), which was over 10 miles wide and lay between the hills of lower Galilee to the north and the mountains of Samaria to the south. It stretched in a north-westerly direction from the Jordan valley to mount Carmel on the Mediterranean coast. Possibly the term is used loosely to refer to the whole of the valley-plain. As it was suitable for the effective deployment of chariot forces, it had been the scene of many military encounters. There is no record of any specific engagement there when the Assyrians seized control of the land. Even so, the fulfilment of this prophecy may be associated with events in 733 B.C. when Galilee became an Assyrian province (cf. Wolff 1974:19–20).

REFLECTION

- Though the monarchs of earth may consider that they are in control of affairs, it is the LORD who is the true sovereign, the 'King of kings and Lord of lords' (Rev. 19:16). It is he who 'removes kings and sets up kings' (Dan. 2:21), for 'the Most High rules the kingdom of mankind and gives it to whom he wishes' (Dan. 4:17). When he resolves that a dynasty has to end, his verdict is final.

- The LORD's judgement is not arbitrary. The northern kingdom sought security through military might (cf. 8:14), and so it was fitting that its downfall was accomplished by military defeat, breaking the bow of Israel (1:5).

(4) Lo-Ruchama: Compassion Withdrawn (1:6-7)

There is no indication of how much time passed before Gomer's second child was born, nor is it spelled out how long will elapse between the naming of the child and the events foreshadowed by her name coming to pass. Possibly the absence of such information indicates that the LORD's forbearance was exhausted right from the moment of her birth. If so, she may have been born during the aftermath of Zechariah's assassination (752 B.C.) when the kingdom began to collapse internally.

1:6 And she conceived again and bore a daughter, and he said to him,
'Call her name Not-Shown-Compassion,
for I will no longer have compassion on the house of Israel,
for I will utterly raise with respect to them.'

When Gomer gives birth to a second child, it is not explicitly stated that Hosea is the father of the baby girl. The omission of 'to him', which was present in 1:3, may well arise from the abbreviated nature of the narrative, in which, for instance, 'the LORD said to Hosea' (1:4) becomes simply ***he said to him.*** That the account becomes progressively more concise is also indicated by the further absence of 'again' in 1:8. So it may be intended that the fact of Hosea being her father should be carried over from the earlier verse. Certainly there is no emphasis on the thought that the child is illegitimate, nor is there anything implied about Hosea's personal disposition towards her.

The focus of the narrative is on the third divine injunction regarding the contrived name the prophet is to give to the girl. The verb 'to show compassion' is derived from a noun meaning 'womb' and 'abdomen', and it denotes a warm, tender attitude welling up from a deep emotional bond, a response of positive feelings and action towards one in need. Though it is often considered to be a term for 'mother love' (cf. Isa. 49:15), it is also used of male figures (cf. Ps. 103:13). Such compassion characterises the LORD's favourable disposition towards his people (cf. Exod. 33:19; Deut. 13:18; Isa. 54:7).

However, the child is here named ***Not-Shown-Compassion*** (Lo-Ruchama, 'she ⌊is⌋ not shown compassion'). This shocking name is not an indication that Hosea refused to treat her with love and affection, but is a sign-name intended to attract the attention of the community and convey to them what awaited them. At first this might seem a more passive, and thus less threatening, message than that of the external disaster indicated by the name Jezreel, but in reality it is spiritually more ominous. What is in view is not just that the people will be scattered in judgement, but that the LORD will no longer view them fondly and mercifully. Previously, he had acted with longsuffering as regards the misconduct of the nation and its kings (cf. with respect to Jehu, 2 Kgs. 10:30; with respect to Jehoahaz, 2 Kgs. 13:4; with respect to Joash, 2 Kgs. 13:23; and with respect to Jeroboam, 2 Kgs. 14:25-27). But those days will come to an end for ***the house of Israel***, which in the light of the contrast found in the next verse refers here specifically to the northern kingdom (cf. 1:4). No longer will the LORD tolerate their disobedience; instead in judgement he will withdraw from them the privileges of the covenant and deprive them of his parental care and oversight.

The rendering of the last line of the verse given above has been deliberately left as awkward as possible in the translation above to indicate the difficulty of determining its meaning. The verb 'to raise' or 'to lift up' in the last line of the verse may be understood in two ways. (1) In 14:2 Hosea employs it along with 'iniquity' (*ʿāwōn*) to signify the removal of guilt and its punishment (cf. Josh. 24:19; Ps. 32:5; 85:3; Mic. 7:18), and even the verb on its own may mean 'to forgive' (cf. Gen. 18:24, 26; Num. 14:19; Ps. 99:8; Isa. 2:9). The introductory conjunction ***for*** (*kî*) would then introduce a consequence clause 'so that I should at all forgive them' (cf. NIV, NRSV, ESV). A more feasible approach would be to take the negative in the previous line as doing double-duty (that is, its negative force is carried over from the first to the second verb: 'for I will certainly not forgive them') and to understand it as an additional reason, couched as a negative counterpart to the character of the LORD which had been revealed in the key passage, Exodus 34:6-7: 'showing compassion … forgiving iniquity' (Fensham 1984:75).

(2) However, a more probable sense is yielded by noting that in 5:14 Hosea uses the same verb in the sense 'to carry off' with respect to the deportation of the people (cf. AV, NKJV, HCSB). ***I will utterly raise with respect to them*** would then present the evidence to substantiate the fact that the LORD will withdraw his compassion: he will exile the people. Possibly, after the preceding negative, the introductory conjunction *kî* then has an adversative sense, 'rather' or 'instead'. The disciplinary discontinuation of divine compassion does not lead to a void in

providence, but to the imposition of dire penalty: 'rather I will utterly carry them off'.

1:7 'But on the house of Judah I will have compassion,
and I will save them by the LORD their God;
but I will not save them by bow or by sword,
by war, by horses or by horsemen.'

The ***but*** with which the verse begins renders an adversative use of the Hebrew conjunction 'and'.[12] ***House of Judah*** denotes the people of the southern kingdom, not merely its ruling dynasty (cf. 1:4). However, most modern commentators view mention of Judah (1:1, 7, 11; 4:15; 5:5, 10-14; 6:4, 11; 8:14; 10:11; 11:12; 12:2) or of David (3:5) as indicative of the interests of later southern editors, and therefore as intrusive in the text of Hosea. Yet the frequency with which such references occur relates rather to the degree of interest that prophets who ministered in either kingdom had in the affairs of the other. This is illustrated in the way in which Elijah, the redoubtable prophet of the north, built an altar of twelve stones on Carmel (1 Kgs. 18:31), and in this way demonstrated his continuing focus on the ideal unity of the twelve tribes even though his immediate ministry was to the north. Whatever tensions existed between north and south, the peoples of the two kingdoms remained brethren (cf. 2 Chron. 28:9-11) who, to some extent at any rate, acknowledged the one God. It is not that Hosea glosses over Judah's sin (5:5, 10) or impending judgement (5:12, 14). Moreover, he also envisages north and south brought together in ultimate harmony (1:11). In this passage Hosea is best understood as prophesying the deliverance of Jerusalem in the Assyrian invasion of 701 B.C.

In addition, Hosea's message here was not without immediate significance for his contemporaries, because at that stage Judah, under Uzziah, was displaying a more responsible attitude towards the covenant. Judah would enjoy salvation not by more clever use of military and political action than the north, but by divine intervention. So the prophet's comparison urges his fellow countrymen to learn from the south and abandon their suicidal policies by returning to the LORD

12. Andersen and Freedman argue that the negative of 1:6 carries over into 1:7—'nor for the state of Judah will I show pity'. In this way the sense of the prophecy is that there will be no exemption for Judah from the fate that will come upon Israel (1980:188–189). The absence of an explicit negative in the last clause of verse 6 makes this suggestion improbable, as does the initial *waw* disjunctive (*waw* followed by a non-verb) of verse 7.

and claiming him as 'their God' (cf. 14:3; Amos 2:13-16). No reason is stated for the divine announcement, ***I will have compassion*** (cf. 1:6). The stress is on the sovereign and effective action of the LORD as the only guaranteed means of deliverance. ***I will save*** comes from the same root as Hosea's own name, and denotes the provision of relief from distress of any type. ***By the LORD their God*** (cf. 12:6; Isa. 10:22) indicates the means employed to effect Judah's deliverance.[13] It is through the instrumentality of God himself that this preservation will be effected. The covenant background of his message influences Hosea's preference for 'the LORD' (Yahweh), the personal, covenant name of God, which he employs 45 times. He refers to the true God as Elohim, 'God', 24 times, and only on five of these occasions is a personal adjective missing. Indeed, nineteen of Hosea's references to Elohim are in a broadly covenantal context. It is from within that relationship, initiated and maintained by divine choice and power, that deliverance will truly arise.

By way of contrast the second half of the verse sets out the means of deliverance which the LORD will not employ. ***Bow*** (cf. 1:5) and ***sword*** were the main weapons of combat, but the LORD was able to work without them. ***War*** may indicate warfare in general, or in this list of military resources it may indicate other miscellaneous implements of war. Though cavalry mounted on individual horses, as distinct from chariotry, were developed by the Assyrians by the end of the eighth century, probably here by ***horses*** Hosea has no more in mind than traditional chariot forces which had become common in Israel from the period of the united kingdom onwards. ***Horsemen*** may designate either charioteers or the teams of horses under their control. Since the LORD will not work through such means, it was pointless for either kingdom to use its resources in accumulating such armaments.

REFLECTION

- Both kingdoms were deficient in exercising trust in the LORD as the King of the covenant to defend them because they were his people. It was easier—but sadly mistaken—to rely on visible resources they gathered for themselves. However, 'no king is saved by his great army; a warrior is not delivered by his great strength. The ⌞war⌟ horse is a false hope for salvation, and by its great might it cannot rescue' (Ps. 33:16-17; cf. Ps. 20:7; 44:3, 6; 147:10-11). Over against these

13. For a third person reference to the LORD within direct divine speech, see on 1:2.

forces which were 'great' in human terms, the covenant people were to rely on the greatness of the LORD who as a man of war exercised his power to ensure their victory over their enemies (cf. Exod. 15:1-3). The lesson was not easy to learn. It took the arrival of his enemy Sennacherib of Assyria before the gates of Jerusalem before the godly king Hezekiah really grasped that 'with him [i.e. Sennacherib] is an arm of flesh, but with us is the LORD our God, to help us and to fight our battles' (2 Chron. 32:8). Though Christian warfare no longer engages in military conflict using weapons of the flesh (cf. 2 Cor. 10:4), it still takes faith to rely on divine intervention and power, and to eschew worldly mechanisms and strategies in the fight of faith.

(5) Lo-Ammi: Estrangement Complete (1:8-9)

There is some indication of the lapse of a period of time before the birth of the third child, a second son. In terms of the events affecting the northern kingdom this probably takes us to the start of Assyrian pressure being felt throughout Syria and Palestine after the accession of Tiglath-Pileser.

1:8 And she weaned Not-Shown-Compassion, and she conceived and bore a son.

Although the narrative is terse, ***she weaned*** (not found in 1:6) indicates the passage of time, probably of as much as two or three years, after which another child was born. Again it is not stated that this son was Hosea's, but this provides insufficient ground for assuming that Gomer had become openly unfaithful to Hosea by this stage. Certainly Hosea still acted as the child's father by naming him. The protracted nature of Hosea's lived-out example to the people would have portrayed the LORD's longsuffering towards them.

1:9And he said,
'Call his name Not-My-People,
for you ⌞are⌟ not my people,
and I ⌞am⌟ Not-I-AM to you.'

For the fourth time the LORD gives instructions to the prophet. As on the previous two occasions, he discloses what the child's name is to be, and he probably also reveals a startling new name for himself. The three negatives in the verse intensify the ominous nature of what is said. Hosea is to call his son ***Not-My-People*** (Lo-Ammi). This need not be a declaration that the prophet does not acknowledge himself as the child's father; the text leaves that open. But it is undoubtedly a prophetic witness to the LORD's perception that relationship between himself and the people is ruptured. 'My people' was a kinship term which was a verbal summary of the bond of the covenant, and encapsulated the privileged status of Israel. 'Then I will take you to myself as a people and I will be to you as God' (Exod. 6:7; cf. Gen. 17:7-8; Lev. 26:12). But now their behaviour had violated the covenant bond, and the boy was to bear a symbolic name which constituted him a living expression of the separation between the people and their God.

For introduces the reason for giving this name. It reflects what has already occurred since Israel had effectively separated themselves from God, disowning the covenant. Here we find the LORD speaking directly to the people for the first time. It is characteristic of Hosea's mode of address that there is such a degree of identification between the LORD and the prophet that the speech of one merges into that of the other.

What is in view is not some momentary lapse in Israel's conduct, but a settled characteristic of their inner orientation and behaviour. ***You*** (plural) ***are not my people*** negates the terms of the ancient covenant relationship. Corresponding to this there is a declaration regarding God's role: 'and I not *ᵓehyeh* to you'. The word *ᵓehyeh* may be identified as a verb form, yielding the translation, 'and I ⌞am the one who⌟ am not to you', or 'I for my part am not yours', where there is omitted a term such as 'God' which might be expected to parallel 'my people' in the first part of the affirmation of the covenant bond ('God' is added here in NIV and ESV). It is more probable, however, that there occurs here a direct reflection on the covenant name of the LORD (Yahweh) by which he had revealed himself to Moses and the people: 'I AM (with the verbal form *ᵓehyeh* functioning as a noun) has sent me to you' (Exod. 3:14). ***I ⌞am⌟ Not-I-AM to you*** is a carefully nuanced expression in which the LORD gives himself a negative name, 'Not-Eyheh' or 'Not-I-AM', corresponding to the negative names he has given to the children.[14] This reverses the covenant declaration, 'I will take you to be my people and I will be your God' (Exod. 6:7). Since he is no longer committed to being their covenant God, they can no longer expect his provision, support and defence. (However, we must note that this ominous name will subsequently be revoked just like those given to Hosea's children, cf. 2:23.)

---

14. The Massoretes indicated that this was their understanding of the term by linking the negative *lōᵓ* to the verb *ᵓehyeh* by a maqqeph, specifying that they are to be read as a compound noun. This holds true even though the preceding compound names are not similarly conjoined.

It is difficult to determine the character and extent of the disrupted relationship: is it to be likened to marital separation, where the benefits of the marriage are suspended, or to divorce, where there is a definitive and irrevocable annulment of the bond? Most probably, despite the seemingly absolute language, the LORD was not abandoning the purposes which he intended to achieve through Israel, but was declaring that their disobedience and lack of repentance meant that fulfilment would be effected by withdrawing his covenant protection and calling down judgement on them rather than avoiding it. For a further discussion of this point, see on 2:2.

REFLECTION

• The name of Hosea's third child signalled the ultimate stage in the LORD's withdrawal of his favour. The people had despised their privileged status in the LORD's sight. Their repeated sin, accompanied by an obdurate refusal to respond to the LORD's entreaties, led to the revocation of their enjoyment of covenant blessing. They became like Cain who was driven out to be 'a fugitive and a wanderer on the earth' (Gen. 4:12) who was hidden from the LORD's face (Gen. 4:14). But even in that dark and dismal condition the LORD's abandonment of them was not absolute (cf. 11:8-9). Disobedience removed every sign of the Father's blessing, but could not annul the underlying relationship instituted by divine grace.

(6) Restoration (1:10–2:1)

Astonishingly the LORD's message was not solely one of impending disaster. While the covenant itself was inviolable, enjoyment of its blessings by any individual or any generation was conditioned on continuing obedience. For those who rebelled against his requirements and refused to repent, the future prospect was dire as the holy God would impose his righteous sanctions on their disobedience. But what would come after that? Indeed, could there be a future beyond the desolating impact of divine judgement?

It is doubtful if in his initial public presentation of the message of impending retribution Hosea mitigated its impact by immediately juxtaposing the prospect of eventual restoration. The pressing need was to alert his audience to the danger they were in and to call them to repentance. From that perspective the sequence of the prophet's oracles is primarily a literary device dating from Hosea's compilation of them into a permanent record for a generation which had already, at least in part, experienced divine judgement. But even so, right from the start of Hosea's activity there would have been a faithful remnant in the north who required encouragement to persevere through the disaster which would engulf them and their community. This oracle of the grand reversal of their national fortunes was therefore an aspect of Hosea's earliest ministry though, to begin with, this message was principally intended for those who remained faithful in the north.

The change of theme at this point is matched by a change in speaker in that it is no longer the voice of the LORD which is heard as in 1:6-7, 9, but rather Hosea relating what has been revealed to him about this time of future blessing. This thematic break is recognised here in the Hebrew chapter division where chapter 2 begins after 1:9 so that the verse numbers for chapter 2 in Hebrew are two greater than those in English translations. However, 1:10–2:1 ought to be associated with chapter 1 rather than chapter 2. The re-use of the children's names in 2:1 constitutes a link with what precedes, even though it is by way of contrast. The pattern of a time of judgement followed by restoration constitutes a basic literary and theological structure in Hosea.

However, while these words about the restored fortunes of the people are undoubtedly fulsome in what is envisaged, they do seem to be expressed in somewhat more impersonal tones than subsequent parallel passages (cf. 2:14-23; 11:9; 14:4-5). Later on Hosea gives greater emphasis to divine involvement and initiative. It is appropriate to surmise that the prophet's perception of the extent of divine grace and love involved in what was to come deepened over the years of his ministry. Certainly the incorporation of this passage is not to be understood as the product of subsequent editors as they reinterpreted Hosea's ministry for a later situation.[15] It is not necessary to suppose that the prophets were ever without a message of salvation. The possibility of deliverance was inherent in any call for repentance in which the people's impending doom was announced to them to induce, if that

---

15. It was a feature of earlier critical thought to regard 1:10-11 'as occupying an impossible place' and so to transfer them to the end of chapter 2 and assign them to a later editor. Even so, Harper acknowledges that each 'contains an important idea, and both together form a splendid unity' (1905:245). 'The fact that the prophecy is a divine restorative confrontation is seen in the inseparable union that exists between the judgement and salvation sections in each cycle. Though the critic's scalpel has sought to incise this unity, the literary structure of Hosea can be verified by observing the formal transitions, vocabulary, symbolism, and thematic development in each of the five cycles' (Wyrtzen 1984:316).

were possible, a change of heart on their part. Similarly the blessings to be enjoyed in a renewed relationship with the LORD might also act to induce a change of heart. Nevertheless, if there was no appropriate response from them, the LORD may abandon and disown one generation—or many more—because of their disobedience, but *his* covenant commitment still stands and he will take action, when he considers it appropriate, to ensure its fulfilment. While an unbelieving generation will exhaust the LORD's patience and draw down on themselves his judgement, there is still hope for a reversal of the people's fortunes, based not on human achievement or attractiveness, but on divine grace and commitment. The great reversal embodies the outworking of the love that refuses to permit sin and rebellion to have the last word on the destiny of God's people.

So this transformation will bring divine punishment to an end and permit renewal of covenant blessing. This will include increased numbers (1:10a), restored and heightened spiritual fellowship (1:10b), harmonious reintegration of separated brethren (1:11a), a single united leadership and new fruitfulness (1:11b). The reversal formulae of 2:1 revoke the judicial sentence embodied in the names of the prophet's children, and show the people interacting in kindly fashion as they acknowledge their joint status in the LORD which is derived from his gracious and compassionate provision.

However, there remains the question of how this prophecy is fulfilled. The Old Testament itself does indeed record various ways in which there was a rapprochement between north and south after the fall of Samaria. In Hezekiah's day there was an invitation extended to those left in the north, and it was accepted by some (2 Chron. 30:10-11, 18). There are also indications that there were refugees from the north residing in the south (2 Chron. 31:6). Later Josiah also took the north into the scope of his religious policy (2 Chron. 34:6), which met with a measure of acceptance from those who lived there (2 Chron. 34:9). During the exile it may well have been that there was further fusion between the peoples of the divided kingdoms. Certainly the restored community thought of themselves as embodying all Israel, as when Ezra arrived in Jerusalem and offered 'twelve bulls for all Israel' (Ezra 8:35).

After the exile the people in Judah and Jerusalem were united to the extent that they no longer lived in separate states, but there was the ongoing problem of the small number of returnees (Neh. 7:4), so that their situation can hardly be said to exhaust the extensive promises given here. Opinions differ as to how that fulfilment will in fact be achieved. In the light of the New Testament appropriation of these promises to the church of Christ incorporating Jew and Gentile alike (cf. Rom. 9:25-26; 1 Pet. 2:10), the view presented here is that their ultimate significance is spiritually realised in the heavenly inheritance of the people of God. See further *Introduction*, pg. 38.

1:10 And the number of the sons of Israel will be as the sand of the sea,[16]
which cannot be measured and cannot be counted;
and it will be that in the place where it was said to them, 'You ⌞are⌟ not my people',
it will be said to them, '⌞You are⌟ sons of the living God'.

The prophet describes the revelation he has been given of what the sovereign intervention of God will restore as regards the status and numbers of the covenant people.[17] ***As the sand of the sea*** deliberately echoes the promises of the Abrahamic covenant ('I will surely make your seed as many as ... the sand which is on the seashore', Gen. 22:17). Other promises of countless offspring include Genesis 13:16; 15:5; 32:12. These are now reaffirmed and their fulfilment forecast for the period after the imposition of punishment. The metaphor points to the large number involved, ***which cannot be measured*** by weight ***and cannot be counted*** by a census.[18] Conscious of the symbolic role being played by his own children, Hosea uses ***sons of Israel***/'Israelites', the traditional phrase for the whole nation viewed as those in covenant union with the LORD. This expression had first occurred in Exodus 3:10, with the plural of the noun 'son' referring, as it often does, to offspring both male and female. In 1:11 (and also in 3:1, 4, 5 and 4:1) the term is specifically used of the people of the north alone, and that seems to be the case here also. However, the original focus on Hosea's audience in their covenantal status is readily extended to all who claim to be in a similar spiritual relationship with God. Indeed, the promise is set in such a wider context in the following verse.

16. It is possible that the initial verb is to be understood in the sense 'and it will come to pass that' which is then followed by 'the number of the sons of Israel ⌞will be⌟ as the sand of the sea.' This would correspond to the rendering of the second line of the verse.

17. Salvation oracles, following messages of judgement addressed to Israel, are found in 1:10–2:1; 2:14–23; 3:5; 11:8–11; and 14:4–8. A second group consists of salvation oracles to Judah, following messages of judgement addressed to Israel in 1:7; 4:15; and 6:11.

18. The two verbs *yimmād* ('be measured') and *yissāpēr* ('be counted') are treated as modal imperfects of capability (*IBHS* §31.4c).

The slaughter in the land due to Assyrian incursions as well as the infighting of the concluding years of the northern kingdom (and also the subsequent deportation of many of its inhabitants) would have made this promise seem even more unattainable by the end of Hosea's ministry. What is envisaged is a renewal of their national fortunes on a Solomonic scale: 'And your servant is in the midst of your people whom you have chosen, a great people, who cannot be numbered or counted for greatness' (1 Kgs. 3:8). It is only divine commitment to the covenant relationship and divine intervention in power that will be able to turn round the condition of the people so effectively.

It was forecast that their fortunes would be reinstated through a changed relationship with God. Increased numbers implied restored political importance, but more significantly there would be spiritual restoration. ***In the place*** points to a geographical location, clearly the land of promise where the curse had been pronounced upon them because of their disobedience. In the very spot where God had once disowned them by declaring, ***You are not my people*** (cf. 1:9), that covenant curse will be reversed. Indeed, what will be restored to them is an enhancement of what had been taken away. It might have been expected that they would again be accorded the designation 'my people', but in a significant extension of their privilege they will be called ***sons of the living God***, picking up on the use of 'sons' in the first line. No longer will the shadow of Baal worship be cast over the land; the name 'children of whoredoms' will be abandoned as obsolete. 'Living God' employs the generic expression for deity (*'ēl*) and differentiates the LORD from the gods of pagan belief as the one who truly is alive and active (Josh. 3:10; Jer. 10:10; cf. similar expressions in Deut. 5:26; Dan. 6:20, 26). He is the ultimate source of all existence and the one who can really impart life to others (Ps. 42:2). Being designated by this title, therefore, indicates that they have been divinely given true life, a fact which calls for joyful celebration (cf. Ps. 84:2; Rom. 9:26).

1:11 And the sons of Judah will be gathered
and the sons of Israel together,
and they will set for themselves one leader,
and they will come up from the land,
for great ⌊will be⌋ the day of Jezreel.

The theme of ***sons***/'children' is continued in a second reminder of the LORD's covenant commitment to Judah and Israel alike (cf. 1:7). It is predicted that the divided communities of north and south ***will be***

gathered … together (cf. Isa. 11:13; Ezek. 37:22). Bitter tensions and animosities will be consigned to the past, and they will act in harmony as they ***set for themselves one leader*** (cf. Ezek. 37:15-17). 'One leader'/'head' (cf. Ps. 18:43) avoids the term 'king', and there are some commentators who take this as evidence that Hosea perpetuates an attitude of hostility towards there being a king in Israel at all because it would compromise the LORD's sole sovereignty over the people. Gideon's refusal to become king (Judg. 8:23) and Samuel's opposition to the request for a king (1 Sam. 8:10-18) are cited as instances of such antagonism. Undoubtedly a king could be asked for from the wrong motives, but there had always been provision made for such a request (Deut. 17:14-20). So when Hosea reminded his hearers of the faults of contemporary kings (cf. 7:3-7; 10:3), he was not being intrinsically anti-monarchical. What he took exception to was the fact that these kings were not conforming to the norms of the covenant institution. Even a passage such as 8:4 refers to the outworkings of kingship rather than the principle. Therefore while Hosea here avoids the term 'king', it may be because of the negative associations deriving from the many ineffectual rulers in the north during its final years of independent rule, or if this vision was granted at an earlier stage, it may reflect on the rebellion by which the north kingdom achieved its separate existence. Certainly he can talk positively about kingship (cf. 3:5). Indeed, though there is no specific identification here of this leader being a Davidic king, that is undoubtedly the conclusion to be drawn from the fuller description in 3:5. The prospect in view is essentially messianic. Acting in terms of the provision that the LORD has made for them, the people will achieve not some temporary political alignment, but the grand unity of the spiritual kingdom (Eph. 4:4-6).

Flowing on from their regained unity is the prospect of what will then be achieved. ***They will come up from the land*** seems to describe a return from exile and dispersion, reversing the judgement of exile in the last line of 1:6. 'The land' points to their places of dispersal, though elsewhere 'the land' without further qualification denotes the land of promise. There are some who take the phrase 'from the land' as equivalent to the underworld (Andersen, et al. 1980:208–209) and the imagery being that of national resurrection similar to Ezekiel 37:1-14), but in the light of the agricultural metaphor implicit in the 'sow' of Jezreel (cf. 1:4) it is more probable that the people are being viewed as a harvest that the LORD will cause to spring up from the promised land (the verb is used in this way in 10:8 and elsewhere in the Old Testament) so that ***great will be the day of Jezreel.*** In this the first symbolic name presaging judgement will have its significance transformed and its threat removed, just as the other names are reversed in the following verse. No longer does Jezreel (*yizrəʿeʾl*) threaten catastrophe (1:4-5), but as restored 'Israel' (*yiśrāʾēl*) it will be enlarged and reinvigorated by divine power. 'Great' conveys ideas of renown and of surpassing growth as the LORD sows prosperity (2:22-23). It is not that the immediate judgement impending on the royal house and on the land will be avoided, but that, after that experience has been endured, there will emerge a time of favour from the God who does not give up on his pledge and purpose.

2:1 Say to your brothers, 'My People',
and to your sisters, 'Shown Compassion'.

The plural terms ***brothers*** and especially ***sisters***[19] indicates that more than Hosea's own family are in view here. ***Say*** is a plural command presumably addressed by the prophet in vision to groups within the restored people who are instructed to announce the reversal of the significance of the other two symbolic names also. The words which they are to utter are not merely an expression of their own aspirations but, in a depiction of the harmony to be enjoyed by the restored community, they are to repeat the message received from the LORD who has once again bestowed on his people the spiritual status and blessings summarised in these names. The negative element in Lo-Ammi (1:9) and Lo-Ruchama (1:6) is dropped to convey the positive message of renewed relationship with God, ***My People***, and restoration to divine favour, ***Shown Compassion.*** Changed names, which had traditionally been associated with transformed covenant status (cf. Gen. 17:5, 15; 32:28), mark the reinstatement of the fallen people because the LORD had not abandoned his commitment to them.

REFLECTION

- Both Peter (1 Pet. 2:10) and Paul (Rom. 9:25, 26) interpret the prophecies of 1:10 and 2:1 as ultimately fulfilled by the incorporation of the Gentiles among those who are included in its scope. This is not an imposition on the ancient promise but a clarification of the implications which had always been present. God's covenant with

19. The LXX obviates this difficulty by reading, 'Say to your brother … and to your sister …', and it is followed in this by the NRSV. Such a reading may well have arisen from the fact that what is said to the sisters is a feminine *singular* form. But the more difficult MT reading stresses that each comprehensively is included in this incorporation.

Abraham was intended as the basis on which spiritual blessing would extend beyond the patriarch's ethnic descendants to 'all the families of the earth' (Gen. 12:3; 22:18; 26:4; 28:14). Whatever measure of fulfilment was achieved at the time of the return from exile in Babylon is to be eclipsed by the numbers of Jews and Gentiles alike brought into the church of Jesus Christ, who is the 'one leader' (1:11) to be acknowledged in that day (Dan. 7:13-14; Rev. 11:15).

- 'In the place' (1:10) may suggest that there is yet to be some local realisation of this promise as regards the Jews, but that most probably confuses the different time horizons on which the multiple fulfilment of Old Testament prophecies occurs. These are not arbitrarily read into the text, but are the natural, organic unfolding of the richness of God's promise, which may be compared to the growth and development of a single flower until it is in full bloom.
- The promise of being 'sons of the living God' (1:10) is achieved only through adoption in Christ. 'See what kind of love the Father has given to us, that we should be called children of God; and so we are' (1 John 3:1; cf. John 1:12-13). The immense spiritual privilege of being a member of the Father's family is enhanced still further by the fact that he is 'the living God'. This title sets him apart from the lifeless and ineffective entities to which the devotees of idols are enslaved (cf. Acts 14:15; 2 Cor. 6:16; 1 Thess. 1:9), but it also holds out the potential inherent in a vital relationship with him (cf. 2 Cor. 3:3; 1 Tim. 3:15; Heb. 9:14).
- Ministry at a time of impending cataclysm has to satisfy two requirements. There must be urgency in warning of the dangers facing a generation and in pressing the need for individual repentance on the spiritually rebellious. Equally there is a need to minister to believers who are struggling to cope with the hazardous and perplexing circumstances confronting them. 'See that no one leads your astray' (Matt. 24:4; cf. Matt. 24:24). There is blessing in conscientious performance of duties in such troubled times (Matt. 24:46). There is also the encouragement to be derived from anticipation of the glorious resolution of the tangled affairs of this life when the Saviour returns (Matt. 25:31).

B. The LORD and Israel (2:2-22)

In many English translations this central section of chapters 1–3 is formally distinguished from the surrounding material by being printed in poetic lines rather than as prose (cf. *Introduction*, pg. 26). However, even apart from analysis of style, it is evident that there is a thematic break in the prophecy after 2:1 because the portrayal of a time of blessing in 1:10–2:1 gives way to scenes of tension, alienation and reproach in 2:2-13. There then occurs the same rapid alternation between judgement and restoration which structured 1:1–2:1, for 2:14-23 moves on to present an overwhelmingly positive picture of the way in which the LORD will resolve the problems affecting the covenant relationship between him and his people, and restore them to enjoyment of his favour.

Hosea's personal circumstances had largely receded into the background by the conclusion of the preceding section, and that prevails throughout this section also. There is an element of continuity with the previous account in that family metaphors are still employed, but that feature is not sufficiently prominent to warrant calling this section 'an account of Hosea's family experience interwoven with the experience of Yahweh and his people'. (Andersen, et al. 1980:218) The focus is now directly on the LORD, who speaks throughout the passage, and who describes his relationship with his people in terms of a tumultuous marriage with an unfaithful wife. The prophet's own difficulties with Gomer (which are elaborated on in chapter 3) would have added a note of poignancy and personal insight to Hosea's delivery of this message, but he does not develop this aspect of the situation.

(1) Israel's Disgraceful Behaviour (2:2-13)

Throughout these verses the LORD himself speaks, and the nation is metaphorically described as the LORD's wife and as the mother of her citizens. First the LORD sets out his complaint at her behaviour (2:2-5) and then warns of the action he must necessarily take against her if she persists in her folly (2:6-13). However, it is noteworthy that he does not speak *to* Israel, rather *about* her as a third party. This reflects the degree of alienation which existed between the LORD and his people: the parties to the covenant were no longer on talking terms.

There is another consequence stemming from the fact that the divine monologue does not directly address the nation and face her with her shortcomings but rather calls upon the citizens of the land as her children to act. This oblique approach invites individual Israelites to stand apart from the community of which they were part, and to view matters more objectively, indeed from the LORD's perspective. It is always easier to see the faults of others, as Nathan notably illustrated in the case of David (2 Sam. 12:1-15). A critique of national behaviour is not immediately confrontational, and we can more readily acknowledge its validity when we adopt the role of a spectator and do not think of ourselves as part of the society being scrutinised. In this way the people might be induced to be more critical of the prevailing national consensus and so become more prepared to dissociate themselves from it. The intended outcome of the LORD's message is not mere description, but a change in personal outlook and behaviour through repentance.

The text is addressed to Israel as they still enjoyed times of material prosperity under Jeroboam II. The nation was, however, being warned that such days are rapidly coming to an end because they had failed to recognise the LORD as the true source of their prosperity and had misused his gifts. The rationale for this passage is comparable to the LORD's later invitation to Judah to reach a settlement in the dispute that had marred their relationship, '"Come now and let us reason together," the LORD keeps saying. "Though your sins are like scarlet, white like snow they can become; though they are red like crimson, like wool they can become"' (Isa. 1:18).

(a) A Plea for National Repentance (2:2-5)

It is difficult to determine the specific setting which is assumed in these verses. Many have detected here a description of formal divorce proceedings. For instance, Wyrtzen argues that what is presented in 2:2-13 is the termination of the marital relationship because of the wife's unfaithfulness. He contends that the terminology of 2:2 'is strange if it is meant to convey only a marital separation but not a divorce. ... In the salvation passage (Hos. 2:14-23) the reunion is not symbolised as the restoration of the previous marriage, the Mosaic covenant, but as the initiation of a new marriage though with the previous partner' (1984:320). Certainly the language of betrothal suggests a radically new beginning.

However, quite apart from the problems Wyrtzen's approach encounters in the divine prohibition on remarriage ('her former husband, who sent her away, is not permitted to take her again to be his wife', Deut. 24:4), the prophets elsewhere do not view the LORD as divorcing his people. Indeed even when the people thought they had been abandoned by the LORD, he issued the challenge, 'Where is the certificate of divorce of your mother whom I sent away?' (Isa. 50:1). That denial of divorce even in the circumstances of exile seems to reflect the attitude expressed here also.

Even in this passage there are clear indications that irrevocable dissolution of the marriage is not in view. If the initial lines of 2:2 announce a divorce, then one would expect the husband to have no further interest in the behaviour of his wife from whom he has split, but the final two lines of the verse express a desire that she change her ways for the better. While 2:3-5 may be interpreted as shaming punishments imposed on an adulterous wife, these verses stop short of the death penalty which was demanded by the law for adultery (Lev. 20:10; Deut. 22:22). More significantly, it is anomalous that a divorced husband is represented in 2:6 as still involved in influencing the future conduct of his wife. It would therefore seem that the analogy of formal divorce proceedings fails to account for all the features of this text.

The LORD's concern is to reclaim. It is indeed a dysfunctional relationship which is described, but it would seem to be one which stops short of an irretrievable breakdown, for the LORD does not give up in the matter and has plans for a future which seems not to be remarriage but restoration of the suspended relationship. After all, Hosea in 3:1 is not called on to 'marry again' but to 'love again'.

There seems to be an analogy with the action of a utility company in cutting off the power supply to a household. It is one thing for the power to be switched off and the meter disconnected; it is another matter to dig up the cabling that connects the house to the mains supply and to declare that the company will never reinstate it. It is the former step that the LORD takes in dealing with his people, retributive and corrective disconnection because of gross misconduct, but not utter abandonment.

2:2[20] Plead with your mother, plead—
for ⌞is⌟ she not my wife
and ⌞am⌟ I not her husband? —
that she remove her whoredoms from her face,
and her adulteries from between her breasts.

While the term ***plead*** (*rîb*; cf. 4:1, 4; 12:3) envisages a situation where one party has a grievance against another, it is not necessarily the case that formal court proceedings are in view. A complaint may be remedied by informally confronting the other party and inducing them through argument and discussion to acknowledge their fault and initiate appropriate corrective action, without recourse to judicial intervention. Bringing the dispute before an outside arbiter may well occur as a last resort once such preliminary attempts at reconciliation have proved unavailing. (Note the sequence in Deut. 25:1-3 where an

20. Though the verse breaks are the same, in the MT chapter 2 begins after 1:9, so that 2:2 in English translations is 2:4 in the MT, and so to the end of the chapter.

unresolved *rîb* ends up before the judges.) What is portrayed here are informal proceedings in which an unidentified group of persons ('plead' and 'your' are plural forms) are urged to take up the LORD's grievance against his wife and to confront her with her conduct in the hope that this will lead to a change of heart on her part.

The role of presenting the LORD's complaint was one that was generally allocated to the prophets, but here it is assigned to a group whose identity has to be inferred from ***your mother***, who is also identified as ***my wife*** by the speaker. Since following verses make it clear that it is the LORD's voice which is being heard, the woman referred to represents the nation considered collectively as the mother of her citizens, while 'sons'/'children' (2:4) reflects the status of individuals who are called on to stand over against the nation as a whole, even though recognition of what is involved in national wrongdoing does implicate them also.

If 'plead with' is understood as 'bring charges against' (cf. NKJV, NLT), then ***for*** could be translated 'that' and introduce the substance of the allegations against the nation. However, the structure of the verse is better understood by taking 'for' as introducing the reason why the LORD calls on this group to plead with the nation as an entity. The obvious translation of the second and third lines is, 'for she ⌊is⌋ not my wife and I ⌊am⌋ not her husband.' Though some commentators have detected here a divorce formula which would be uttered by the husband, whose wife had no option but to acquiesce in his declaration, it is more probable that the words present the practical outcome if she persists in her current behaviour, and that the call to 'plead' is designed to avert this result.

However, there is a further approach to this expression which is more satisfactory than either of the foregoing interpretations, and that is to take the words as an unmarked rhetorical question: ***for ⌊is⌋ she not my wife, and ⌊am⌋ I not her husband?*** Originally the interrogative note would have been conveyed by a rising intonation in the speaker's voice. It is not difficult to hear Hosea, who delighted in word-play and rhetorical devices, uttering such words ironically or with a negative, questioning inflection. Unmarked questions in the Old Testament are more common in conversation—which is in effect what we have here. This approach was adopted by the NEB: 'Is she not my wife and I her husband?' It has been recently revived by Liang (2009), who is seemingly unaware of the NEB rendering. The rhetorical question (cf. 6:4) would expect the answer 'Yes indeed, she is', and would provide more than adequate grounds for the request to urge her to change her ways and to avoid the disasters which will otherwise come on her.[21]

That she remove is a purpose clause depicting the desired effect of the intervention the LORD pleads for.[22] He compares Israel to a wife whose conduct has been wanton, but whom he still wishes to reform her ways and live in obedience to him. ***Whoredoms*** and ***adulteries*** are plurals, the latter occurring only here. The former term refers to sexual immorality in general (cf. 1:2), whereas adultery is specifically a violation of the bond of marriage (cf. 3:1). As in 1:2, the plural may indicate how often she had acted in this way, or how characteristic such conduct had become for her. Alternatively, given the two references to her body in ***from her face*** and ***from between her breasts***, these plurals may refer to the various cosmetics with which prostitutes habitually adorned their faces and to the jewellery which hung down from their necks (cf. 2:13; Jer. 4:30; Song 1:13). At any rate, mention of her face indicates the brazen lack of embarrassment with which she acted (cf. Jer. 3:3), and mention of her breasts also signifies the shamelessness of her conduct. It is only if she solemnly renounces such behaviour that the way to reconciliation would be opened up.

The analogy of the wayward wife has, of course, ultimate reference to Israel and her misconduct. The spiritual significance of the allegations levelled against her is spelled out in 2:5, 8, 12-13.

2:3 lest I strip her naked,
  and make her as on the day of her being born,
and set her as the wilderness
  and put her as parched land
  and kill her with thirst;

---

21. It is a recognised feature of Hebrew that questions need not have an explicit interrogative marker (GKC §150a; Joüon §161a). This seems to be especially true in speech (as here) where intonation plays a major part in conveying the sense. It is, however, a serious decision for a translator to take, that a seemingly negative declaration should be translated in such a way as to convey a positive assertion. Liang (2009:6) lists five passages where a negative sentence may be understood as an unmarked question (Exod. 8:26; 2 Sam. 23:5; 2 Kgs. 5:26; Job 2:10; Jonah 4:11). This is the rendering adopted by the translators of the NIV, NRSV and ESV in each of these texts. Instances of unmarked positive questions are more common.

22. After a volitive, a simple *waw* with a jussive verb may express a purpose or wish (GKC §165a). Since *wətāsēr* is ordinary *waw* followed by a jussive hiphil with the volitive *rîbû*, 'plead', as the lead verb, it is preferable to identify that construction here rather than to treat the jussive as expressing a quite separate thought, 'and let her remove' (cf. NIV).

Lest introduces a series of five clauses of increasing intensity which describe the outcome awaiting wayward Israel if she rejects the overtures that the LORD has initiated and fails to mend her ways. ***Strip … naked*** is the same verb as was used of the forcible removal of Joseph's garment (Gen. 37:23). Israel had started on a display of vulgar ostentation, making no attempt to conceal her conduct, and so her punishment extended her shame even further than she would have wished. Public exposure was part of an Assyrian punishment for harlots who broke the law, and something similar may have occurred in Israel (cf. Ezek. 16:37; 23:10; see also Jer. 13:26-27; Nah. 3:5-6). 'Food, clothing and marital intimacy' (Exod. 21:10) were listed as three rights to be accorded to an Israelite concubine or secondary wife. Here the LORD removes the benefits a wife would ordinarily have bestowed on her by her husband because she is no longer acting as a true wife should.

Make her as on the day of her being born forms an obvious parallel with 'strip naked', newly born and not yet clothed. 'Make' may convey the idea of 'expose' or 'exhibit' as in 'He has made me as a byword for people, and I am one in whose face they spit' (Job 17:6). This pictures both shaming punishment (cf. Mic. 1:11) and extreme need (Job 22:6; 24:7, 10; Amos 2:16) for the wayward wife.

The second part of the verse develops the image of 'the day of her being born' by considering the circumstances in which the nation of Israel first came into existence. ***As*** is probably used in a compressed sense equivalent to 'as in'. Rather than denoting a period when drought will afflict the land, ***the wilderness*** (cf. 2:14) and ***parched land*** look back to the journey up from Egypt. So the nation which turned its back on the covenant would experience a reversal of covenant blessing and endure once more former hardships and deprivation (cf. Jer. 2:6 for a description of those times, but now the LORD will not be present to help them). She had then suffered thirst there (cf. Exod. 17:1-7; Num. 20:2-13), and the largely synonymous terms, ***set*** and ***put***, point to the LORD's decisive action if she continues to reject him. He would take from ***her***, that is, the people, all that they had and leave them to endure the curse of the broken covenant. 'Because you did not serve the LORD your God with joy and gladness of heart because of the abundance of everything, you will serve your enemies whom the LORD will send against you in hunger and in thirst and in nakedness and in want of everything' (Deut. 28:47-48). While ***kill*** might imply the death through thirst of some of the nation, more probably what is intended is that extreme suffering will be imposed on them.

2:4 ⌞lest⌟ also on her sons I do not show compassion,
for they ⌞are⌟ sons of whoredoms.

The force of 'lest' at the beginning of 2:3 carries into this verse also, but with the difference that now what is in view is the individual, rather than the general, impact of the people's refusal to repent and amend their ways.[23] What comes upon their 'mother', the nation as a whole and its institutions, inevitably affects ***her sons***, the persons who comprise that nation (cf. 2:2). Although Scripture clearly teaches the responsibility of each human being to turn to the LORD and secure their eternal destiny through trust in him (cf. Ezek. 18:4), it equally clearly reveals the social dimension of humanity, organised in families, communities, nations, and indeed as one racial entity. No individual can abstract himself from the bonds which generically and societally link him with others. A community cannot be judged by God without each member of it also experiencing the temporal consequences of divine judgement, quite apart from how they have personally behaved (note the LORD's discriminating provision for Ebed-Melech and Baruch, Jer. 39:16-18; 45:5). ***I do not show compassion*** (cf. 1:6) describes the LORD withholding his provision and protection, exposing all to the rigours of his chastisement whether through natural calamity as in famine or through the vicissitudes of war and enemy invasion.

Here, however, the LORD goes further than tracing out the corollary of the societal interconnection of humanity; he also adds ***for they are sons of whoredoms.*** A similar expression, 'children of whoredoms', has already been used in 1:2, where their mother's repeated misbehaviour not only blackened the name of her offspring but also influenced them for ill. 'Her sons' in the previous line has already intimated that the LORD, who is here speaking in the role of the nation's husband, does not recognise them as true children of his own. By inclination and participation they are all complicit in their mother's guilt, and so it is right that they will all share her doom.

2:5 For their mother has committed whoredom;
she who conceived them has acted shamefully,
for she has said, 'Let me go after my lovers,
who are giving ⌞me⌟ my bread and my water,
my wool and my flax, my oil and my drinks.'

---

23. The initial *waw* disjunctive breaks the sequence of verbs following *pen*, 'lest', in 2:3, not to introduce a new train of thought but to indicate a set of concurrent circumstances. Alongside the national experience of the LORD's wrath, individuals will also endure his judgement.

For introduces an explanation of the description 'sons of whoredoms' at the end of the previous verse. The children's character has been moulded by the conduct of ***their mother*** (= the nation), who ***has committed whoredom*** (cf. 1:2), which is more specifically identified in the second part of the verse. ***Acted shamefully*** describes brazen conduct which defies all propriety.[24] ***She who conceived them*** attributes to the nation as a whole responsibility not only for the existence of her citizens but also for the character they displayed. Individuals and the people communally have brought disgrace on themselves by their sin.

For at the beginning of the third line presents the evidence which substantiates the allegations against Israel. The device of personifying the nation is used to bring out the inner motivation which informed her conduct. This is the first of three such speeches in the chapter (also in 2:7, 12), which vividly represent the mood of the community rather than claim to reproduce sentiments that they actually uttered. It presents their misconduct not as accidental or a momentary aberration, but as deliberate adoption of the behaviour and religion of the Canaanites so as to enjoy the prosperity which was attributed to worshipping their gods. The present perfect translation ***has said*** (rather than simply 'said') indicates that the attitude she embraced in the past is on-going.

My lovers are 'those I love' (cf. Jer. 2:25; Ezek. 16:37) rather than 'those who are loving me'. This is an continuing disposition[25], and the plural describes the various local manifestations of the god Baal, who was the Canaanite god of fertility (cf. 2:8, 13). The term is unlikely to refer primarily to the bull-calves of Dan and Bethel (cf. 8:5), or, in this context, to foreign nations (cf. Jer. 22:22; Lam. 1:2; Ezek. 16:33), because that does not fit the circumstances of Jeroboam's reign when Israel was strong and not dependent on alliances with surrounding nations. Rather Israel was infatuated with the Baals to whom she openly attributed the agricultural prosperity of the land, and to whom she devoted herself (cf. the statement of the women in Jer. 44:15-19).

---

24. The hiphil of *bôš*, 'be ashamed, fall into disgrace', has two grammatical forms: (1) *hēbîš* has the expected causative sense 'be put to shame'; (2) *hôbîš*, as here, carries the sense not so much of finding oneself engulfed by a situation of disgrace as of bringing it upon oneself by one's own action (*TDOT* 2:59).

25. The piel participle is generally used with a pejorative meaning, 'lover', 'paramour' (*TLOT* 1:47). Macintosh (1997:48) notes that it is difficult to resolve whether the piel is intensive, denoting their passionate character, or causative, the paramours caused her to love them by their gifts.

Go after (cf. 2:13) describes an inner desire translated into ardent striving to achieve fellowship and satisfaction. The idiom is employed of commitment either to the LORD (Deut. 13:5; 1 Kgs. 14:8) or to false gods (Deut. 4:3; 6:14). The underlying metaphor is similar to that used in 'from after' in 1:2 (cf. 11:10). ***Are giving*** is a participial expression which is reminiscent of the hymnic participle in which praise was accorded to the LORD (cf. Ps. 136:25). That was what the nations around her believed, and Israel had adopted their worldview.

The repeated ***my*** in the last two lines indicates the materialistic focus of Israel's thoughts. Not only did she misattribute the source of these gifts; she viewed them both as constituting the essentials of her life and as hers by right. Three pairs of commodities are listed. ***Bread*** was the staple foodstuff of the land, and ***water*** was not only for human consumption but for crops and livestock too (Deut. 9:9, 18; 1 Kgs. 18:13). Without it the whole agricultural economy would collapse. The ***wool*** and ***flax***/'linen'[26] were materials for clothing, the first being of pastoral origin, while the latter was a plant cultivated for its fibres. ***Oil*** was olive oil, used in a multitude of ways, for cooking, lighting, cosmetically, medicinally, and ritually; especially it was a major item of trade (cf. 2:8; 12:1). ***Drinks*** are not necessarily alcoholic, but convey the notion of liquid refreshment of any sort (cf. Ps. 102:9; Prov. 3:8). Hosea is not countering Israel's misattribution of the source of these blessings by advocating entire prohibition of their use. They are God's gifts and to be used, but with thanks to the one true 'God, who lavishly provides us with all things for our enjoyment' (1 Tim. 6:17).

The description of Israel's religious outlook given in this verse may be described as 'baalisation', that is, attribution of the well-being of the nation to the Canaanite gods so as to marginalise and effectively deny the power of the LORD (see *Introduction*, pg. 33). It is improbable that it involved an outright abandonment of the worship of the LORD (cf. 2:11, 16). That challenge had been countered at the time of Elijah, but Canaanite influence had not been extirpated from the land and it remained a major factor in the religious thought and practice of the

---

26. The singular form of the noun *pēšet*, 'flax', occurs only here and in 2:9. Although it has been suggested that the pronominal suffix should be amended to the form found with a plural noun (*pištay* instead of *pištî*) to match the form of 'my drinks' (*šiqqûyāy*), that is not really required and the Massoretic text ought to be retained. Macintosh considers the possibility that the Massoretes preserved a dialectal form (1997:48).

north. Nominally and formally they worshipped the LORD, but in reality their ideology had been so debased with Canaanite ideas that it was Baal they were worshipping.

REFLECTION

- The use of 'mother' (2:2) and 'sons' (2:4) to refer to different aspects of the life of the northern kingdom highlights the difficult question of what an individual's conduct should be when society as a whole no longer respects God or his word, and when the life of the nation no longer observes divine norms. While there are circumstances where silence may be appropriate (cf. 4:4; Amos 5:13), the prophetic role accorded to the church, and especially to those who are leaders in it, requires that suitable warnings be issued of God's verdict on sinful misconduct (cf. Ezek. 3:18-21). But such pleading is not to be done in a harsh or self-righteous spirit, but in a way that befits one who claims to speak on behalf of Christ (cf. John 17:18; 2 Cor. 5:20).
- 'Is she not my wife and am I not her husband?' (2:2). The mutuality which should structure and uphold the marriage bond has to be activated by both parties to the union. 'In a marriage a partner should return the other's love, and, the prophets point out, God seeks love from his people. The very use of this imagery [of a bride and a wife] contains an implied demand for love, a demand which is for the most part not met' (Morris 1981:60).
- Israel's sin was that of syncretism in which her religious views were an amalgam of what the LORD had revealed and the debased concepts of surrounding pagan peoples. Her portrayal as an adulteress (2:2) suggests that she had not totally repudiated her bond with the LORD but was seeking to deceive him (and in measure herself) as to where her true attachment lay. But it is impossible to combine loyalty to the LORD and to other gods because the uniqueness of the LORD leaves no scope for compromise. 'The LORD is God; there is no other besides him' (Deut. 4:35). Furthermore the LORD requires absolute and undeviating commitment to him alone. 'You shall have no other gods before me' (Exod. 20:3). The exclusiveness of Christianity is not derived from intolerance towards particular individuals, social classes or ethnic groups—the gospel invitation is sincerely given without discrimination—but from its demand that a choice has to be made (cf. Josh. 24:15; 1 Kgs. 18:21).

(b) Wandering Frustrated (2:6-7)

Israel's aberrant conduct inevitably provoked a response from the LORD, but he did not immediately overwhelm them in judgement.

Instead in his longsuffering he employed less stringent measures towards his wandering people, to frustrate their ill-conceived ambitions, to prevent further deterioration in their behaviour, and to draw them back to himself.

2:6 Therefore, I am about to hedge up
  your way with thornbushes,
 and I will build a wall about her
  so that she will not find her paths.

Therefore (*lākēn*) frequently introduces the divine verdict on the people's conduct, but here what is in view is not so much punishment but preventative measures which the LORD is ***about to***[27] impose on her[28] because he has resolved to restrain her behaviour.

Although ***hedge up*** is used positively in Job 1:10 to describe a barrier against external assault, what is in view here is something to curb Israel's propensity to wander. The picture is an extension of the previous verse where the people are determined to go after the Baals, presumably by travelling on pilgrimages to sacred sites where those gods were worshipped. Instead the LORD will prevent Israel going off in whatever direction she pleased by the ***thornbushes*** of his providence. A thornbush was a low, prickly shrub, often trained over the top of stone walls to prevent animals either entering or leaving a field (cf. King 1988:123). Israel would be treated as an animal whose instinctive urge to wander, either from the field in which it has been placed or into a forbidden field from the path along which it is being herded, will be hampered. The LORD ***will build a wall about her*** (literally, 'wall a wall'), again not to protect her from others but from herself. The path which she had rebelliously selected for herself will be effectively blocked by a stone wall constructed by the LORD ***so that she will not find her paths.***[29] This action is not so much retributive as preventative. In his loving commitment to the people the LORD first

---

27. The use of *hinnēh* with the participle is an instance of the *futurum instans*, conveying the ideas of certainty and immediacy (*IBHS* §37.6f).

28. 'Your' in 'your way' is a second person feminine singular form, referring to Israel as a whole. There is no difficulty in Hebrew style that there is then a switch to third person references, '*her* path', '*she* will not find' and '*her* paths' (GKC §144p). English prefers more regular pronominal references; hence translators often change the initial 'your' to 'her' (cf. NIV, ESV). There is no need to emend the text as is suggested in *BHS*.

29. The *waw* disjunctive with which the last clause begins probably indicates that this is the purpose of the LORD's action. Less probably the *waw* may indicate a coordinated (rather than consequential) action.

seeks to restrain their folly and keep them in *his* path which he wishes them to follow.

2:7 And she will pursue her lovers, but will not catch up with them;
and she will seek them, but will not find ⌞them⌟.
And she will say, 'Let me go
and return to my first husband,
for it ⌞was⌟ better for me then than ⌞it is⌟ now.'

The first two lines are a parallel picture of the frustration the LORD will impose on the people to discipline them and to recall them to himself. ***Her lovers*** remain the Baals (cf. 2:5), and ***pursue***[30] and ***seek*** show that her desire to worship them remains as strong as ever. 'Pursue' is the language of the hunter and, though often used in negative contexts, it may denote an ardent quest for what is legitimate (cf. 6:3; Ps. 34:14; 38:20; Prov. 15:9). 'Seek' is used elsewhere to describe religious devotion to the LORD and the desire for fellowship with him (cf. 5:6). But Israel will not be successful in accomplishing her own plans because the LORD will put impediments in her way. The absolute ***will not find*** may indicate failure to locate not only those whom she sought but also any other source of satisfaction. Her conduct is utterly futile, and her ill-informed endeavours result in her finding nothing at all. Though it is possible to interpret this and the previous verse as anticipating the siege of Samaria and the deportation of Israel from her territory, what was principally in view was probably the deterioration in the internal situation in the land even before the emergence of Assyrian aggression.

The second part of the verse relates what will happen when Israel finds herself unable to acquire security and prosperity through devotion to the Baals. As the LORD's restorative discipline begins to have an impact, his wayward wife will acknowledge, to some extent, the realities of her situation. Again (cf. 2:5) insight into her attitude is provided by presenting what it is envisaged ***she will say. Let me go*** echoes her earlier utterance in 2:5, but now there is a marked difference in where she resolves to go—not to the false gods, but ***my first husband***/'man' (*'îš*, cf. 2:16). 'First' is not used in contrast to 'second', as if it were being conceded that Baal was her second husband. Her relationship with Baal was illegitimate from start to finish. 'First', with the sense 'original', looks back to her initial union with the LORD.

Return (*šûb*) is basically a verb of motion, which is used in a variety

30. The piel form *riddəpâ* may have intensive force, either 'she will repeatedly pursue' (*HALOT* 1192) or 'she will ardently pursue' (BDB 922).

of extended senses. The verb occurs 22 times in Hosea, most significantly to describe a spiritual return (cf. 5:4). However, it does not appear that the situation described here is one of genuine repentance.[31] The stimulus for her changed conduct is her perception that ***it was better for me then than it is now.*** 'Then' looks back to the whole period when they could be said to have served the LORD, days of obedience and covenant loyalty, which certainly included the period in the wilderness when she enjoyed the LORD's provision for her despite difficult surrounding circumstances. Her argument seems more than a little tinged by materialistic self-interest. If the Baals are not providing her with what she expects, then perhaps it would be better for her to try the LORD again (cf. 'I was better off with him', NEB). There is no expression of allegiance to the LORD, or regret for her actions. Even so, at one level the LORD's discipline of frustrating judgements has had an impact. She is no longer blindly committed to following the Baals, and has been brought to reappraise her conduct, though in a self-centred fashion. Deeper spiritual insight is still required.

REFLECTION

- When the LORD's people wander spiritually, he may discipline them by bringing hardship and misfortune as warnings that they are off the right road which leads to himself and that they have aligned themselves with those who have rebelled against him. Pitting oneself against the LORD leads to suffering and frustration. 'It is hard for you to kick against the goads' (Acts 26:14). 'Good understanding wins favour, but the way of the treacherous is hard' (Prov. 13:15). Roadblocks in the path an individual has chosen for himself may a sign of divine concern as God encourages a backslider to reappraise his conduct and return in repentance. 'When you are in distress and all these things have come upon you, in the latter days you will return to the LORD your God and obey his voice' (Deut. 4:30).
- In the volumes on the Minor Prophets which he contributed to *The Expositor's Bible* of 1899, George Adam Smith developed a suggestion of Jerome and entitled his comments on Hosea 1–3, 'The Story of the Prodigal Wife'. This was an evident allusion to the parable found in Luke 15:11-32, but though the calamities which befell the lost son led him to reconsider his situation and return, the stark

31. 'This is no genuine repentance (cf. 6.1-3), but only a desire for change, because change is expected to bring relief' (Harper 1905:237).

outcome of Israel's history shows that no such reaction was forthcoming in her case.

(c) Disloyalty Punished (2:8-13)

Israel did not come to appreciate how serious her situation was, and so did not in fact utter the words of 2:7, or anything like them. Since repentance, no matter how deficient, was still a long way off, a further indictment is lodged against the LORD's errant wife—that she fails to acknowledge the true source of her prosperity (2:8). Consequently, as a second stage in the LORD's recovery programme, he will take back the gifts he has already provided for the nation (2:9) and expose it to shame (2:10), joylessness (2:11), and utter ruin (2:12-13). 'Love is never harsh, but it can be stern' (Morris 1981:18).

2:8 But as for her, she does not know that I ⌞am the one who⌟ gave her
the corn and the new wine and the olive oil,
and silver I multiplied for her
and gold ⌞which⌟ they offered to Baal.

But as for her turns the spotlight back to Israel's present attitude, which is far from what should characterise a loyal follower devoted to the LORD. The focus falls on the fact that ***she does not know.***[32] 'Know' is a key term in Hosea (cf. 2:20; 4:1, 6; 5:3,4; 6:3, 6; 13:4, 5), and includes not merely possessing information about God, but acknowledgement of what he has done, expressed in thanksgiving, obedience and true intimacy. Israel was no longer living as the covenant partner of the LORD, but had instead embraced a perverted understanding of him and the world derived from Canaanite ideology in which the Baals, the gods of fertility, were worshipped because they were conceived of as the source of every material blessing. Whatever perception the people had of their relationship with the LORD, their infatuation with all things Canaanite had blinded them to the fact that they were living in the world which the LORD had created and which he continued to control (cf. Jer. 5:24). Their mental and spiritual block did not, however, alter the reality of the situation. ***I ⌞am the one who⌟*** reflects the emphatic use of the first person pronoun 'I', so that the

32. The perfect aspect of the verb *yādaʿ*, 'to know', may be used to denote an ongoing state of mind which requires a present tense translation, 'she does not know' (Joüon §112a). A past translation is also possible, 'she did not know', but that is less likely in that her lack of acknowledgement still continues.

statement is virtually equivalent to 'I and I alone', and not those who have been mistakenly identified as bestowing these gifts (cf. 4:6; 5:3, 14; 7:15; 12:10; 13:5; 14:8).[33]

No doubt David's psalms continued to be sung in the worship of the northern kingdom. With their lips they would proclaim that the LORD satisfies the desire of every living think with his bountiful provision (cf. Ps. 145:16), but they had become mere words which no longer reflected what they actually thought.

The staple agricultural commodities were blessings they enjoyed from God, stemming from his goodness as their covenant Overlord. The people were in 'a land which the LORD your God cares for' and to which he had promised that he would give 'rain in its season, early rain and later rain, that you may gather in your grain and your wine and your oil. And I will give grass in your fields for your livestock, and you will eat and be full' (Deut. 11:12, 14-15; cf. Deut. 7:13). The first three blessings in this verse are different from those found in 2:5. Here the reference is to newly harvested commodities, freshly given by God, and not yet processed. ***Corn*** consists of grain gathered from a variety of crops, principally wheat, but also barley, millet and spelt. Such cereals would grow in the valleys. Vines and olive trees would be found on the terraced hillsides. ***New wine*** probably points to freshly pressed grape juice. It is unclear to what extent, if any, fermentation had occurred (cf. 4:11). ***The olive oil*** is a different term from that found in 2:5, and probably relates to freshly pressed oil from olives. Olives were not grown in either Egypt or Mesopotamia, and their oil was a valuable export commodity. These three products formed the basis of Israel's national well-being and prosperity.

From their agricultural abundance there flowed commercial success. The LORD also added ***silver and gold*** to their national assets, commodities which were not naturally found in Canaan, but which Israel acquired through trade with foreign nations. ***Multiplied***/'made much/many' (cf. 10:1) implies that the LORD was unstinting in his provision, and so their wealth had grown substantially.

However, it was a measure of Israel's spiritual insensitivity that they had not just misused these resources, but had also abused them. The plural subject ***they*** in the last clause of the verse goes beyond the

---

33. The emphatic use of the pronoun 'I' (*ʾānōkî*) is readily identified because the accompanying verb form already incorporates the sense of 'I'. Separate expression of the pronoun is equivalent to the use of a close-up in photography (Joüon §146a).

metaphor of Israel as the LORD's wife to make clear reference to the individuals who comprised the community. There is also here the first explicit naming of Baal, the Canaanite god. For the significance of the term, see on 2:16.

The precious metals which God had given the Israelites ***they offered to Baal,*** literally 'made to Baal'. Though it has been suggested that this involves converting the metals into statues of the god (cf. Ezek. 16:17-18), the phrase 'to make to/for' God (or a god) is idiomatic for giving something by way of dedication or sacrifice. For instance, in Exodus 10:25 Moses asked Pharaoh for animals 'that we may make them to the LORD our God', by which he meant offering them in sacrifice to him (cf. this use of 'make' for 'sacrifice' in 2 Kgs. 17:32; 2 Chron. 24:7). So in their perverseness Israel did not just omit to thank the LORD for his goodness; they insulted him more deeply by returning thanks to another god and dedicating the gifts they had been given to another deity.

2:9 Therefore I will return and take away my grain in its time
and my new wine in its season,
and I will remove my wool and my flax
⌞intended⌟ to cover her nakedness.

Therefore again (2:6) introduces the LORD's verdict in these circumstances, as he resolves to punish Israel appropriately for her perverse misattribution of his blessings. He too can ***return*** (cf. 2:7). The thought may just be that of the LORD's renewed involvement with the people after a period when he had left them to their own devices to expose the inadequacy and folly of their ways. But, additionally, 'return' may express the reversal of an action, 'I will take back' (cf. ESV).

When the LORD does so, he ***will take away*** the gifts which have been misunderstood and misused (cf. 9:2). Four times the use of ***my*** emphasises from whom the commodities really came, and counters the misguided attitude of the people who had looked on them as rightfully and intrinsically their own (cf. '*my* grain' etc., 2:5). ***Grain*** and ***new wine*** are also present in the list of the preceding verse. ***In its time*** and ***in its season*** show that these crops were going to fail just when they were due to be harvested, grain in May to June, and grapes in July to September. The background to this might be drought which inhibited the crops from maturing, but it could also occur through destructive enemy action. Armies typically went to war in the late spring so that their troops could forage for provisions and also inflict maximum damage on the economy of the land they were invading. This would also apply to the ***wool*** and ***flax*** (terms taken from the description of 2:5). Young lambs would be eaten by enemy forces and the fields of flax destroyed.

But this outcome is not just the result of human devastation. Invading armies were the instruments through whom the LORD would forcefully operate to impose the curses of the broken covenant (cf. Deut. 28:18). ***Remove*** may refer to snatching something out of the firm grip of another (cf. 2:10; 'rescue', 5:14). ***My*** again asserts that these commodities are rightfully the LORD's. His action in retrieving them would bring shame and disgrace upon the people. ***To cover her nakedness*** shows how, without the provision the LORD had made for her needs, Israel would be totally and shamefully exposed without clothing (cf. Ezek. 16:8).

2:10 So now I will expose her shame before the eyes of her lovers,
and no one will remove her out of my hand.

The introductory 'and now' does not signify, as it often does, the introduction of a new subject or the next phase in a developing scenario, but rather functioning as ***so now*** it elaborates on what God has resolved will occur. ***I will expose her shame*** threatens that she will be stripped completely naked (cf. 2:3 and Deut. 28:48 cited there). The word 'shame' (*nablût*) occurs only here, and may punningly allude also to folly or stupidity (as indeed the term is understood in the Vulgate). It is related to words that describe wanton, lewd or immodest conduct, and so the one is presented as the appropriate penalty for the other. Such exposure was viewed as a source of utter disgrace for an individual (cf. Lev. 20:17; 1 Sam. 20:30; Isa. 20:4; 47:3; Lam. 1:8; Ezek. 16:35; Nah. 3:5), and applied metaphorically to a nation it described it as without resources to sustain its population or to maintain an adequate defence against external aggression (cf. Gen. 42:9). There may well be a further hint as to how this will occur in that the verb 'to expose' also has an associated sense of 'to exile'. The nation's shame will be seen when they are marched off as naked captives into exile. She will then be liable to ridicule and contempt ***before the eyes of her lovers.*** As in 2:5, 7 they are the Baals, who are presented as powerless spectators of her humiliation.

No one will remove her out of my hand expresses the finality of the LORD's intervention. 'Remove' uses the same term as in the previous verse, but now the process is reversed. In view are possible attempts of others—especially the Baals—to extricate Israel from her dire and shameful state. They will be ineffective because no power is stronger than the LORD and so none is capable of prising her from his grasp (cf. 5:14). In the ultimate analysis he alone is the one who determines her destiny. He will not revoke his decree and he possesses the strength to enforce it.

2:11 And I will cause all her joy to cease,
her festivals, her new moons and her sabbaths,
and all her appointed feasts.

The LORD's action against Israel will not overlook her religious celebrations which played a central role in her national life. Though they afforded her ***joy***, they were detested by the LORD. He declares that he ***will cause to cease*** (cf. 1:4) these ceremonial observances because, although originally divinely appointed as occasions in which joyful praise would be accorded to the LORD for his goodness (cf. Num. 10:10; Deut. 12:12), they had been corrupted by assimilation to the materialistic paganism of Canaan. It is indeed significant that in Israel there were still ***festivals,*** the annual events which should have been accompanied by pilgrimage to Jerusalem (cf. Exod. 34:22-23; Deut. 16:16-17), ***new moons***, the time of rejoicing associated with the start of each month (cf. 1 Sam. 20:5; Amos 8:5), and the weekly recurring ***sabbaths*** (cf. Exod. 23:12; 34:21).[34] These three terms occur together as a standard way of referring to all religious festivals (cf. 1 Chron. 23:31; 2 Chron. 2:4; 8:13; 31:3; Neh. 10:33; Ezek. 45:17). There is a tragic echo between 'cause to cease' (*hišbattî*) and 'her sabbaths' (*šabbattāh*). These ordinances of the Mosaic law had been maintained in the north after the break with Jerusalem, but they were a shell without substance. Again repetition of the possessive adjective is employed to make a point. ***Her*** indicates the element of will-worship that was involved: the LORD no longer recognised them as 'the appointed feasts of the LORD ... my appointed feasts' (Lev. 23:1), truly dedicated to him. By introducing pagan elements ***all her appointed feasts*** had become unacceptable to the LORD, and so they would be swept away.

2:12 And I will ravage her vines and her fig trees
⌞of which⌟ she has said,
'They are my reward
which my lovers have given to me.'
But I will set them as scrubland
and the wild animals will eat them.

---

34. 'Festivals', 'new moons', 'sabbaths', and 'appointed feasts' are all singular nouns used collectively (Joüon §135).

The LORD's anger will also be evident in his treatment of the land's agricultural resources, whose fertility was so closely linked with Baal in Canaanite thought. The LORD asserts who was really in control. ***I will ravage*** promises severe destruction for ***her vines and her fig trees,***[35] which are symbolic of Israel's prosperity and satisfaction (cf. 1 Kgs. 5:5; Jer. 5:17; Joel 2:22; Mic. 4:4; Zech. 3:10). No longer will the people be able to sit in the shade afforded by the fig tree; no longer will the grapes and figs be harvested in the autumn, followed by the Feast of Ingathering/Booths. It is not spelled out how the LORD would bring about this change, but it is evident that it is not one adverse season which is in view, but ongoing desolation.

What is made abundantly clear is why this change will occur. '*Her* vines and *her* fig trees' continues the sequence involving 'her' from the previous verse. Israel entertained mistaken beliefs regarding ownership of these resources. ***She has said*** (cf. 2:5, 7) reveals how she continued to think that they were inalienably hers. Indeed her outlook was even more flawed than that because she attributed their produce to the Baals which she worshipped: ***They are my reward which my lovers have given me.*** 'Reward' occurs only here and is probably a play on the similarly sounding word 'fig tree'.[36] It is derived from a verbal root (cf. 8:9, 10) which indicates paying for services rendered. Her 'lovers' are again the Baals (cf. 2:5) to whom she professed allegiance and devotion, and in accordance with Canaanite ideology she considered them as having gifted to her the produce of the land.

The LORD, however, had another view of the matter, and he would therefore ***set*** aside what she regarded as trophies which her lovers had awarded her for her devoted service. Economic catastrophe will require a complete reassessment of Israel's lifestyle and allegiance. The LORD will reduce ***them***, that is, the nation's vineyards and orchards, so that they become ***scrubland***, overgrown thickets with untended and entangled plants struggling to survive invasive weeds—a sign of desolation

---

35. The two nouns 'vine' and 'fig tree' are singular terms, used collectively. Moreover, while they are elsewhere treated as feminine nouns, in Hosea they are masculine as the following masculine 'they' (*hēmmâ*) attests and also the masculine pronominal suffixes on the two verbs in the final line of the verse. This is almost certainly an indication of Hosea's northern dialect rather than evidence of textual corruption requiring emendation.

36. 'Reward' is *ʾetnâ* whereas 'fig tree' is *təʾēnâ*. A further wordplay arises from the fact that *ʾetnān* is used elsewhere for what is paid to a prostitute (cf. 9:1; Deut. 23:19; Ezek. 16:31).

(cf. Isa. 5:6; 7:23; Mic. 3:12). Such fruit as is produced ***the wild animals will eat***, because, with no one to tend the plants or repair the protective walls, they are left open to the depredations of foraging beasts. 'Eat' as a verb generally refers to the physical consumption of food by man or beast, but the term can also have negative connotations and refer to destructive activity, when the rendering 'devour' is more appropriate (cf. 7:7). More seems to be involved here than agricultural failure; there is also the devastation and depopulation of enemy invasion.

2:13 And I will bring her to account for the days of the Baals
to whom she would burn incense,
and she adorned herself with her ring and her jewellery,
and went after her lovers but me she forgot,
declares the LORD.

I will bring her to account describes a superior assessing and rewarding the activities of a subordinate (cf. 1:4). The reckoning God here instigates leads to punishment of his wife's unfaithful ways. ***The days of the Baals*** points to the occasions of her appointed feasts (2:11) which she had contaminated by her syncretism, effectively devoting them to Baal worship. The plural term 'Baals' (also used in 2:17; 11:2) points to the multiplicity of local manifestations of the deity. Mention of Canaanite goddesses is avoided as not fitting in with the prevailing husband/wife metaphor.

Would burn incense[37] renders a verb which basically signifies 'to send a sacrifice up in smoke'. While the root can be used with a specific offering as its object (cf. Lev. 1:9) or in connection with cultic activity in general (cf. 2 Chron. 25:14), because words such as 'incense' and 'incense altar' are derived from it, it is appropriate to understand it as referring to burning incense unless the context indicates otherwise.

Israel did not spare herself in her worship of these false gods. Mention of adornment connects back with 2:5. ***Her ring*** refers to an ornament worn either in the nose (Gen. 24:47; Isa. 3:21) or on the ears (Gen. 35:4; Exod. 32:2-3), and which may well have been made from gold (cf. Exod. 35:22). ***Her jewellery*** indicates a finely crafted item, which may have formed part of her dress for worshipping idols. Certainly she ***went after her lovers*** (cf. 2:5) in infatuated devotion to the pagan gods. The terse, emphatic statement ***but me she forgot***

37. The imperfect is used to denote repeated action in past time (Joüon §118n).

indicates that her outlook was quite the opposite of that devoted and familiar knowing of the LORD which she should have cherished (cf. 2:20; 6:6; Jer. 18:15). In this way the practice of the people embodied a rejection of all that the LORD had done for them, failure to recognise his claims upon their loyalty and a resolve to live as though God did not exist. The solemn ***declares the LORD*** marks an authoritative and determinative pronouncement which emphasises the gravity of the offence and the danger of the position into which it had brought the people. While a common phrase in other prophets, it is used rarely by Hosea (also in 2:16, 21; 11:11). Here, as in 11:11, it occurs at the end of a discourse and serves to mark the end of the subsection.[38]

REFLECTION

- 'She does not know' (2:8) does not record an overnight change in Israel's religious perception, but the outcome of a gradual, but nonetheless, deadly process of decay. Those whom the devil captures to do his will (cf. 2 Tim. 2:26) he first desensitises to the truth and then allures by the bogus claims of an alternative lifestyle which is promoted as glamorous and satisfying. Recovery is possible. The pathway set out for the Christian ministry in such circumstances is to correct with gentleness those who have wandered from the right path of the truth and to aim at bringing them to their senses through a renewed appreciation of the truth (cf. 2 Tim. 2:24-26). However, God himself may employ harsher remedies to destabilise the complacent coalition of his backsliding people with the powers of darkness.
- The gravity of sin does not principally arise because it leads to deprivation of blessing, exposure to disgrace, or liability to punishment. The heinousness of sin springs from the insult it delivers to God, and the sheer ingratitude that it displays to his goodness. It is this element of personal affront that adds pathos to the declaration, 'But me she forgot' (2:13).
- 'Me she forgot' does not point to a loss of memory of the name of God, or even to forgetfulness of the history of his dealings with his people. It may co-exist with continuing participation in religious worship. But what it lacks is genuine spiritual attachment. Scripture is treated as mere literature, appreciated for its aesthetic qualities without hearing God speaking through it and with no inner inclination to observe its moral injunctions. Heart detachment from God

38. The Massoretes additionally indicated a break here by inserting a paragraph marker after 2:13 (2:15 in the Hebrew verse enumeration).

leads to a practical amnesia so that God's known requirements no longer mould conduct or determine the goals to which our lives are dedicated.

- How rarely the hand of God is recognised in business or economics! Company profits and national economic growth are alike attributed to entrepreneurial acumen and adroit implementation of government policy. Yet both are subject to events beyond human control, and both may be undermined from within by greed or complacency. Divine governance of material prosperity is effected through inherent moral forces and also by providential intervention to bring to account for the days in which God is forgotten (2:13). It remains as true now as it did in Hosea's time that God blights the economic advance of individuals and nations to force them to reassess their priorities and give first place to spiritual prosperity. 'But seek first the kingdom of God and his righteousness, and all these things will be granted to you as well' (Matt. 6:33).

(2) Love's Initiative (2:14-23)

In a manner reminiscent of the change which occurred in 1:10–2:1, there now breaks into the bleak scenes of Israel's perfidious obsession with the gods of Canaan the light of the LORD's sovereign restoration of his people. Only through his gracious initiative can the exclusive relationship of the LORD and Israel be put on a proper basis and their fellowship resumed. The components of his blessing are marked out by repetition of 'on that day' (2:16, 18, 21). The fourfold presentation shows that divine intervention will involve a period of training in the wilderness for the people (2:14-15), eradication of all that had been contaminated by Baal worship (2:16-17), security in the land through restoration of the LORD's protection towards those whom he takes as his own (2:18-20), and the all-encompassing blessings of the renewed covenant (2:21-23).

(a) A New Exodus (2:14-15)

2:14 Therefore I am about to allure her
    and bring her ⌊into⌋ the wilderness
    and speak kindly to her.

After the preceding exposures of Israel's misconduct, a third repetition of ***therefore*** (cf. 2:6, 9) leads us to anticipate an announcement of impending doom. Instead, there is a startlingly unexpected disclosure of the LORD's initiative to bless and restore his errant wife.[39] Hosea's paradoxical presentation emphasises that from a human perspective there are no grounds from which such an action can be logically inferred. It is utterly inexplicable and entirely unmerited. There is not the least hint that restoration will occur because of Israel's desires or her efforts. All is attributed to the abiding commitment of divine grace and love which is displayed by the sovereign LORD as he reclaims his people (cf. the divine speech in 11:8–11; 14:4–8).

I am about to[40] points to impending divine intervention. ***Allure*** is the language of persuasion, enticement, or even seduction (cf. Judg. 14:15; 16:5; 1 Kgs. 22:20-22; Jer. 20:7; Ezek. 14:9). Israel's persistent misconduct has made it abundantly clear that she has no desire to return, but the LORD will not permit that state of affairs to continue. He will act in an irresistible and compelling fashion to overcome her reluctance and evoke a response from her.

Furthermore it is the LORD's intention to ***bring her into the wilderness.*** But which wilderness is intended? In the light of the following verse the reference is obviously to the one between Sinai and Egypt, but this is used as a metaphor to explain how the LORD is going to act in the current circumstances. The wilderness does not picture oppression such as that which they had experienced in Egypt, and which they would again undergo when their land was subjugated by Assyria (cf. 11:6). Indeed, reference to the wilderness is not primarily a matter of physical, geographical location. It speaks rather of the spiritual conditions which the LORD will recreate. They will be patterned after the way he made his will known to the people at Sinai and tested them to prove their heart allegiance to him (Deut. 8:2-5). That had been particularly needed in the light of the undue hold the affluence of Egypt had exercised on their hearts (cf. Num. 11:4-5) as well as the debased conceptions of God they entertained (cf. Exod. 32:1-4). Parallel circumstances had again arisen in that the agricultural fertility and wealth enjoyed in Samaria had corrupted their national life, and their religious understanding had been debased. There was again need for a time of wilderness discipline and stringency in which they would be separated from the paganised environment of the Baal groves of

---

39. 'The third ('therefore') speech is entirely out of character; it is not a judgement speech at all, and must be seen as a delightful reversal of the expected, a bold rejection of the causal nexus between sin and punishment. ...Yahweh's answer to Israel's ignoring him will be to turn the clock back and let her begin her history with him all over again' (Clines 1978:86).

Canaan and forced to survive in conscious reliance upon the LORD and his providential provision, listening anew to his word and rededicating themselves to his service. This would prevail wherever the people were scattered after the Assyrians invaded their land.

The LORD will ***speak kindly to her***, that is, 'speak to her heart' (Gen. 34:3), uttering words of tenderness and encouragement (Judg. 19:3; Gen. 50:21; Isa. 40:1), designed to console. 'Heart' imagery recurs throughout Hosea (cf. 4:11; 7:6, 11, 14; 10:2; 11:8; 13:6, 8). What is looked for here is inner change in which the people are responsive to God's inner pleading with them and once more adopt a basic attitude of dependence on him no matter what outward situation prevails.

2:15 And I will give her her vineyards from there
and the valley of Achor for a door of hope;
and there she will respond as ⌞in⌟ the days of her youth
and as ⌞in⌟ the day of her coming up from the land of Egypt.

The LORD further elaborates on his programme of spiritual recovery and training for Israel by mentioning how much more ***he will give her*** when she progresses ***from there***, that is the wilderness, to the next class in this recapitulation of her spiritual experience. ***Vineyards*** were one feature of Canaan which initially attracted Israel's attention (cf. the cluster of grapes from the valley of Eshcol, Num. 13:23). Indeed the terraced vineyards clinging to the hillsides were a notable feature of the land as distinct from the wilderness.

However, recalling ***the valley of Achor*** ('trouble') acts as a reminder that all did not advance smoothly on that first journey. As a matter of geography Achor was located north of Jericho, in the tribal territory of Judah near its boundary with that of Benjamin (cf. Josh. 15:7), but here it is its spiritual significance which is uppermost. After Israel's entry into the land, this was the place where Achan brought disaster upon the community by his covetousness (Josh. 7:26). The parallel will not be fully worked out because, on this second entry into the land of promise, in a further instance of the reversal of the significance of names (cf. 1:10–2:1), what had been a place of ill omen will be transformed into ***a door of hope*** (cf. Isa. 65:10). A 'door' may refer to the entrance into a territory (Mic. 5:6), and in that respect the term fitted the valley of Achor through which access was gained into the hill country of central Palestine. But the 'hope' entertained here is that of an eager expectation of enjoyment of close fellowship with God. Achor will no longer be thought of as the place where sin led to estrangement between the LORD and his people, but as the entry point into the territory where 'they may have life, and have it to the full' (John 10:10, NIV). For this to be so they would have to renounce their materialistic hankering after the physical abundance of the land and their deluded attribution of its gifts as given to them by the Baals.

And there probably takes up where the last line left off, at the entrance into the land of promise.[41] No longer will Israel misunderstand or misattribute all that the LORD has done on her behalf. There is a measure of uncertainty about the dominant characteristic of her reaction because the root of the verb employed here has a variety of meanings, including 'to answer'/***respond*** and 'to sing' (NIV). As is frequently the case in Hosea, he probably intended to convey both ideas, though primarily the former. What will be looked for from Israel will be a genuine and joyful response to the LORD's dealings with her, paying close attention to the situation in which they have been placed, a meaning similar to that in 2:21-22, where the same word is used five times. 'Respond' may well recall the willing devotion expressed at Sinai. 'And all the people responded with one voice and said, "All the words which the LORD has spoken we will do" ' (Exod. 24:3) and 'we will be obedient' (Exod. 24:7).

In the days of her youth looks back on the immediate post-Exodus period as a positive time (cf. 11:1). Hosea was well aware that not everything had not gone well in the wilderness. For instance, he mentions Baal-Peor in 9:10. But it had been a time of intimacy when relationships developed between the LORD and his chosen people as they learned how to please him. Jeremiah would later reflect on this period in a similar way, and record the LORD's appraisal of it: 'I remember about you the devotion of your youth, the love of your betrothals, your walking after me in the wilderness in a land not sown. Israel ⌊was⌋ holiness to the LORD, the firstfruits of his harvest' (Jer. 2:2-3; cf. Jer. 31:2; Ezek. 20:10-38). ***In the day of her coming up from the land of Egypt*** recalls the same time from the perspective of a dark and dismal past from which the LORD had delivered them (cf. 11:1; 12:9, 13; 13:4). While Israel had then made many mistakes, on the whole she had been on a learning curve marked by faltering progress. In that respect it was unlike the later period when the worship of Baal had become endemic among the people.

---

40. For 'about to', see footnote 27.

41. *šammâ* is strictly 'to there', but the force of the directive ending is frequently attenuated.

REFLECTION

- After a major physical illness, a period of recuperation and rehabilitation is required. The same holds true spiritually: recovery takes time. Furthermore the parallel between the two situations extends to the nature of what has to be regained to effect a comeback. After a time of prolonged physical weakness or inability a person has to learn again how to perform the elementary tasks of everyday life. So too spiritual rehabilitation does not consist of novel experiences, but of retracing with deeper understanding and intensity the old ways, which were the true ways in any case. 'Thus says the LORD, "Stand by ⌊the⌋ ways and see, and ask for the ancient paths, where the good way ⌊is⌋, and walk in it! and you will find rest for yourselves" ' (Jer. 6:16).
- 'A door of hope' (2:15) testifies to the transforming power of God. When his people master the spiritual lessons he is teaching them through his providential intervention in their lives, he gives opportunities for spiritual progress which are not to be despised. When the sins of the past are identified and repudiated, the mistakes of the past will not be repeated, and even the experience of defeat may be used as the basis for confident advance. There remains the need to perceive the doors he opens and to be willing to take advantage of the direction he gives (cf. Acts 14:27; 1 Cor. 16:9; 2 Cor. 2:12).

(b) Abandonment of Baal (2:16-17)

The relationship which the LORD restores with Israel as his wife will be purged of all grounds of confusion (2:16) and of every opportunity to slip back into their former evil ways (2:17). There will be a clear separation from anything associated with the worship of Baal.

2:16 And it will be on that day, declares the LORD,
that you will call me 'My husband'
and will not call me any more 'My lord'.

On that day acts as a unifying indicator in this section (cf. 2:18, 21), pointing to the time when the LORD will restore Israel to obedient fellowship with himself (cf. 3:5; 11:10-11; 14:4-7). His promise is accompanied by the authenticating mark ***declares the LORD*** (cf. 2:13), which gives an unequivocal pledge as to its achievement.

One notable feature of this verse is that the LORD now addresses Israel directly. With the exception of 2:8a he had maintained a detached stance regarding Israel throughout the chapter, pleading with her through third parties and speaking about her in the third person.

Now the days of estrangement are over. After the wife's true response (2:15), the marriage partners are again talking to each other.

But care will have to be exercised regarding the language which the wife is to use in speaking of the LORD. The term *baʿal* could be used of any superior, whether a husband, owner, or lord. It was also commonly employed as a descriptor of deity, and had originally been used of Yahweh himself as the lord and master of all he had created and also of his role in the special covenant relationship he had instituted with Israel ('It is he who made us, and we are his', Ps. 100:3). Names such as Esh-Baal ('man of the Lord', 1 Chron. 8:33), Merib-Baal (possibly, 'The Lord defend me', 1 Chron. 8:34) or Beeliada ('the Lord knows', 1 Chron. 14:7) had not reflected devotion to Baal, even although later scribes understood them in that way (cf. 2:17). However, when the dominant reference of the term *baʿal* became Baal, the Canaanite god of storm and fertility, and his many localised representations, it turned into a source of confusion for the same word to be used of the LORD—a confusion no doubt exploited by the proponents of the syncretistic state religion of the north to encourage the notion that the LORD might be worshipped as one of the many manifestations of Baal. To prevent any possibility of blurring the two, instead of *Baali*, ***my lord***, it is declared that the people must say *Ishi*, ***my husband*** (*ʾîš*, cf. 2:7). There is also a warmth and closeness in the latter term (cf. Gen. 2:23-4; Isa. 54:5), but even so it is probable that the main point being made is the rejection of any misunderstanding fostered by the Baal cult. ***You will not call*** shows that there some who were already doing so, conceiving of the one true God in a way corrupted by Canaanite ideology.

2:17 And I will remove the names of the Baals out of her mouth,
and they will no more be remembered by their name.

Switching back to third person language, the LORD declares his resolve to take away ***the names of the Baals***.[42] 'Names' points to various epithets used to describe the god, and also place designations such as

---

42. Possibly this verse combined with 9:10 gave rise to the scribal practice of changing names which had *baʿal* as their theophoric element, e.g. Ish-Bosheth ('man of shame'; 2 Sam. 2:8-11) compared with Eshbaal ('man of the Lord'; 1 Chron. 8:33; 9:39), where the Chronicler, though the later author, retains the earlier form because Baal worship was no longer a threat in the post-exilic community for whom he was writing. A similar practice may well have given rise to the New Testament Beelzebub (Baal-Zebub, 'lord of the flies'; Matt. 10:25) in place of Baal-Zebul ('Prince Baal', or 'Baal of the lofty abode').

Baal-Gad (Josh. 11:17), Baal-Hazor (2 Sam. 13:23), or Baal-Peor (9:10; Deut. 4:3). ***Out of her mouth*** indicates the speech of Israel will be purged of mentioning such a god or place. In particular this foretells the removal of Baal worship from amongst the people so that there will be no occasion to name such a god.

Furthermore the outlook of those who had forgotten the LORD (2:13) in their headlong pursuit of the Baals will be so transformed that the Baals ***will no more be remembered by their name***, and the people's conduct would conform to the standards of the covenant ('and the name of other gods do not cause to be remembered: it will not be heard upon your mouth', Exod. 23:13; cf. Deut. 12:3). 'Remember' may be used in cultic contexts, for example, 'in every place where I cause my name to be remembered'/'invoked' (Exod. 20:24), or 'in the name of the LORD we will cause to be remembered'/'trust' (Ps. 20:7; cf. 1 Chron. 16:4; Isa. 26:18), and so mention of Baal is particularly banished from Israel's worship. The singular 'name' points to the god Baal apart from the local epithets and designations which were used to distinguish the various manifestations of Baal at different shrines. Perhaps the emphasis on 'names' and 'name' suggests that all that really existed was just the sound of the word with no corresponding reality behind it. So there will be no trace left of the misguided and ultimately empty devotion of their past.

REFLECTION

- Words and the way we use them are important because they shape as well as express our perception of reality. Words can provide an Orwellian mode of thought control which earthly authorities may use to modify and control responses and attitudes. At an individual level, the Christian has to avoid all improper and debased use of language (Eph. 5:3-4, 29), especially language which relates to God (Exod. 20:7; James 5:12). In 2:16 we have an instance of a word changing its significance over time. It is essential that we monitor our speech patterns to detect words which, though we may be familiar and comfortable with them, no longer communicate accurately with others. When the one word is used in different senses in religious circles, confusion reigns and it is easy to worship a false god of our own devising.
- Fellowship with God involves an ever deepening process of sanctification whereby the believer dissociates from past futile conduct and is inwardly renewed in true righteousness and holiness (cf. Rom. 12; Eph. 4:17-23). This process is evident outwardly in speech because

'out of the abundance of the heart the mouth speaks' (Matt. 12:34). But what is involved is not just filtered speech to conform to God's requirements, but inner change whereby former debased life practices 'will no more be remembered' (2:17) because intense, total inward focus on Christ and appreciation of his grace and steadfast love leave no place in thought or affections for any other.

- Mention of the Baals (2:17) tends to make Hosea's message seem remote and disconnected from a modern audience, just as New Testament references to idolatry may be passed over as of little relevance. However, Paul's explanation that one who is covetous is an idolater (Eph. 5:5; cf. Col. 3:5) points to what is really involved. The Baals (and idolatry) are particular manifestations of a deep-seated perversion of the fallen human heart which focuses its affections and desires on anything other than God. When mankind invent gods for themselves, they project their fallen aspirations onto their idols, gain religious sanction for their sin, and reinforce their debased lifestyles. The modern gods in whatever philosophical, political or cultural guise they are presented distort a nation's understanding of what is true and are obstacles blocking the way to true satisfaction. Indeed, they are guaranteed sources of great disappointment when God intervenes to judge what has gone wrong.

(c) Security and Betrothal (2:18-20)

Another vista of what the LORD will bestow on his recovered people is expressed in terms of covenant (2:18) and betrothal (2:19-20). The ravaging of wild animals (2:12) will be reversed to ensure that the people are free from external threat, and they will be brought into an eternal relationship with the LORD.

2:18 And I will make a covenant for them on that day
with the wild animals and with the birds of the sky
and with the reptiles of the ground,
and bow and sword and war
I will break from the land,
and I will make them lie down in safety.

On that day reflects the period of Israel's restoration which was first mentioned in 2:16. This is a description of freedom from external threat achieved through the reversal of the covenant curse (cf. 2:12). Marauding animals will no longer pillage their crops, possibly in the aftermath of an enemy invasion (cf. 2:12; Isa. 11:6-9; 35:9; 65:25; Ezek. 34:25, 28). Furthermore no military invasion will occur as the LORD ***will break*** 1and so do away with such weaponry ***from the land***

(cf. 1:7; Ps. 46:9; 76:3; Isa. 3:25; 21:15). Consequently the area which had frequently been beset by ***war*** would find it banished from their midst. In this way their divine Overlord and Protector ***will make*** his people ***lie down in safety.*** This picture of rest and repose goes beyond an absence of disturbance to include total well-being and uninterrupted enjoyment of all the blessings of the covenant. In Leviticus 25:18-19 'safety'/'security' is envisaged principally as freedom from famine (cf. Isa. 14:30), whereas in the following chapter the picture is extended to include absence of enemy aggression and attacks by wild beasts (Lev. 26:5-8). The LORD's provision is not stinted or half-hearted.

Moreover God undertakes to ***make a covenant,*** that is, to 'cut' it, the usual language for covenant formation/inauguration (cf. Jer. 34:18). ***For them***[43] indicates that the people are beneficiaries of this covenant, not directly parties in it. Instead the LORD imposes his requirements on ***the wild animals and with the birds of the sky and with the reptiles of the ground***, terms that come from the creation account (cf. Gen. 1:21, 24, 30). The situation is reminiscent of the Noachic covenant (Gen. 9:9-10; cf. Ezek. 34:25), and indicates resumption of the harmonious world-order which prevailed in Eden before the irruption of sin (cf. Isa. 11:6-9). This provides the setting for the LORD's future spiritual dealings with his people, anticipating the fuller revelation of the 'new covenant' (Jer. 31:31-34) and the 'covenant of peace' (Ezek. 34:25-31; 37:26-28).

2:19 And I will betroth you to me for ever,
and I will betroth you to me in righteousness,
and in justice and in steadfast love and in compassion.
2:20 And I will betroth you to me in faithfulness,
and you will know the LORD.

But it is not just a covenant with the physical realm that the LORD has in view. Taking up the thought of 2:16 he uses the formal language of betrothal and speaks not about Israel ('them', 2:18), but again directly to them ('you', feminine singular, cf. 2:16), personally and warmly. The tenderness and sincerity of his approach are also conveyed by the use of the marriage metaphor for the envisaged relationship.

In Hosea's day betrothal resulted from a conventional set of negotiations leading to an agreement between a bride's parents (or their representative) and a suitor regarding a suitable bride-price. When that had been arranged, the woman was recognised as irrevocably committed to

43. The NRSV reads 'for you', but this is an unnecessary change though it yields a smoother flow in terms of English style (cf. footnote 28, pg. 84).

her husband-to-be, even though the marriage would not be fully formalised until later. Only cohabitation remained after this step (cf. Deut. 20:7). ***I will betroth you to me*** points to the establishment of a new, unsullied relationship which is yet to be fully consummated. But ***for ever*** shows that this bond has finality and will not be revoked. The situation is not perceived of as a modification or reversal of the marriage previously envisaged between the LORD and Israel. Consequently what is described is not remarriage of formerly divorced partners; the metaphor is used to set out an altogether new relationship, starting without hang-ups or recriminations over past failures (cf. Vos 1975:293). Furthermore, the use of the language of betrothal also allows for there being a period between betrothal and consummation of the marriage.

The threefold repetition of ***I will betroth you to me*** indicates the intensity of the LORD's commitment to the relationship, not three successive actions. Although there is no explicit connection made with the covenant, the terms in which the description is couched are all covenantal. ***For ever*** reminds that covenant arrangements were expected to last in perpetuity. They had not in the past, but the LORD's initiative would ensure that matter developed differently in future. Then five terms are used to set out the nature of the relationship that is initiated; together they depict true and lasting commitment in every aspect of the covenant bond.[44] These qualities are, in the first instance, those of the LORD, but he bestows them on his bride-to-be and so infuses the whole relationship with them.

---

44. The force of the preposition *bə* (repeated four times in 2:19 and once in 2:20) is uncertain. In the context of betrothal and the payment of a bride-price, Macintosh (1997:83) identifies it as *beth pretii*, so that the price paid by Yahweh are the gifts listed, indicating the quality of the marriage that he will enter into. Alternatively, it may be an instance of *beth instrumenti*, that is, the betrothal will be characterised by these elements which had been significantly absent from Israel's past conduct. To translate the preposition as 'in' might point to these qualities as accompanying the marriage and they would in that case apply equally to either partner, though of course provided by the LORD. 'With' would suggest that this is how the LORD betroths Israel, in the sense, that these are the bride price. Though a combination of both senses might be involved, it is unwise to press the metaphor of betrothal too far. Otherwise one might end up asking nonsensical questions such as who are the bride's parents. The simplest understanding is to take these qualities as the betrothal price handed to the bride herself, as might indeed happen in ordinary life (cf. Gen. 24:53).

Righteousness describes conduct which does not deviate from a norm. Yahweh commits himself to be true to all that his covenant role requires of him, and so too should his covenant partner. This is brought out in the parallel psalms, 111 and 112, which portray in similar terms the righteousness of the LORD and the righteousness of the individual who fears him. Righteousness is not a matter of rigid performance of duty, but an exercise of graciousness and warm compassion which endure for ever (compare especially Ps. 111:3-4 and Ps. 112:3-4).

Justice relates to God's equity in reaching decisions and administering affairs scrupulously, not just secular affairs but every aspect of the covenant stipulations. Again this is what is desired in the people: that their decisions are fair, and that they achieve this by reflecting divine standards. 'Let justice roll down like waters, and righteousness like an ever-flowing stream' (Amos 5:24).

Steadfast love (*ḥesed*) is the covenant loyalty which is prepared to go beyond the strict terms of the engagement in its desire to promote the interests of the other party. In the Old Testament it is generally employed of the LORD's enduring love for the people, but the covenant was not intended to be one-sided in its operation. The LORD's covenant partners were expected to reciprocate his level of commitment, but the sad fact was that they rarely did so (cf. 4:1; 6:4, 6).

Compassion echoes the name of Hosea's daughter (1:6-7; 2:1) and describes the deep and warm concern which God shows for his people, and which they are required to display to others. 'Walk in love, as Christ loved us and gave himself for us' (Eph. 5:2).

The repetition of the verb, ***I will betroth***, sets ***faithfulness*** somewhat in a category of its own. It is a matter of the dependability and consistency which should pervade the preceding characteristics. The LORD's commitment will not and cannot vary in its intensity or in its aim, and the ideal is that the commitment of the people should not do so either. As they reflect the character of God himself, so will the potential of their relationship with him be realised.

The consummation of this betrothal is in the experience of the bride: ***you will know the LORD.*** 'Know' is used of the intimacy of marriage (Gen. 4:1; Num. 31:17; 1 Kgs. 1:4), and provides an appropriate culmination to this divinely instituted arrangement in which the bride is endowed with the aptitude to reflect the character of her husband and so to be taken into close fellowship with him. This reverses and dispels the previous 'she does not know' (2:8) and 'me she forgot' (2:13). Knowledge is a theme taken up extensively in the remainder of the prophecy (cf. 4:1; 6:3).

REFLECTION

- When the LORD restores his fallen creation, he provides a fitting environment for his people to live in, and also ensures that they are fit to live in that new environment. The land where Israel enjoyed fellowship with the LORD was in measure restored to them in the return from the exile, but the fulness of what is described here awaited the coming of the Messiah whose work is the only basis for ensuring the harmony here described (cf. Isa. 11:6-9; 55:13; 65:25). When he comes a second time, he will inaugurate his eternal kingdom with the formal marriage ceremony to his bride with whom he has been so long betrothed (cf. Rev. 19:6-9).
- As regards the holy city, the new Jerusalem, 'nothing unclean will enter it, nor anyone who does what is detestable or false' (Rev. 21:27), and so Christ has equipped and made ready his betrothed through the ministry of the Holy Spirit. The qualities set out in 2:19-20 are mediated by the Spirit to each one in whom he implants new life. Whereas the new birth is, as the metaphor implies, a matter of a moment, becoming proficient in the aptitudes which the Spirit bestows requires a lifetime's training. 'If we live by the Spirit, let us also walk by the Spirit' (Gal. 5:25). But the task of 'perfecting holiness in the fear of God' (2 Cor. 7:1) is one which the God of peace will ensure is brought to completion so that all who are Christ's are kept blameless at his coming (cf. 1 Thess. 5:23).

(d) Harmony Restored (2:21-23)

The details of this section often seems somewhat obscure, but it leaves the metaphor of the marriage relationship to one side and develops the picture of the total and final security promised in 2:18. What is to come is a time when the LORD's willing and bountiful bestowal of blessing on his people will be indisputably present, as it is seen descending from on high (2:21-22). The repeated use of 'respond' probably indicates that this occurs as an answer to prayer. 'It is a beautiful picture of the harmony between the physical and the spiritual spheres, Jezreel (i.e. Israel) asks its plants to germinate; they call upon the earth for its juices; the earth beseeches heaven for rain; heaven supplicates for the divine word which opens its stores; and Jehovah responds in faithful love' (Cheyne 1884:56). There are parallels in the descriptions of agricultural abundance in Amos 9:13-15 and Joel 3:18, but here there is the additional dimension of answered prayer. Finally the LORD reinstates the people in his favour and they gratefully acknowledge him (2:23).

2:21 And it will be on that day that I will respond,
declares the LORD.
I will respond to the heavens,
and they for their part will respond to the earth.

Declares the LORD links with 2:16 as does the reference to the time of restoration, ***on that day*** (also in 2:18). This is a further aspect of the definitive prospect that the LORD holds out to his people, but it is presented in highly figurative language. ***I will respond***[45] sets out the LORD's reaction to the way in which the people have acknowledged him, whether this is viewed as evident in the way they are conducting their lives in obedient imitation of him or in the prayer they address to him. However, what is described is a sequence of responsive actions, and this is traced from heaven to earth so as to emphasise the LORD's sovereignty and initiative in all that occurs. The needs experienced below are met by action from on high (cf. 14:8; Ps. 20:1, 6). All that is needed for blessing to be bestowed is that he speaks the word.

The heavens which had been restrained from sending rain on the earth are now divinely permitted to fulfil their natural purpose, and in this scene of cosmic harmony they react to the needs of earth below by sending rain. The restraint had been caused by the sin of the people, and when that has been dealt with and a true relationship with the LORD restored, the channel for divine blessing is opened up. Although the same Hebrew word signifies 'the land' and 'the earth' (cf. 4:1), when it occurs alongside 'the heavens', ***the earth*** is the appropriate translation. This transformation will occur on a cosmic scale.

2:22 And the earth will respond to the corn
and the new wine and the olive oil,
and they will respond to Jezreel.

Tracing the chain of causation further down to the source of the need, ***the earth*** (less probably 'the land') will display renewed fertility in ***the corn and the new wine and the olive oil*** (cf. 2:8). This is a general reference to all the agricultural produce which was the foundation of Israel's economy (cf. Deut. 12:17; 14:23; 2 Chron. 32:28; Jer. 31:12). Under God's beneficent rule, from the earth there will spring up a copious provision to respond to and meet the needs that are prevalent. The days of recourse to Baal for fertility have gone.

---

45. The verb *ʿānâ*, 'to answer', need not imply that there is preceding speech. Its basic signification seems to be 'to react' in word or deed, generally in a beneficial sense (*TLOT* 28).

The mention of ***Jezreel*** again applies to restored Israel (cf. 1:11), who will be the recipients of the bounty of the land when 'God sows' not judgement but blessing. In terms of the development of the theme of the prophecy Jezreel also points back to the name of Hosea's first child, and so to the disaster which the LORD had there predicted he would bring upon the people (1:5). This opens the way to reversal of the significance of the other names in the next verse and also to resumption of consideration of Hosea's family circumstances in the following chapter.

2:23 And I will sow her for me in the earth,
and I will show compassion to Not-Shown-Compassion,
and I will say to Not-My-People, 'You ⌞are⌟ my people',
and he will say, '⌞You are⌟ my God'.

I will sow her is a wordplay on Jezreel, 'God will sow' (cf. 1:4). No longer is the reference negative; it now reflects the number and material prosperity of the people (cf. 1:11). ***Her*** refers to the nation in terms of the betrothed of the LORD, a concept which finds its consummation in the bride of Christ (Eph. 5:22-33). ***In the earth*** is again ambiguous, quite possibly 'in the land' is intended, but 'earth' in 2:21 is the counterpart of 'heaven', and in this context there is no specific mention of a return from exile which 'the land' would require. This is probably an application of the Gentilic promise of the Abrahamic covenant (Gen. 12:3). The sowing of the people of God points to a massive increase in their numbers which was associated with the ingathering of the Gentiles.

The reflection on the reversal of the ominous significance of Jezreel leads into the affirmation that the other two curse names are also revoked. The LORD ***will show compassion*** on Not-Shown-Compassion (cf. 1:6-7; 2:1) and will also reinstate ***Not-My-People*** (cf. 1:8-9; 2:1). This final act of deliverance evokes a response from the one who was formerly Not-My-People. ***He will say, 'You are my God'.*** The masculine is now used because Lo-Ammi was a son. Here the mutual pledges of a renewed relationship replace the former words of alienation and reproof. The two parties are again reaffirming the terms of the bond uniting them in a mutual, perpetual and solemn commitment.

REFLECTION

• Though the prophet was initially addressing the people of the northern kingdom of Israel, the vision granted to him was shaped by God to reflect the totality of his redemptive provision. Although the language was drawn from the typical revelation which had been granted at that stage of the disclosure of the divine plan, the ultimate reality was to be grander and more extensive. The LORD's dealings with Israel (whether the northern tribes or the covenant people as a whole) foreshadowed what would be achieved through the one who was the ultimate embodiment of all that Israel should have been. Through identifying himself with 'Not-My-People' he became 'Not-My-Son' ('My God, my God, why have you forsaken me?' Matt. 27:46), and 'humbled himself by becoming obedient to the point of death, even death on a cross' (Phil. 2:8). In this suffering he assumed a guilt not his own and paid its penalty so that divine compassion may be extended without compromising divine justice.

• Christ also broke down 'the dividing wall of hostility' between Jew and Gentile (Eph. 2:14) so as to 'create in himself one new man in place of two' (Eph. 2:15), and on that basis both Paul (Rom. 9:25) and Peter (1 Pet. 2:10) have no hesitation in seeing the fulfilment of 2:23 in the blessing achieved in the unity of the church of New Testament times. Let us make sure that as individuals we by faith respond with reverent submission, 'You are my God.'

C. Reclaiming Love (3:1-5)

To complete the framing effect in the first division of the book, further reference is now made to Hosea's marital circumstances, balancing the information given in chapter 1 (cf. page 43). This change has been in part prepared for by the resumption and reversal of the names of the children at the end of chapter 2. As well as being integrated into the chiastic (cross-over) structure of chapters 1–3, chapter 3 shares the same inner literary pattern of earlier sections in that there is a movement from judgement to salvation. Here judgement is already evident in the abject circumstances in which Gomer is found, and much greater attention is given to the way in which restoration will be effected, first for Gomer in 3:1-3 and then for Israel in 3:4-5.

But is the unnamed woman of this chapter to be identified as Gomer? Furthermore, even though the literary organisation of these chapters is fairly clear, that does not in itself require the underlying incidents to be sequential. So a further question may be posed. Did the events of chapter 3 occur after those of chapter 1, or are they the same story told from another point of view?

It has been observed that this section is autobiographical whereas chapter 1 is a biography, written in the third person. This has led to scholarly speculation that chapters 1 and 3 may have been edited together from a number of sources. If that were the case, then 'again'

(3:1) might not relate back to chapter 1, but be a feature inadvertently retained from, and relating to the structure of, a different earlier source. However, this is implausible both as regards subsequent redactional activity playing a significant role in the composition of the book and as regards the lack of literary skill displayed in leaving such an unconnected allusion. A robust case can be made for the prophecy being shaped by Hosea himself, who here incorporates material from an account he had written at an earlier date into this final carefully-arranged literary structure. That being so, whatever precise sense is attached to 'again' in 3:1, a sequential understanding of these events is required, though the timeline involved is obscure.

Furthermore, although some commentators argue that mention is made here of a second woman (cf. Stuart 1987:64–69), the introduction of an additional character into the symbolism of the prophet's action is clearly at variance with the main point being illustrated. Hosea's life has been divinely shaped to mirror the LORD's dealings with Israel. Since there is only one people of God, introducing another woman into Hosea's life would distort the message portrayed by his marriage and would undermine the effectiveness of his presentation. The description 'adulteress' (that is, one who is unfaithful in marriage) reinforces the identification of the woman as Gomer.

Even so, there is much that remains unclear. Though some have tried to glean information about Gomer from 2:2-22, the focus there is clearly on Israel considered as the wife of the LORD, and it is hazardous to try to reconstruct anything about Gomer's life from that section. We should recognise that we are simply not informed about her story in the interval between chapter 1 and chapter 3.

Though Gomer had been characterised as a 'wife of whoredoms' (1:2), up to this point there has been nothing explicitly recorded of the nature of her reprehensible behaviour. It is debatable whether her conduct had begun to deteriorate openly after the birth of her first, or after that of her third child. Now, however, she is characterised as 'an adulteress' (3:1) who has deserted her husband. She may still have been living with another man, but the fact that Hosea had to buy her back (3:2) probably indicates that her situation had further worsened to such an extent that she had sold herself into slavery. But, as in chapter 1, it is a deliberate feature of the narrative that only sketchy details are provided regarding the prophet and his wife. The paramount theme is the costly redemptive love exhibited by Hosea as a telling depiction of the LORD's dealings with his wayward wife, Israel.

(1) The Restoration of Hosea's Wife (3:1-3)

From the high point of future restoration chapter 3 abruptly returns to the reality confronting Hosea—and the LORD. Some hints are provided about the troubled relations between the prophet and his wife, but the main point of the narrative is Hosea's initiative, in accordance with God's instructions, to love her again (3:1), to reclaim her (3:2), and to institute arrangements for her complete restoration (3:3). All this pictures how the LORD will act to remedy the fractured relationship between himself and Israel.

3:1 And the LORD said to me,
'Again go, love a woman
loved of a friend and an adulteress,
just as the LORD loves the sons of Israel
though they keep turning to other gods
and ⌊are⌋ lovers of cakes of raisins.'

Again is positioned ambiguously, and it cannot be decided on grammatical grounds whether the thought is 'the LORD said to me again, "Go, love ..." ' or ***the LORD said to me, 'Again go, love'***,[46] just as he had done once before in first marrying her (1:2, 3). Most English translations prefer the latter rendering (the NRSV being a notable exception), but in either case the description is of a subsequent stage in Hosea's marriage. The indefinite 'a woman' does not refer to another woman, but corresponds to the original indefinite 'a wife/woman' of 1:2, possibly with the sense 'such a woman'. Through her misconduct

46. A translation taking the adverb 'again' (*'ôd*) with the verb of speech is similar to 'And the LORD said to him again' in Exod. 4:6, whereas the adverb being construed with the following imperative is paralleled in 'And the LORD said to me, "Again take ..." ' (Zech. 11:15). Such ambiguity was presumably evident to ancient hearers also. Two strategies might have been adopted to avoid doubt. By placing 'again' after 'go' the sense would have been resolved as 'Go again', but this would have necessitated separating the two imperatives, and that is avoided elsewhere in this construction where 'go' is used to intensify the following exhortation. By placing 'again' as the second word of the sentence (after 'and he said' and before 'the LORD') the sense would have been indubitably 'and the LORD again said'. Since this word order, though clumsy, is possible (cf. 'and he said again God to Moses', Exod. 3:15), it renders 'again go' more probable as the intended sense than 'said again'. The accents of the MT are ambivalent as regards their reading, but the LXX and Peshitta favour 'Go again'. *'ôd* is separated from 'love', and so it is improbable that it has a continuative sense ('still'; with a negative 'no longer', cf. 1:6), 'continue to love'.

she has forfeited her right to the designation 'your wife'. 'Go' is used in an idiomatic manner as a summons to action which is then more precisely specified in the second imperative 'love'.

'Love' (*ʾāhēb*) has a broad range of meaning, being used both of emotional attachment to a person and also, as with the 'cakes of raisins' later in this verse, of liking some object (cf. *NIDOTTE* 1:277-299 and also the first *Reflection* below). Although Hosea later portrays God's love in terms of a parent's love for a child (11:1, 4), the comparison which is dominant is with the love of a man for his wife (cf. 9:15). Love opens a new door in interpersonal relationships while closing other doors, or at any rate lowering the significance of some (cf. 'leave', Gen. 2:24) and giving exclusive dominance to a new central relationship (cf. 'cling to'/'hold fast to', Gen. 2:24). The qualities of this attachment are positive, affectionate and caring. Although love may remain unrequited, it always seeks reciprocation and is not fully consummated without it. Love has an enduring quality which does not let itself be deflected by external circumstances and which persists despite inner anxieties and pained emotions. 'Many waters cannot extinguish love and rivers cannot wash it away. If a man were to offer all the wealth of his house for love, it would be utterly scorned' (Song 8:7). So Hosea is called on to display his continuing attachment to Gomer despite the provocation of her behaviour towards him. Once more he is to take care of her and to act to secure an appropriate response from her.

The phrase ***loved of a friend*** may be understood in a variety of ways because the term 'friend', 'companion' or 'neighbour' is one of wide significance. 'Without expressing a particular legal relationship, [it] means those persons with whom one is brought into contact and with whom one must live on account of the circumstances of life' (*HALOT* 3:1254). The range of meaning associated with the term can be see in Jeremiah 3 where it is first used of paramours, 'You have committed whoredom with many friends' (Jer. 3:1), but later of a husband, 'Instead, ⌞as⌟ a treacherous wife ⌞goes⌟ from her friend, so you have been treacherous to me, O house of Israel' (Jer. 3:20). The interpretation favoured by Calvin, following the medieval Jewish scholar, Rashi, is that 'friend' refers to Gomer's husband, that is, Hosea himself (cf. 'loved by her husband', NASB; Calvin 1986:123). Despite the fact that he continues to love her, she has intensified the enormity of her conduct by becoming an adulteress. This certainly fits the sense of the passage and the parallel regarding Israel and the LORD.

However, it is more probable that 'loved of a friend' and 'adulteress' express the two aspects of Gomer's illicit relationship, with the euphemistic 'friend' (perhaps the modern use of 'partner' catches something of what is in view) portrayed as enamoured of Gomer who is living in an adulterous relationship with him.[47] So there are three parties: the prophet, Gomer and the paramour. This corresponds to the three parties in the relationship being illustrated: the LORD, Israel and Baal. Just as Gomer had turned to another man, so Israel had turned to other gods. It is significant that the term ***adulteress*** is used here (cf. 4:2) because it reinforces the perception that Gomer is in view. The term is a participle, which describes not a temporary lapse, but habitual conduct that deliberately and persistently violates the marriage bond. The narrative gives the clear impression that Gomer's conduct was not news to Hosea in the way that the LORD's instructions to him were.

If Hosea's world had been turned upside down by God's initial demand that he marry a 'wife of whoredoms', here he is called to a still more difficult task, that of putting to one side the wrong he had suffered through his wife's infidelity and also his sense of personal dignity and propriety as he, the injured party, goes in search of her. But Hosea was to pattern his conduct not in accordance with merely human notions of appropriateness, but after the standard God himself displays: ***love ... just as the LORD loves the sons of Israel.***[48] The LORD's love is his inexplicable attachment to Israel which welled up from within the divine being when he set his heart on them (cf. Deut. 7:7; 10:15). His love for them formed the basis for his electing choice of them to be his people (cf. Deut. 4:37; 10:15), those whom he would protect, those for whom he would provide, and those from whom he demanded exclusive loyalty in return. Once the LORD had committed himself to them by covenant, his love for them continued constant and unbroken (but note 9:15 as regards the continuing beneficent provision of that love and its approval of their conduct), always seeking to bring back to himself the people whom he had chosen as his own (cf. 1:10).[49]

---

47. A third approach is found in the early versions (LXX, Peshitta, Vulgate) which read an active participle 'loving' (*ʾōhebet* rather than *ʾăhubat*). This may be reflected in the NRSV, 'who has a lover'. Additionally, the LXX describes the woman as 'loving evil', possibly reading *ʾōhebet rōaʿ* rather than the Massoretic *ʾăhubat rēaʿ*.

48. 'According to the LORD loving the sons of Israel': 'loving' is an infinitive followed by a subjective genitive 'the LORD'. An appropriate temporal supplement has to be added in translation.

49. The use of 'the LORD' within divine speech does not constitute a problem in Hebrew idiom (cf. 1:2).

God's love continued despite two counter phenomena, the first of which is presented in ***though they keep turning to other gods.*** The participle indicates their ongoing action in 'facing towards' these deities as they worship them and orient their lives in accordance with the ethos of their devotees. After the repeated use of Baal and Baals in chapter 2, 'other gods' here deliberately points back to the first commandment: 'You shall have no other gods before me' (Exod. 20:3). Hence it is despite their glaring defiance in spurning the very first requirement of the covenant that the LORD displays his love in that he does not give over in his determination to act in their best interests.

The extent of Israel's folly and of the gulf between the divine and human involvement in the situation is further brought out by the behaviour of the people, who are ***lovers of cakes of raisins.***[50] This refers to compressed cakes of sun-dried grapes, which were considered to be a delicacy (cf. 2 Sam. 6:19). It may be that they were brought as offerings to pagan gods, and perhaps part was returned to the worshipper who would eat them, possibly in the expectation that they would increase sexual prowess (perhaps alluded to in Song of Solomon 2:5). The figure of speech known as metonymy is used to select this feature as typical expression of the perverse practices of the illicit shrines, all of which Israel was addicted to. It is a sarcastic exposure of how little it took to divert Israel from the LORD: a trivial sop to satisfy their appetites was sufficient to motivate them to be inconstant and treacherous in their behaviour.

3:2 So I bought her for myself for fifteen ⌞shekels of⌟ silver and a homer of barley and a letek of barley.

Hosea records his immediate and uncomplaining compliance with the divine directive (cf. 1:3), but the terse narrative does not reveal the whole story. If 3:1 records all that the LORD said on this occasion, then in the light of his knowledge of his own circumstances Hosea has to translate the divine command into practical steps which will achieve its fulfilment. His love was to be revealed in action which embodied his attachment and commitment. And what he had to do was costly. This was how the prophet was brought to understand what love like that of the LORD for Israel entailed. It is not stated that Hosea was prompted by such a love apart from the divine pattern being enjoined on him.

---

50. Medieval Jewish commentators favoured understanding *ʾăšîšâ* as a 'flagon of wine' rather than a 'cake' (cf. AV, NJPS), but the root *ʾšš* may well indicate 'to press' or 'to compact'.

I bought her for myself.[51] Again there is no record of Hosea's feelings on the matter, just a simple statement of the action he took. The best explanation of why this should have been necessary seems to be that Gomer had been reduced to slavery because of indebtedness and that she had become the concubine of some man from whom her release had to be effected by purchase. Hosea may have reimbursed her paramour for the outlay he had incurred when he had bought Gomer. The complex nature of the payment in a narrative which is so sparse in other details suggests that it is of some significance. The fact that Hosea had to make up the total in such a mixed fashion indicates the struggle he had to gather sufficient resources. It has been suggested that combined the payment amounted to thirty shekels of silver, the compensation paid for the loss of a slave (Exod. 21:32), but the calculations are uncertain.[52] A ***homer*** was a dry measure used for grain, perhaps about 48 gallons (220 litres), and a ***letek*** (found only here) is generally assumed to be half a homer.[53] Though ***barley*** was an important crop, it was less valuable than wheat. So Hosea's love and resources were tested to the limit by obeying God's command, and in this way the prophet procured the release of his wife from the degrading position into which she had brought herself.

---

51. There is some dispute as to the root with which the form *wāʾekkərehā* should be associated because there is a *dagesh* in the *kaph*. This might indicate the presence of an assimilated *nun* so that the root is *nkr*, but this does not occur in the qal and its basic sense of 'to recognise' is inappropriate in the context. Identification of the verb as *kārâ*, 'to purchase, buy, conclude a transaction', is almost certainly correct, and the presence of the *dagesh* is then to be explained as an instance of *dagesh forte dirimens* (GKC §20h), possibly to indicate that the *shewa* is vocal before the following *resh*.

52. 'The word "lethech" occurs only here. Its meaning is uncertain, but it has been generally assumed to be half a homer. A homer and a half amounts to forty-five seahs. In 2 Kings 7:1, 16 it is stated that immediately after the siege of Samaria a shekel would buy two seahs. If in normal times the price was somewhat lower, say a third of a shekel for a seah, then a homer and a lethech would be valued at fifteen shekels, and the total price paid for Gomer would be thirty shekels, which was the value of a female slave according to Ex. 21:32 (cf. Lev. 27:4)' (Anderson 1975:428). Many precarious assumptions are made, particularly the stability of prices over an extended period.

53. The NRSV 'a measure of wine' follows the LXX, but it is probably a marginal gloss indicating an alternative understanding of the last phrase of 3:1 and wrongly inserted here.

3:3 And I said to her,
'⌊For⌋ many days you will dwell as mine.
You will not commit whoredom
and you will not be for a man;
so I also ⌊will be⌋ towards you.'

This verse presents a heightened role for the prophet. The restrictions he imposes are not presented as divinely dictated but as arising out of his personal perception of what was appropriate in the circumstances. Hosea's understanding of love patterned after that of the LORD has affinities with Moses' presentation of love in Deuteronomy. 'You shall love the LORD your God and keep his injunction, his statutes, his judgements and his commands always' (Deut. 11:1; cf. Deut. 30:16), but if love is not translated into obedience, then the LORD will be provoked to anger (cf. Deut. 32:21) and 'the anger of the LORD will be kindled against you' (Deut. 11:17; cf. Deut. 30:17-18).

So in displaying love that requires purity and seeks for reciprocal affection, Hosea lays down the terms on which Gomer would again become his wife. Many details only become clear in the light of the parallel arrangement which the prophet knew that the LORD would impose on Israel (3:4-5). ***Many days*** points to an extended but limited period of time. It is difficult to establish the force of the verb, ***you will dwell***. It is not just that Gomer is to stay 'with' the prophet, but that she is to remain true to him. The idea may be that of 'sit still' (as in Isa. 30:7; Jer. 8:14) rather than engage in the frenetic activity she had recently undertaken, and so it would be a discipline to prepare her for resumption of her former position as his wife. (This interpretation is reinforced by the parallel in 3:4 of a period of deprivation for Israel.) ***As mine*** (literally 'to me') denotes possession, specially set apart as Hosea's. During this period Gomer's activity would be restricted so as to curb and eradicate her promiscuous tendencies. ***Commit whoredom*** is the broader term for unacceptable sexual behaviour (cf. 1:2). ***You will not be for a man*** forbids intimacy with any man, including Hosea himself. For the Hebrew expression, compare Ruth 1:12. ***So I also will be towards you***. Hosea also would not have intimate relations with her, nor would he enter into a relationship with any other. While Hosea would provide for Gomer, there would not be a full resumption of the marriage relationship during this extended probationary period.

REFLECTION

- Since Hosea is restrained in his use of the term 'love', it is all the more remarkable that in 3:1 he employs it in four different ways. The theologically fundamental use is in 'as the LORD loves', where it describes the constant affection, demanding attachment and propensity to forgive which God voluntarily and sovereignly displays towards his people (see below). This establishes the pattern after which all human relations are to be modelled, and so it gives content to the requirement imposed on Hosea, 'love a woman'. Unfortunately, our sinful emotions readily set aside divine norms and express themselves in ways God has vetoed. This is seen in 'loved of a friend' (understood to refer someone other than the prophet), which is a euphemistic description of a relationship that breaks the bounds of the ordinance of marriage (cf. Gen. 2:24; Exod. 20:14). Furthermore, the debasing effect of sin is grossly evident in the incongruous behaviour to which it leads: 'lovers of cakes of raisins'. They are innocent enough trifles in themselves, being part of the everything which God has richly given us to enjoy (cf. 1 Tim. 6:17). But as associated with pagan worship or as motivating conduct in terms of immediate physical gratification, they have been demeaned by becoming part of Satan's foul strategy to induce mankind to sin. What had been good is rendered deceitful when it is cloaked with a seductive allure which overwhelms the emotions, blots out the fear of the LORD, and takes captive those who have suppressed their rational faculties by ignoring God's rule in their lives (cf. Gen. 3:6; 1 John 2:16). True love conforms to God's pattern and requirements.

- Hosea acted in accordance with the stated norm, 'as the LORD loves the sons of Israel' (3:1), but even the prophet did not then know the full cost of God's love. 'In this love is ⌊evident⌋, not that we have loved God but that he loved us and sent his Son ⌊to be⌋ the propitiation for our sins' (1 John 4:10). The measure of God's reconciling love is the selfless sacrificial love of Christ providing for his church and entering into an abiding, close relationship with it. His is a committed love despite the erring ways of the other partner in the relationship (cf. Eph. 5:22-33). 'Jesus Christ, who became incarnate, was present and functioning in his preincarnate state. It was he who called Hosea to serve as his prophetic agent and thus Hosea functioned as "the secondary messianic/mediator" ' (Van Groningen 2003:59).
- 'Many days' (3:3) reflects the fact that the LORD's love for his people is not an undemanding acceptance of everything they do or want, but a committed ardour which desires to see them cleansed of all unrighteousness and living in faithful obedience to him. No matter how long it takes, he is prepared to punish so as to work holiness in

them by purging away all that defiles until the outcome he desires is achieved (cf. Mal. 3:2-4). Though he acts in love, the God who cannot change does not compromise on his unvarying standards. He is not prepared to take an easy way out for a peaceful life. 'Do not become proud, but fear. If God did not spare the natural branches, neither will he spare you' (Rom. 11:20-21). Instead, he labours in love to achieve his goal of his people entering into perfect union and harmony with himself (cf. 2 Pet. 1:3-11).

(2) The Restoration of Israel (3:4-5)

Hosea now turns from his own marriage to consider the relationship between the LORD and Israel. He envisages that the LORD's discipline of them will require that they endure a period of minimal existence as a nation without a king and as a people without atoning access to God. This punishment, imposed by the LORD in his loving concern for the well-being of the people, was designed to eradicate unwholesome influences from their midst, to induce true spiritual change in their thinking and habits, and to achieve complete restoration which is described in messianic terms.

3:4 For ⌞for⌟ many days the sons of Israel will dwell
without a king and without a leader
and without sacrifice and without standing-stone,
and without ephod and teraphim.

For connects this description to Hosea's actions which had symbolically reflected the way the LORD would deal with his people. They too are going to ***dwell***, that is, live in a restricted fashion, ***for many days*** (cf. 3:3). But there is no hint here as to where they would live, whether in exile or in the land of promise.

The sons of Israel (cf. 1:10) describes the people in terms of their covenant relationship with God. For the prophet and his contemporaries those specifically in view were the ten northern tribes, but the southern tribes were following on their heels as regards their infidelity to the LORD and the similar doom that would overtake them. The description is not one of annihilation, but of deprivation and abstinence. What they had misused and disparaged will, under the judgement of God, be withdrawn from them in every form.

The fivefold repetition of ***without*** (*ʾên*, 'non-existence of') denotes a period of intense destitution both as regards political cohesion and religious observance. There are three pairs of items. ***King*** and ***leader*** (cf. 7:3) are associated with nationhood and effective civil government. Israel will be forced to exist without legitimate marks of identity and cohesion as a political force, possibly because those who held these offices had so often acted in defiance of the LORD. Hosea did not think of monarchy as evil in itself. It was the abuse of the office which had to be corrected in this way.

The next two items are of religious significance. ***Sacrifice*** played a significant role in ancient worship. It also is not here banned as inherently unlawful, but it is foretold that the circumstances of the people will be such that they would not have the opportunity or resources to engage in sacrificial ritual, whether the sacrifices were offered to the LORD or to the gods of Canaan. The ***standing-stone*** refers to a memorial pillar such as was found in early times (Gen. 28:18, 22; 31:13; Exod. 24:4). However, it was increasingly identified as an aspect of pagan worship and banned from use in Israel (10:1; Exod. 23:24; 34:13; Lev. 26:1; Deut. 7:5; 12:3; 16:22). It is significant that the term is carefully avoided in connection with the erection of the memorial stones in Joshua 24:26 and 1 Samuel 7:12, though it does describe Absalom's monument in 2 Samuel 18:18. It seems to be the compromised sense which is intended here, so that the two items reflect the mixed-up nature of the syncretistic worship of the north. Throughout the period envisaged Israel will not be permitted to engage fully in the worship of the LORD, nor will she participate in heathen worship either.

The third pair of items is related to various aspects of the cult, and the absence of a sixth 'without' suggests the pair were easily thought of in combination, possibly in connection with gaining information about the future. The ***ephod*** was one of the high priest's garments (cf. Exod. 28:4), and attached to it was the breastpiece with pouches to contain the Urim and Thummim used to inquire of the LORD (cf. 1 Sam. 30:7-8). Its absence would point to the lack of a priesthood or, at any rate, of one which could carry out the full ritual of the law. However, the term 'ephod' was also used for another object or garment associated with illegitimate worship (Judg. 8:27; 17:5; 18:14-20), and that is more probably intended here. ***Teraphim*** are generally understood as household gods (Gen. 31:19, 34; 1 Sam. 19:13, 16). Possibly 1 Samuel shows they were of human shape, and they were closely linked with the idolatrous ephod in Judges 17 and 18 (cf. also 2 Kgs. 23:24). So mention of this pair of cultic objects probably points to the suspension of all the debased worship practices of Israel. What is foreseen is a period of minimal existence which will purge from the collective psyche of the people any propensity to engage again in the malpractice of the past.

3:5 Afterwards the sons of Israel will return and seek
the LORD their God and David their king,
and they shall fear the LORD
and his goodness at the end of the days.

Afterwards signifies that the dire period of deprivation will come to an end. It will not lead to reinstatement of their former rebellious ways, but to a renewal of true devotion to the LORD. Once more (cf. 3:4), the ***sons of Israel*** views the people in their capacity as the covenant community. The sense of the word rendered ***return*** is unclear. When the verb *šûb*, 'to return', is linked (as here) with an immediately following verb, it frequently functions as auxiliary term indicating resumption of a previous action (cf. 11:9), and that sense is appropriate here, 'once again seek'. However, a stronger sense is more probable. While the term may envisage that their punishment was going to be accompanied by dispersal from their land so that 'return' points to a return from exile (cf. 1:6), the idea of a spiritual 'return' from apostasy to the LORD fits in well with Hosea's message as a whole (cf. 5:4; 6:1; 12:6; 14:1-2). ***Seek*** conveys a devoted eagerness to consult the LORD and conform to his will—just the response he is waiting for (5:15). Their former hankering for idol worship (2:7) is going to be reversed through the discipline of deprivation, and in repentance they will once more desire fellowship with the LORD whom they acknowledge as ***their God.***

It is probably an instance of zeugma (cf. 1:2) that ***David their king*** occurs as a second object after 'seek' because the verb is not used elsewhere for seeking a king (but note that in Jer. 30:9 the combination 'serve the LORD and David' is found). It is, however, an apt usage in that in seeking God the people will acknowledge that they have to fall in with his directions regarding their constitution. Because the house of David had remained in control only of the south, 'David their king' presupposes a reunification of the two kingdoms. So the old division is done away with, and there is renewed harmony (cf. 1:11). But what is envisaged is more than reunion of the divided people under 'the house of David'. The emphasis on 'David their king' is the clearest messianic expression in Hosea's prophecy. For such a use of 'David', compare Jeremiah 30:9 and Ezekiel 34:23-24. The phrase anticipates the appearance of a specific figure who will truly function as the LORD's duly appointed king whose rule will be divinely established to supply what had been previously missing from the life of the people.

Israel's attitude towards God will then be completely changed. ***They***

shall fear the LORD describes a right attitude of reverential awe and careful obedience, but it does not employ the more common Hebrew term for 'fear' (cf. 10:3). This synonym basically denotes 'to shiver' or 'to tremble' with intense emotion, whether of joy or terror. Here it is accompanied by the preposition 'to', which gives rise to translations such as 'come in awe' or 'come trembling' (cf. Mic. 7:17).[54] Though the idea of a return from exile might possibly be in the background, it is more probable that the thought is of gathering to worship. ***His goodness*** is connected to 'fear' by a zeugma (cf. 1:2). While 'goodness' may refer to the inherent character of God (Ps. 25:7), here it describes the outward consequences of God's inner disposition as revealed in the totality of the covenant blessing which the LORD extends to his people (Ps. 27:13; 31:19). 'And they shall come and sing on the height of Zion, and they shall flow ⌊as streams⌋ to the goodness of the LORD—because of the grain and because of the new wine and because of the oil, and because of the young of the flock and the herd … "My people shall be satisfied with my goodness," declares the LORD' (Jer. 31:12, 14). ***At the end of the days*** refers to a distant time when the process of discipline and recovery shall have been fully worked out, and balances the 'many days' at the beginning of 3:4. It also indicates the same time period as 'afterwards' at the beginning of the verse (Willis 1979:64).

REFLECTION

- The policy of the Assyrians, and after them the Babylonians, was to deprive peoples they conquered of a national identity by deporting them from their homelands and incorporating them into an undifferentiated population spread throughout their empires. These displaced and disoriented peoples would no longer have local loyalties to compromise their total dependence on the central authority for their existence and well-being. Other people groups did not survive this treatment and vanished from the pages of history as their descendents were absorbed into the amorphous mass of the empire. Not so the sons of Israel. Doubtless many of their offspring intermarried with other peoples, but an ethnically separate remnant were preserved. During and after the exile people from north and south coalesced and became known by the term 'Jew', which was derived from the name Judah, the dominant southern tribe. The Jews have been preserved

54. Certain prepositions such as *ʾel*, 'to', and *min*, 'from' (cf. 11:11), are used with verbs which do not in themselves express motion to form a pregnant construction implying movement towards (or from) a goal (cf. GKC §119g, x; Joüon §133b).

through many national vicissitudes from the time of Hosea to the present, and their continuing existence testifies to the veracity of Scripture and the continuing faithfulness of God in preventing their assimilation and annihilation.

- It is a mistaken notion to suppose that the reversal of the fortunes of the Jews will occur apart from their returning and seeking David their king (3:5). It is Jesus the Messiah who is the true Son of David. He is the Deliverer who will come from Zion and banish ungodliness from Jacob (Rom. 11:26). Whatever measure of national recognition and advance may be achieved by the Jewish people, it cannot be the fulness and acceptance prophesied for them until they recognise Jesus as their Messiah. The sentence of deprivation will stand until the veil which lies over their hearts is removed (2 Cor. 3:14-15), and Christ is acknowledged and confessed as the fulfilment of the promises of Scripture.

II. Waiting for Repentance

(4:1–6:3)

OUTLINE

A. Religious Degeneration (4:1-19)

1. Indictment of the land (4:1-3)
2. A Community without True Knowledge (4:4-6)
3. A Community without Satisfaction (4:7-10)
4. Debased Worship (4:11-14)
5. A Warning to Judah (4:15-19)

B. Internal Chaos (5:1-14)

1. Failed Leadership (5:1-7)
2. Wars and Warmongering (5:8-14)

C. Penitence? (5:15–6:3)

1. The LORD's Withdrawal (5:15)
2. An Exhortation to Return (6:1-3)

Hosea's marriage, which figured so prominently in the message of chapters 1–3, remains in the background in the remainder of the prophecy, though there continue to be references to the nation as a mother with children (cf. 4:5), and to the people's sin as spiritual whoredom (the last of these occurring in 9:1). However, Hosea had still to grapple with the problem of addressing a hostile and unreceptive audience. Now, instead of symbolic actions being used to attract and hold their attention, numerous vivid similes and metaphors are employed to make the message memorable.

It is difficult to be certain precisely when in Hosea's ministry the sayings collected in chapters 4–14 were originally uttered. There are clear indications that his marriage took place in the closing years of Jeroboam II, before the nation descended into internal squabbling and strife, and before it had to face mounting pressure from Assyria, and so chapters 1–3 may be approximately located in the decade 755–745 B.C. It is probable that the material found in 4:1–5:7 derives from the same period before Assyrian aggression came to dominate the nation's affairs. Assyria is first mentioned in 5:13, and so 5:8–14:9 must be dated after 745 B.C. Commentators have attempted to identify certain allusions in these later chapters, but none has been established with any certainty. Perhaps it is warrantable to detect a generally chronological order, with later chapters increasingly reflecting the turbulent conditions of the 730s and then the confusion and plotting of Hoshea's reign.

There are three ways of understanding the structure of chapters 4–11. (1) The remainder of the prophecy may consist of largely unconnected oracles of judgement, with certain brighter elements interspersed, but the record has not been ordered in terms of any specific sequence. (2) Another approach is to identify in chapters 4–14 two overviews of Israel's destiny, each of which begins with her present tragedy and impending judgement (4:1–11:7; 11:12–13:16) and ends with her future restoration, at first glimpsed in 11:8-11 and then set out more fully in 14:1-9. This is a repetition of the thematic pattern found in the first three chapters. In this way chapters 4–11 are taken as a core collection of prophetic sayings, brought to an end by 'declares the LORD' (11:11). (3) However, it is also possible to subdivide the central chapters, depending on what view is taken of the meaning of 6:1-3. If this oracle is read positively, then chapters 4–14 may contain three divisions, with each progressing from present condemnation through impending judgement to a positive future scenario—and that is the outline adopted here. It may further be argued, as in Laetsch 1956:41

and Kaiser 1985:48, that the three divisions correspond to the three allegations levelled against Israel in 4:1: no knowledge (4:2–6:3); no steadfast love (6:4–11:11); no faithfulness (11:12–14:9). That interpretation is, however, less securely established.

The present division of the prophecy (4:1–6:3) may be readily analysed as possessing a tripartite structure. In 4:1-19 the prophet lodges the LORD's complaint against the religious practices of the land, whereas 5:1-14 is concerned rather with the infighting which characterised the northern kingdom and depicts the LORD's judgement as soon to come on them. The final section (5:15–6:3) may be interpreted in somewhat brighter terms as it points the people to the way of escape from the danger they were in. Here the prophet urges them to return to the LORD in repentance. But there is no indication that they responded to this message, nor is any hint given that they ever would. Indeed, the following division of the book reverts to a sombre intimation of divine rejection and indicates that more than Hosea's counsel and exhortation was needed to turn the situation around.

A. Religious Degeneration (4:1-19)

The start of a new section of the prophetic record is marked by a change from third person description of Israel's future (3:4-5) to direct, second person address of the people, accompanied by a change of theme from restoration to condemnation of their present conduct, with a clear introductory summons to 'hear the word of the LORD' (4:1).[1] A similar invocation to 'hear' in 5:1 indicates the start of the next section.

In this section the focus is primarily, though not exclusively (4:15), on the religious decline of the northern kingdom. The unremitting drift in their loyalty away from the LORD brought in its train grievous consequences for the land. The sins of omission and commission found in 4:1-2 are elaborated on in subsequent passages in this division of the book. However, until the war summons of 5:8, there is no hint of the political crises and international tensions which occurred later. So, while chapter 4 predates the Assyrian resurgence from 745 B.C. onwards, it probably dates from earlier than that. The politically untroubled and economically prosperous conditions strongly suggest the closing days of Jeroboam II's reign before 753 B.C.

It was, however, far from the case that Jeroboam's reign was free of problems. Wealth was concentrated in the hands of a few who abused

1. The start of a new section is also indicated by a Massoretic paragraph mark after 3:5.

their position to exploit their fellow countrymen. The desire for self-advancement drowned out concern for the less advantaged in the land. Such decay in social attitudes and justice stemmed from the religious decline of the nation. One feature of the charges levelled in this section concerns the role of priests and prophets in this process. While they are criticised for taking the initiative in abandoning the standards of the covenant, there is no suggestion that the people were reluctant to follow their example. Indeed, the reverse seems to have been true. The religious leaders were only providing what the people wanted to hear. 'Like people, like priest' (4:9) sums up the reciprocal spiritual connection which sucked both parties ever more deeply into a downward spiral of apostasy and strife.

(1) Indictment of the Land (4:1-3)

The term 'covenant lawsuit' has been used to describe this and similar passages in other prophecies (e.g. Isa. 1:2-3; Jer. 2:12; Mic. 6:1-2). The scenario envisaged is that the prophet as the messenger of the LORD engaged in a formal legal process with the people, setting out how their conduct had offended their Overlord, and announcing to them the penalty he would impose on the nation if they remained intransigent. In this procedure the LORD was in effect acting as both pursuer and judge.

However, there are deficiencies in such an understanding of the passage. The term 'lawsuit' is itself somewhat inappropriate in that it envisages two parties bringing a matter before an independent arbiter for resolution—which is hardly the case when the LORD is involved. Furthermore, there is no record of a speech for the defence or announcement of a verdict in the dispute. Rather what we have is one party to an agreement (which in this case is the covenant between the LORD and Israel) giving notice to the other party of a grievance against their conduct, seeking to convince them that they are in the wrong, and urging them to take action to remedy the situation.[2] One way of viewing these verses is to take them as an example of how Hosea on his part sought to fulfil the injunction recorded in 2:2 to plead with the nation. As the LORD's legal agent he urges the people to recognise that they have failed to meet their obligations, and that what they were already experiencing was a precursor of worse to come if they did not amend their ways.

---

2. See DeRoche 1983. For a detailed analysis of these three verses, see also Bosma 1999.

4:1 Hear the word of the LORD, sons of Israel,
for the LORD has a complaint with those who dwell in the land,
that there is no faithfulness
and there is no steadfast love
and there is no knowledge of God in the land.

The initial call for attention alerts the people to the gravity of the issues being brought before them. The message is nothing other than ***the word of the LORD*** (cf. 1:1), relayed to them through the prophet (cf. Num. 12:6; 1 Kgs. 22:19; 2 Kgs. 7:1). Possibly 'word' here also carries with it overtones of the ten words of the LORD's covenant requirements (cf. Exod. 34:28; Deut. 4:13). The prophets frequently took the covenant as the basis on which they demanded that they be given a hearing by the people (cf. Isa. 1:10; Amos 4:1; Mic. 6:1). Hosea likewise did not remonstrated with Israel on the basis of new demands being imposed on them for the first time, but in terms of the recognised requirements of the Sinai covenant.

Sons of Israel/'children of Israel' (linking back to previous chapters, cf. 1:10) is a designation for the whole nation, particularly in their covenant relationship with the LORD. In the light of 4:15 where Israel is distinguished from Judah it is appropriate to take the reference here to be specifically to the people of the northern kingdom viewed in their religious relationship with the LORD.

While the term rendered 'land' is equivocal, as it may also convey the sense 'the earth' (cf. 2:21-23), it is clear that ***those who dwell in the land*** designates the covenant community as the recipients of the divinely-bestowed right to inhabit the land of promise and enjoy all the blessings which were entailed in that. Since their tenancy had been granted to them by the Sovereign to whom the territory still rightfully belonged, there was an obligation on the people to ensure that their behaviour in the LORD's property complied with the terms of the lease on which he had made it available to them (cf. Num. 35:33-34). Consequently they now needed to listen to what was being said ***for*** their conduct had been such that the LORD ***has a complaint***/'accusation' (*rîb*, cf. 2:2) against them of breaching the terms of their tenancy. The basis of the dispute is expressed negatively in the remainder of the verse and positively in 4:2. The judgement to be imposed (or possibly the action already being taken against them) is set out in 4:3.

There were three acute aberrations which the LORD had detected in the behaviour of the community.[3] The life of the nation had degenerated and disintegrated, and the absolute character of the first two allegations probably indicates a deficiency in their conduct with respect both to God and to fellow members of the community. The emphatic threefold repetition of ***no*** (*'ên*, cf. 'without', 3:4) depicts the empty shell that their religion had become. Despite the fact that the people still considered themselves to be loyal worshippers of the LORD, their conduct was grossly at variance with their self-perception.

Though ***faithfulness*** may be rendered 'truth' (AV, NKJV, HCSB), it is not to be understood primarily in the sense of propositional accuracy, but rather as personal truthfulness and integrity.[4] Such reliability in word and conduct is characteristic of those who take care to ensure that their speech conveys the truth and that they adhere to the commitments into which they have entered. Without faithfulness in public and private life the bonds which unite individuals into a society are loosened, and a nation becomes inwardly unstable and liable to collapse. A related noun is used in 2:20 to describe the nature of the LORD's commitment to Israel and what, by implication, he expects from her. But that had not been forthcoming. So faithfulness is presented here with a negative to lodge an accusation of infidelity to God and untrustworthiness to one another.

Steadfast love (*ḥesed*, cf. 2:19) refers to the mutual commitment which should characterise the parties to a covenant—an inner attitude which should be evidenced by appropriate outward action. Fundamentally, steadfast love should shape the relationship between the LORD and his people, but its scope was wider than that. The common allegiance of the members of the covenant community to the LORD created a spiritual bond of brotherhood between them, and that ought

---

3. The introductory term *kî* may introduce another clause of reason, this time explaining why the LORD has a controversy (cf. NASB). More probably, *kî* introduces a subordinate noun clause setting out the substance of the LORD's dispute with the people of the land (cf. NIV, NKJV).

4. 'Faithfulness' (*'ĕmet*) and 'steadfast love' (*ḥesed*) frequently occur together as a conventional pair for the enduring nature of the commitment with which the LORD adheres to his covenant pledges (cf. 2 Sam. 15:20; Ps. 40:11; 85:10; 89:14; Prov. 3:3; 14:22). This pairing is based on the foundational self-revelatory description 'abundant in steadfast love and faithfulness' (Exod. 34:6-7). Here, however, there is a triplet, each item of which is accompanied by the negative 'there is not', and so the distinctive force of the separate terms should be preserved.

to have manifested itself in a caring and loving reciprocity. The way the LORD had behaved towards them set the standard for their conduct. Steadfast love was essentially a compassionate reaction which was stirred up by perceived need and which refused to be curtailed by rigid and mechanical adherence to a set of regulations. But in Israel covenant norms had been disregarded and the dictates of love suppressed. They lacked steadfast love towards the LORD (cf. 6:6), and that led to a degeneration of their conduct towards one another.

Probing further, this inadequacy in their behaviour is identified as arising from the absence of ***knowledge of God***, which is another significant theme in Hosea (see 2:20; 6:6; 14:9). The fact that it is 'God' (and not Yahweh, the personal covenant name of the LORD) that is employed here may well indicate that the people displayed ignorance of fundamental religious truth regarding his character and sovereignty. Moreover, 'know' functioned as part of the vocabulary of ancient international treaties which are used in Scripture to illustrate God's covenant with his people, and in that context 'know' pointed to personal recognition of the overlord's rights. Whatever claims Israel made as regards her relationship with God (cf. 8:2), they were not substantiated by her conduct because true heart acknowledgement would flow into behaviour patterns which pleased him. Furthermore, 'know' in Hebrew also possesses a sense of intimacy and personal relationship (cf. 2:20).[5] The people were devoid of living attachment to God, and the situation was made worse by the fact that this prevailed ***in the land*** which the LORD had granted to them as their inheritance in their capacity as his covenant vassals.

4:2 Swearing and lying and murder
  and stealing and committing adultery:
they have broken out,
  and bloodshed has reached to bloodshed.

There is no such thing as a spiritual vacuum: if virtues are absent, then they are replaced by vices . Hosea lists in summary fashion five representative covenant commands which were being ignored in the community. The final three terms are precisely those of the Decalogue, though the order varies (3, 9, 6, 8, 7 being the order in which the

---

5. For a defence of the view that knowledge of God is 'conduct that issues out of and is appropriate to covenantal devotion to the Lord and rooted in Yahweh's divine teachings. It implies action: that is, the practice of moral qualities that reflect commitment to the will, person, and nature of Yahweh', see Carew 2009.

commandments of Exodus 20 are cited here). Indeed, evidence of breaches of these covenant requirements points to rejection of the covenant in its entirety (cf. Jas. 2:10). Critical scholarship, of course, is only prepared to concede that this is evidence of an early form of the Decalogue existing in Hosea's day, but throughout his prophecy Hosea displays such a detailed acquaintance with the five books of Moses that it undermines critical reconstructions (cf. 12:3-6). Furthermore he takes it for granted that his contemporaries were also familiar with the content of these books, which could be appealed to as a standard of truth. Moreover, on the basis of his audience's acquaintance with the Decalogue, it is probable that Hosea has deliberately distorted its sequence to reflect his theme regarding the disordered state of society around him. The form of the presentation is not an arbitrary embellishment, but has been designed to reinforce the message.

Rejection of covenant standards had led to a widespread deterioration of public conduct. ***Swearing*** refers particularly to taking false oaths (cf. Exod. 20:7), unworthily associating the name of the LORD with their profane acts (cf. 10:4; Exod 21:17, 20; Judg. 17:2), and probably also maliciously (that is, in a way contrary to the covenant) invoking the name of Yahweh to call down calamity on one another. Thus even when they gave the outward impression of piety, they were really debasing the name they confessed. ***Lying*** involves giving false testimony so as to trick others or defraud them of their legal rights (7:3; 9:2; 10:13; 11:12; Exod. 20:16). ***Murder*** is the taking of human life without regard for legal processes (6:9; Exod. 20:13). ***Stealing*** is seizing for one's own the property of others (7:1; Exod. 20:15). ***Committing adultery*** (cf. 3:1; 4:13-14; 7:4) denotes violating the bonds of marriage (Exod. 20:14). In this context it is not primarily a reference to Israel's spiritual apostasy but to the breakdown of married life in the community which no longer recognised the LORD's standards as relevant to their personal conduct. The staccato way in which these offences are listed[6] presents them vividly, and the disordered sequence also suggests the lack of social coherence which prevailed. Hosea holds up a mirror before his countrymen and urges them to recognise the disintegration of their land, and he explains that they are in process of imploding as a society because of their individual and collective failure to recognise and observe the boundaries the LORD had ordained for loyal and cohesive life in his land.

---

6. The Hebrew consists of a series of infinitives absolute, which provide 'a lively narration … even of what is still taking place' (GKC §113ff).

The five violations of the covenant have been stated abruptly, stabbing at Israel's self-assurance. It is unclear how these misdemeanours are related to the following verb, ***they have broken out.*** The offences may form the subject of the verb (cf. GNB, NJPS, NRSV, HCSB), and show that such violations had become widespread in the community.[7] Alternatively 'they' might refer to the people as a whole (cf. NASB, NIV, ESV), in which case the accusation is that throughout society there have been widespread breaches of all constraints. Most probably the reference is prospective to the ***bloodshed*** of the final line, which describes acts of murder, so that the two lines focus on a serious aspect of the chaos in the land.[8] ***Has reached*** suggests that no sooner has one incident occurred than another follows in what seems to be an unbroken succession—and that this has not yet ended.[9] Unlike the first part of the verse where there is a disjointed series of offences, the final two lines display a connection, but one that is ominous in the extreme.

4:3 On account of this the land mourns,
and everyone who dwells in it pines away,
with the wild animals, and with the birds of the heavens—
and even the fish of the sea are taken away.

Though the verb forms in this verse may refer to the present (e.g. NIV, ESV) or the future (e.g. LXX, AV), ***on account of this*** (*ʿal-kēn*) generally differs from 'therefore' (*lākēn*, cf. 2:6) in that it points to a situation which has already occurred rather than to a future state which is the impending outcome of previous conduct, and so the verbs are rendered

7. The LXX takes the five preceding infinitives absolute as the composite subject of the following verb: 'Swearing and lying and murder and theft and adultery have broken out in the land.' The Massoretic accents instead indicate that the five infinitives absolute stand on their own, and the following verb is to be read separately.

8. Since murder has already been listed, it has been suggested that what is referred to here is some form of state sponsored violence. Hubbard views favourably Andersen's suggestion of 'the activity of armed troops breaking into households to seize victims for the human sacrifices that fed the altars of Baal, a savage breach of divine law like that described in Psalm 106:37-39' (Hubbard 1989:98). Stuart (1987:76) endorses proposals that the word *dāmîm* or *dōmîm* represents 'idols': 'The idols crowd against one another.' This would point to a violation of the second commandment. But in neither case is it necessary to depart from the traditional view of the words.

9. The two correlated perfects are instances of a persistent (present) perfective usage of a 'situation that started in the past but continues (persists) into the present' (*IBHS* §30.5.1c).

as relating to an existing calamity. ***The land mourns*** is an instance of personification which serves to bring out the intensity and totality of the plight being described.[10] Notice how ***everyone who dwells in it*** echoes 'those who dwell in the land' (4:1), and brackets these verses together as a distinct section.[11] ***Pines away*** or 'withers' also suggests a drought. The verbs 'mourn' and 'pine away' frequently occur in combination (cf. Isa. 24:4; Jer. 14:2; Lam. 2:8), and reflect the interconnection between mankind and their environment. It is not just the people who are grief stricken, but the whole realm of nature has been engulfed by this catastrophe.

At one level a severe drought has sapped the vitality of the people (cf. Joel 1:10-12, 17), but this is not to be considered as merely a natural disaster. It had been imposed by the LORD in his displeasure at the people's misconduct and as a means of disciplining and reclaiming them (for drought as a covenant curse, cf. Lev. 26:19; Deut. 28:22-24). ***Are taken away*** points to death. 'Sea' may be used in Hebrew to refer to extensive bodies of inland water, which surprisingly (note ***and even***) are also adversely affected. However, ***the fish of the sea*** may be part of a hyperbolic expression indicating a reversal of creation (DeRoche 1981), a judgement greater than that of the Noachic flood. Certainly the description reflects negatively the picture of covenantal renewal set out in 2:20, for the same realms which were blessed there are here overwhelmed by the consequences of human abandonment of the divine order.

The whole description is based on the interrelation of every aspect of the world's existence. Mankind were originally appointed rulers over God's creation, and their downfall impacted all the realm entrusted to them (cf. Gen. 3:17-18), just as the failure of an earthly monarch has grave implications for the well-being of all his subjects. Similarly, Israel as the redeemed people of God were given a special role as tenants in the land of promise, which pointed back to what was lost in

---

10. 'Mourns' (from the root *ʾābal*) is often understood in the sense 'is dried up' when it is applied to inanimate objects (cf. TNIV, NIV margin). There is scholarly dispute as to whether there are two homonymous roots (*HALOT* 1:6-7 notes the existence of an Akkadian root *abālu*, 'to dry out'), or whether applications to objects such as 'the earth' are metaphorical (*NIDOTTE* 1:244).

11. Equally it is possible to render the phrase as 'everything which dwells in it' and understand the preposition before 'wild animals' and 'birds' as *beth* of specification, listing the constituent parts of the preceding composite expression (cf. Gen. 7:21).

Eden and prefigured what would be regained hereafter. If they failed to order their lives by God's standards, the impact of their rebellion extended to all that God had placed under them.

REFLECTION

- Nowadays an audience is apt to be more concerned with the quality of the presentation which a speaker delivers to them than with the quality of their personal reaction to it. But the prophetical call to hear (4:1) is focused on the need for hearers to respond correctly given the origin of the message before them. 'Take care then how you hear' (Luke 8:18). Ignoring a warning sent by God is to draw disaster down upon oneself.
- Covenant relationship has implications which should structure every aspect of personal living. Those who are children of light are urged to regard as valuable what is pleasing to the Lord (Eph. 5:10). True wisdom accepts his standards, and genuine love delights to conduct itself in imitation of him (Eph. 5:1-2).
- When a nation is deprived of moral standards based on God's moral law, it no longer has a fixed set of reference points to guide its conduct, and it enters a world of ethical confusion and social disintegration. Norms of conduct which are based simply on prevailing majority opinion are essentially transient, and also without any solid foundation, being the products of the wisdom and prejudices of imperfect human perception. The ethical relativism espoused at present in western civilisation has survived for a while because it has inherited the heritage of a Christian past, just as the life in the northern kingdom was for a while partially illumined by the standards of the covenant. But the capital of such a spiritual legacy is soon depleted if there is not a resurgence of personal recognition of God and heart commitment to him.
- Since God's creation is one interconnected reality (cf. 4:3), environmental concerns have a necessary and legitimate place in a Christian worldview. This is not based on some pantheistic perception which deifies the earth, nor does it arise from a racial concern for survival. Christian environmentalism is based on the creation mandate to control and utilise the resources of the earth for the good of mankind and the glory of the Creator (cf. Gen. 1:28). Mankind as God's appointed rulers in his kingdom (cf. Ps. 8:5-8) are answerable to him for the way in which they attend to their responsibilities. It is this acknowledgement of God's sovereignty which has been lost by mankind's sinful rebellion. It is only with the complete fruition of the

divine redemptive agenda that the created realm will be released from the oppressive and exploitative propensities of fallen humanity (cf. Rom. 8:18-22).

(2) A Community without True Knowledge (4:4-6)

The rhetorical analysis of DeRoche (1983:187) has provided good grounds for delimiting 4:4-6 as a unit within this chapter by identifying the repetition of five key words in each pair of lines: 'contend' (4:4), 'stumble' (4:5ab), 'destroy' (4:5c, 6a), 'reject' (4:6b,c), and 'forget' (4:6d,e). This literary feature establishes the propriety of considering these lines together, but, of itself, it does not clarify what their theme is.

Many modern commentators and translations (cf. REB, NRSV, ESV, HCSB) view these verses as an indictment of the priesthood of the northern kingdom because their inadequate teaching and leadership had led to a systemic religious failure on the part of the people who consequently were deprived of true knowledge. While it is clear that the prophecy, which is clearly about Israel as a whole in 4:1-3, does turn at some point to focus on the priests, identification of the change as occurring at 4:7 (rather than at 4:4) avoids the need for emending the earlier verses in the interests of clarity. So here God continues to address his wayward people. He reproves their contentious spirit (4:4) and warns of impending disaster (4:5). The root cause of their downfall is their rejection of true knowledge which consists of continued national allegiance to him as evidenced by faithful compliance with his commands (4:6).

4:4 Yet let not a man contend, and let not a man reprove,
but your people are like those who contend with a priest.

Translations of this verse differ because of the variety of ways in which the overall theme is understood. 'But it is not for mankind to bring charges, not for them to prove a case' (REB) adopts the approach of Pusey that God has a controversy with his people which he has taken into his own hands and it is inappropriate for anyone else to interfere (Pusey 1885:1:47). Alternatively, what is pointed out may be how inappropriate it is for there to be mutual reproof because all were to blame (cf. NLT), or again how wasted any effort at reproof would be in such a morally corrupt society (Keil 1977:51–52). Most probably, however, the divine critique of the nation which had broken through all bounds by its wickedness (4:2) is extended to the contentious and unruly spirit of those who were forever bickering and engaging in feuds.

Yet (*ʾak*) may on occasions function asseveratively ('surely'), but here it seems to be restrictive. Despite the conditions which prevail, it would be improper for an individual to ***contend***/'enter a complaint', that is, notify a neighbour of a grievance which he has against his conduct (cf. 4:1) or ***reprove***, that is, confront another with his wrongdoing with a view to correcting him, even though such action would be in accordance with the covenant requirement, 'You shall reprove your neighbour' (Lev. 19:17). However, the context has changed. Covenantal reproof assumes that both parties accept the LORD's norms as a basis for their living, but in a disordered society which recognises no boundaries to its conduct such reproof engenders not repentance, but further profitless strife. Amos had already conveyed similar advice: 'Therefore at such a time whoever is prudent will keep silent, for it is an evil time' (Amos 5:13).

This leads into the statement of the second line which amplifies the reason why such action should be avoided, ***but your people are like those who contend with a priest*** (cf. NIV, NASB, NKJV). 'Your people', rather than 'my people', serves to distance the LORD from Israelite society which refused to submit to any superior religious or moral authority. This reflects on the stipulation of Deuteronomy 17:12: '⌞As for⌟ the man who acts with insolence so as not to listen to the priest who stands to serve the LORD your God there, or to the judge, that man shall die and so you shall purge the evil from Israel.' The lawless self-assertiveness of the people exposed them to death because of their rejection of true authority just as surely as an individual who refused to accept the verdict of the courts of the land was condemned to death.[12] However, their quarrel was not now with any earthly court, but with the LORD himself, and he would act decisively in the situation.

One difficulty which arises in connection with this interpretation is ascertaining to whom 'your' (singular) applies. While it is possible to take this as referring to the Israelites collectively, many find this awkward. They also consider the expression as a whole is obscure, and so offer a translation such as 'With you is my contention, O priest', which serves to focus this section on the priests collectively, or possibly on a

---

12. Although the use of the preposition *kə* may be treated as an instance of *kaph veritatis* (cf. 5:10), that is unlikely here since there was no tension between the people and the priests (cf. 4:9). The preposition functions to institute a comparison.

specific high priest in the north.[13] There is no textual evidence to support the emendations required by this approach, and it is difficult to establish a link between the two lines of the verse without still further change (DeRoche 1983:188).

4:5a,b And you will stumble in the day,
and a prophet also will stumble with you at night.

Because the people reject the LORD's warning, they can only expect judgement to befall them. ***Stumble*** does not suggest some minor loss of balance, but a major, potentially fatal, disaster which befalls those who abandon the way of God (cf. 5:5; 14:1, 9). There are three parts to stumbling: striking an obstacle while one is moving; staggering and being unsteady as a result; and possibly lying prostrate on the ground ('stumble and fall', e.g. Jer. 46:6). Stumbling is a precursor to total destruction (cf. Ps. 27:2; Jer. 50:32), and here it does not just assert that the people as a whole ('you' continues to be singular) will act sinfully, but that their misconduct will inevitably bring with it divine retribution. ***In the day*** and ***at night*** constitute a distributed expression indicating that this disaster will be unremitting, occurring both in the darkness when stumbling might be expected, and in the light of day, rather than suggesting one party will suffer by day and another by night.

The mention of ***a prophet*** here has caused difficulty.[14] The reference is to prophetic figures who were not true spokesmen of the LORD (cf. 9:7), but prophets 'who teach lies' (Isa. 9:15). Baal worship also had prophets who claimed to speak on behalf of the god (cf. '450 prophets of Baal and 400 prophets of Asherah', 1 Kgs. 18:19), and so the compromised worship of the north had associated with it those who

---

13. Finding the priests addressed in 4:4 requires two textual emendations: changing 'your people' (*ʿamməkā*) to 'with you' (*ʿimməkā*); and dividing 'like those who contend with' (*kimrîbê*) into two words 'indeed my controversy' (*kîmā rîbî*), or some other variant. *kōhēn*, 'priest', is then treated as a vocative (cf. Andersen, et al. 1980:344–351). For further discussion of the passage see Lundbom 1986. The difficulties with the verse do not, however, arise from the words of the text, which is actually quite clear, but from the difficulty we have in grasping the situation in which they were spoken.

14. To ease the perceived difficulty DeRoche (1983:190) offered the suggestion that 'prophet' here refers to the prophetic status of the nation, even though he admits the concept is rare in the Old Testament (Num. 11:29; Joel 2:28-29). This certainly accords with the subsequent mention of their priestly role (4:6), but even DeRoche does not seem to regard it as more than a distant possibility.

falsely claimed to be spokesmen of the LORD (cf. 1 Kgs. 22:6, 11). Micah's description of the conduct of a similar group in Jerusalem (Mic. 3:5-7, 11) provides a background for supposing that such prophets in the north were also careful to toe the establishment line and to give oracles that people wanted to hear. Their counsel was devoid of insight into the spiritual condition of the nation, and so failed to provide any genuine guidance about how they should behave or what lay ahead of them. Hosea wishes to make it clear that neither the prophets nor the people should think that those who took it upon themselves to advise the nation would be exempt from the coming disaster.

4:5c And I will destroy your mother—
4:6a my people have been destroyed through the lack of the knowledge.

The threat is clearly one that is uttered by God and not by Hosea. But who is ***your mother***? While some of those who interpret these words as addressed to a chief priest argue that the reference is to his actual mother, this seems far-fetched.[15] It is quite out of keeping with the general nature of the accusations that the prophet is presenting. Hosea has already used the terminology of 'mother' (2:2, 5) to refer to the nation as a whole, and that understanding is reinforced here by the divine 'my people' (cf. 4:8, 12) in the parallel colon.

My people (*ʿammî*) echoes the name of Hosea's son, and its employment contrasts with the dissociative use of 'your people' in 4:4. ***The knowledge*** which they lack is that which had been observed to be absent in 4:1. This is clearly true knowledge of God, based on personal acknowledgement of him and leading to action in conformity with his expressed will.

I will destroy is a threat regarding what God is going to do, and the verb points to coming to an end in a way which is almost always violent. However, ***have been destroyed***[16] conveys a somewhat different sense: their lack of spiritual integrity and faithfulness has undermined the cohesiveness of Israelite society which has already turned in on itself in a self-destructive fashion.

---

15. 'Analogously with the king's mother (e.g. 1 Kings 16.7), she may be a sacred functionary, and thus represent a matriarchal origin of the priesthood that would demystify its masculine exclusiveness' (Landy 1995:55).

16. The perfect verb *nidmû*, 'they have been destroyed', is plural because 'my people' is treated as a collective noun, and the verb is taken as a present perfect conveying the ongoing consequences of a past occurrence.

4:6b-e Since you yourself have rejected the knowledge,
I reject you from being a priest to me.
And ⌊since⌋ you have forgotten the law of your God,
I will forget your sons—I in turn.

Though the repetition of 'knowledge' links the first two lines of 4:6, the main pattern in the final two couplets is that provided by the recurrence of 'reject' and 'forget'. In these couplets the initial line continues to be a statement of the offence of the people, and is followed in the second line by the corresponding punishment. The repeated verb brings out the way in which the punishment fits the crime. ***You yourself*** (= 'my people' of the preceding line) clearly points to their personal action as the cause of the broken relationship. ***Reject*** is a strong term for turning away from someone or something with disdain and loathing.[17] ***The knowledge*** clearly refers to the 'knowledge of God' (4:1), his character and his demands, as mediated principally through God's self-disclosure to Moses. So this lack of knowledge was not God's fault, but theirs. They had neglected and despised the revelation which had been given to them, and would not desist from the sins introduced by Jeroboam I. This led to more than internal decay (4:6a): it occasioned the withdrawal of divine privilege, ***I reject you from being a priest to me.*** It had been at the core of Israel's covenant status that they were 'a kingdom of priests and a holy nation' (Exod. 19:6; Isa. 61:6), but when his priests neglect what God requires, he withdraws that status from them. This principle had already been activated as regards divine withdrawal of recognition of Saul as king (cf. 1 Sam. 15:26).

The picture of mutual rejection is reinforced by one of mutual forgetfulness. Israel had ***forgotten the law of your God***, that is, the teaching he had given regarding conduct of which he approved. In the light of Hosea's citation from the Decalogue in 4:2, this coheres with a reference to the Pentateuch. (For ***forget***, see on 2:13.) The final and emphatic ***I in turn*** (cf. 2:8) balances the 'you yourself' of the preceding couplet, and stresses the personal dimension of the interaction. Those who disregarded their Overlord's requirements were not just spurning a series of regulations, they were spurning the King whose

17. The verb form *wəʾemʾāsʾkā*, 'and (*waw* of apodosis) I reject you', is difficult to explain, particularly the presence of the third aleph. It may be the remains of an emphatic form, which perhaps survived in the north, or, more probably, it may represent an early scribal mistake, as is suggested by the qere *wəʾemʾāsəkā*.

will those laws expressed. They had ruptured their relationship with the LORD and could no longer enjoy his favour. Divine forgetfulness of their ***sons***/'children' (cf. 1:10) points to the withdrawal of God's protection and blessing with all the dire consequences which would follow from that. So their action has repercussions for the well-being of subsequent generations to whom they bequeath a legacy of rebellion and alienation (cf. Exod. 20:5).

REFLECTION

- Contending with a priest (4:4) is symptomatic of rejection of all authority. Fallen mankind refuse to recognise external constraints, whether imposed directly by God or mediated by him through the structure of the family (cf. Exod. 20:12) or of civil government (cf. Rom. 13:1-6). All such rebellious conduct is produced by the same inner rebellion. 'You shall not revile God, nor curse a ruler of your people' (Exod. 22:28). Those who despise authority act in a bold and wilful manner which undermines righteous conduct (cf. 2 Pet. 2:10), and asserts the ultimacy of personal choice and the corrupt desires of our sinful nature. God calls on his people to separate from these defective behaviour patterns. When Christ is acknowledged as 'the head of all rule and authority' (Col. 2:10), then there is respectful acknowledgement of all authority derived from him and exercised in accordance with his requirements, whether in the civil sphere (cf. Tit. 3:1) or in the life of the church (Heb. 13:7, 17).
- Rejecting 'the knowledge' (4:6) is not a matter of familiarity with facts or with doctrine. Knowledge of the truth is essentially a matter of personal encounter with God and submission to him. Those who hate knowledge are those who do not choose the fear of the LORD (cf. Prov. 1:29; 2:5-8). True knowledge is supremely that which is bestowed by divine enlightenment in 'the light of the knowledge of the glory of God in the face of Christ Jesus' (2 Cor. 4:6). It is a dynamic possession with which the believer may be 'filled' (Col. 1:9), in which they may 'increase' (Col. 1:10), 'be renewed' (Col. 3:10) and have 'full assurance of understanding' (Col. 2:2). Such deepening understanding and perception leads to 'a knowledge of the truth which accords with godliness' (Tit. 1:1) and provides a defence against the impoverishment and decay experienced by those who think they can live apart from the knowledge which God alone can give.
- Forgetfulness of the law of God (4:6) sets the stage for all sorts of lawlessness. When an individual or a community is no longer

prepared to recognise the divinely set boundaries for their behaviour, sin proliferates. 'Everyone who keeps practising sin also keeps practising lawlessness; sin is lawlessness' (1 John 3:4). Furthermore this is not a static situation for whoever presents himself as a slave to sin is also enslaved to 'lawlessness leading to lawlessness' (Rom. 6:19 ESV). Lack of recognised norms is an aggressive condition which does not terminate until it is fatal (cf. Jas. 1:14-15). Also, Christ envisaged a future situation where such conduct had repercussions for others: 'Because lawlessness will be increased, the love of many will grow cold' (Matt. 24:12). The only remedy is to stand firm in asserting and practising the divinely disclosed norms for human conduct. Such righteousness leads to holiness which is associated with the free gift of God which is eternal life in Christ Jesus our Lord (Rom. 6:23).

(3) A Community without Satisfaction (4:7-10)

The structure and theme of this section are not immediately obvious with singular (4:9) and plural (4:7-8, 10) pronominal references not being clearly identified. Again, DeRoche (1983:193–198) has proposed a literary analysis to help clarify the situation by detecting a chiastic structure centred on 4:9. While not as convincing as his approach to the previous section, it may be adopted with some modifications. The chiasm would consist of (a) 4:7 which balances (a') 4:10c, and refers to the whole community, whereas (b) 4:8 and (b') 4:10a,b would focus on the priests with the verb 'eat' forming a link between the two couplets. The centre of the chiasm (c) 4:9, then, contains the main message of the section, that there would be no difference in the way the LORD dealt with the priests and with the community as a whole.

4:7 The more they increased, the more they sinned against me;
their glory I will change into shame.

On the hypothesis that preceding verses describe the priests, ***they*** continues the same subject.[18] However, the natural antecedent for 'they' is 'your sons' at the end of 4:6. This is not a reference to descendants of the priests, but to the offspring of the whole nation. Identifying 'they' in this fashion fits in with the chiastic analysis mentioned above, namely, that this verse is concerned with all Israel and corresponds to the conclusion of 4:10.

---

18. The NIV's 'the priests' is interpretation rather than translation. The text has no more than 'they'.

The more they increased (literally 'according to their becoming many/great', a standard way of introducing a comparison) refers mainly to their numbers, but in the ancient world, if natural conditions were favourable, population increase also implied national expansion, economically and territorially. For the root 'to be many', see on 10:1. Israel had enjoyed such growth in numbers, prosperity and national prestige during the reign of Jeroboam II. However, this covenantal blessing had not been properly appreciated, and instead of leading to obedient thankfulness it had increased the rebellious conduct of the people who ***sinned against me*** by attributing the abundance to the Canaanite gods they venerated and not to the LORD (cf. 2:5, 12).

The LORD therefore will act in judgement. ***I will change*** points to divinely imposed reversal of their circumstances.[19] ***Their glory*** is unlikely to be a reference to the LORD himself, and is instead a sarcastic reference to what they pride themselves in, their increased numbers (cf. 9:11), along with all that entailed.[20] The LORD will show who is really in control of events by bringing an end to their expansion and wealth (cf. 2:9-12), and substituting ***shame*** for it. 'Shame' does not primarily reflect a subjective response of feeling ashamed, but the imposition of a penalty which is shaming. The downturn in their national circumstances, and eventually the defeat, slaughter and capture they will experience, would mean that they would be unable to increase in numbers (cf. 9:11-14, 16). In addition, such divinely originated change would expose the impotence of the Canaanite gods whom they had regarded as the source of their growth and affluence.

4:8 The sin of my people they eat,
and to their iniquity they ⌊each⌋ lift up his soul.

This verse constitutes the (b) section of the chiastic poem (see introductory comments above), which deals with the corrupt conduct of the priests. We can gain some insight into the motivation of the priesthood in the northern kingdom at this time from the interaction between the

---

19. 'They exchanged' (NIV) reflects a textual tradition found in the Targum and the Peshitta which understand 'their glory' as a reference to the LORD whom they have forsaken, and 'shame' as pointing to Baal after whom they have gone. However, the context does not provide an obvious link for the latter reference, and the text can be understood as it stands since it fits in with an alternating pattern of exposure of sin and threatened judgement, which is found in the following verse also.

20. There is probably a punning allusion in 'their glory' (*kəbôdām*) to 'according to their increasing' (*kərubbām*).

prophet Amos and Amaziah, the priest of Bethel, which took place shortly before Hosea's ministry (Amos 7:10-17). Amaziah served at the shrine founded and maintained by the kings of Israel, and comes across as an establishment figure committed to the preservation of the status quo and of his own career. He had no regard for truth, but only for a quiet life, and viewed Amos as motivated by mercenary motives as much as he himself was. After he had informed king Jeroboam about Amos, he warned the prophet to flee to Judah, not from a desire to save his life, but as a politically convenient solution to an awkward problem. His opposition to Amos led to the promulgation of an oracle of severe judgement against him and his family. Amaziah provides insight into the calibre of the priesthood in Hosea's day.

The background to this indictment is to be found in the fact that the priests were divinely entitled to ***eat*** portions of many sacrifices (cf. Lev. 24:9). The ***sin*** of the people may well refer to their 'sin offerings' since the same word describes either the offence or the sacrifice offered to atone for it. Moreover, though ***their iniquity***/'guilt' (cf. 7:1) is not used elsewhere to refer to guilt-offerings, it may do so here. Sin and iniquity are also mentioned together by Hosea in 8:13; 9:9; 13:12. These offerings would be made whenever Israel gathered for worship. Consequently, if the priests lacked spiritual motivation, they could easily develop an interest in keeping up the number of sacrifices. Most probably this was a consequence of Israel's religiosity, sacrificing without inner loyalty to the LORD (cf. 6:6), rather than from conviction of their sin and a desire for forgiveness. Even so, what mattered to the priests was the number of offerings (and hence the size of their own income), and their vested interests meant that they would not say or do anything to correct the moral situation in the land.

They ⌞each⌟ lift up his soul therefore portrays them as setting their desire on something (cf. Deut. 24:15; Prov. 19:18; Ps. 86:4). The use of the singular 'his' along with a plural verb 'they lift up' is a idiom with distributive force, indicated by the addition of 'each'. Motivated by mercenary and materialistic considerations, the priests possessed no incentive to rebuke sin. A decadent priesthood was condemned for its preoccupation with personal gain, not with the spiritual reformation of those whose well-being they were supposed to advance. In such a situation of corrupt religious leadership it is possible to detect an element of mitigation of the community's culpability in the LORD's use of the term ***my people*** (cf. 4:6). Notwithstanding all that was wrong with the people's conduct, they had been deprived of the teaching and warnings which ought to have been given.

4:9 And it will be: like people, like priest.
I will bring him to account for his ways,
and I will repay him for his deeds.

This verse contains the triplet at the centre of the chiasm (c). It begins with an adage, ***like people, like priest***, which points to the two-way interaction between the groups, neither of which was without blame in the prevailing religious disloyalty in the land. If the priests behave with unprincipled greed (4:8), how could it be expected that the people to whom they were supposed to give religious guidance would behave any differently? Furthermore, a spiritually debased people will get the religious leadership they deserve: not one that challenges their wrong-doing, but one that is complicit in it.

The switch to singular references in the second and third lines of the verse may just be a stylistic device to mark the central portion of the chiasm in which case the singular 'him' and 'his' have the same referents as the surrounding plurals. However, the change probably also serves to modify the thematic focus by making clear that no individual, whether from the laity or from the priesthood, will be spared divine scrutiny. The ***ways*** each had personally selected will be examined by the standard that the LORD had set, and ***deeds*** too, especially any which were contrary to what the covenant King had prescribed, would be inspected. When the LORD ***brings him to account for*** his behaviour, there is no doubt that his scrutiny will result in punishment (cf. 1:4; 2:13). This will be done in accordance with strict justice, in that ***repay*** indicates bringing back on them the consequences of their own actions (cf. 12:2, 14).

4:10 They will eat, but they will not be satisfied;
they have encouraged whoredom, but they will not break out,
for ⌊it is⌋ the LORD they have abandoned paying regard to.

Reversion to a plural subject at the beginning of the verse indicates a further change of focus. In terms of the chiastic structure of the section (b'), those in view are again the priests as in 4:8, and this connection is additionally indicated by the repetition of 'eat'. ***They will eat*** leads to the covenant curse of frustration being imposed on the priests: ***they will not be satisfied*** (cf. Lev. 26:26). To eat and be satisfied with the produce of the land was a sign of covenant blessing (cf. Deut. 8:10, 12; 11:15), but this would only be achieved if there was true loyalty to the

LORD. ***They have encouraged whoredom***[21] (whether literal, spiritual or both) might have led to an expectation that their numbers would increase but, with an ironic reflection on 4:2, it is declared ***they will not break out***, that is, there will be no increase in numbers that will require expansion of their villages and cities to accommodate their off-spring.

The final line of the verse completes the chiastic structure which has been proposed (a') by reverting to the behaviour of the people (see the introduction to this section). ***They have abandoned*** denotes an act of departure from the LORD and of renunciation of the covenant. Such apostasy plagued Israel throughout its existence (Deut. 29:25; Judg. 2:12; Jer. 22:9; 1 Sam. 8:8; 1 Kgs. 11:33). This is the only use of the verb by Hosea, presumably because it was so close in meaning to his usual mode of expression, 'commit whoredom'. Here, however, he may well have employed this variant because it carried with it overtones of how the LORD would react: 'You have abandoned me; therefore, I now abandon you' (2 Chron. 12:5; cf. Deut. 31:16-17).

The ending of this verse is a source of ongoing textual perplexity. Literally it reads, 'for the LORD they have abandoned to keep'. It would be expected that an object would be expressed after the final infinitive, and that is often found by transferring the first word of the following verse to read 'to keep whoredom' (cf. RSV). That expression is, however, as awkward and unusual in Hebrew as it is in English, and 'whoredom' fits better with the theme of 4:12-14 than with that of the preceding verses.[22] Another approach is to read the two verses together and/or transfer 'to keep' to the next verse (cf. NIV, ESV). It may be that 'to keep' is used absolutely (Hosea does employ it in this fashion in 12:13), or, more probably, that it is used in the sense of ***paying regard***

---

21. The verb *hiznû* is a hiphil form which elsewhere has the sense 'to cause another to commit whoredom' (cf. 2 Chron. 21:11, 13). It is often claimed that here (and also in 4:18 and 5:3) Hosea uses the hiphil intransitively as equivalent to the qal in a simple, active sense (cf. Macintosh 1997:147). However, Moughtin-Mumby (2008:64) argues persuasively that the hiphil forms in 4:10 and 5:3 have causative force. 'The causative reading of the Hiphil allows us to read "They will encourage prostitution, but not increase" in parallel with "They will eat but not be satisfied" with the priests as the subject of both threats' (2008:65). Indeed 'increase' might play on 'increase in number' and 'increase in wealth' as the priests are warned that they will no longer gain as a result of encouraging the people to sin.

22. The LXX retains 'whoredom' as part of 4:11, and this is also supported by the presence of the conjunction 'and' before 'wine'.

to (cf. 'those who pay regard to worthless idols', Ps. 31:6). The sense of 'devoting oneself to' for this verb may be a feature of Hosea's northern vocabulary. So the problems besetting the kingdom have this as their root: the apostasy of the people who no longer have any genuine regard for the LORD and his ways.

REFLECTION

- Increase in numbers and wealth is rarely conducive to an increase in spirituality. Instead material affluence blinds individuals and communities to their true spiritual condition. They are apt to conclude regarding themselves in the complacent manner of the Laodicean church that 'I am rich, I have acquired wealth, and I need nothing' (Rev. 3:17) or like the rich fool who said to himself, 'Soul, you have many good things laid up for many years: relax, eat, drink, be merry' (Luke 12:19). Such superficial self-assessment will be exposed as 'worthless in the day of wrath, but righteousness delivers from death' (Prov. 11:3).
- Religious leaders must always remember that they are not answerable primarily to those who are in their flock, but rather to the chief Shepherd. It is to his verdict on their conduct that they are to pay attention, and it is to the reward of the unfading crown of glory that he bestows that they are to have regard (cf. 1 Pet. 5:4). Aiming for his approval, they are not to be motivated by shameful gain, nor domineering, but rather exemplary in their conduct (1 Pet. 5:2-3). They are ever to be mindful of the saying of the Lord Jesus, 'It is more blessed to give than to receive' (Acts 20:35), and so to emulate the self-denial of the Saviour himself (cf. Phil. 2:5-11) .

(4) Debased Worship (4:11-14)

This section contains a series of exposes of the debased nature of Israelite worship: divination (4:12a), idolatrous worship (4:12b-13), sexual promiscuity (4:14). There are no explicit pronouncements of judgement. The whole section is framed by initial (4:11) and concluding (4:14e) proverbial sayings which point to the mindless behaviour of those who act in this fashion. Indeed it is possible that these two lines originally formed a single saying.[23] The central oracle (4:12-14d) should be taken as divine speech throughout.

---

23. Lundbom suggested that two parts of a proverbial saying bracketed this section, adjusting verse 11 to read 'New wine takes away the mind of my people' and taking verse 14e as 'A people without sense will be thrust down' (1979:303–305).

4:11 Whoredom and wine and new wine takes away the heart.

The proverbial saying lists three factors which are considered as one (and hence there is a singular verb). In the proverb itself ***whoredom*** may originally have indicated physical prostitution, but used before the following prophetic description it is employed here to target spiritual infidelity. Indeed, McComiskey (1992:66) contends that this form *zənût* is always used in a metaphorical sense of unfaithfulness to God either in the national sphere (Ezek. 23:27) or the religious sphere (Num. 14:33; Jer. 3:2, 9). ***New wine*** has already been mentioned by Hosea as part of the LORD's provision for his people that they have mistakenly attributed to the Baals (2:8, 9, 22).[24] It is probable that such wine was consumed as part of the harvest festivals at which Baal was honoured. New wine generally refers to fresh wine or even newly pressed grape juice (cf. Prov. 3:10; Isa. 65:8) whereas ***wine*** has fermented for a longer period. Together this potent cocktail of sexual and alcoholic indulgence ***takes away the heart***, where 'the heart' refers to an individual's capacity to react in a rational and emotionally sensitive manner (cf. 7:11; 10:2). At a physical level they are robbed of understanding and sound judgement; but participation in the Baal cult robs them of more than that since they lose their ability to see clearly the reality of the LORD, his provision for them and demands on them. Once their faculties have become dulled in this way, the people are open to further debased conduct.

4:12 My people ask ⌊counsel⌋ at their tree,
and their staff informs them,
for a spirit of whoredoms has made ⌊them⌋ wander,
and they have committed whoredom away from their God.

The initial ***my people***[25] (cf. 4:6) highlights the incongruity of the people of the LORD, who should have known better, being so deficient in discernment that they ***ask ⌊counsel⌋ at their***[26] ***tree.*** There is probably an implicit word play here between 'counsel' (*ʿēṣâ*) and the similarly

24. Transferring 'whoredom' to 4:10 leaves only references to wine and new wine, but it is whoredom which is the theme of the following verses. If any emendation of the MT is required, the most probable is that there should be two occurrences of *zənût*, one in each verse, of which the first has been omitted by haplography.

25. It is grammatically feasible to take 'my people' as the last word of 4:10 (cf. NIV), but this is less likely if 4:11 is in fact a proverbial saying.

26. 'Their' and the following plural pronouns are in fact singular in Hebrew agreeing with the singular collective noun 'my people'.

sounding 'tree' (*ʿēṣ*), to which the Israelites mistakenly resort for guidance. 'Tree' may refer to some sacred tree such as the wooden pillars erected to represent the goddess Asherah at Canaanite sacred sites (cf. 'stone and wood/tree', Jer. 3:9), or it may be a more general derisive reference to an idol made of wood (cf. NIV). ***Their staff*** denotes a smaller piece of wood like a walking stick. It would be whirled round and thrown down so that the direction in which it fell could be taken as a divine sign to ***inform them*** how to proceed (cf. Ezek. 21:21). Trusting such divinatory techniques showed the extent to which the people of God had forgotten that he alone knows the future and that it is from him alone that they should be seeking direction (cf. Deut. 18:1-14). In their folly they have taken the staff upon which they physically rely to walk as spiritual guide—and that is not a recipe for spiritually balanced conduct.

For introduces the reason for such crass and perverse behaviour: the loyalty of the people is no longer to the LORD. ***Away from their God***, literally 'from under their God' (cf. 'subdued peoples under me', Ps. 18:47; compare also 1:2), points to the fact that they have repudiated his authority over them, and instead they have been induced to ***wander***.[27] This is not so much an idle, unstructured roaming as the deliberate, flawed action of those who have rejected the one true focus of life and so have lost their spiritual bearings (cf. Prov. 7:25). Their disorientation has been occasioned by ***a spirit of whoredoms*** (cf. 1:2) which has them in its grip. This describes an inner propensity which leads them to identify other gods and lifestyles as attractive, and disposes them to follow the gods of the nations rather than remain loyal to the LORD.[28] Their heart inclination is soon translated into outward rebellion. ***They have committed whoredom*** by participating in the Baal cult, and violating the integrity of their pledge to be faithful to the LORD alone.

4:13 On the tops of the mountains they sacrifice,
and on the hills they burn incense—
under an oak or a poplar or a terebinth,
for its shade is pleasant.

27. Unlike the imperfect verbs of the first two lines, 'has made wander' and 'have committed whoredom' are perfects. This indicates both that the action of these verbs has been completed prior to the crass misconduct of the first two lines and that the disposition described by these verbs continues to be active in their lives.

28. 'The whoredom is represented as a demoniacal power which has seized upon the nation' (Keil 1977:80).

On account of this your daughters will commit whoredom,
and your daughters-in-law will commit adultery.

Baal worship was conducted on elevated sites, originally close to mountain tops where the worshippers were deemed to be nearer to the gods (cf. Isa. 57:7). Later 'high places' might just be artificially heightened sites in more accessible locations. There those who participated in the Canaanite cult engaged in the two major activities, to ***sacrifice*** and to ***burn incense*** (cf. 2:13).

Many sacred sites were surrounded by groves of trees (cf. Deut. 12:2; Isa. 57:5; Jer. 3:6; Ezek. 6:13). Of the three trees mentioned, the ***oak*** and ***terebinth*** (the latter a large, leafy tree not positively identified) provided ample shade. The ***poplar*** is probably to be identified in this mountain-top setting with the storax, which has white leaves and clusters of white flowers and contributed beauty and fragrance to the scene (King 1988:122). It is not clear if Hosea is merely recording the reason for choosing such sites as being the relief they provided from the scorching heat of the sun, or if he is hinting sarcastically that shade was the only pleasant thing that could be expected there. There is probably also a play on 'under': those who slip out from under divine authority (cf. 'away from' 4:12) are found instead under trees. ***Its*** suggests that the trees formed a single protective hedge round the sacred enclosure. ***Shade*** often expresses the spiritual protection afforded by being close to God (cf. Ps. 36:7; 121:5), but now all they have secured is merely physical relief from the glare of the sun. Even so, ***pleasant*** shows that the Baal cult had an aesthetic attractiveness which would appeal to the senses. The sacred area was attractively cool, the burning incense would give off a pleasing fragrance, and there would be meat to eat from some of the sacrifices.

On account of this (cf. 4:3) refers to the totality of their worship and introduces not a divinely imposed penalty, but the inherent consequences of the people indulging in Baal worship at the Canaanite shrines. The plural ***your*** (that is, 'your very own') emphasises how their conduct strikes at their own family circles. Their ***daughters*** and ***daughters-in-law*** had become ensnared by the practices of the lascivious cult and had not preserved their purity. For ***play the whore*** and ***commit adultery***, see on 2:2. Note that it is the daughters-in-law, as married women, who are said to commit adultery. Dalliance with the deviant practices of Baal worship undermined the sanctity of their marriage vows.

4:14 I will not bring your daughters to account because they commit whoredom,
or your daughters-in-law because they commit adultery,
for⌊the men⌋ themselves go aside with whores,
and offer sacrifice with cult prostitutes—
indeed, a people who do not understand will be trampled on.

The expected verdict is surprisingly withheld. The LORD does not ***bring to account*** and so punish (cf. 4:9) their repeated and on-going misconduct. Since there is no hint in the context of forgiveness or acceptance, it may be that this is a relative rather than an absolute statement: that is, the LORD declares that it is not on them that his anger and punishment would primarily fall.

The reason for divine restraint is introduced by ***for***, which shows the divine finger of blame pointed at ***the men themselves*** (literally, 'they', a masculine plural pronoun). It is their perfidy which has set the corrupt example for others to follow. They ***go aside***, that is, quietly separate themselves from the group they are with so that they may engage in sexual activity ***with whores***, probably ordinary prostitutes, and what is more ***they offer sacrifice with cult prostitutes,*** literally, 'holy ones' who offered their services as part of the fertility cult practised at Baal shrines.[29] Portions of the sacrifices offered would have

29. There was a scholarly consensus that *qədēšâ*, 'holy one', referred to a 'cult prostitute', who participated in the fertility rites at Canaanite shrines. Certainly 'holy ones' performed a role that was forbidden to both male and female members of the covenant community (Deut. 23:17), and reforming kings sought to remove such cultic personnel (1 Kgs. 15:12; 22:46; 2 Kgs. 23:7). However, nowhere is the Biblical text explicit about the activities of such persons.

Modern scholars have questioned if the cult officials known as 'holy ones' actually engaged in sexual activity. Similar terms are employed in other ANE sources for officials associated with priests, but without indicating that was the role assigned them. Yee argues that 'the biblical text is simply too polemical, revealing more about the prophetic mind that leveled the accusation than about actual practices in the cult itself' (Yee 1996:241). Adams claims that this passage has been generally misunderstood as a literal description whereas it is in fact a metaphorical presentation of the women who engaged in Canaanite worship (Adams 2008, who also provides extensive current references on both interpretations).

However, while the ordinary word for a 'prostitute/whore' (*zōnâ*) is used to describe Tamar in Genesis 38:15, a few verses later the term *qədēšâ*, 'holy one', is employed (Gen. 38:21-22). It is difficult to evade a connection

been returned to the worshipper to consume. The picture is one of a banquet with an accompanying sexual orgy (cf. Deut. 23:17; Amos 2:7). This picture is not necessarily of an explicit Baal shrine; it would seem that such practices had invaded sites where it was ostensibly Yahweh who was worshipped.

The concluding proverb (cf. 4:11) returns to the theme of the mindlessness of a society which engages in such behaviour.[30] The reference to ***people*** may well also look back to verses 6 and 9. To ***understand*** was a mark of the wisdom which the seers of Israel sought to inculcate (cf. 14:9; Prov. 1:6), but the conduct of the people showed that they were completely lacking in spiritual discernment. Their fate was therefore to ***be trampled on.*** We do not really know the meaning of this verb (which occurs elsewhere only in Prov. 10:8, 10), and translators have to engage in informed guesswork. But the experience intended was certainly an unwelcome one.

REFLECTION

- Isaiah reflected extensively and sardonically regarding the spiritual blindness of those who worshipped pieces of wood (Isa. 44:9-20). When a generation or an individual has become spiritually insensitive, they will resort to all sorts of expedients for guidance in their lives, while they reject the one true and lasting source of light in God himself and his word. Blinded by the god of this world (cf. 2 Cor. 4:4), they lose their spiritual bearings and rather than turn in reliance to God they plunge into gross immorality (cf. Eph. 4:17-19; 1 Thess. 4:5).
- The pleasantness of the groves of Baal worship (4:13) is an instance of how carefully Satan sugars the pill of rebellion which he induces mankind to swallow. Eve 'saw that the tree was good for food, and

---

between the two, though admittedly there is no sacred site mentioned in the context. The two designations are also found in successive verses in Deut. 23:17-18. Furthermore, in this passage the term occurs in parallelism with both whoredom and adultery, and whether or not the reference is metaphorical and polemic, it still strongly supports a connection between the term *qədēšâ* and illicit sexual activity so that the translation 'cult prostitute' remains valid. While the evidence for the reconstructions of the activities of the 'holy ones' is not extensive, illicit sexual liaisons seem to have played a significant role in Canaanite worship (cf. *NIDOTTE* 3:886).

30. The final line begins with a disjunctive use of *waw* plus a noun. Here it probably functions epexegetically to present an alternative analysis of the preceding situation. If two parts of the one proverb are present in 4:11, 14, then *waw* in that context would have originally had coordinating force.

that it was a delight to the eyes' (Gen. 3:6). Lady Folly announces that 'stolen water is sweet, and bread eaten in secret is pleasant' (Prov. 9:17).

(5) A Warning to Judah (4:15-19)

The behaviour described in this section is the same as that in 4:11-14, but the matter is viewed at the level of the covenant people as a whole. The southern kingdom of Judah was not at this stage so immersed in pagan practices as Israel to the north, and Hosea urges them not to become contaminated by assimilating to the situation in the more prosperous north. His language is scathingly sarcastic in an attempt to penetrate the insensitivity of his own countrymen and alert them to the folly of their conduct.

4:15 Though you, Israel, are committing whoredom,
let not Judah become guilty.
And do not enter Gilgal,
and do not go up to Beth-Awen,
and do not swear, As the LORD lives.

Critics are suspicious of the first two lines because of the mention of Judah and their view that Hosea's ministry was confined to the north (cf. 1:7). But the advice is stated in an oblique fashion. Though it is ostensibly addressed to ***Israel*** as an entity (***you*** is masculine singular), it was the southern kingdom of ***Judah*** which was in fact being advised not to adopt the ways of the north. Possibly Hosea puts matters this way to provoke the people of the north by presenting them as a potential source of contamination for their southern neighbours. A verbal link with the preceding verses is provided by ***committing whoredom***, which repeats the charges of sexual immorality and of apostasy (4:11-12). ***Become guilty*** (*'āšam*) may indicate performing an action which infringes divine standards and so renders an individual or nation liable to punishment (cf. 5:15; 13:1). It is less likely here to indicate suffering the penalty imposed by the LORD on their transgression.

In the second part of the verse the commands are plural, and may be addressed to pilgrims from both parts of the divided nation who went to sacred sites reverenced by people from north and south alike. Both Amos (4:4; 5:5) and Hosea (cf. 5:8; 10:5) mention Gilgal and Bethel as sites to be avoided. Though other places had the same name, the ***Gilgal*** in view here was where the Israelites first encamped after crossing the Jordan (Josh. 4:19-20; 5:9). The site has not been conclusively identified, but it lay between Jericho and the Jordan. It remained the site of the sanctuary (Josh. 9:23, 27) before it was moved to Bethel. After the collapse of Shiloh, Gilgal again regained prominence (1 Sam. 7:16; 1 Sam. 11:14-15). With the division of the kingdom, the exact line of demarcation between north and south through the territory of Benjamin was a source of ongoing dispute, but it would appear that Gilgal lay just within the kingdom of Israel at this juncture. Hosea regarded Gilgal as a centre of pernicious influences (9:15), especially connected with the bull worship there (12:11), and, like Amos (Amos 5:5), he foresaw that only destruction would eradicate its influence (12:11).

Beth-Awen ('house of malicious conduct/wickedness',[31] cf. Amos 5:5) is a deliberate and sarcastic deformation of Bethel ('house of God'), which commemorated Jacob's vision of divine presence and protection (Gen. 28:10-22). There was a town of that name close to Bethel ('Beth-Awen, east of Bethel', Josh. 7:2; cf. Josh. 18:12; 1 Sam. 13:5; 14:23), and perhaps the name was so spiritually fitting that the prophets employed it more widely. More probably, Hosea adopted the name from Amos' saying, 'Bethel will come to nothing/disaster (*'āwen*)' (Amos 5:5). If the evil behaviour referred to is idolatry, then 'the house of God' had indeed degenerated into 'the house of the idol'.

Bethel was situated 10 miles north of Jerusalem, and was the chief sanctuary of the northern kingdom (cf. Amos 7). It too had been an important site in the history of God's people (Gen. 28:11-18; 36:13). The caricature of its name expresses Hosea's view of the shrine Jeroboam I had set up there to rival the Jerusalem Temple (1 Kgs. 12:29-33). ***Go up*** reflects the fact that Bethel was situated over 2,400 feet high. It was, like Gilgal, in the border zone between the two kingdoms.

Do not swear urges avoidance of the habit of using the name of the LORD lightly in connection with commitments they had no intention of keeping (cf. 4:2). ***As the LORD lives*** was frequently employed as an oath (e.g. Ruth 3:13; 1 Sam. 14:39; Jer. 38:16). Jeremiah 4:2 also urged a return to a right mode of oath taking, but the nub of the criticism is the fact that the oaths were being used to bolster assertions and promises which lacked substance.

4:16 For like a stubborn cow
  Israel is stubborn.
Now the LORD will shepherd them
  like a lamb in a broad ⌞pasture⌟.

---

31. For a discussion of this term and in particular denying the idea of 'emptiness, insubstantiality' which is often associated with it, see *NIDOTTE* 1:312-4.

For introduces the reason why the prophet is issuing this warning. After mentioning Bethel with its bull-calf, Hosea may have felt drawn to describe Israel in terms of a cow. Keeping domestic animals was a major part of the agricultural economy of Israel, and Hosea uses two similes drawn from this background to emphasise the wilful nature of Israel's rebellion. Israel is ***like a stubborn cow*** (a similar image is also found in 10:11), obstinately refusing to comply with her master's instructions. 'Stubborn' points back to the description of the stubborn and rebellious son who will not obey his parents (Deut. 21:18-21; cf. 9:15; Isa. 1:23; Jer. 5:23). It may be that there is a double wordplay here: 'cow' (*pārâ*) sounds somewhat similar to Ephraim (*ʾeprayim*), and 'stubborn' (*sārar*) is not dissimilar to Israel (*yiśrāʾēl*). She will not be led where her owner wants her to go, and therefore cannot enjoy what he would give her.

The second half of the verse may be read as an unmarked rhetorical question (cf. 2:2), 'So now, will the LORD shepherd them like a lamb in a broad pasture?' (cf. NIV, ESV) indicating that a stubborn cow should not expect the blessings accorded to the obedient. While this has the advantage of keeping the usually positive note associated with 'broad' (cf. Ps. 31:8; 118:5; Isa. 30:23), it is more probable that the lines contain another caustic jibe with the introductory ***now*** voicing an element of frustration. The metaphor of a shepherd is frequently employed for the LORD's rule over his people, but if they wished to benefit from it, they had to act like sheep and heed his commands and desires. Their refractory behaviour means that the imagery takes on a negative significance, and ***the LORD will shepherd them*** but only in the sense that the provision he will make is for their deportation to the ***broad pasture*** of Mesopotamia, to let them find how little there is to enjoy in its exposed expanses.[32]

4:17 Ephraim is joined to idols:
leave him to himself!

This is the first of thirty-six instances in which Hosea uses ***Ephraim*** to refer in some way to the northern kingdom. Ephraim was the dominant tribe in the north, and its traditional territory formed the heartland of the kingdom. ***Joined to idols*** may imply that the people had politically 'allied themselves' with idolatrous nations. More probably the thought

32. Stuart (1987:85) suggests that the 'broad pasture' refers to the underworld and that this is an expression of the mortal consequences of Israel's transgression.

is that of 'spellbound to idols', which would point to a condition similar to that induced by the spirit of whoredom (4:12).[33] Ephraim had been beguiled and they had lost their capacity to think straight. 'Idols' refers to objects which have been shaped and manufactured (cf. 8:4), and as such they were merely human inventions and products. Therefore the people of Judah are commanded as a group (the imperative is singular) to ***leave him to himself.*** Words will not get through to him, and those who seek to engage in dialogue with him will be exposed to his pernicious ways and liable to become corrupted by them. This warning was issued in recognition of what the LORD himself would do; Ephraim's punishment was imminent.

4:18 Their drink has come to an end;
they continually encourage whoredom;
their rulers intensely loved shame.

The picture is of the people of the north having banqueted until ***their drink*** (probably a beer fermented from grain, cf. Isa. 1:22) ***has come to an end.*** There is a finality in the verb 'come to an end' which suggests that this is not just temporary exhaustion of the provisions made for a specific banquet, but a complete end to their orgies. The same verb is found in 'Therefore they will now go into exile as the head of those who go into exile, and the celebration of those who stretch themselves out *will come to an end*' (Amos 6:7). In their inebriated and befuddled state they ***continually encourage whoredom.*** [34] Although the words may describe the physical behaviour of the inhabitants of the north, it is their spiritual condition which is primarily in view.

In ***their rulers*** 'their' is literally 'her', retaining the feminine imagery of the cow in connection with Israel (cf. 4:19). 'Rulers' is literally 'shields', which may possibly view them as those who are responsible for protecting the community. They ***intensely loved***[35] ***shame***, a reference to Baal worship with which they were infatuated.

---

33. Again there may be a word play between 'joined' (*ḥābûr*) and 'broad' (*merḥāb*).

34. For the hiphil form of the verb, see note 21, pg. 145.

35. The Hebrew expression *ʾāhăbû hēbû* ('they dearly loved') is obscure. Of the many suggestions as to how this phrase should be understood, two would support an intensification of the verb. It is possible that the second word is a northern abbreviated verb form with a meaning similar to the preceding word. Alternatively, there may only be one word, a reduplicated pealal form, *ʾăhabûhăbû*. All proposals have attendant difficulties.

4:19 A wind has wrapped them up in its wings,
and they will become ashamed because of their sacrifices.

Them, the object of the first verb, is literally 'her', probably a reference to Israel/Ephraim as the heifer of 4:16, and thus equivalent to a plural 'them'. ***A wind*** involves a play on the double reference of the Hebrew word (*rûaḥ*) which may also be rendered 'a spirit'. 'Wind' is more probably the primary reference because of the following ***wings*** (cf. Ps. 18:10; 104:3). ***Has wrapped them up***[36] might indicate a protective embrace ('wings' often has connotations of protection, cf. Ruth 2:12; Ps. 17:8; 36:7), but 'wind' probably has overtones of the spirit of whoredom (4:12), and denotes an overpowering influence which has taken hold of them and constrained their freedom of action so that they are being carried incapacitated towards their doom.[37] It is improbable that the thought here is specifically that of the wind of divine judgement sweeping them away to an undisclosed destination—a veiled threat of exile? Rather the description is of a nation which, by engaging in false worship, particularly ***sacrifices*** (cf. 4:13),[38] has become intractably enmeshed in a contrary course of conduct. Their stubborn persistence in apostasy has set in train a sequence of events which will not stop until ***they become ashamed***, disappointed as regards the outcome they desired and exposed to the bitter consequences of their unfaithfulness when the LORD acts in judgement against them.

REFLECTION

- 'Leave him to himself!' (4:17) is not to be confused with the LORD's withdrawal from the rebellious nation (cf. 5:6, 15). This is prudential advice to Judah which, though not as far advanced in its defection from the LORD (cf. 1:7; 6:11), was still weakening in its devotion. Further contact with the north would hasten the spiritual decline of Judah. 'Let them alone; they are blind guides. And if the blind lead

---

36. There is a grammatical problem in that *rûaḥ*, 'spirit', is a feminine noun and the verb *ṣārar* is a masculine form.

37. Again there is a connection through similarity of sound between 'has wrapped' (*ṣārar*) and 'to be stubborn' (*sārar*, 4:16). This hints at a causal connection: the one has led to the other.

38. The reading of the LXX provides a basis for emending *mizzibḥôtām*, 'from/because of their sacrifices', to *mimmizbəḥôtām*, 'from/because of their altars' (cf. NRSV). The overall sense is not unduly affected, and the change is not required.

the blind, both will fall into a pit' (Matt. 15:14). The contaminating power of sin (cf. 1 Cor. 5:6) is such that Paul counselled the Corinthian church, 'Do not be deceived: "Bad company ruins good character" ' (1 Cor. 15:33).

- Mention of Gilgal and Bethel (4:15) reminds us that places with an illustrious past may become corrupt and unhealthy. While we may retain fond memories of what they once were and give thanks for what was achieved there, our present association with such locations must recognise their changed circumstances. They are a potential danger not only to our own spiritual health but to the message which our going there would communicate to others.

B. Internal Chaos (5:1-14)

(1) Failed Leadership (5:1-7)

Though various commentators differ as to the significance they attach to these verses, most acknowledge that they constitute a separate unit in the prophecy, with an introductory call for attention and a Massoretic paragraph marker at the end. Though this passage deals with similar themes to those in preceding sections, the figure of the king is introduced in 5:1, and this anticipates subsequent critiques of Israel which focus on its corrupt leadership as well as on its apostasy. At present, however, despite the mention of the king, the spotlight still falls mainly on the corruption of the nation's spiritual life.

The background to this section is to be found in the troubled years after the death of Jeroboam II.

5:1 Hear this, O priests,
and pay attention, O house of Israel,
and listen, O house of the king,
for the judgement ⌞is⌟ for you:
for you have been a snare for Mizpah
and a net spread on Tabor.

Hear (cf. 4:1), ***pay attention***, and ***listen*** are three synonyms which combine to emphasise that those addressed need to concentrate on the message which is being brought to them. The imperatives also serve to mark this as a new section, with ***this*** referring to what follows. ***Priests*** elaborates on the reference to them in 4:9 because at the heart of Israel's problems is an inadequate, disintegrating relationship with the

LORD.[39] The compromised priesthood founded by Jeroboam I (1 Kgs. 12:31) considered themselves as worshipping the LORD, but they had readily adopted innovations drawn from Canaanite practice. ***House of Israel*** is most probably a reference to the northern kingdom as a whole (cf. 1:4),[40] as distinct from ***house of the king***, which would refer to the administrative class in the north (cf, 'rulers', 4:18), including the monarch himself, other members of the royal family, personal advisers, and lesser officials. The people are listed between the two—influenced by both, but by neither of them for good. It is not possible to determine who was on the throne when this message was initially proclaimed.

The repetition of ***for*** (cf. 5:3, 4, 7) is a minor feature of this passage which brings out the reasoned nature of the LORD's assessment. Here it introduces the reason why they should listen, though this is deliberately expressed in a form that is capable of two meanings. It might convey the thought (similar to that of Mic. 3:1), 'the right to judge has been entrusted to you', where 'you' is plural and refers to the royal administrators and probably also to the priests, who under Mosaic law formed an appeal court for general legal cases (cf. Deut. 17:9). If understood as a reference to the way justice was dispensed, this would inevitably be a source of surprise: Has Hosea become an establishment figure, acknowledging the responsibilities of those in government and so legitimising the regime and its policies, religious or otherwise? But such a possibility is no sooner hinted at than it is quashed. The immediate mention of two notorious incidents makes it evident that the prophet's message in fact centres on ***the judgement*** which is the divine assessment of the regime's plans and conduct. Hosea has been called on to remind those involved that there is no escaping the LORD's scrutiny of what they have been about, and that his verdict on them is one of doom.

The second occurrence of ***for*** introduces the justification for the LORD's negative evaluation of their conduct. ***Mizpah*** ('watchtower') is probably the significant settlement which had been associated with

39. Of course, those who have found repeated references to the priesthood, especially the high priest, throughout 4:4-19 find them continuing here, with the plural indicating that all the priests come within the scope of this critique.

40. Though a reference to the elders of the community is often detected in 'house of Israel' (cf. Wolff 1974:97; Macintosh 1997:175–176), a similar passage in Mic. 3:1, 'Hear, you heads [rulers] of Jacob, and leaders of the house of Israel' shows that the 'heads' are not to be equated with Jacob, or the 'leaders' with 'the house of Israel'.

Bethel and Gilgal in Samuel's circuit as a judge (1 Sam. 7:16), and so lay near the southern boundary of Israel in the territory of Benjamin. McComiskey (1992:75) favours Mizpah in Gilead, a lofty mountain to the east of the Jordan (Judg. 10:17; 11:8, 11), but such a distant reference seems improbable. ***Tabor*** was a prominent hill near the plain of Jezreel on the boundary between Zebulun and Issachar, or less probably (***on*** fits a mountain better) a Levitical city of the same name in the territory of Zebulun (1 Chron. 6:77), though there was also an area near Bethel called Tabor (1 Sam. 10:3).

Snare (9:8) and the larger ***net*** were means of trapping birds (cf. 7:12; Ps. 124:7, 10; 140:5; Isa. 8:14). This portrays the people as easily captured by the combined stealth of priests and politicians, who worked closely together in that the cult in the north was state sponsored (cf. Amos 7:10-11).

However, lack of information makes it difficult to assess why these particular locations are named in connection with the culpability of Israel's rulers. In Hosea's prophecy allusion is often made to events in the people's past. If that is so here, Samuel's call for the community to return to the LORD at Mizpah (1 Sam. 7:3-6) and the battle at Tabor which took place in the days of Deborah and Barak (Judg. 4:6, 12-16) are incidents which might be relevant. However, though these episodes include certain negative features (the need for repentance, and the failure of certain tribes to assist Barak), their overall significance is positive, and that does not fit this passage which sets out grounds for condemnation. This makes it more likely that Hosea's original hearers would have recognised recent scandals in these two places. Moreover, King notes, 'As at many sites, figurines of Astarte, the Canaanite goddess of fertility, were found at Mizpah; Hosea may have been alluding to the presence of fertility cults there' (1988:49). If so, his choice of sites was based not on specific events, but on what typically occurred there, with a northern and southern location in Israel selected to represent the national impact of the misguided policies promoted by the king and his court. By encouraging the populace to resort to these places and engage in the debased rites which took place there, the leadership of Israel were ensnaring the people in conduct which drew down on itself the LORD's judgement.

5:2 And those who turn aside have gone deep ⌊into⌋ slaughter,
but I ⌊will be⌋ chastisement for them all.

This verse is closely linked to the preceding, and its first line most probably is a more literal statement of what Hosea has just presented metaphorically.[41] Unfortunately ***those who turn aside*** is itself an obscure term, but it may well relate to unfaithful behaviour (cf. the unfaithful wife in Num. 5:12; devotion to religious falsehood in Ps. 40:4; avoidance behaviour in Prov. 4:15). It does not seem to describe rebels against the ruling authorities in Israel, but to the rulers, political and religious, who have themselves deviated from whole-hearted allegiance to the LORD. They ***have gone deep into slaughter***, that is, they have become deeply involved in it, presumably through policies which brought death to the people, not just by a single unfortunate misjudgement, but because of a long-term disposition to act in this way (cf. 9:9; Isa. 31:6). The suggestion has been made that the reference is to the imposition of child sacrifice on an unwilling people but, while possessing a measure of plausibility, the evidence is scanty (cf. Andersen, et al. 1980:380). More probably what is in view is the loss of life in the turmoil which engulfed the nation after the death of Jeroboam, a significant instance of which is to be found in Menahem's brutality against Tiphsah (2 Kgs. 15:16).

The LORD asserts that he will be ***chastisement***, correction which both instructs and disciplines (cf. 'correction', 5:9; the associated verb is found in 7:12, 15; 10:10). This will extend to ***all*** who have behaved in such a disgraceful and unprincipled fashion, not just the leadership. By acting in this way the LORD intends to bring them to their senses and put a stop to the prevailing anarchy. It does not appear that the LORD is proposing to impose at this stage the devastation which would shortly occur at the hands of the Assyrians, but rather such hardship as would be brought about by withdrawing their previous prosperity and causing drought and famine (cf. 2:9; 4:3).

5:3 I myself know Ephraim,
and Israel is not hidden from me,
but now, Ephraim, you have encouraged whoredom,
Israel has become unclean.

41. A translation such as 'a pit dug deep in Shittim' (NRSV; cf. NLT) takes the initial noun *šaḥăṭâ* as a form related to *šaḥat*, 'pit', and reads *šiṭṭîm* ('Shittim', 'acacia trees') for *śēṭîm*, 'those who turn aside'. A third reference to a place may suggest that the line should be added to, or read in conjunction with, the previous verse. Again it is difficult to establish any immediate relevance for such a mention of Shittim (on the west bank of the Jordan, Josh. 2:1) in the contemporary circumstances of the prophet. A translation such as that of the NIV, 'the rebels are deep in slaughter' (cf. ESV), does not require the text to be emended, though there are unusual aspects to the vocabulary.

The divine saying of verse 3 and the prophetic comment of verse 4 form a single literary entity bracketed by 'know' in the first and last lines, and also by the repetition of the concept of 'whoredom'. There is a contrast between the LORD's knowledge of the people (5:3) and their lack of knowledge of him (5:4). The emphatic ***I myself*** (cf. 2:8) decisively distinguishes the LORD's awareness and so vindicates his action from allegations of being arbitrary and unfounded. His verdict is based on good evidence, because they cannot conceal their misconduct from him. ***Know*** in this instance does not convey any implication of approval or intimacy (cf. 2:20).

Though ***Ephraim*** (cf. 4:17), the leading tribe in the north, may function here simply as a synonym of ***Israel***, the northern kingdom, what is intended may be a distinction between the rival regimes of Menahem in the west and Pekah in the east (discussed further at 5:5). Neither regime is exempt from scrutiny—or judgement. ***Is not hidden*** repeats the thought of the first line in a negative form to emphasise that no area escaped the LORD's inspection. While the translation 'I have cared for Ephraim and not neglected Israel' (REB) overstresses one implication of the LORD's knowledge, it does bring out the fact that divine scrutiny, even at its most searching, is not carried out just to find grounds for criticism (cf. Ps. 139).

But ('for', *kî*) does not introduce the reason for the preceding statements; instead, after the negative, it presents a contrast. The people of the LORD should have been aware that 'his eyes see, his eyelids try, the sons of mankind' (Ps. 11:4; cf. Ps. 33:13-15; 94:7), and should have framed their conduct accordingly. ***Now***, however, their guilty conduct is exposed, and Ephraim is confronted with the accusation: ***you have encouraged whoredom***,[42] because the royal establishment and the priests of the north have promoted Baal worship (cf. 1:2). ***Israel has become unclean*** employs a cultic term which in the first instance denotes a state of external, ceremonial impurity. This debarred an individual from approaching the sanctuary and God who is present there (cf. Lev. 15:31), and also pointed to moral pollution (cf. Num. 35:33-34; Isa. 6:5; Ezek. 14:11), particularly that associated with idolatry (cf. Lev. 18:21; 19:31). Moral, not ritual, defilement constituted the fundamental barrier to their acceptance with God (cf. 6:10; 9:3-4). If

---

42. For the hiphil of *zānâ*, see note 21, pg. 145. Moughtin-Mumby (2008:66) argues that 5:3 echoes 4:10, and 'it is the leadership, and particularly the priesthood, of Israel who are responsible for the people's outrageous behaviour.'

Ephraim refers to the tribe, then the thought may be that it led the rest of the nation into adopting Canaanite ideology and practices. More probably, the two components of the description are distributed, so that both parts of the land are charged with promoting alien beliefs and conduct, and with being impure in God's sight.

5:4 Their deeds do not permit them
to return to their God,
for a spirit of whoredoms ⌞is⌟ in their midst
but the LORD they do not know.

From this point to the end of the section in 5:7, the prophet himself speaks, and comments with the discernment that the LORD has given him on the tragic circumstances into which the people have fallen. ***Their deeds*** (cf. 4:9; 7:2; 9:15; 12:2) may refer to actions good or bad, though here Hosea obviously uses the term to summarise all that has gone wrong in the north, particularly their infatuation with Baal worship. The root ***to return*** is used in a variety of senses, but at this point it is spiritual return to God which is in view (cf. 2:7; 3:5; 7:10; 12:7; 14:1-2). 'To allow' (or as here with a negative 'not to allow') is a recognised usage of the common verb 'to give'. At one level it was open to them to return in repentance to the LORD, but at another level the legacy of past years and generations had moulded the thinking of the people, lowered their spiritual sensitivity, and enmeshed them in the practices of Canaan. The disastrous outcome was that they were practically incapable of acting in their own best interests. For a similar description of their lack of spiritual ability, see 11:7.

Their inability to return is probed further by disclosing that ***a spirit of whoredoms*** (cf. 4:12) ***is in their midst.*** The nation was collectively addicted to the seeming pleasures and benefits of Baal worship, and they were powerless to extricate themselves from this communal mindset. Indeed they had no desire to do so because their repeated indulgence in such behaviour had desensitised them as to how heinous their lifestyle was in God's sight. They were without any inward qualms regarding their conduct and considered their lifestyle to be natural—it was just the way people thought and acted. But as a result, ***the LORD they do not know***, an expression forming an inclusion with the first line of 5:4. The covenant people were no longer functioning as such because there was no inner desire to acknowledge the claims of the LORD upon them (cf. 4:1). Their outward actions were simply the fruit of hearts alienated from God.

5:5 And the pride of Israel will testify against him,
and Israel and Ephraim will stumble in their iniquity,
Judah also shall stumble with them.

The initial ***and*** indicates that what follows is a consequence of Israel being helpless in the grasp of sin. ***The pride of Israel*** is the self-assertive and self-sufficient spirit by which they threw off all allegiance to God and reliance upon him for their well-being (cf. 7:10). This was a distorted response to their population growth, economic prosperity, military prowess, and religious blindness. ***Will testify*** imparts a legal air to what is being said. Evidence to substantiate the allegations made is being accumulated, and it is principally found in the conduct and bearing of the accused. The meaning 'testify' seems somewhat different in 7:10 where the testimony is constituted by the evident decay in all the outward good fortune that Israel had formerly enjoyed. Here the spirit of arrogance with which they have rebelled against Yahweh is held on record against them. ***Against him*** (literally 'in his face') shows that no further witnesses need be called to substantiate such evident misconduct.

The autonomous mindset they displayed would lead to the downfall of the northern kingdom. While it is possible to argue that ***Israel and Ephraim*** constitutes a joint subject (Israel, even Ephraim; cf. 5:3[43]) rather than two designations, there are grounds for differentiating between the names. Certainly in 13:1, 'He [Ephraim] was the one who exalted himself in Israel', a distinction is made between the dominant tribe, Ephraim, and the rest of the nation. That probably prevails here also, and may well reflect the rival kingdoms of Pekah and Menahem (see *Introduction*, pg. 14). They ***will stumble*** (cf. 4:5) ***in their iniquity*** (cf. 7:1). Hosea uses 'stumble' in 4:5; 5:5; 14:1; 14:10 (six times in total) to denote the judgemental consequences of sin rather than the sinful act itself. It may be a development of the thought of the LORD's vengeance bringing about 'the time when their foot will slip' (Deut. 32:35).

Furthermore the prophet's description extends to Judah (cf. 1:7). Evidently Hosea perceived the state of the southern kingdom had deteriorated from the time of the warning given in 4:15. It ***also shall stumble with them*** (a prophetic perfect of what shall certainly come to pass). This statement is often taken as an addition by a southern

43. That idea seems to underlie the ESV rendering of 'their guilt' as 'his guilt', i.e. 'his iniquity'. The RSV and NRSV delete the second occurrence of 'Israel' to obtain a similar rendering.

redactor seeking to apply the prophet's message to the later circumstances of his own day.[44] However, the same spirit of self-reliance was already evident in the south, and, even without supposing that Hosea escaped to Judah after the fall of Samaria, there is no reason to deny that he would be concerned with her fate as well as that of Israel. 'Also' may well function as a textual indicator of a remark which was not part of his initial message to the north (cf. 6:11a), but which Hosea subsequently included when drawing up this record of his ministry.

5:6 With their flocks and with their herds they will go
to seek the LORD,
but they will not find ⌊him⌋—
he has withdrawn from them.

The picture is of the people (perhaps Judah as well as Israel) preparing to make abundant sacrifices to the LORD. The imperfect verbs 'will go' and 'will find' may have a present frequentative sense: 'they keep going' and 'they keep not finding him'. Formally there was no lack of religion in the land. Many sacrifices were offered at great cost, and many miles travelled on pilgrimages to sanctuaries (cf. Amos 5:4-5). This was all done because the people had adopted the perspective of Canaan that sheer volume of sacrifices would placate the deity and render their entreaties effective. They ***seek the LORD,*** ostensibly desiring to know his will and enjoy fellowship in his presence through sacrifice (cf. 3:5; 5:15; 7:10). However, it is a mockery, because there is no heart engagement with him. There was no perception of his uniqueness, and they would have equally gone to worship Baal. Furthermore, the people of the north were not going to authorised shrines, but those set up in rebellion against the Jerusalem Temple. So from the start their worship was flawed because it was not that prescribed by the LORD. Above all, their hearts were disaffected: they were living in rebellion; they had allied themselves with heathen modes of thought; they had adopted the deluded conviction that their syncretistic practices would bring blessing. For further development of 'seek', see on 5:15.

It is therefore no surprise that their religious endeavours will fail (cf. 2:7). ***They will not find him***, no matter that they are coming with great material wealth and offering many sacrifices. Their hearts are

44. Note, however, the comment of Harper (1905:270): 'These words are suspected as a gloss by some without sufficient reason. An occasional side glance at Judah, a people so intimately connected with his own, must not be denied to the prophet'.

estranged; they are not offering themselves. Consequently, the LORD would not presence himself with them. ***He has withdrawn from them***, an act of separation like taking off and laying aside clothes (cf. 3:3; 5:15; Deut. 25:9-10). The LORD leaves them to fend for themselves and experience the outcome of the decisions they have made.

5:7 With the LORD they have dealt treacherously,
for they have given birth to strange sons.
Now a new moon will devour them with their allotted property.

Dealt treacherously describes their infidelity to the LORD (cf. Jer. 5:11). They cloaked over or dressed up their true attitudes with a plausible disguise, professing to serve the LORD but infatuated with Baal (cf. 2:8; 10:1). As a result they had defrauded the LORD of what was rightfully his: their obedient service. ***For*** indicates that the evidence to substantiate the charge of treachery lies in the fact that ***they have given birth to strange sons***/'children'. 'Strange' implies that they are illegitimate, not the offspring of a true union (cf. 1:2; 2:4), but rather originating from outwith the regular family circle. The reference is not to physical birth, but to the spiritual degradation of a generation caused by the evil influence of apostate parents on their offspring.[45] Their children were brought up without respect for the LORD and without the positive example of parents who had regard to his covenant, and so the religious and social fabric of the community had been torn apart.

Now draws the sorry conclusion from all this, but the language is less than clear. 'A new moon' may just indicate a period of a month, and the subject of the verb 'devour' may be the LORD himself, so that what is foretold is that very soon, in just a month (reinforcing the temporal sense of the initial 'now'), the LORD will take from them their ancestral territory.[46] Somewhat more likely is the view that ***a new moon*** refers to

45. It would be placing too great significance on these words to infer that Hosea was aware that his second and third children by Gomer were illegitimate.

46. The TNIV rendering, 'When they celebrate their New Moon feasts, he will devour their fields', comes between the two approaches discussed above. It adopts the suggestion that the *mem* at the end of *yōʾkəlēm*, 'he will devour them', is not a pronominal suffix but an enclitic *mem* so that there is only one object to the verb. (Andersen, et al. 1980:396) Further, 'new moon' is taken to refer to religious celebrations, the subject of the verb is identified as the LORD himself, and *ʾet*, 'with', is identified as the object marker rather than a preposition.

religious festivities associated with the arrival of a new lunar month, though what is in view is not a celebration authorised by the LORD, but its corrupt northern counterpart. This monthly ceremony may stand for all their religious worship, which the people consider will provide them with divine acceptance and relief from the woes which have beset them. Hosea prophesies that the outcome will be quite the reverse. All their ill-conceived worship ***will devour***/'eat' (for this sense of the verb, see on 7:7) ***them with their allotted property*** ('their portions'), that is, the ground assigned to their families when the land was divided among the tribes. Far from ensuring their security their rebellious and debased religion will ensure their ruin. In view would seem to be the encroachments on their territory from the north by the Assyrians, leading eventually to total subjugation and annexation.

REFLECTION

- 'Their deeds do not permit them to return' (5:4) illustrates the hardening impact on an individual or a community of persistent indulgence in sinful conduct. Those who are enslaved by sin have seared consciences (1 Tim. 4:2) which are incapable of appreciating the enormity of their misbehaviour, and so they 'hold fast to deceit' and 'refuse to return' (cf. Jer. 8:5). The only way forwards is by divine emancipation which frees from the bondage of sin (cf. John 8:32; Rom. 6:18) and by divine transformation whereby God creates a new heart within us, and puts a new and willing spirit within us (cf. Ps. 51:10; Jer. 31:33–34; Ezek. 36:26; 11:19–20).
- Proliferation of sacrifice and observance of religious ceremonies have to be evaluated by the standard of 'to obey is better than to sacrifice' (1 Sam. 15:22). This does not assert that sacrificing was in itself wrong; it had after all been divinely mandated, and that requirement remained in force throughout Old Testament times. However, the ritual law was given to the people as a means of expressing genuine heart loyalty. Without inner commitment merely being present at a sanctuary and engagement outwardly in ritual observance were a mere charade. It required covenant faithfulness evidenced by lives lived in obedience to God's standards to impart true meaning and significance to the prescribed worship of tabernacle and temple.

(2) Wars and Warmongering (5:8-14)

Again a Massoretic paragraph marker and an introductory imperative mark the start of a new section. At this point there is also a thematic transition to military metaphors, and the scope of the prophecy extends to include the political chaos and instability of the regimes of the closing years of the northern kingdom. New features in this section include tension and border skirmishes between Israel and Judah (5:8, 10), and additionally there is the first mention of Assyria (5:13). This is the Assyria of Tiglath-Pileser III, who came to power in 745 B.C. (see *Introduction,* pg. 15-16). However, the keynote of the previous section is not forgotten. The problems facing the land are at root spiritual. Attention is not drawn to the specifics of their misconduct, but rather the direct divine speech which is found throughout this section warns north and south alike of the gravity of the disasters about to engulf them, and declares that they have been imposed by the LORD himself.

Though the oracles seem to have originated in specific situations, we no longer possess sufficient background information to determine their setting with any exactitude. The detail about Ephraim sending tribute to Assyria (5:13) has often been connected with Hoshea's payment after the death of Pekah in 732 B.C. (cf. the discussion of Alt's thesis below). However, circumstances a decade earlier provide a more plausible background in Menahem's submission around 743 B.C. (2 Kgs. 15:19). Also, the evidence of friction between Judah and Israel (5:10) need not relate to the events of the Syro-Ephraimite war (cf. pg. 17), but to earlier troubles during Menahem's reign. While the sequence and dating of events in this period is so confused that the allusion cannot be pinned down precisely, a broadly chronological presentation of Hosea's ministry also favours an earlier date.

This passage begins with a dramatic summons to muster the local defence forces because of the threat of invasion (5:8-9). It is then made clear that the LORD would be behind this turn of events because of his unfavourable assessment of the behaviour of both Judah and Israel (5:10-11). Though his verdict was severe, announcement of it was designed to shock both north and south into awareness of the gravity of their situation, particularly the folly of trying to seek remedies from alliance with Assyria (5:12-14).

5:8 Blow a horn in Gibeah,
 a trumpet in Ramah!
Raise a cry ⌊in⌋ Beth-Awen,
 'Behind you, Benjamin!'

A break may be confidently detected at this point, as the scene switches from empty religious celebrations to one of military tension. Even so, there is potential ambiguity in the way this verse starts. The command, ***Blow a horn!***, could well signal a religious festival, as in 'Blow the horn at the new moon, at the full moon, on our feast day' (Ps. 81:3). While the reference to the 'new moon' in 5:7 suggests that these words might initially have been heard as such a summons, it soon becomes clear that the horn in fact is functioning as a military alarm to summon the local militia and to warn the populace of an impending attack. In times of conflict it was usual for those who worked on the land to abandon their farming and take up arms. Such conscripts formed the bulk of armies at this period.

The commands which are issued are plural, as several individuals, possibly the watchmen of the named cities, are called on to sound a ram's ***horn***, an instrument with a limited musical range, or a ***trumpet***, made of metal. Since both instruments might signal danger, their unexpected use would induce fear among the citizenry (cf. Amos 3:6). The verb, ***raise a cry***, does not make specific what type of shout is involved, but a 'war cry'/'alarm' seems probable (cf. 1 Sam. 17:20; 2 Chron. 13:15), possibly to muster those of military age for battle.

Three places are named, the first two of which were in the traditional tribal territory of Benjamin (cf. Josh. 18:28). The precise site of ***Gibeah*** (cf. 9:9; 10:9) is disputed. Formerly it was generally identified with Tel el-Fûl, 3 miles (5 km) north of Jerusalem, but more recently Jabaʿ, 5½ miles (9 km) north-east of Jerusalem has been preferred (*ABD* 2:1007-08). ***Ramah*** was probably situated 4½ miles (7 km) north of Jerusalem. ***Beth-Awen*** had been used by Hosea as a contemptuous designation for Bethel, because of its cultic malpractice (cf. 4:15), but it was in the tribal territory of Ephraim. Quite possibly the reference here is to the actual Beth-Awen (Beth-aven), located slightly further north than Gibeah (Jabaʿ), and so 6 miles (10 km) north of Jerusalem. On this basis all three towns lay in Benjamite territory.

The words, ***Behind you, Benjamin***, are readily understood as a warning of a unsuspected threat from their rear. However, the same words are also found in Judges 5:14, where they suggest that certain tribes would follow Benjamin into battle (cf. 'Lead on, O Benjamin', NIV), but that seems implausible here because the tribe of Benjamin did not possess sufficient military strength to play a leading role in mounting a campaign against the south.

There are two scenarios in which the words may be taken as

incorporating a warning. (1) Albrecht Alt in 1919 proposed that the Gibeah (Tel el-Fûl), Ramah and Beth-Awen (Bethel) represented the line of attack of troops from Judah seeking to regain territory in the border zone to the north of Jerusalem (cf. Wolff 1974:111–112; Hubbard 1989:118–122). This area would have been occupied by Israelite forces during the Syro-Ephraimite war. It is, however, unlikely that, even though Samaria had been weakened, Ahaz would have done anything to infringe on the settlement imposed by Assyria on the area after 732 B.C.

(2) An earlier incident presents a more plausible conjecture. After the division of the kingdom on Solomon's death the tribe of Benjamin had remained with the southern kingdom (1 Kgs. 12:21), but since its territory lay between Israel and Judah, it became in effect a buffer zone between the two, coming under the control of one kingdom or the other as their respective fortunes fluctuated. It is generally supposed that from early in the eighth century Benjamin fell under the sway of Israel, having been lost by Amaziah, king of Judah, after his rash challenge of Joash to battle (cf. 2 Kgs. 14:8-14). If that was so, Hosea's words may be understood to come from the time of Menahem, and to warn that Judah, taking advantage of the weakness and instability prevalent in the north (cf. 5:10) was attempting to regain lost territory.

5:9 Ephraim will become a desolation
in the day of correction;
among the tribes of Israel
I have made known what is certain.

In this section ***Ephraim*** is distinguished from Judah, and so here a warning of impending judgement is first of all issued to the northern kingdom. ***Desolation*** describes the dismay which would arise from the utter wasting of the land.[47] ***Correction*** in the phrase 'the day of correction' (cf. Isa. 37:3) is associated with a verb meaning 'to rebuke, to punish' (cf. 4:4), and refers to the LORD's covenantal reprimand and discipline (cf. Lev. 26:18, 28; Ps. 50:8, 21).[48] Thus Ephraim is not here

---

47. The verb 'will become' is most probably third feminine singular, implying the suppression of the headword 'land of', rather than being a reference to the people. If it is taken as second masculine singular, then Ephraim would be a vocative: 'You, O Ephraim, will become a desolation'.

48. In 5:2 the root *yāsar*, 'to chastise' had been employed; in 5:9 the root is *yākaḥ*, 'to correct'. 'But whereas *yāsar* has the notion of paternal chastisement, ... *yākaḥ* denotes education and discipline as a result of God's judicial actions' (*TWOT* 1:377).

threatened with the final annihilating judgement of Assyrian invasion, but with the beginning of a process of divine chastisement. Their situation is not yet viewed as entirely without the possibility of recovery. It will be possible for those who are punished to recognise their wrongdoing and repent. However, if they do not, the LORD will inevitably proceed to impose more punitive measures (contrast 5:12 with 5:14).

The ancient phrase, ***the tribes of Israel***, alludes to the former united status of the covenant people. So all twelve tribes are in view (not just those of the northern kingdom), and this links in to the following condemnation of Judah's conduct. The picture is of the nation assembled as one, and jointly confronted with the declaration, ***I have made known*** (or possibly a performative perfect, 'I hereby make known'). None should be surprised at what will occur because it ***is certain***. The curses of the broken covenant had been part of what the LORD had revealed from the time of Moses (cf. Lev. 26:14-39; Deut. 27:15-26; 28:15-68), and now, through the prophet, he has declared his intention to impose these sanctions progressively upon those who have violated their covenant commitments.

5:10 The leaders of Judah have become
like those who move a boundary marker;
upon them I will pour out
like water my indignation.

The speech of the LORD in the remaining verses of this section may be analysed as consisting of three strophes (5:10; 5:11-12; 5:13-14), in each of which an accusation against the covenant people is followed by a divine threat expressed in the first person using metaphorical language (cf. Good 1966:276–277). In this verse the first two lines constitute the accusation, and the second two lines the resultant threat. Here ***the leaders of Judah*** (cf. 7:3) are singled out for rebuke. The governing classes of the land (either named in their own right, or standing for the population as a whole) are accused of conduct similar to ***those who move a boundary marker.***[49] Such behaviour was included among the solemn curses uttered on Mount Ebal: 'Cursed be anyone who moves his neighbour's boundary marker' (Deut. 27:17; cf. Deut. 19:14). When unscrupulous individuals tried to extend the holding allotted to their family in the division of the land, their encroachment on their neighbour's inheritance violated God's disposition of his gift to his covenant people.

---

49. Alternatively the *kaph* may be *kaph veritatis* (GKC 118x), that is, the leaders of Judah are precisely that.

But what is intended by the accusation here? While it might accuse the powerful in Judah of grabbing land from their less influential brethren, Hosea does not raise concerns for social justice within the community (north or south) at this stage of his prophecy. ***Like*** indicates the use of a simile which extends the curse against an individual in Deuteronomy to an international level. The leadership of Judah is accused of annexing territory from Benjamin. As was argued above (cf. 5:8), it is implausible to locate such action in the 730s. A decade earlier does, however, provide a suitable background. That it is various leaders who are implicated in this activity, and not the king, indicates unofficial action by some who took advantage of the internal turmoil in Israel to encroach on Benjamite territory to enlarge their own estates.

Whatever the precise nature of their misconduct, the LORD disapproved and was roused to ***indignation*** (cf. 13:11), a term which refers to what overflows or passes over. ***Like water*** is not intended to convey a picture of a minor spill from a vessel used to carry water, but of a sudden, copious flood which sweeps everything away (cf. Isa. 8:7-8). Just as thoroughly will the enemy carry away from Judah its wealth and resources. ***I will pour out*** indicates that the impending and deliberate unleashing of this torrent on the underhand behaviour of the leadership of Judah will be inflicted by the LORD. Though the description is of a severe judgement, it is one which stops short of predicting the total overthrow of Judah. It may have been fulfilled either in the Syro-Ephraimite war (cf. 2 Chron. 28:5-7, and especially the prophetic declaration, 'the LORD, the God of your fathers, was angry with Judah' in 2 Chron. 28:9) or slightly later through the tribute imposed on Judah by the Assyrians (cf. 2 Chron. 28:20-21).

5:11 Ephraim ⌊is⌋ oppressed, crushed ⌊in⌋ judgement,
for he was keen to walk after filth.

Verses 11 and 12 may be read together as a description of the northern kingdom (5:11) followed by divine action against them (5:12). Here it is not the misconduct of ***Ephraim*** which is being reported, but the consequences which have already followed from it. Although the absence of a finite verb allows for a future supplement (cf. NLT), passive participles generally describe an existing condition. Furthermore, while the participles do not specify who has brought about this state, there is no doubt that it is the LORD's verdict which has been imposed on the northern kingdom. ***Oppressed*** (cf. 'exploit', 12:7) and ***crushed*** may be used in relation to internal misrule and exploitation (cf. Amos 4:1), but this would be intensified when they also had to cope with the tyranny and cruelty of foreign aggressors (cf. 2 Kgs. 15:19-20).

For introduces the reason for the LORD's verdict on the misconduct of the community who were ***keen to walk after filth.*** 'Walk after' suggests religious devotion (2:5, 13), and 'keen' reflects the determination of the community to persevere in their chosen course of action.[50] However, it is unclear what goal they are pursuing. The Hebrew noun (*ṣaw*) occurs elsewhere only in Isaiah 28:10, 13, where it may be understood as either a 'precept' or a mocking sound. In this passage three options have been proposed: (1) 'precept' as in Isaiah 28, taken in the sense of a merely human command, here the royal edicts which set up the alternative worship of the north; (2) 'filth' (Vulgate, ESV), a contemptuous reference to a pagan deity; (3) as a corrupt form of a noun 'emptiness' or 'vanity', also used to describe an idol (cf. Ps. 31:7; Jer. 18:15).[51] Clearly, whatever understanding is adopted of the noun, the root of Ephraim's misconduct lay in the false worship of the golden bull-calves.

5:12 But I ⌞am⌟ like a moth to Ephraim,
and like decay to the house of Judah.

Turning from the situation that prevailed in Ephraim, the LORD employs two remarkable similes regarding himself as the real antagonist in the affairs of the land.[52] Both comparisons indicate that there will be a build-up in the intensity of his action. It may not be noticed at all at present, or dismissed as trivial, but the LORD will work without faltering or compromise to impose his punishment unless they repent.

In clauses of this sort the verbal supplement required in an English rendering is a matter of the translator's judgement, with standard versions using either a present or a future tense. Instead of ***moth*** some

---

50. Though there are two finite verbs *hôʾîl*, 'he was keen', and *hālak*, 'he walked', there is no need to emend the second to an infinitive since *yāʾal*, 'to be keen', is found elsewhere with a finite verb (cf. Deut. 1:5).

51. The first proposal relates the noun to the root *ṣwh*, 'to command'; the second proposal connects it to the root *ṣwʾ*, 'to be foul' (BDB 844), but with the aleph missing; and the third approach (cf. *BHS*) emends *ṣāw* to *šāwʾ*, 'worthless', 'futile' (cf. 12:11), which may be supported by the LXX and Peshitta. The last proposal is most commonly adopted in English translations, but it has no compelling advantage over the other two.

52. 'The metaphors used for the work of Yahweh are shockingly bold and abrasive, even for Hosea. God is putrefaction and bone rot in the body of both peoples' (Mays 1969:90).

identify a homonym meaning 'maggots' (NRSV) or 'pus' in an open sore as more in line with the parallelism, and also with the military context set by the introductory imperatives; but 'moth' is attested elsewhere as a meaning for this term (Job 13:28; Isa. 51:8). The clothes moth was a major pest in the ancient world, silently but steadily devouring garments. With a present tense supplement the reference is to what the LORD has already done. The tensions which had already arisen in the land had caused it to disintegrate internally. But the holes which had appeared in Ephraim's garment would increase in number and size when Assyria annexed much of their territory—and eventually there would be no garment left at all.

Not just the north will experience the LORD's chastisement. In a similar figure of gradual, progressive, relentless deterioration the LORD compares himself to ***decay***, which may refer to an external attack such as a bacterial infection, or it may be an internal wasting away (cf. 'decay/rottenness in his bones', Prov. 12:4). This may well describe what happened in the reign of Jotham with attacks on Judah from Aram and from Pekah (2 Kgs. 15:37), possibly beginning at the time he dominated only Gilead, attacks which intensified early in the reign of Ahaz (2 Chron. 28:5-8, 17-18).

5:13 And Ephraim saw his sickness
  and Judah his sore;
then Ephraim went to Assyria
  and sent to the king of Jareb.
But he is unable to heal you
  and he will not cure you of your sore.

This verse and the following are again paired. ***Sickness*** is a word for general illness, though it may refer to a wound. A ***sore*** was an open, infected injury which oozed pus (Jer. 30:13). So there existed a weakening, potentially life-threatening condition which required immediate attention. This was so obvious that both kingdoms recognised their debilitating condition, but neither looked in the right direction for relief. Rather than returning in repentance to God, ***Ephraim went to Assyria***. The phrase indicates an acceptance of vassal status, and probably relates to Menahem's payment to Tiglath-Pileser on his first campaign in Syria-Palestine in 743 B.C. 'So that his hand might be with him to strengthen his hold on the kingdom under his hand' (2 Kgs. 15:19) may involve more than Assyrian recognition of Menahem as their vassal. It probably indicates that other threats existed to his regime, possibly from Pekah in Gilead.

The phrase ***sent to the king of Jareb*** contains two difficulties: the identity of the subject of the verb, and the identity of the king of Jareb. The balancing of Ephraim and Judah in previous lines has suggested to some commentators that Judah may be the singular subject of 'sent', in reference to the action of Ahaz (2 Kgs. 16:7-9), though an even earlier possibility also exists (cf. pg. 16). However, it is more probable that Hosea is describing only what Ephraim did in 743 B.C. ***Sent*** would refer to an initial approach to Tiglath-Pileser for assistance with an appropriate gift—Assyria did not extend aid for nothing.

There are no records of a king Jareb. Perhaps Jareb is to translated as 'he will contend' and seen as an ominous reference to the bellicose Assyrian king. However, a more viable approach is to redivide the consonants of *melek yārēb*, 'king Jareb', and read instead the 'Great King' (*malki rāb*, where the adjective is the same as that used of Solomon in the Aramaic of Ezra 5:11) which might be a northern rendering of an attested mode of address for the Assyrian emperor.[53] The Great King's dominion extended over the realms of many minor figures who were also known as 'king' by their own subjects, and hence the need for a distinguishing epithet for the emperor.

But he is an emphatic contrast, which underscores the discrepancy between the claims embodied in Tiglath-Pileser's title and what he could in fact accomplish with respect to the ***sore***. It is the same word as earlier in the verse, though now descriptive of Israel's condition. The metaphor involves a deep abscess requiring to be cleansed, which stood for the condition of the land, especially spiritually. This was beyond the capability of any earthly physician or monarch to ***heal*** or ***cure*** (the second word occurs only here, but its meaning is established by the parallelism with 'heal'). The switch from third person statements to direct address in ***you*** is an accepted feature of Hebrew style (cf. 6:5; GKC §114p). The pronoun is plural and refers to individuals in Hosea's audience. Whatever panacea they supposed Assyria might possess was an illusion. The assertion that human expedients were incapable of remedying the weakness of the regime or dealing with the problems posed by the heart delinquency of the people prepares the way for 6:1.

---

53. The problem with this approach is to explain the additional *yodh*. To treat it as an old genitive ending, a *yodh compaginis*, is awkward in that this is not normally found apart from a construct form or a participle. It may have been introduced to facilitate pronunciation of the consonantal cluster in an original *malk rab*.

5:14 For I ⌞will be⌟ like a lion to Ephraim,
  and like a young lion to the house of Judah.
I, I myself, ⌞am the one who⌟ will tear and go ⌞away⌟;
  I will carry off and there ⌞will be⌟ no one to rescue.

For introduces the reason why appeals to Assyria would be ineffective. Though Tiglath-Pileser was a mighty monarch, he was still only an instrument in the hands of God. Israel's affairs were under the sovereign rule of the LORD, and as long as they continued to defy him, they would find themselves confronted by his power and determination to punish them.

The supplement ***will be*** is suggested by the verbs later in the verse. The time is about to come when the LORD will move on from his policy of gradual discipline of the people (5:12) to more ferocious, sudden action ***like a lion*** and ***like a young lion*** (cf. Prov. 30:30). Two further terms for a lion are used in reference to God in 11:10 and 13:8. A young lion is not to be thought of as a lion cub. Though not fully mature, it was already strong enough to hunt prey. The reliefs which adorned the palace walls of Assyrian kings often portrayed them displaying their strength and courage by hunting lions, but the LORD is the lion whom none can overcome. No longer will the kingdoms be faced with the slow decline of moths and decay; instead they will be confronted with the swift ferocity of sudden attack.

In ***I, I myself, ⌞am the one who⌟*** the emphatic use of 'I' is further strengthened by the repetition of the pronoun. There must be no confusion about who is really in control of the international political scene. Neither kingdom should be so taken up with the visible threat posed by the king of Assyria as to be oblivious to the fact that what will come upon them is imposed by none other than the LORD himself who as the covenant King controls the affairs of his errant and ungrateful people (cf. Lev. 26:22; Deut. 32:24). ***I will tear and go away.*** The outcome is presented as a bleak prospect: savage attack followed by departure. More than that, ***I will carry off***/'raise' repeats the use of the verb found in 1:5 with respect to Israel's deportation from the land. In view is not just weakening onslaught, but exile as the LORD takes them from the land. ***There will be no one to rescue.*** 'Rescue' is the same verb as 'remove' (2:9). There will be no one who can forcibly extricate them from the grasp of the divine lion (cf. 2:10) who has taken his mauled prey out of the land.

This prophecy was fulfilled on two occasions when the LORD acted through the instrumentality of the Assyrians, and in both episodes inhabitants of the northern kingdom were forcibly removed from the country. It is recorded in the context of the invasion of 733 B.C. that Tiglath-Pileser 'deported the people to Assyria' (2 Kgs. 15:29), and again a similar removal took place after the fall of Samaria, when the king of Assyria 'deported the Israelites to Assyria' (2 Kgs. 17:6). Thinking only of the first of these makes a difference to the interpretation of what follows (see below), but in fact the prediction anticipates both events.

REFLECTION

- Tension and fighting often characterised the relationship between the two kingdoms which ostensibly worshipped the same God. Such internecine rivalry was not confined to God's people of Old Testament times, but still continues to mar and weaken the church (cf. 1 Cor. 6:1-8). Paul warned the Galatians 'if you keep on biting and devouring one another, watch out that you are not consumed by one another' (Gal. 5:15). Brotherly love is an index of true Christianity because whoever does not love his brother still walks in darkness (cf. 1 John 2:9-11). It is imperative to maintain such a spiritual attitude (cf. Heb. 13:1; 1 Pet. 1:22), and this can only be sustained by recognising it as a basic requirement of the Lord himself and a constitutive feature of likeness to him (John 13:34).
- In this passage there is a progressive intensity in divine remonstrance. When the gentler rebukes of 5:12 fail in their objective, more serious inflictions take their place when the LORD comes as a lion against his people. There is a constant need to interpret correctly the Father's discipline of his sons and to respect the warnings he gives before the situation deteriorates further (cf. Heb. 12:5-11). King Ahaz at this period provides an example of one who misinterpreted God's admonitions. 'In the time of his distress he became yet more unfaithful to the LORD' (2 Chron. 28:22; cf. Isa. 7:11-13). Ignoring serious problems does not solve them; it may well lead to an even more intense catastrophe. We need to be given spiritual perception to see our situation in its true light.
- If we heard God compared to a moth or decay and we were unaware of 5:12, our conclusion might well have been that these were the musings of some avant-garde theologian. However, such unusual and startling language reminds us that human words can never totally represent divine reality, and that we would do well to remember that God shatters our comfortable notions of his character (cf. Heb. 12:29).

- Judah too would find out by bitter experience that attempts to find a human remedy for a spiritual problem are doomed to fail (cf. 5:13). When Ahaz requested Assyrian assistance and paid tribute, Tiglath-Pileser 'came against him and afflicted him instead of strengthening him' (2 Chron. 28:20). The sorry verdict on Ahaz's diplomacy was 'it did not help him' (2 Chron. 28:21). This serves as a warning to individuals and communities of the inadequacy of solutions to the problems of life which do not take the divine dimension into account and stop short of commending a right relationship with God (cf. Jer. 2:13; 17:13; Luke 12:20-21). The mistake is often made of thinking our problems arise from our economic circumstances or from external threats. Our problems generally arise from what we are in ourselves, especially in relation to God—and in that respect only his help is able to provide a remedy.

C. Penitence? (5:15-6:3)

Hosea has often set out his material without clearly demarcated divisions, and so it can be extremely difficult to decide just where one theme ends and another begins. 'No one to rescue' (5:14) had conveyed a note of finality. If it was merely the deportation of 733 B.C. that was in view in 5:14, then this section might be understood as holding out the gracious prospect of avoidance of judgement if only the remnant still left in Samaria responded to divine discipline by repenting. However, the absolute imagery of the lion carrying a corpse off as prey (5:14) leaves no room for national survival, and the perception of the nation as dead is reinforced is 'revive' (6:2) has in view revivification rather than recovery from serious illness. The time frame of Hosea's vision in this section is to be understood as after the fall of Samaria when the nation as a whole is in exile. However, even then there is the prospect of relief beyond the imposition of penalty. This introduces the theme of the repentance which should be forthcoming as the impact of divine discipline becomes effective.[54]

Furthermore, interpretation of this section varies as regards the significance of 6:1-3. While these verses are relatively optimistic in tone, it is disputed whether they portray the prophet inviting the people

54. 'Hosea 5:15–6:3 should be regarded with 10:12 and 11:10-11 as the first in a series of contrapuntal voices strategically arranged by a later redactor to prepare for the conclusion of the book. These voices may be original to the prophet Hosea, but their present position is clearly secondary, though consistent with the overall thrust of Hosea 4–11' (Yee 1996:249).

to imitate him in a prayer of repentance, or whether they record the people's facile resolve as to renewing their relationship with God. The latter interpretation would fit in with a setting in the last decade of the northern kingdom rather than the later perspective adopted here.

(1) The LORD's Withdrawal (5:15)

In this transitional verse there recurs the theme of divine withdrawal causing an absence of blessing (2:9; 3:3-4; 5:6). This has now, however, become more devastating than crop failure or spiritual emptiness as the nation engaged in worship. They are captive in a foreign land, deprived of the blessings of nationhood and undergoing exploitation. Divine withdrawal was not of course absolute: God did not abdicate as ruler of heaven and earth. It is a mode of speech to indicate his punitive withdrawal of his favour. This inevitably led to increased troubles and suffering for the people, but in and through all their deprivation and misery God was still at work. His control shaped events to induce in them greater spiritual awareness.

5:15 I will go ⌞away⌟; let me return to my place
until they recognise their guilt and seek my face.
In their distress they will earnestly search for me.

I will go away picks up on 'I ... will ... go away' in the previous verse, but this does not of itself imply the verse ought to be taken only with the preceding. As a transitional statement, it also possesses links with what follows. After the fierce attack Israel has experienced, there will be a period when the LORD will leave them to let their situation come home to them (cf. 3:4). The main thought is expressed by the second verb, ***Let me return to my place*** (with 'return' [*šûb*] anticipating 6:1),[55] possibly to the Jerusalem Temple (not the corrupt sacred sites of the north), but more probably in this oracle addressed to the northern kingdom, to God's heavenly throne, of which the Temple was an earthly extension (cf. Isa. 26:21; Jer. 7:12; Mic. 1:3). The metaphor of the previous verse may continue to be felt: the lion after its attack returns to its den.

Then from a distance (cf. Ps. 14:2; Isa. 18:4) God will observe their affairs, not intervening for good or ill while he awaits the outcome he requires, that is, ***until they recognise their guilt*** (*ʾāšam*). This verb often has the sense 'to suffer the penalty incurred by their offence' (cf.

55. The cohortative form *ʾāšûbâ*, 'let me return', suggests that the initial *ʾēlēk* might be understood in a similar fashion, 'Let me go'. What is then expressed is the will or resolve of the speaker (Joüon §114b).

10:2; 13:16). In that case there is a prediction that after punishment has been imposed the people will come to their senses spiritually and so seek to resume an intimate relationship with the LORD. However, most translations understand the verb here as involving an admission of guilt, presumably because that is a precursor to ***seek my face*** (cf. 3:5; 5:6; cf. Ps. 24:6; 27:8), truly desiring renewed fellowship with the LORD on his terms. This use of the term occurs in the regulations for the guilt offering where an individual who 'has sinned and has realised his guilt' (Lev. 6:4) is directed how to find forgiveness by compensating those he has wronged and by offering the prescribed sacrifice.

In their distress, anguish caused by adverse circumstances, borrows an expression from Deuteronomy to set out a basic feature of the covenant programme for spiritual recovery. Moses envisaged that because of their rebellion the people would be banished from the land and undergo exile among the nations. He then predicted, 'And from there you will seek the LORD your God and you will find him, if you look for him with all your heart and with all your soul. *In your distress,* and when all these things have happened to you in the latter days, you will return to the LORD your God and obey his voice' (Deut. 4:29-30). ***Earnestly search*** (cf. Job 24:5; Prov. 1:28) is not the same word as in 5:6, but carries forward the theme of the need for a right approach to the LORD. It indicates that they will then engage in a thorough and well-motivated quest for renewed fellowship with God (cf. Ps. 63:1; 78:34; Isa. 26:9).[56] There is no indication when this will be realised, whether after the exile or under a messianic king (3:5).

REFLECTION

- The ultimate stage in the LORD's dealings with his people occurs when he abandons them to what they have chosen for themselves so that they might experience the full consequences of their rebellious choice and obstinate refusal to respond to his gracious overtures. 'But my people did not listen to my voice; Israel would not submit to me. So I gave them over to their stubborn hearts, to follow their own plans' (Ps. 81:11-12; cf. Ezek. 20:39). It is possible that a similar disciplinary process was in view when Paul handed Hymenaeus and Alexander 'over to Satan that they may learn not to blaspheme' (1 Tim. 1:20).

---

56. The verb *šāḥar* may be connected with the noun 'dawn', in which case the metaphor was originally one of looking for something with the intensity with which the dawn is awaited (BDB 1007), but this association is now widely denied and a number of homonyms are detected.

- In his dealings with his people the LORD sets a limit on the outpouring of his wrath (Isa. 54:8). His discipline achieves its purpose when the sinner returns in repentance to God because of the severity of what he imposes on them. 'O LORD, in distress they sought you; they poured out a whispered ⌊prayer⌋ ⌊when⌋ your chastening was on them' (Isa. 26:16; cf. Ps. 50:15; 78:34; Isa. 26:9). A notable Old Testament instance of one who was brought by distress to humble himself before the LORD is Manasseh (2 Chron. 33:12-13).

(2) An Exhortation to Return (6:1-3)

If the words of 6:1-3 are understood as a report of the people's self-exhortation, question inevitably arises as to whether their utterance was well meant or not. The rejection of Ephraim and Judah in 6:4 has suggested to many that this speech which is to be attributed to Hosea's audience is flawed and inadequate. The major deficiency is often identified as a lack of confession of sin and contrition for their wrongdoing, and unfavourable comparison is made with 14:1-3. Though the people knew that they were hurting, and so sought relief from the LORD, it is argued they still did not comprehend the gravity of their offence, and therefore they came in a somewhat flippant and superficial spirit (like the morning cloud or the dew mentioned in 6:4), expecting God to change his disposition towards them as readily and automatically as day dawns and the seasons change (cf. GNB). Such a presumptuous attitude would then explain the LORD's exasperated rejection of their shallow response in 6:4-6.

On the other hand, while reading the passage as a flawed response is a plausible approach, many features of the preceding verses are echoed in this exhortation, and this suggests that it was not a course of action which the people framed, but a proposal which the prophet made to them that, in the light of his message, they should conduct themselves in this way. A similar, but less likely, approach is that found in the NRSV which follows the Septuagint (and also the Peshitta and Targum; see *Introduction*, pg. 23) by introducing 'saying' between 5:15 and 6:1 to indicate that these words are a direct expression of the reaction the LORD is waiting for from the people. On either of these interpretations, the words express genuine sentiments of repentance in which the people are earnestly exhorting one another to seek the LORD. If this approach had been adopted before Samaria was finally overwhelmed, the catastrophe would have been avoided, but the prophet's counsel fell on uncomprehending ears. The only possibility left for it being implemented would then be after the imposition of judgement.

Furthermore, if the analysis is accepted that throughout Hosea there is a repeated thematic progression from indictment through penalty to future blessing (cf. *Introduction*, pg. 25), then this division of the prophecy is brought to an end on a positive note, though not yet attaining the heights reached elsewhere. On that understanding, the LORD's rejection of the people's conduct as recorded in 6:4-6 does not arise because of the insincerity of what has been said in 6:1-3, but because of the fact that these words, or others like them, were not uttered at all. Therefore, on balance, it is appropriate to take these verses as embodying an example proposed by Hosea to the people, but not immediately adopted by them.

6:1 'Come and let us return to the LORD,
for ⌊it is⌋ he ⌊who⌋ has torn so that he may heal us,
he has struck so that he may bind us up.'

Come uses the same verb as in 'Ephraim went to Assyria' (5:13), and in the LORD's *going* to his place (5:15), but now the exhortation has as its intended outcome, ***Let us return to the LORD*** (cf. 14:1). The only remedy for their situation lies in the hands of the one who has imposed it. Moreover, although the LORD had gone away from the people, this had been his reaction to their prior spiritual departure from him, and 'return'/'turn around' (*šûb*, cf. 2:7; 14:1[57]) points to the repentance they must exhibit towards him if they are again to enjoy fellowship with him. The use of the personal name of the LORD, and not the more general term God, clearly guides their thoughts away from pagan gods to the true and living covenant King. They are being urged to set their hope for the future on being in a right relationship with him so that his lovingkindness and commitment towards them, and not on their own competence or worthiness, would determine their destiny.

For introduces the reason why such a course of action should be adopted. The emphatic ***he*** shows the people that they are to recognise the LORD's ability to intervene in their circumstances and his effective control over them. ***Has torn*** uses the same verb as described the attack of the LORD who is a lion (5:14), and the past tense indicates that this experience has already occurred by the time these words would come to be used. They are to acknowledge that the calamity which had engulfed their nation been sent by God to achieve his purposes. ***Heal*** indicates the therapy the LORD can provide, a remedy which was

57. For the significance of *šûb*, 'to go back', 'to turn around', 'to return', as a major link providing thematic continuity throughout the Minor Prophets, see Bowman 2006.

unavailable from earthly sources such as the Assyrian emperor (5:13). The blow indicated by ***struck*** may be fatal (cf. Exod. 2:12) or non-fatal (cf. Exod. 2:11, 13).[58] It is conjoined here with ***bind***, which is used of caring for a wound (cf. Isa. 61:1; Ezek. 30:21), and this suggests a serious, though not necessarily mortal, injury. ***Us*** identifies the prophet with the people in what is a tender, compassionate plea. Hosea acknowledges that the LORD has inflicted the curse of the covenant on the people when he chastised them with severe blows, but ***so that*** shows his aim has been that through this process they may be restored.[59] Despite all that has come upon them, there is still the potential of his grace to revive and reinstate the covenant bond if only the people respond to his entreaties and acknowledge him.

6:2 'He will revive us after two days;
on the third day he will raise us up,
and we will live before him.'

While ***revive*** may convey the thought of preserving life in one who is weak or ill (cf. Judg. 15:19; Isa. 38:9), and so the nation would be envisaged as at the point of death, the term is also used of the restoration to life of one who has died (cf. 1 Kgs. 17:22; 2 Kgs. 13:21). That is more appropriate in this context where a lion has mauled its prey, carried it off to its den and there is no one to rescue (5:14). There is no need to spell out that the situation is irrecoverable. Here, however, Hosea holds out before the people a prospect which stretches beyond what had humanly seemed final, and invokes a yet more distant period of renewal. Some scholars interpret this in the light of the emphasis on rising from death to life in the seasonal agricultural cycle which was the focus of the Canaanite fertility cults, but that hypothesis seems improbable in such an anti-Canaanite prophet as Hosea. Many take this

58. The verb *yak* is a short-form imperfect hiphil from the root *nākâ*, 'to strike', but in this context it is difficult to interpret it as an imperfect (cf. 11:4). A *waw* may have been dropped from the text, which would then originally have read *wayyak*, 'and he struck'. However, for poetic reasons Hosea may have deliberately abbreviated the construction to use the imperfect form in its archaic preterite sense, 'he struck'.

59. In the second line of the verse a perfect verb is followed by ordinary *waw* with an imperfect. It is unlikely that the second verb functions as a simple future (NRSV, HCSB). The unusual construction may indicate a contrast, 'but he will heal us' (cf. Joüon §119y). Alternatively, the idea may be to convey intention or consequence (RSV, ESV). The same would also apply to the further instance of ordinary *waw* with an imperfect in the final line, 'that he may bind us up', though here RSV and ESV opt for a simple future.

as restoration to health after severe illness, but that again fails to do justice to the finality of the previous description. The most satisfactory explanation is that this is covenant language. 'Life' is enjoyment of the favour of the covenant overlord, and 'death' is the withdrawal of his favour. The nation as such dies when because of its sin the LORD withdraws from it and refuses to treat it as his own. But that need not be the end of the story. What happens next depends on the action of the overlord who has been ofended (Wijngaards 1967), and here the covenant God is the one who has declared, 'I ⌊am the one⌋ who kills, and I make alive; I wound, and I ⌊am the one who⌋ heals' (Deut. 32:39). It is to that declaration they are exhorted to attach their faith.

After two days anticipates what will happen ***on the third day***. This rhetorical device is not necessarily setting out a precise timetable, but is using a poetic doublet to express a short period of time, not dissimilar to our 'in two or three days', indicating speedy closure of an episode. ***He will raise us up*** refers to the re-establishment of the vigour and vitality of the nation when the LORD shines the light of his countenance upon them and communicates new life to them.

And we will live before him. The result of the LORD's action in raising them from their national grave will be restoration of what is truly life, enjoyment of covenantal blessing and relationship (Deut. 8:1; 16:20; 30:18; Amos 5:14). 'Before him' is literally 'to his face', and it may be that the literal sense is, at least partly, intended so as to reflect on the desire that they 'seek my face' (5:15). It certainly conveys the idea of living in harmony with his will and enjoying his blessing (cf. Gen. 17:18; Acts 23:1).

The prayer which Hosea is here teaching the people gives rise to two questions. (1) Does it reflect a belief in life after death for the individual? (2) How does 'on the third day' relate to Jesus' resurrection?

(1) Though many scholars doubt the existence of a belief in personal resurrection in Israel in Hosea's day, that view is far from being established. The language of national 'resurrection' is certainly more accessible if there is a prior belief in personal resurrection, and there are many Old Testament passages which point to *post mortem* existence (e.g., Job 14:7-14; 19:23-27; Pss. 16:9-10; 17:14-15; 49:14-15; 73:24; Prov. 12:28) (cf. Kaiser 1978:180–181.). Even so, though life after dead was anticipated as the divine provision for God's people as individuals, and so provided a basis for this description of restored covenant life for the resurrected nation, it is unlikely that the prophet was here directly teaching regarding the destiny of individuals. Both he and his contemporaries would have understood his words as pointing

to a collective experience rather than an individual one.

(2) However, that perspective is significantly expanded by New Testament teaching. Hosea 6:2 is often considered to be the passage referred to by Paul when he cites the early testimony regarding the essence of the Christian faith: 'he was raised on the third day in accordance with the Scriptures' (1 Cor. 15:4). The connection between Paul's citation and this passage is much controverted, but if the phrase 'in accordance with the Scriptures' simply qualifies the lapse of time 'on the third day' and is not taken with the clause as a whole referring to the resurrection, then there is no other single passage to which the allusion can be readily traced.

It is probable that 'the third day' reflects a theme found throughout the Old Testament. God appeared to Israel on Mount Sinai on the third day (Exod. 19:10-16). The third day is represented as one of crucial decision-making (1 Kgs. 12:12; Est. 4:16; 5:1), of healing and sacrifice (Lev. 7:17-18, 19:6-7; Num. 19:12, 19-20). It was also the day of Hezekiah's recovery (2 Kgs. 20:8) and Jonah's deliverance (Jonah 1:17).

Furthermore, Jesus repeatedly emphasises his resurrection on the third day: 'The Son of Man ... will be raised on the third day' (Matt. 17:22-23; cf. Matt. 12:40; Mark 8:31; 10:34; John 2:19-22). In particular it is documented as part of his post-resurrection teaching of the disciples that 'the Christ should suffer and on the third day rise from the dead' (Luke 24:46; cf. also Luke 24:21, 27). 'If this passage from Hosea is indeed what underlies this teaching, then a prediction which ostensibly concerned the restoration of *Israel* has now been applied by Jesus to his *own* resurrection' (Walker 2000:107). As a feature of the essential continuity between the LORD's dealings with Israel and with the One who identified with Israel and came as their sinbearer, the ultimate horizon of the passage is then indeed the individual resurrection of all those who are in Christ and so incorporated into the new Israel of the people of God.

6:3 'And let us know—let us press on to know the LORD.
As certain as the dawn ⌞is⌟ his going forth,
and he will come like rain for us—
like spring rain ⌞which⌟ waters the earth.'

And let us know introduces an exhortation which follows logically from the preceding expression of hope. 'Know' is used in its Hoseanic sense of faithfully acknowledging the covenant King (cf. 4:1; Jer. 31:34). Perhaps it echoes and reverses the condition described in 5:4.

Press on indicates an enthusiastic and unremitting 'pursuit' of the LORD, as well as an admission that the goal has not yet been adequately attained and requires resolution and effort for success. This is in contrast to their previous pursuit of the Baals (2:7), and it is not a matter of mere survival, but of spiritual fellowship and harmony, which is achieved collectively on the basis of individual repentance and restoration.

They are assured that they will be successful in such endeavours because the character of the LORD is constant. ***His going forth*** employs a term which describes the rising of the sun (Ps. 19:6), and it points to something as being as regular and certain as the coming of ***the dawn*** (cf. Isa. 58:8; Mal. 4:2). Here it reflects the LORD's intervention in the flow of history as he imposes his will upon the affairs of earth. His coming brings benefits in its train. ***Rain*** is a general term for rain, and the metaphor combines the ideas of regularity and refreshment (cf. Deut. 32:2).[60] It is the latter idea which is especially brought out by ***like spring rain***, falling in March and April, which matures the crops and ensures a bountiful harvest (cf. Joel 2:23). The desirability of rain possibly reflects on the drought that the land was experiencing (2:12; 4:3), and the use of such natural and agricultural phenomena is a virtual rejection of the outlook of the Canaanite cult. Enjoyment of blessing is the outcome when there is true submission to the sole covenant King.

REFLECTION

- One reason why the people of the north disregarded Hosea's message and did not make immediate use of the model prayer he set before them was their confidence that they could cope on their own by developing strategies which would relieve their distress (5:13). Another aspect of their refusal was that they did not consider that the call to 'return' (6:1) applied to them, for they did not acknowledge that they had really departed from the LORD. They had forgotten what was involved in a right relationship with God, and in their spiritual blindness they were insensitive to the fact that they had

60. Though the NIV renders the first occurrence of *gešem* as 'winter rains', *yôreh* is the specific term for that and it is less likely that the structure is 'winter rains ... spring rains' than that the parallelism is that of a general term followed by a specific instance of the general phenomenon. The form *yôreh*, 'which waters', that occurs here is to be understood not as the noun 'winter rains' (so NKJV) but as a hiphil imperfect of the root *yrh*, probably a northern byform of *rāwâ*, 'to drink one's fill, to be saturated' (cf. 10:12).

slipped so far away from God and could not see that there was any need for them to repent and return. It is only through the divine endowment of true wisdom that the rod of his chastisement and who has appointed it are truly perceived (cf. Mic. 6:9). Then awareness of separation from God impels to true repentance (cf. 1 Kgs. 8:47; Jer. 31:19; Ezek. 18:28; Luke 15:17).

- When the people become aware of their need, their desire for a true relationship with the LORD is expressed in terms of knowing him (6:3). This goes beyond acquaintance with his character and purposes as set out in Scripture to include an unreserved and trusting response to that information. With godly zeal they resolve not to give up in their pursuit of the goal they have set before themselves of actualisation of the covenant relationship (cf. Jer. 31:34). It is now clear that this intimacy with God cannot be achieved apart from Jesus Christ. 'This is eternal life, that they know you the only true God, and Jesus Christ whom you have sent' (John 17:3; cf. Eph. 3:19). This statement embodies a significant link between the full Scriptural implications of 'know' and the enjoyment of the life of the new creation. While at present this knowledge is partial, it will be complete in heaven when all that is procured through the resurrection of Christ is fully and permanently realised (cf. Isa. 11:9; 1 Cor. 13:12; 1 John 3:2).

III. The Forgetful People

(6:4–11:11)

OUTLINE

A. The Problem Faced by the LORD (6:4-6)

B. Domestic Transgression (6:7–7:7)

1. Treachery and Outrage (6:7-11a)
2. Restoration Stymied (6:11b–7:2)
3. The Heated Oven (7:3-7)

C. External Problems (7:8-16)

1. The Half-Baked Loaf (7:8)
2. Grey Hairs (7:9-10)
3. The Naive Dove (7:11-13)
4. The Defective Bow (7:14-17)

D. Reaping the Whirlwind (8:1-14)

1. The Broken Covenant (8:1-3)
2. Spurious Leadership (8:4a)
3. The Bull-Calf of Samaria (8:4b-6)
4. Ungodly Alliances (8:7-10)
5. Illicit Worship (8:11-13)
6. The Divine Verdict (8:14)

E. Days of Reckoning, not Rejoicing (9:1-9)

1. Abandoned Festivals (9:1-6)
2. Prophetic Misdirection (9:7-9)

F. Failed Prospects (9:10–10:15)

1. Grapes in the Wilderness (9:10-17)
2. A Luxuriant Vine (10:1-8)
3. A Trained Heifer (10:9-15)

G. Restoration (11:1-11)

1. A Father Remembers (11:1-4)
2. The Punishment Imposed (11:5-7)
3. Divine Reluctance (11:8-9)
4. Restoration Envisaged (11:10-11)

While the insertion of a major thematic heading at this point may be challenged as unduly disruptive of the flow of the prophet's material, if 6:1-3 has been correctly identified as essentially positive in tone, then there is a step back to the harsh reality of the spiritual inconstancy and blindness which existed in the land throughout Hosea's ministry. This division of the book is bracketed by the questions of 6:4 and 11:8 where the LORD expresses astonishment at the people's fickle superficiality and outright intransigence.

Moreover the division possesses the structure which is a recognisable feature of the way the prophet ordered his material by progressing from exposure of misconduct through announcement of impending punishment to a concluding glimpse of divinely bestowed relief and blessing (see *Introduction*, pg. 25). As Hosea grappled with the task of convincing the nation of how far they had strayed, his main theme was undoubtedly their aberrant conduct and its consequences. After their shallow responses have been highlighted in 6:4-6, there is extensive examination of how this had given rise to misjudgement and mismanagement in the internal affairs of the land (6:7–7:7) and in its external dealings (7:8-16). In both 8:1-14 and 9:1-9 the nation's woes are portrayed as stemming from violation of the covenant, which inevitably incurs condemnation and brings catastrophe. Since Israel had repeatedly failed to live up to the privileges bestowed by God, they could not expect anything other than sweeping disaster (9:10–10:15). The only possible alternative scenario was that the LORD would intervene in grace. As the Father of the people whom he had called to himself, he would not permit judgement to have the last word on their national existence. However, it is only after imposing on them the penalties associated with breach of covenant that he would provide relief for them despite their rebellion (11:1-11).

This analysis of the LORD's dealings with the northern kingdom is a case study in his interaction with those who in any generation despise his word and his goodness. As well as yielding insights into the events of that particular historical epoch, it reveals fundamental spiritual principles of God's dealings with anyone who fails to appreciate 'the riches of his kindness and restraint and patience, not realising that God's kindness is leading you to repentance' (Rom. 2:4). Since God does not change, and since our attitude towards him is still warped by our fallen nature and sinful reactions, there are lessons here of ongoing relevance. Supremely there is the wonder of God's love shining upon a canvass of such human folly, ingratitude and perversity.

A. The Problem Faced by the LORD (6:4-6)

This section is a link passage in that it follows on from the preceding exhortation to prayerful repentance (6:1-3). Significantly, there is no record that the people at that time acted on the basis of the prophet's recommendation. Instead, it is clear that whatever good resolutions Ephraim or Judah made were superficial and transient. So rather than moving on to chart the LORD's gracious response to the remorseful and penitent, the prophet has to return once again to his task of piercing the spiritual complacency of his contemporaries. He relays the LORD's disappointment that they were incapable of keeping their promises (6:4) despite prophetic warnings about the outcome and despite divine imposition of judgement (6:5). Even under Hosea's ministry the people refused to see past a religion focused on outward appearance and ritual performance, and so fell short of yielding heart allegiance to the LORD (6:6).

6:4 What am I to do with you, Ephraim?
What am I to do with you, Judah?
Your steadfast love ⌞is⌟ like a morning cloud,
and like the dew ⌞which⌟ goes away early.

There is an unmarked transition from the speech of the people in the previous verse to the LORD's address to them, a transition similar to those found elsewhere (e.g. 1:10; 3:1; 4:1). Hosea does not spell out how the people responded to his exhortation (6:1-3), but the context implies that at most they agreed that what he had said sounded fine, but showed themselves incapable of following through on the urgent exhortations they had received.[1] Consequently the LORD's rejoinder highlights the perversity of their lack of response to his urgent message. He asks rhetorical questions (cf. 8:5), which are not designed to elicit information as if the speaker is unaware of the answer which should be supplied, but which are rather a device for forceful presentation of a point of view. So the translation of the verbs requires more than a simple future, 'What will I do with you?', which might convey the notion that God was at a loss to know how to act next in respect of

---

1. 'Hosea called Yahweh's bride. Between verses 3 and 4, the second proposition of the syllogism is not stated. "Israel would not listen; she would not return; she would not acknowledge her husband, the covenant Lord." The response to this negative reaction came from the loving, yet pained and grieving husband but was actually spoken by the mediatorial prophetic spokesman' (Van Groningen 2003:59).

their conduct. Rather the repeated question, ***What am I to do with you?***, is intended to convey to them how far God had gone in his forbearance with their obstinacy and to alert them to the dire situation in which they had placed themselves. This emotionally charged interrogation anticipates a passage such as 11:8-9 where God again poses questions, though there addressed to himself, as to what he should do next with the two rebellious nations. Neither ***Ephraim*** in the north nor ***Judah*** (cf. 1:7) in the south had exhibited any real understanding of their predicament. There had been no repentance, no return to the LORD, despite his patience in dealing with them.

Your is a plural form, covering both Ephraim and Judah. ***Steadfast love*** (*ḥesed*, cf. 4:1) entails a demonstration in outward act of the inward hold the covenant has taken of the hearts. However, the conduct of the people lacked the essential quality of being steadfast because they lacked true love towards the LORD himself. There may have been fitful protestations of good intentions, but they were not grounded in revised inner allegiance to the LORD which would be evidenced by consistent action as they worshipped him, and also by consistent conduct towards fellow members of the covenant community. Their solemn words of commitment ('All that the LORD has spoken we will do and will be obedient', Exod. 24:7) vanished like an early ***morning cloud*** once the heat of the day intensified (cf. 13:3). ***Like the dew ⌞which⌟ goes away early***[2] refers to a feature of the Mediterranean coast whereby in summertime moisture to sustain vegetation largely depends on night dew brought in by on-coast winds. The comparison with 'dew' initiates a mini-theme in the prophecy which is developed further in 13:3 and 14:5. Here this nature-based imagery is applied to the transitory response of the two kingdoms, north and south. To qualify as genuine, loyalty must continue; it must not vanish as quickly as they saw the dew depart once the sun came up.

6:5 On account of this I have hewn ⌞them⌟ by the prophets,
I have slain them by the words of my mouth,
and your judgements ⌞are⌟ light ⌞which⌟ goes forth.

---

2. The precise thought in *wəkaṭṭal maškîm hōlēk*, 'and like the dew, doing early, going', is difficult. The participles are without the article and there is no conjunction joining them. They may be taken as constituting one composite thought, 'like the dew which early goes' (REB, NRSV, ESV), or one may be acting adjectivally 'your steadfast love ... like the early dew going away' (NIV, NKJV, HCSB), though the absence of the article with the first participle makes such an attributive use unlikely.

The LORD switches from speaking to the people to speaking about them—an acceptable feature of Hebrew style (cf. 5:13). He testifies to the repeated warnings he had given to the people. ***On account of this*** (cf. 4:3), that is, their shallow commitment and outright disobedience, the LORD had been unable to bless them as he would have wished, and had instead to remonstrate with the people regarding their infidelity. ***The prophets*** were the instruments the LORD used to warn about the judgement that would come on those who defaulted on their covenant commitments (cf. 12:10, 13). 'Yet the LORD warned Israel and Judah by every prophet and every seer ... but they would not listen' (2 Kgs. 17:13-14; cf. Amos 2:12).

It was more than verbal warnings that were issued. The gravity of their repeated misconduct required the imposition of punishment on the nation to impress on them how flagrantly they had transgressed and to induce them to repent. ***Hewn*** is a verb used of cutting wood with an axe (cf. Isa. 10:15) or of digging out cisterns in rock (cf. Isa. 5:2). The prophet's message was effectively ***the words of my mouth***: he relayed what God had revealed to him. Announcement of the word which expressed the verdict of the sovereign and all-powerful God both foretold what would happen and began the process of implementing the sentence on their misconduct. ***I have slain them*** points to the bitter outcome of their intransigence in the face of prophetic warnings.

In ***your judgements*** the pronoun is singular, considering the people as one, and the reference is to each occasion on which the LORD had announced his verdict against them (cf. 'the judgements on you', NASB). Alternatively, the Hebrew consonants may be redivided so that the last letter of the first word is read at the beginning of the second word. After adjusting the vowels, this yields 'My judgement like light will go forth' (cf. NIV, NRSV, ESV, HCSB), and agrees with how the early translations (LXX, Peshitta and Targum) understood the line.[3] 'Light' is then taken as a reference to 'lightning' (cf. Job 36:32; 37:11) or perhaps to the sunrise to cohere with the reference to judgement. Both readings of the text emphasise that God has acted in unmistakeable fashion against them. ***Goes forth*** echoes the language of 6:3, but with the twist that the ***light*** is not a word of covenant blessing (cf. Ps.

3. The change assumes that the *kaph* in *ûmišpāṭêkā ʾôr*, 'and your judgements light', has been misidentified in the consonantal text as the pronominal suffix and should instead be taken as the inseparable preposition placed before the following word, *ûmišpāṭî kāʾôr*, 'and my judgement like light'.

97:11) which proceeds from the LORD; instead it is his searching, clear and inescapable verdict on their conduct.

6:6 For ⌞it is⌟ steadfast love I desire and not sacrifice,
and knowledge of God rather than burnt offerings.

For picks up the theme of 6:4, and shows why God's judgement, though severe, was not without reason. What had been consistently lacking in the people's disposition was the basic heart orientation of ***steadfast love*** (*ḥesed*, cf. 6:4) which God ***desires***/'finds acceptable'. ***Not sacrifice*** is not intended as an absolute disparagement of the Old Testament sacrificial system: Hosea undoubtedly recognised the divine mandate for it.[4] Moreover both lines of the verse show clearly that sacrificial worship to the LORD was being practised in both kingdoms. So the verse is not about worship of pagan deities, but about how to approach the one true God in a manner acceptable to him.

However, the LORD had never intended that sacrifice would be a ritual which would exist on its own, because that would lead to its being viewed as a means of manipulating God, something closer to pagan ideology and tantamount to magic. For sacrifice to the LORD to be meaningful it had to be accompanied by, and expressive of, right heart attitudes. Such inner loyalty would be displayed not in perfunctory ritual performances, but primarily in obedience to God's commands (cf. 1 Sam. 15:22-23). Only on that basis would they be able to offer sacrifice in the sanctuary in a manner which would be acceptable in the highest and only proper sense (cf. Ps. 51:17; Isa. 1:11; Mal. 1:10). So, what is declared here is that their sacrifices and the performance of religious rituals could not make up for an absence of genuine attachment to God.

Knowledge of God resumes a theme which occurs frequently in Hosea. Along with 'steadfast love' its absence has already formed the substance of the divine complaint in 4:1, and achievement of it was the goal of the prophetic proposal in 6:3. ***Rather than*** is a privative use of the preposition 'from'. Again it is important to realise that the idiom expresses relative worth in God's sight, and does not dismiss the less

---

4. Though Macintosh (1997:234) continues the earlier critical assessment that 'Hosea repudiates radically the whole sacrificial cult with its licentious feasting', this results from an overly literal reading of the text and from assuming that there was tension between prophets and priests in this regard. It is spiritually empty sacrifice, not the institution itself, which the prophets critique.

favoured item as having no worth at all (cf. Luke 14:26).[5] ***Burnt offerings*** had been instituted as the basic form of sacrifice (Lev. 1), but they had to be offered in a context of covenant loyalty. No matter how careful the people adhered to the prescribed rituals, their worship could be authentic only if they gave priority to acknowledging the LORD's sovereign rights by obedience in every aspect of their lives.

REFLECTION

- The divine questions of 6:4 (and also of 11:8) are not to be misconstrued as expressions of surprise at unanticipated human conduct or of bafflement at what God should do next. God knows both how mankind will behave and also how he himself will rule and overrule in the affairs of earth so that he can truly say, 'My counsel will stand, and I will do all my purpose' (Isa. 46:10; cf. Ps. 33:11; Prov. 19:21). But it is not to be supposed that his government of mankind is harsh and insensitive, or that he is unconcerned about the outcome of our actions. These questions are rhetorical devices to convey a sense of his compassionate concern at the extent of the folly of the spiritually recalcitrant. By bestowing blessing on them God has exposed them to his inducements to right conduct; by issuing warnings he has informed them of the outcome if they persist in their obstinate rebellion. In sorrow at their blindness God pleads with them to view matters as he sees them, and such entreaty is continued when the gospel is presented by those who 'are ambassadors for Christ, as though God is making his appeal through us. We implore you on behalf of Christ: Be reconciled to God' (2 Cor. 5:20).
- 'A morning cloud' and 'the dew' (6:4) vividly capture the transience of much religious experience. Being swayed by an emotional appeal augurs well for the future, but in itself it cannot be enough. A genuine commitment to God must capture the heart to avoid a superficial, short-lived response. 'I go, sir' is of little worth if the outcome proves to be 'but he did not go' (Matt. 21:30). Indeed, guilt is increased by a good resolution which is not followed through. What may have been a sin of ignorance becomes a sin of culpable

5. 'In Hos. 6.6, the difference between the two members of the sentence is a difference in form but not in reality. The meaning is not that when mercy comes under consideration, God absolutely rejects all sacrifice ("mercy and not sacrifice"), whilst, when it is a matter of knowledge of Himself, He has only a relative preference, which does not absolutely reject the sacrifice ("knowledge of God more than burnt offerings"). There is here simply an idiomatic variation of the same thought in both clauses' (Vos 1975:269).

ignorance. Moreover repeated professions of obedience followed by repeated failure to act increase spiritual hardness and unfruitfulness (cf. Mark 4:13-20).

- Jesus twice cites 'I desire mercy and not sacrifice' (reflecting the Septuagint translation of 6:6) to establish the ethos of his kingdom in which true inner concern for others takes precedence over merely formal expression of devotion. In Matthew 9:13 his focus is on the love of God reaching out to those who need forgiveness. As the divine physician Jesus approaches those who are morally sick to cure them, whereas the Pharisees are hidebound by their ideas of propriety and religious decorum and so are incapacitated from taking the action which is so greatly needed. In Matthew 12:7 he uses it to condemn the Pharisees' rigid insistence on their version of the Sabbath law over against the humanitarian needs of those who are hungry. This was not to denigrate the Sabbath, for 'the Son of Man is lord of the Sabbath' (Matt. 12:8), but to emphasise the need for appropriate priorities springing from loving concern for others. The lesson to be learned still applies when a Christian community uses its traditions to block interaction with others and to ignore their needs. A spiritual heritage must be used correctly, for, if it is not improved on, greater condemnation follows.

B. Domestic Transgression (6:7–7:7)

(1) Treachery and Outrage (6:7-11a)

This section follows on closely from what precedes. The basic theme of the LORD's speech is that the behaviour of the people is at variance with what he desires (6:6). Apart from the concluding words of 6:11a, the focus is on the internal state of the northern kingdom. A catalogue of the people's sin, both in general (6:7) and with specific supporting evidence (6:8-9), is followed by a comprehensive condemnation of them for the heinousness of their conduct (6:10). There is then a brief extension of what has been said to show that the warnings apply to Judah also (6:11a).

6:7 But they ⌞are the ones who⌟ like Adam have transgressed a covenant;
there they acted treacherously against me.

The subject of the verse is left unspecified as ***they***, but the place-names in 6:8-9 indicate that it is primarily the citizens of the northern kingdom who are in view. ***But*** indicates that their behaviour has been contrary to what pleases God since, instead of complying with the structures and obligations of the covenant, they have ridden roughshod over them and so ***have transgressed a covenant*** (cf. 8:1). The verb conveys the idea of moving beyond a limit or overstepping a boundary, and the past tense shows that there had already occurred.

The phrase ***like Adam*** has provided an ongoing source of difficulty for interpreters. The Septuagint understood 'Adam' as a common noun meaning 'man', and translated 'But they are like a man transgressing a covenant' (cf. also AV). However, this fails to do justice to the fact that 'transgressed' is a plural verb form.

A perceived problem with the long-standing interpretation that the comparison is with Adam's rebellion in Genesis 3 is the absence elsewhere in the Old Testament of an explicit reference to a covenant between God and Adam. Furthermore, in the light of ***there*** in the second line of the verse, and of the place names mentioned in succeeding verses (Gilead, 6:8; Shechem, 6:9), the preferred option among recent commentators has been to emend the text to read 'at Adam' (cf. NRSV, TNIV), which is identified as the place in the Jordan Valley mentioned in Joshua 3:16, possibly near the confluence of the Jabbok and the Jordan.[6] Such a situation in the territory of Gilead would fit in with the reference in the following verse.

But, while it is often asserted that 'there' requires a place to be designated in the context, it is also possible that the word may function in poetry as an exclamatory particle equivalent to 'Look!' (cf. Pss. 14:5; 36:13; 48:7; 66:5; Zeph. 1:14). In that case, the need to identify a location in 'like Adam' is weakened. Instead, the reference would be to the state of those who have violated the covenant. Also, a specific offence, most probably one by the nation as a whole in defiance of the requirements of the covenant, committed at Adam remains conjectural.

The analogy with the fall is appropriate because of the extent and gravity of the rebellion and offence of the northern kingdom. Israel had quite lapsed from the obligations imposed on them by the Mosaic covenant, and had jeopardised their whole relationship with God.

The ***covenant*** mentioned here is unlikely to have been a treaty between Israel and a foreign nation. Even though Israel would have affirmed its commitment to such a treaty by using the name of the LORD, it would hardly have been 'treachery' in Hosea's eyes to have

---

6. The REB reads 'at Admah', which was one of the cities of the plain (also mentioned in 11:8), but it was not an Israelite settlement. As well as reading the preposition *bə* rather than *kə*, this approach requires a further emendation of the text.

broken a foreign alliance which he would have condemned in the first instance. What is in view is a covenant between the LORD and his people, something which is spelled out more clearly in 8:1. This primarily corresponds to the arrangements instituted at Sinai under Moses. Possibly ***transgressed a covenant*** points to offences which violated the terms of the covenant, but which did not utterly nullify it in the sense that there is still held out the possibility of amendment of their ways. ***Acted treacherously*** is the same verb as is used in 5:7, and it may well allude to some recent specific breach of covenant faithfulness during the political upheavals which wracked the land at this time.

6:8 Gilead ⌞is⌟ a city of those who work wickedness,
deceitful because of bloodshed.

Gilead was the territory of the tribes of Reuben and Gad, a highland region on the east bank of the Jordan, lying between the river Yarmuk to the north and the city of Heshbon to the south. Since Gilead was not the name of ***a city***, the reference may be to Ramoth-Gilead, the principal town of the area (cf. Josh. 20:8; Judg. 10:17; 12:7). Its population is described in general terms as ***those who work wickedness***, a participial expression indicating that they characteristically engage in wrongdoing, which is then more specifically identified as involving ***bloodshed***, that is, murder. ***Deceitful***, which qualifies 'city', comes from a root which signifies 'to catch by the heel', and Hosea uses it of Jacob's behaviour (12:3). Here it may be employed metaphorically of uneven ground which catches the traveller's foot and trips him. Alternatively, the phrase may have conjured up a picture of rough ground through which tracks can be identified because there are footsteps stained with blood.[7] We do not know what assassination or murder had been perpetrated by the Gileadites, but it is clear that Hosea is pointing to some recent event. Perhaps the background to these words is to be found in Pekah's coup against Pekahiah where mention is made of fifty men from Gilead (2 Kgs. 15:25; cf. Mays 1969:101).

6:9 And as one from robber gangs would lie in wait,
⌞so do⌟ a band of priests;
they murder on the way to Shechem,
for they commit outrage.

Again in this verse no information has come down to us as to what incident Hosea had in mind, but even so there is no doubt that what is

7. This approach redivides *ʿăqubbâ middām*, 'deceitful because of blood', as *ʿiqqəbêhem dām*, 'their footprints of blood'.

being described is a land, wracked by turmoil and treachery, on the verge of inner collapse. ***Shechem***, which lay between Samaria and Bethel, had an distinguished past. It had been the place of assembly for Joshua's ceremony of covenant renewal (Josh. 24), and had even earlier patriarchal associations (Gen. 12:6-7; 33:18-20). It was also a traditional Levitical city and a place of refuge (Josh. 21:20-21), and had been the site of a major convocation at the division of the kingdom (1 Kgs. 12:1). However, it is not Shechem itself that is the focus of Hosea's condemnation. ***On the way to Shechem*** is expressed somewhat unusually, possibly 'at the roadside, to Shechem', but that does not make clear the direction of travel or the business of those attacked.[8]

The comparison with ***one from robber gangs*** portrays an individual waiting to ambush a hapless traveller.[9] But the actual banditry is carried out by ***a band of priests.*** Probably this does not allude to their activities at a sanctuary, but to a specific plot to assassinate someone who was travelling ***to Shechem***. However, the verb 'murder' is intensive and characteristic. Perhaps the priests were in favour of one party in the internecine warfare in the land and acted surreptitiously to waylay and assassinate those who opposed their viewpoint.

Outrage is a strong term for shameless sexual misconduct, generally with overtones of deliberately planned acts. Certainly this is so with the phrase 'to commit/do outrage' (Judg. 20:6; Ezek. 16:43; 22:9; 23:48; cf. Lev. 18:17; 19:29; 20:14). In this passage, however, we do not know the precise nature of the crime in view. Even if it were a religious crime, it need not have been to do with idolatry. But it was certainly one whose nature occasioned divine revulsion. ***Commit*** is a perfect form and may indicate a past action, whereas ***murder*** is an imperfect form, indicating that such behaviour is still occurring. Possibly the verbs do not refer to quite the same thing.

6:10 In the house of Israel I have seen something horrible:
there Ephraim's whoredom ⌊is⌋;
Israel has become unclean.
6:11a Judah also—he has set a harvest for you.

---

8. This translation follows that of the Massoretic accents. It is also possible to take *derek* as an accusative of respect with the preceding line, '⌊so do⌋ a band of priests at the roadside; they murder to Shechem.' The meaning is not significantly different.

9. Translations such as 'As marauders lie in ambush for a man' (NIV) are less probable in that the subject of an infinitive construct (written with final *yodh* rather than the expected *he*) is not usually separated from it. It is more likely that 'one/a man of robber gangs' is a construct chain.

The first person pronouns of 6:4-7 clearly indicated divine speech, and that is also true of 6:11b. It is therefore probable that only 6:11a is prophetic speech, as indicated by the third person reference to the LORD, and that in 6:10 ***I have seen*** stresses that the LORD himself (not the prophet) has been aware of what has been going on in the land (cf. 5:3). Three entities are mentioned. ***The house of Israel*** may well refer to the northern kingdom as a whole (cf. 5:1) since the next line refers to ***there***/'in that place'. ***Ephraim*** would then be the territory to the west of the Jordan, which had been controlled by Pekahiah, whereas ***Israel***, if it refers to a separate entity and is not a parallel reference to Ephraim, would be the land to the east of the Jordan under the control of Pekah (cf. 5:5).

Wherever he looks, the LORD's verdict on what he perceives is that there is ***something horrible*** (cf. Jer. 18:13), causing disgust and revulsion.[10] This probably refers to the shrines at Dan and Bethel (cf. 8:5). ***Whoredom***, referring to the religious infidelity of the land (cf. 4:11), is located specifically (***there***, or else 'look!', cf. 6:7) in the central tribe of Ephraim, but from there contamination had spread throughout the kingdom. ***Has become unclean*** (cf. 5:3) does not just point to ceremonial defilement, but to moral pollution. The moral degeneration of a nation which repudiated the covenant had excluded Israel from its benefits, and they could therefore only expect divine punishment.

The first part of 6:11 is often taken as a addition made by redactors in Judah as they attempted to apply the prophet's message to their own later circumstances (cf. 1:7). However, such an assessment mainly commends itself to those with a prior commitment to the text having a long and involved redactional history. There is no compelling reason to depart from the assumption that Hosea even as a northern prophet was concerned about the situation in the south as well as in his own land. ***Judah also*** (cf. 5:5) indicates Hosea's additional comment that there too the covenant was being violated. ***Set a harvest*** uses potentially ambiguous imagery because 'harvest' has many positive associations (cf. Deut. 28:4; 30:9; Ps. 4:7; Isa. 9:3), but here it points to a time of impending judgement (cf. Isa. 18:5; Jer. 51:33; Joel 3:13; Amos 8:2) which will affect south and north alike. There is no doubt about the ***he*** who is responsible for ordaining this arrangement.[11]

---

10. The kethib *šaʿărîrîyâ* and the qere *šaʿărûrîyâ* are spelling variants.

11. The words may also be understood as an instance of an impersonal construction, 'one has set', which is equivalent to a passive (GKC §144d). Even so, this would be an oblique reference to divine action.

REFLECTION

- The covenants of the ancient world formalised solemn pledges which were instituted to regulate in perpetuity relationships between the parties to the covenant. So God's covenantal arrangements are designed to be 'everlasting' (cf. Gen. 9:16; 17:7; Isa. 24:5; 55:3; Jer. 32:40). If it is true that 'even with a man-made covenant, once it has been ratified, no one annuls it or adds to it' (Gal. 3:15), how much more heinous is the conduct of those who breach commitments which they have undertaken not only before God but with him. 'Treachery' (cf. 6:7) intensifies their offence by implying that they deceitfully keep up a pretence of faithfulness while secretly violating the terms of the agreement.
- The misconduct of the priests on the road to Shechem (6:9) is sadly but one instance of many where those who have held office and taught in the church of God have subsequently acted contrary to the teaching they claimed to espouse and have thereby inflicted great damage on the cause they once promoted. Judas is the pre-eminent example of one who was numbered among the Twelve and enjoyed personal, familiar contact with the Lord himself—and yet betrayed the Lord (cf. Acts 1:16-17). Those who are in positions of authority are especially vulnerable to temptation. 'Let anyone who thinks that he stands take heed lest he fall' (1 Cor. 10:12; cf. Gal. 6:1).

(2) Restoration Stymied (6:11b–7:2)

Although it is possible to understand this section as making general observations regarding how the spiritual insensitivity and perversity of Israel kept them from enjoying the full blessing that the LORD would bestow on them, it does seem that in the first instance the passage reflects a specific stage in the LORD's attempts to draw the people back to himself. At the beginning of the eighth century B.C. Israel suffered a period of intense external pressure, particularly from the Arameans of Damascus to their immediate north, but the situation was turned round in the reign of Jeroboam II when the land enjoyed a period of prosperity and territorial expansion (cf. *Introduction*, pg. 11). Despite the fact that Jeroboam continued to do evil in the sight of the LORD, this time of blessing was no chance occurrence, but took place 'according to the word of the LORD, the God of Israel, which he spoke through his servant Jonah, son of Amittai, the prophet, who was from Gath-Hepher. For the LORD had seen the suffering of Israel, ⌊that it was⌋ very bitter, with neither bond nor free left, and there was no helper for Israel. But the LORD had not said that he would blot out the name of Israel from under the heavens, and so he saved them through Jeroboam, son of Joash' (2 Kgs. 14:25-27). Relief from oppression and prosperity was designed to induce to Israel to amend their ways through gratitude, but they failed to respond to the challenge. Instead, enjoyment of favourable material circumstances only served to expose how deep seated their sin and perversity had become.

6:11b When I would restore the fortunes of my people,
7:1 when I would heal Israel,
then the iniquity of Ephraim kept being revealed
even the evil acts of Samaria,
for they have practised deceit,
and a thief enters in,
a gang has plundered in the street.

It is generally agreed that the last part of 6:11 should be linked with what follows.[12] The first two lines set out the divine programme for the period. God desired to see Israel prosper spiritually and, having tried to bring them to their senses through adversity, he next provided a period of relief and prosperity to induce them to turn to him in gratitude. Although the phrase ***restore the fortunes*** may point to a return from captivity (e.g. Jer. 29:14), it is a broader term than that (cf. Job 42:10; *NIDOTTE* 4:58-59) and is a common prophetic expression for national renewal in general (cf. Jer. 33:11; Joel 3:1; Amos 9:14). The Hebrew construction with ***when*** and an infinitive does not specify if this restoration is past, present or future; that is determined by the following finite verb which indicates that this sequence had occurred a number of times.[13] The LORD had acted out of loving concern for the good of ***my people***, a positive description of them as his partners in the bond of the covenant (cf. 2:23). ***Heal*** looks back to the descriptions of 5:13 and 6:1, and portrays the LORD as intending to do more than initiate an

12. This follows the lead of the LXX which linked the last line of 6:11 and the first line of 7:1, though it read both in conjunction with the first part of 6:11.

13. It is not uncommon for a temporal expression involving *kə* and an infinitive to be followed by *waw* of apodosis indicating the accompanying event (cf. GKC §164g). What is at first surprising here is that *wəniglâ* is a perfect form which might suggest the translation ought to be 'then it will be revealed'. However, the imperfect *yōʾmərû* in 7:2 may be taken in a frequentative sense, and that is probable for the perfect here also (cf. GKC §112e).

upturn in their economic and political situation. This restoration was also to be spiritual, but for that to come into effect there had to be genuine repentance on their part (14:4).

However, the improvement in the external circumstances of the north did not have the desired impact (cf. 12:7-8). Security and affluence only served to ***reveal*** (cf. 6:10) the underlying problem by exposing ***the iniquity of Ephraim.*** 'Iniquity' (*'āwōn*) points to corrupt deviance from the set standards of the Mosaic covenant (cf. 4:8; 5:5; 8:13; 9:7, 9; 12:8; 13:12; 14:1-2), whether the wrongful act itself, the guilt incurred in committing it, or even the punishment imposed as a consequence. The present parallelism with ***the evil acts of Samaria***, the capital, suggests that it is principally wrongful deeds which are in view here. From passages such as Amos 5:10-12 and 8:4-6 it is clear that the wealth which flowed into the land was concentrated in the hands of a few who abused their position and riches to exploit their fellow countrymen and gain even greater control and wealth.

For introduces the evidence the LORD adduces to substantiate his allegations. ***They have practised deceit*** in the past and at present. 'Deceit' covers uttering lies (Prov. 17:4), giving false testimony under oath (Exod. 20:16), and breach of faith in general (Ps. 7:14). It describes a dysfunctional society where an individual's commitment cannot be relied on. The land was permeated by attempts at self-advancement without regard to the interests or suffering of others. Truth, if inconvenient, was simply ignored. In particular, the grasping attitudes of Ephraim are disclosed by the prevalence of theft. Mention of ***a thief*** implies a high crime rate in general. It may link back to the robbery of 6:9, and be associated with the priests in particular, but given the degeneracy of the times there is unlikely to be any specific connection. ***Enters in*** points to an action which takes place repeatedly over a period of time. ***A gang*** is the singular form of the word rendered 'robbers' in 6:9, but again there is no need to assume anything more than a land where law and order has broken down, and people cannot find security at home or in the streets.

7:2 And they are not saying to their heart
that I remember all their evil.
Now their deeds have surrounded them;
they have come before my face.

Civil lawlessness and societal breakdown are produced by lack of spiritual awareness. ***They are not***[14] ***saying to their heart*** is a description of inward insensitivity and incomprehension. It is a reminder of the need for human beings, as moral agents, to evaluate their behaviour inwardly. As a matter of fact Hosea's contemporaries did not deny the existence of the LORD; they just ignored him when it came to ordinary living. Quite heedless of divine scrutiny of their actions and motives, they were without conscience regarding their conduct. This is practical atheism which pays no regard to the fact ***that I remember all their evil***, repeating the word found in 7:1, not now as 'evil acts' but as 'evil' viewed abstractly. Even so, 'all' emphasises the inclusiveness of God's examination; nothing escapes him. Furthermore, 'remember' involves more than a mere act of mental recall: appropriate measures will inevitably be instigated (cf. 8:13; 9:9).

Now (cf. 2:10; 5:7; 8:13; 10:2; 13:2) points to the prevailing ominous situation. Though they are unaware of what has happened, the LORD certainly is not. ***Their deeds*** (cf. 4:9), all their evil actions, are compared to an army besieging them so that they are ***surrounded*** and have no scope for manoeuvre. Furthermore their rebellious actions ***have come before my face*** (cf. Ps. 90:8). The Sovereign Judge has the evidence laid out in front of him, and he will inevitably act against them. This is what has come from their misunderstanding of the LORD's goodness and their wilful refusal to repent.

REFLECTION

• While 'to remember' may simply refer to inward recall of past events and situations (e.g. Ps. 137:8), such renewed awareness and attention is often associated with taking appropriate action. 'Remember the Sabbath day' (Exod. 20:8) is immediately clarified by 'to keep it holy' (cf. 'observe the Sabbath day', Deut. 5:12). When all the ends of the earth 'remember' the LORD, they turn to him in repentance and adoration (Ps. 22:27). If God is the subject of the verb 'to remember', the emphasis inevitably falls on divine intervention, for the omniscient One can never be unaware of events and relationships. For instance, when it is recorded that 'God remembered Noah' (Gen. 8:1), it is not implied that for a while he had been oblivious of his circumstances and needs, but that the right time had arrived for divine action (cf. Exod. 2:24). God's remembrance of his people means that blessing flows to

14. The poetic negative particle *bal* is used here to achieve assonance with *lilbābām,* 'to their hearts'.

them (Ps. 115:12; 136:23). However, the fact that God remembers sin (cf. 7:2) implies that his forbearance is exhausted and his intervention is imminent, whether by withdrawing the blessings he bestows or by imposing punishment. 'Now he will remember their iniquity and punish their sins' (Jer. 14:10), and disabuse them of the idea that he is indifferent towards their conduct. Contrariwise, for God not to remember sin is an act of gracious pardon in which, while it cannot be said that the facts are expunged from the divine record, there is no longer any threat of the corresponding penalty being imposed and divine compassion prevails (cf. Ps. 79:8-9).

(3) The Heated Oven (7:3-7)

The final verse of this section makes it fairly obvious that what is described is the political turmoil which existed in Samaria, the capital of the northern kingdom. While we do not possess sufficient information to determine precisely which incident is in view, a somewhat more coherent account can be built up than was the case with the allusions in 6:7-10. The passage talks about a *coup d'état* in which courtiers succeeded in plotting against the existing regime, but the king's identity remains a matter of conjecture. There were, after all, four royal assassinations in the closing years of the kingdom. Possibly the occasion is Hoshea's conspiracy against the rabidly anti-Assyrian Pekah in 732 B.C. (2 Kgs. 15:30; favoured by Mays 1969:104–105), but Pekah himself had succeeded Pekahiah by conspiracy, and there is the additional fact that he had been a member of Pekahiah's court, probably his adjutant or his chief military officer (2 Kgs. 15:25). A plot by an insider seems to mesh with the details of the passage. At any rate, the focus is not on the specific circumstances of any particular conspiracy. While there are obscure features in the metaphor of the baker's oven, the imagery conveys the fever pitch at which Samaria's ruling classes lived and engaged in their confused intrigues while the nation plunged from one crisis to the next. The use of 'our' in 7:5 indicates that this section is a prophetic description, possibly until the last line of 7:7 where 'me' occurs as a divine complaint against the people is cited.

7:3 By their evil they make a king glad
and by their lies leaders.

Their evil provides a thematic link with the preceding section (7:2; cf. also 'the evil acts of Samaria', 7:1), but it is not clear whether this verse continues the general indictment of the nation or whether it relates to a specific incident—and if so, whether the king spoken of is the one favoured by the plotters or the one whom they have ousted. While ***a king*** may a generalising use of the singular to take in a number of different rulers of Israel, the passage as a whole is better understood as moving from a specific figure towards a concluding general review in 7:7. The word 'king' recurs in verses 5 and 7 and (along with 'oven') links the passage together. ***Leaders***, traditionally rendered 'princes' (also in 7:5), are not necessarily members of the dynasty, but comprise the administrators of the king's court who implemented his policy and controlled the civil and military life of the country.

As well as the king and the leaders, there is a third group in the verse, indicated by ***they*** and ***their***. Had 'they' been explicitly identified, it would have considerably reduced the number of possible interpretations of the passage. Equating 'they' with the people in general supports the view that this is an initial summary verse dealing with the decline in the standards of public administration and justice in the land. However, reading the verse as part of the following story, 'they' are the unidentified conspirators. Some commentators are confident that more can be said about them. '*They, their* and *them* point uniformly to the priests who stood as the centre of the conspiracy' (Hubbard 1989:132). That, however, seems to go further than the text warrants. Though 'a king' here may be the new king who is ***made … glad*** by those whose plotting has cleared the way for his accession, a more plausible approach is to read 7:3 in the light of 7:5. This implies that the king who is made glad by evil and the leaders who are similarly deceived into being joyful are the current regime who have been lulled into a false sense of security by the deceptive tactics of the conspirators. From the evidence of 7:5 it is probable that among the royal administrators were some who were plotting against the king and who had hoodwinked their colleagues.

7:4 All of them are adulterers,
 like an oven heated by a baker;
he ceases stoking ⌞the fire⌟
 ⌞and⌟ kneading the dough until it is leavened.

While ***all of them*** might continue the general references to the people begun in 7:1-2, it is more probable that 'them' indicates the conspirators, who are denounced as ***adulterers***. Although this may point to sexual misconduct (cf. 3:1; 4:14), a metaphorical usage is more suited to this context. Perhaps surprisingly in Hosea, it is not religious deviance which is in view, but the treachery of those who pledged their loyalty to the current king while they actively plotted to overthrow the existing regime and to establish a rival on the throne. The accusation of betrayal and perfidy conveyed by the term adultery (from the root *nāʾap*) opens the way for the development of the theme of a baker (from the root *ʾāpâ*)—and in addition the two consonants involved in this wordplay are constituents of the name Ephraim (*ʾeprayim*).

Different views are taken of the significance of the simile, ***like an oven heated by a baker.***[15] Baking bread was ordinarily a woman's task, but here the term 'baker' is masculine, indicating that a professional baker is in view. Consequently the oven is not a small portable device, but a larger, permanent one, built from clay bricks in a rounded or bee-hive shape. A fire was kindled on the oven floor, and after the whole structure had become sufficiently hot, the ashes were removed, a top vent was closed over, and flat cakes of dough were placed on the base and sides of the oven to cook in the residual heat.

The point of the comparison is embodied in the closing lines of the verse. Baking bread was not a task to be undertaken on the spur of the moment. It required pre-heating the oven and also, once the leaven had been kneaded into the flour, leaving the dough to rise. It was probable that this often took place overnight; certainly it required several hours. In preparing bread therefore there came a point at which a baker ***ceases stoking*** (literally, 'rousing' or 'keeping alert') ***the fire and kneading the dough*** while he waits for the appropriate time to proceed with his task. So too the conspirators. For a while they did not appear to be doing anything untoward, but they were biding their time. Whether it was resentment or ambition which stoked their fury, their outward demeanour concealed an intense inner fire, ready to flare up when the opportunity for action arose.

7:5 On the day of our king
leaders made ⌞him⌟ ill with the glow from wine;
he stretched out his hand with scoffers.

In this verse the imagery of the baker and the oven gives way to plain speech. ***On the day of our king*** may refer to a birthday celebration, or

15. Redividing *bōʿērâ mēʾōpeh*, 'heated by a baker' (MT), yields *bōʿēr hēm ʾōpeh*, so that the thought would be 'like a blazing oven they are. A baker ceases stirring' (or being alert). The MT has a feminine participle agreeing with a masculine noun 'oven', and it is difficult to see what role a baker plays in the comparison being made.

more probably to the anniversary of his coronation. While the phrase itself might have been a standard Israelite expression for such an occasion, it is clear that use of 'our king' indicates Hosea's northern identity. On what would have been an occasion for rejoicing and festivity, especially at the royal court, the conspirators put their plans into action. ***Leaders made ⌊him⌋ ill with the glow from wine***, or possibly 'poison from wine' (NJPS). In the light of 7:3 not all the leaders were involved in the coup, but those that were made sure the king was very drunk—and presumably his entourage as well. The clause may also be rendered, 'leaders became ill with the glow from wine' (cf. Isa. 28:7-8). This would point to the conspirators anticipating the drunken nature of the celebration and using that to give them the opening needed to mount a successful coup.

The last line of the verse shows how completely off guard the hapless monarch was: ***he stretched out his hand with scoffers.*** This signifies more than becoming befuddled with wine and joining them in their drunken carousal. It is an action of drawing them into a cordial embrace: after all, were they not his courtiers celebrating his reign? The term ***scoffers***[16] is used elsewhere of those who do not recognise God and are incapable of learning (Prov. 9:8; 15:12). Here it is the prophet's commentary on the real attitude of the plotters: they despised the king and secretly mocked his person and policies.

7:6 For they approached with hearts ⌊heated⌋ like an oven in
their ambush.
All the night their baker slept;
in the morning it ⌊was⌋ burning like a flaming fire.

They approached[17] indicates that they have begun to execute their plot. Presumably their approach was to the king to assassinate him, though that is never said. What concerns Hosea is their inner attitude, ***with hearts heated like an oven***. They are consumed with intense emotion as they carry out their scheme. ***In their ambush*** points to the fact that they waylaid the king and his entourage when their reactions were dulled as a result of the banquet.

---

16. The translation of *lōṣəṣîm* as 'scoffers' identifies the word as a polel form from the root *lûṣ*, but there may have been a root *lāṣaṣ*, otherwise unattested, but with a cognate Arabic root indicating 'to act stealthily', 'to deceive' or 'to rebel' (cf. *NIDOTTE* 2:811). This yields a similar picture.

17. A literal translation reflecting the piel form *qērəbû*, 'they brought near' rather than 'they approached' would yield 'they brought near as an oven their heart in their ambush'.

All the night their baker slept possibly refers back to the heating of the oven in 7:4. The baker would be a reference to the conspirators' obsession which had been suppressed until the right moment. Another possibility is that 'their baker' refers to the ringleader of the conspiracy, who had waited till he judged it right to give the order to attack. But most translations emend the text to read 'their anger' slept.[18] ***In the morning it was burning like a flaming fire***, and so inflamed by their resolve they brought their plot to a conclusion.

7:7 All of them are hot like an oven,
and they have devoured their judges.
All their kings have fallen;
there is no one among them who is calling out to me.

All of them (cf. 7:4) probably changes the focus somewhat from the particular conspirators of preceding verses to all the leadership class in Samaria. They were similarly ***hot like an oven***, consumed with intense emotion and furiously intent on carrying out their schemes no matter who or what the opposition. As a result, ***they have devoured their judges.*** 'Judges' were not merely courtroom officials; their role included general administration of the affairs of the land (cf. 13:10). From this period, evidence of the purges of officialdom which accompanied regime change is provided by the Samaria Ostraca, a collection of 66 pen-ink inscriptions on potsherds, receipts for quality wine and fine flour received in the capital, probably as payment of taxes. One set of ostraca seem to come from Menahem's reign, and the others six or seven years later from Pekah's reign in Samaria, after Pekahiah's assassination.[19] The recipients of the texts were royal officials, and it is probably significant that there was no overlap in the names of the two groups. Scholars have speculated that there were no survivors from the regime under Menahem once Pekah had dealt with them as he had with Pekahiah. It is also interesting that some names recorded on the ostraca are compounds employing Yahweh, while others employ Baal as the theophoric element, probably reflecting the mixed nature of religious allegiances in the land.

---

18. Because *ʾōpēhem*, 'their baker', seems awkward in the context, many translations accept the reading of the Peshitta and Targum, and emend the word to *ʾaphem*, 'their anger' (NRSV, ESV) or 'their passion' (NIV). This has the advantage of providing an antecedent for *hûʾ*, 'he/it', in the last line, so that it is their anger which becomes inflamed in the morning. Still 'anger' is not quite the emotion conspirators would be expected to display.

19. See Shea (1977), or for a different assessment Kaufman (1982).

All their kings have fallen. Kings and officials alike were casualties of the intense political upheaval in the north as the nation imploded on itself. The land was left without any coordinated response to the crises into which it was plunged.

After the description of the conspiratorial conditions in the north, there is a brief emphatic conclusion. The LORD reveals why conditions in the land had degenerated to such an extent: ***there is no one among them who is calling out to me.*** This speaks of a persistent lack. 'Them' may be successive kings of the north, but the contexts suggests it is the leadership of the land which is in view. These advocates of doing things their own way had lurched from one expedient to another while avoiding the one true source of relief. ***Calling out*** implies seeking help (cf. Prov. 21:13; Isa. 58:9), and only the LORD could successfully provide that.

REFLECTION

- Scripture values highly good government in a country and presents it as a key theme for prayer (cf. 1 Tim. 2:1). When rulers do not live up to their responsibilities, the result may be dire. 'Woe to you, O land, when your king is a child and your officials feast in the morning! How blessed you are, O land, when your king is a son of noble birth and your officials feast at the proper time, for strength and not for drunkenness' (Eccl. 10:16-17). Holding high office exposes individuals to increased temptation and the opportunity to indulge their weaknesses. Scripture particularly sounds an alert regarding excessive consumption of alcohol. 'It is not for kings, O Lemuel, it is not for kings to drink wine, or for rulers to take strong drink, lest they drink and forget what has been decreed and pervert the rights of all the afflicted' (Prov. 31:4-5). But the warning is not confined to rulers. 'Wine is a mocker, strong drink a brawler, and whoever is led astray by it is not wise' (Prov. 20:1).
- When the LORD sorrowfully notes that no one calls out to him, what is in view is prayerful presentation of need, beseeching divine intervention to remedy their situation. 'Call on me in the day of trouble; I will deliver you, and you will glorify me' (Ps. 50:15). However, the people no longer recognised the sovereignty of the LORD over them or his capacity to extricate them from their difficulties. The opinion formers in Samaria were so sure of themselves and their scheming, and so used to ignoring the spiritual dimension of life, that prayer to the LORD did not figure on their agenda at all. Throughout the kingdom the pernicious influence of Baal worship had so undermined the

people's faith in the LORD and their piety that the land had become prayerless. Such practical atheism worked itself out in national anarchy and social failure.

C. External Problems (7:8-16)

In this section Hosea moves on from the internal politics of Israel to focus on the blundering and inept foreign policy of the north. He uses a series of metaphors drawn from everyday life to caricature the incompetence of the state officials, and to bring out the debilitating and disastrous impact of disloyalty to the LORD on the life of the nation. It did not take much in the way of common sense to realise that Israel's efforts at international diplomacy were doomed to failure in the face of Assyrian aggression. However, it took the insight given to Hosea as a prophet to appreciate that the true crisis facing the north was that their refusal to acknowledge the LORD deprived them of the ultimate strength and protection they so desperately required.

(1) The Half-Baked Loaf (7:8)

Hosea was adept at using familiar scenes to press home his message. Here he presents another metaphor drawn from the preparation of food. The focus is no longer on the baker's oven, but on what was produced in it. Bread which is only half-baked is unfit for consumption. So too Ephraim with its politics of compromise had lost its true identity and had become unfit for purpose, that is, for serving the LORD and bearing testimony to him among the nations.

7:8 Ephraim—among the peoples he is mixing himself;
Ephraim has become a loaf which has not been turned.

Ephraim is used to refer to the northern kingdom as a whole. The introductory 'Ephraim' is an instance of fronting for emphasis (*casus pendens*, cf. Joüon §156a) where the noun stands apart from the grammatical structure of the clause but introduces its theme (cf. 9:11, 13; 12:8; 14:8). There were two aspects to the international policy of the north. The first is brought out especially by the verb in: ***Among the peoples he is mixing himself.*** 'Mix' also occurs in passages describing the mixing of flour with oil in the preparations for sacrifice (cf. Exod. 29:2; Lev. 2:4-5; Num. 7:13; 28:5). Here it develops an idea suggested by a baker blending ingredients to prepare bread. This does not refer to the future dispersal of Ephraim among the nations when they are deported from their land, but to the outcome of their current propensity to deny that they were a people uniquely separated by the LORD to serve him (cf. Lev. 20:24, 26) and destined to dwell apart (cf. Num. 23:9). Conforming to the practices of surrounding nations and relying on alliances with them to ensure their security, Israel had deliberately abandoned their distinctive role as the people governed by the LORD, dedicated to his service, and in turn upheld and defended by him. They had rendered themselves no different from other peoples.

The repetition of ***Ephraim*** resumes the reference broken off in the previous line, and points to the second, related aspect of the situation: the nation which has thoughtlessly abandoned the LORD already ***has become*** fit only for rejection. This is portrayed by the telling metaphor of ***a loaf which has not been turned.*** A flat circular lump of dough would placed on the preheated side of the oven (cf. 7:4). If through oversight the dough was left unturned, one side would become charred and inedible, while the other would be virtually raw, uncooked. This unbalanced development does not provide a picture of something which is only partially usable; it is rather a matter of being irrecoverably unfit for use.[20]

REFLECTION

- Israel 'mixed with the nations and learned to do as they did' (Ps. 106:35), and drew down on themselves the judgement of God. It was just as great folly then as it remains today to suppose that anyone can serve two masters. Compromise between God and mammon (worldly wealth) is impossible (cf. Matt. 6:24). Israel's attempts to do so were therefore inevitably doomed, and still serve as a warning to avoid any similar clash of loyalties. Though still in the world and therefore not in a position to separate completely from the ungodly (cf. 1 Cor. 5:10), the Christian community is to maintain a holy separation and so prove that they are sons and daughters of God Almighty (cf. 1 Cor. 10:21; 2 Cor. 6:14-18). When an individual believer or a church as a body compromises in its fidelity to the revealed standards of God and seeks security and success by employing worldly strategies, the folly of half-baked Ephraim is replicated.

(2) Grey Hairs (7:9-10)

Hosea now uses a metaphor drawn from the onset of old age. He imagines someone who is unaware of the change taking place in

20. 'It may not be pushing the imagery beyond its bounds to say that Ephraim's side that was turned towards the nations was badly burnt, while the other side — the unpalatably weak commitment to Yahweh — was underdone' (Hubbard 1989:137).

himself and who consequently is unable to grow old gracefully. By continuing to behave in a way that had been possible earlier (perhaps in the days of Jeroboam II), the nation was trying to do more than it remained capable of. Overreaching itself and neglecting its God, it was doomed to fail disastrously through its lack of self awareness.

7:9 Strangers have devoured his strength,
but he himself does not know ⌞it⌟;
also grey hairs are sprinkled on him,
but he himself does not know ⌞it⌟.

The repeated remark, ***but he himself does not know it***, emphasises how completely the people had failed to grasp the decline which had occurred in their national vitality and capability. They would not acknowledge the devastating extent of their current political weakness and tried to behave as though they still had a significant influence on the international scene. ***Strangers*** who constituted the Assyrian armies had ***devoured his strength***. 'Devour'/'eat' probably does not continue the previous picture of the half-cooked bread (it was inedible), but looks back to the occurrence of the same verb in 7:7. It is not just the rulers of the land who are vanishing; the nation as a whole has been eaten away. 'Sap his strength' (NIV) conveys the sense well, but fails to alert to the connection with the use of the same verb in 7:7. With the relentless southwards advance of the Assyrians in the decade after 745 B.C., the economic resources which had been built up in the prosperous years of Jeroboam II had been ruined by invasion and dissipated by harsh demands for tribute, and large parts of their territory had been annexed (2 Kgs. 15:19-20, 29). Others could clearly perceive how this had impacted on Israel's status and strength, but the people themselves were oblivious to it.

Also indicates that the second part of the verse intensifies the image of the first. ***Grey hairs are sprinkled on him*** may refer either to mould growing on bread[21] or, more probably, since mould can easily be seen, to signs of age which are visible to others even though an individual himself remains unaware of how his hair now looks. In other contexts grey hair was viewed as venerable (cf. Lev. 19:32; Prov. 16:31; 20:29), but that does not constitute a conclusive objection to the second interpretation. Though the people were no longer what they had once been,

---

21. Evidence for an Akkadian root signifying the grey hairs of mould was suggested by Paul (1968:119–120) and has been accepted by various commentators (e.g Andersen, et al. 1980:467–468) because it continues the culinary metaphors.

they had not updated their perception of themselves. Decrepitude and even death were approaching, yet the nation was blind to their relentless encroachment.

7:10 And the pride of Israel will testify against him,
but they have not returned to the LORD their God,
and they have not sought him in all this.

Hosea had previously summarised the situation which awaited the people in the same terms: ***the pride of Israel will testify against him*** (cf. 5:5). Again 'the pride of Israel' is not the LORD, but their own conceited reliance on their own resources—economically, politically and intellectually. The outcome of their policies had already yielded clear evidence as to their inadequacy, and would continue to do so.

But despite the obvious signs of decline and divine displeasure the community had not learned the spiritual lesson. ***They have not returned to the LORD their God*** in repentance (cf. 3:5; 5:4; 6:1). The outward reversal of their fortunes had been designed to induce them to consider who they really were and where the true source of their prosperity lay. Yet, in their arrogant self-reliance, they did not think themselves in need of learning any lessons, far less returning to the LORD in humility. ***They have not sought him in all this***. Even though there had been extensive warnings given to them and increasing calamities had afflicted them, still they saw no need to turn to the only source of assistance (cf. 13:4, 9). 'To seek God' embodies a significant aspect of a positive response to his providential dealings with an individual or a nation, desiring spiritual fellowship with him and deeper knowledge of his will (cf. 3:5; 5:6, 15; 10:12).

REFLECTION

• It is folly to look in a mirror and then go away and forget what one is like (cf. James 1:24). Ephraim's conduct had degenerated one stage further—he did not even look in the mirror—and so he was in denial about the blows he had already suffered and the present weakness of his situation (cf. Prov. 23:35; Isa. 42:25; Rev. 3:17). The only remedy for such a lack of awareness is ongoing self-examination in the light of Scripture (cf. Job 13:23; Ps. 77:6; Lam. 3:40; 2 Cor. 13:5). It continues to be incumbent on the church to examine itself for 'grey hairs' lest it is unwittingly beguiled by the deceitfulness of adversaries, human or demonic, and compromises its testimony by conformity to current cultural standards of behaviour (cf. 2 Cor. 11:1-3; 1 John 2:15). How easy it is for a church to be merely an empty shell while it deludes itself that it is serving the Lord! How easy it is for an individual to succumb to pressures to adopt current social norms and so drift from the Lord!

(3) The Naive Dove (7:11-13)

7:11 And Ephraim has become like a dove,
easily deceived, without understanding:
they called to Egypt,
they went to Assyria.

The people are next compared to a dove, which is viewed as so familiar with humans that it trusts them too readily.[22] ***Easily deceived*** refers to the simple, who are readily duped into following a course of action (for a more positive use of the term, cf. 'allure' in 2:14). It does not take much to induce the gullible into adopting a self-destructive policy because they are ***without understanding*** (literally 'heart', cf. 4:11), lacking the intelligence and perception to assess strategies in any depth.

This deficiency in Israel was evident in the political incompetence the rulers displayed in lurching frantically from one policy extreme to another. ***They***[23] ***called to Egypt*** for help, and in doing so showed they had rejected calling to God (7:7). Egypt at this period was suffering from internal division and weakness, and, while they might encourage unrest in the minor states of Syria-Palestine as a means of frustrating Assyrian expansionism, they did not have sufficient resources to intervene decisively there. After looking to the south Ephraim swung round to the north and ***went to Assyria***, again rather than returning to God. Assyria would not provide them with genuine assistance; it was all out for its own ends. For the events of history corresponding to these charges, see *Introduction*, pg. 16.

7:12 According as they go, I will spread my net over them;
like a bird of the heaven I will bring them down;
I will chastise them according to the message ⌊given⌋ to their congregation.

22. Seow notes that 'Outside of this passage, there is no reference anywhere in the ancient Near East to the stupidity of such birds. One can only conjecture here that in the popular proverbs of Israel, doves were said to be easily lured and trapped' (1982:218). Garrett advances the notion that 'the dove here is probably a homing pigeon, but it is an especially stupid one, since it cannot find its way home. In the metaphor Yahweh is the home to which it should fly' (1997:171).

23. This is an instance of construction according to sense where a collective noun (here Ephraim) is first treated as a singular and then, as the thought develops, as a plural (cf. 8:5, 8; 9:16; also GKC §145g).

A divine pronouncement of impending judgement further develops the avian imagery of 7:11 (cf. 9:11; 11:11 for the development of this mini-theme). The LORD now threatens Ephraim with his personal intervention to frustrate their plans. The self-deluded people will be trapped and punished by the divine bird-catcher. A fowler (cf. 9:8; Ps. 91:3; 124:7; Prov. 6:5) practised a recognised occupation in the ancient world by catching birds for food. He used a variety of implements in his work, and mention is made here of a net while the second line of the verse alludes to a bow and arrow.

According as they go, that is, 'whichever way they go' (cf. NKJV, REB) is the sense rather than 'when they go'. Whether they turn north or south to seek assistance, God declares that he will act like as a fowler: ***I will spread my net over them*** (cf. 5:1). In this way any bird feeding or resting on the ground would be caught under it and trapped. The action of spreading (*ʾeprôś*) is appropriate to dealing with Ephraim (*ʾeprayim*). ***I will bring them down*** probably refers to shooting an arrow at birds in flight so that, dead or injured, they would fall to the ground. Since the Israelites had turned their backs on the LORD, he would frustrate the alternatives they were pinning their hopes on.

The third line summarises the impact of the first two lines: ***I will chastise them*** (cf. 5:2; 7:15). This threat still holds out the potential for learning by means of the disciplinary punishment imposed. The significance of the additional phrase, ***according to the message ⌞given⌟ to their congregation***, is obscure.[24] It might relate to the recital of the message of the covenant in the religious assemblies of the north (cf. Deut. 30:9-13), warning them of the curses which would come on transgressors, but one wonders to what extent that requirement would have been actually observed. Furthermore, 'their congregation' suggests a public assembly convened by the rulers of the north, and 'message' or 'report' is not the usual term for the divine word but rather suggests news conveyed by a messenger. Possibly what is being said is that news of the way in which their plans had been frustrated would be announced to this public gathering, and so it would be

24. In place of the MT *ʿadātām*, 'their congregation', RSV reads *rāʿātām*, 'for their wicked deeds' (cf. 7:1, 2, 3). Other emendations have also been proposed, generally supposing that the word 'congregation' is a jumbled form of a term for 'affliction' or 'trouble' (cf. LXX). The NIV is more adventurous in its reading, 'When I hear them flocking together, I will catch them', reading the root *ʾāsar*, 'to catch' instead of *yāsar*, 'to chastise'. While this continues the avian imagery, it does not seem necessary.

evident that further calamity was impending. The phrase may possibly relate to the arrival of intelligence regarding the failure of Hoshea's diplomatic approach to Egypt to secure military assistance (2 Kgs. 17:4) with the inevitable consequence of being left unsupported to face the might of Assyrian reprisals.

7:13 Woe to them! for they have wandered from me.
Devastation to them! for they have rebelled against me.
But I ⌞am the one who⌟ would ransom them;
however, they for their part have spoken falsehoods against me.

The LORD denounces their folly with ***Woe to them!*** (implying that their misguided policies would have fatal consequences; cf. 9:12) and with ***Devastation to them!*** The second term (cf. 9:6; 10:14; 12:1) refers more specifically to a general collapse of the social and economic structures of the nation (cf. Isa. 13:6; 16:4; 22:4; Jer. 48:3; Amos 5:9).

The three elements in the indictment against Ephraim reflect the underlying religious misconduct of the nation. (1) ***They have wandered***. While the verb can refer to the fluttering of a bird (Isa. 10:14), what is described here is deliberate evasion of another party, that is, rebellious departure from God. ***From me*** shows Ephraim's tragedy is fundamentally spiritual. They have not sought the presence of the LORD and fellowship with him, but have gone off on ways of their own choosing (cf. 2:5, 7). Hosea will further reflect on the outcome of this wandering in 9:17. (2) ***They have rebelled***, that is, they revolted against due authority over them. This was not just a matter of insurrection against their Assyrian overlords to whom they had been forced to pledge loyalty. The real rebellion was their refusal to recognise the LORD's suzerainty over his people. Instead they substituted their own plans and lifestyle for that which he required. Their choices were not neutral but ***against me***. Again it is emphasised how at the root of their troubles was their repudiation of their covenant relationship with God. (3) In the last line of the verse a further charge is levelled: ***they have spoken falsehoods*** (cf. 12:1). This goes beyond the widespread disregard for truthfulness in the community (4:2), beyond even making insincere promises of fidelity to the LORD. It rather points to utterances to promote the syncretistic cult of the north (2:5-13) and to denigrate the LORD's covenant provision and goodness, possibly asserting that he would (or could) not provide for them as the Baals could. ***Against me*** again stresses the personal nature of the injury done to their relationship with the LORD.

The Israelites' rejection of the LORD makes his reaction even more startlingly gracious (cf. 11:8-9). ***But I ⌞am the one who⌟*** (emphatic 'I', cf. 2:8) ***would ransom them.***[25] There was still a possible way of escape from the disaster which had already begun to engulf the nation. The LORD would pay a price to deliver them from catastrophe (*pādâ*, cf. 13:14). In his love he had done so before when he 'brought you out with a mighty hand and ransomed you from the house of slavery, from the hand of Pharaoh king of Egypt' (Deut. 7:8; cf. Deut. 9:26; 13:5; 15:15; 21:8; 24:18). But the people were set in their ways and unresponsive to his pleas to return to him. So the blows which came on them did not represent God's preferred option for their national destiny, but the outcome of their folly.

REFLECTION

- While there is a place for 'simplicity and godly sincerity' (2 Cor. 1:12) in the Christian's conduct, even Christ advised his disciples to be 'as shrewd as serpents and as innocent as doves' in their dealings with those who gave a hostile reaction to the gospel (Matt. 10:16; cf. Matt. 7:6). Being peace-loving and gentle is not the same as permitting oneself to be taken in by the unscrupulous and the deceptive. The balanced conduct which is required can only be achieved by the empowering of the Holy Spirit.
- Those who fail to cultivate spiritual discernment expose themselves to influences which cause them to wander and bring evil on themselves (cf. Isa. 3:9; Jer. 14:10). Refusal to listen to the truth results in becoming embroiled in vain discussion (1 Tim. 1:6; 2 Tim. 4:4), and the love of money causes others to wander away from the faith and to pierce themselves through with many sorrows (1 Tim. 6:10). 'Those who cling to worthless idols forfeit the grace that could be theirs' (Jonah 2:8 NIV). To counteract such tendencies it is necessary to grow in the faith and in spiritual maturity, welcoming deeper knowledge of the truth as a bulwark against error. 'Give ⌞instruction⌟ to a wise person, and he will become still wiser; inform a righteous person, and he will learn even more' (Prov. 9:9).

---

25. Andersen and Freedman (1980:473) argue that the imperfect verb *ʾepdêm* should be translated as a past tense from *pādâ*, 'to ransom', and that this looks back to the LORD's action at the Exodus (cf. Deut. 7:8; 9:26). The imperfect is more naturally taken in a modal sense, 'I would ransom them', though perhaps not going as far as the NIV's 'I long to redeem them'.

- 'Ransom' (7:13) was originally a commercial term indicating a transaction in which a stipulated sum was paid to transfer ownership (cf. the release of a slave girl, Exod. 21:8), and in many religious contexts in the Old Testament the idea of payment is still present (Exod. 13:13; 34:20; Num. 18:15-16). However, when God ransoms his people, the concept of payment or price recedes and the emphasis is on liberation from distressing or restricting circumstances, such as when Israel was brought out of the servitude of Egypt. The Psalmists also plead for deliverance from danger or oppression using this term (cf. Pss. 25:22; 26:11; 31:5; 119:134). In Psalm 130:7-8 reference is made more specifically to ransoming from sin. For the more specific term 'redeem', see on 13:14. In the New Testament, the cost involved in the ransom paid to effect salvation is made clear. 'You were ransomed from the futile ways inherited from your forefathers, not with perishable things such as silver or gold, but with the precious blood of Christ, like that of a lamb without blemish or spot' (1 Pet. 1:18-19).

(4) The Defective Bow (7:14-17)

7:14 And they have not cried to me in their heart,
  instead they wail on their beds:
about grain and new wine they assemble themselves,
  they turn away against me.

The LORD describes the inappropriate responses of the people to the widespread difficulties facing them. There was nothing wrong with crying out to God in time of trouble (cf. 8:2), seeking his intervention and relief. But the LORD's complaint is that their reaction had not been sincere: ***they have not cried out to me in their heart***, though they may have done so in other ways. There was no inner acknowledgement of his rights or desire to comply with his requirements.

They wail on their beds may be understood in two ways. ***Instead*** renders *kî*, usually 'for', but here after a negative it introduces a contrasting situation (cf. 5:3). Because of their lack of heart recognition of the LORD all that their prayers amount to is a pained expression of grief and despair in which they are consumed by their own feelings and the tragedies that have come upon them. They are like petulant children who complain that they have not got what they wanted and who refuse to accept any personal responsibility for the situation which had beset their land. 'On their beds' refers to the hours of the day when they could engage in undisturbed reflection and meditation (cf. Pss. 4:4; 16:7).

An alternative, but somewhat less probable, approach is to regard the description as being of some heathen ritual, with 'their beds' being a reference to reclining at an orgy. This fits in with a translation of the following words as: 'about grain and new wine they gash themselves' (NRSV, ESV, HCSB).[26] Acts of self-mutilation were a Canaanite device to attract the attention of the gods and to add to the effectiveness of prayers to them (cf. 1 Kgs. 18:28). Since such behaviour was forbidden to true worshippers of the LORD (Deut. 14:1), those who engaged in it incur divine displeasure because ***they turn away against me.*** At a physical level the verb 'turn away/aside' (*sûr*; compare the synonymous *šûb*, 'to turn round/back', 14:1) may indicate leaving the road one is on (Judg. 18:3) or no longer engaging in an activity (Exod. 3:4). Spiritually the term indicates deviation from a commitment entered into. This had been true of Israel after the Exodus when the LORD complained that 'they have been quick to turn away/aside from the road that I commanded them' (Exod. 32:8). The same rebellious inclination had surfaced once more in both the false worship and the foreign alliances of the north.

Translating the line as ***about grain and new wine they assemble themselves*** (cf. NIV, NKJV) is, on balance, to be preferred. It fits in with the preceding description of the immaturity of the Israelites which evidences itself not only self-centred complaints, but also in the materialistic focus of their lives (cf. 2:5-13). There was no difficulty in getting a crowd to gather in the market place to stock up on supplies. Or was the gathering more sinister in that it was to engage in Baal pagan rites to ensure a fruitful harvest? In either event it was the behaviour of those who 'turn away against me'. The LORD was not at the centre of the life of the nation whose conduct was instead a personal affront to him (cf. 7:13).

7:15 But ⌞it was⌟ I who trained them;
I strengthened their arms,
but against me they devise evil.

---

26. This verb is difficult to analyse. The MT has *yitgôrārû*, which is a hithpolel form from *gûr* I, 'they dwell together', possibly 'they assemble themselves', or *gûr* II, 'they excite themselves', or even *gārar*, 'they drag themselves off'. Commentators often argue that none of these is intrinsically probable, and so following a few Hebrew manuscripts and the evidence of the LXX, they read instead *yitgôdādû*, 'they gash themselves'. It is easy to mistake the Hebrew letters *daleth* and *resh*.

But again (cf. 7:13) marks out the contrast between the rebellious behaviour of the people and the provision the LORD himself made for them. Once more there is a note both of divine wistfulness and of divine complaint about their inconsiderate conduct. ***It was I who trained them*** as a loving parent seeking to bring up his children to know and practise what is right (cf. 11:3). 'Train' is rendered 'chastise' in 5:2 and 7:12, but here it denotes the whole educative process designed to nurture spiritual and moral vigour.[27]

I strengthened their arms refers to their limbs (not weaponry), but probably it denotes more than imparting physical power to their bodies. This is the all-encompassing prosperity with which the LORD had blessed the nation's endeavours, but which had been misunderstood and misused (cf. 2:8, 12). Instead of devotion to their benefactor, ***against me they devise evil*** uses the same preposition 'to me' as in the first clause of 7:14 in a hostile sense, and forms an inclusion round the two verses, though the term is preposed in this clause to yield an emphatic contrast. Their wrong-doing had not simply breached some abstract moral law; rather they had slighted the God who had dealt with them graciously. Such behaviour has inevitable consequences.

7:16 They keep returning, ⌞but⌟ not ⌞to him who is⌟ on high;
they have become like a slack bow.
Their leaders will fall by the sword
because of the insolence of their tongue.
This ⌞will be⌟ their derision in the land of Egypt.

While ***return***/'come back' is precisely the response that was required (cf. 3:5; 6:1; 14:1), Ephraim persisted in getting it wrong.[28] They reoriented their ways, possibly seeking to renew failed or rejected alliances, ***but not to him who is on high***[29] (cf. 11:7). Because of their failure to

---

27. There may well be an intended contrast between Israel's turning away at the end of the previous verse (*yāsûrû*, from *sûr*, 'to turn aside') and the LORD's training (*yissartî* from *ʾāsar*, 'to rebuke, teach').

28. The imperfect *yāšûbû* probably conveys the idea of repeated past action continuing into the present.

29. The significance of *lōʾ ʿāl* is much debated. The two most probable options are a name for God, related to *ʿelyôn*, 'Most High' (NIV), or an adverbial usage 'not upwards' (cf. NASB; ESV). Some, however, see here a reference to Baal: 'they return to Baal' (cf. *BHS*, RSV). This follows the LXX: 'they turned aside to Nothing', perhaps taking *lōʾ ʿāl* in the sense 'not-god' in reference to Baal. The rendering, 'to that which does not profit' (NRSV) instead emends to a noun derived from *yāʿal*, 'to profit'.

return to a right relationship with God, the people lacked the capacity to direct their own affairs effectively and they are compared to ***a slack bow***, that is, 'a treacherous/deceitful bow' which was incapable of operating reliably because its frame was warped or its bowstring was not suitably taut.[30] The outcome of using such a faulty bow was unpredictable: it was improbable that an arrow from it would reach its target and, more than that, wielding such a bow was downright dangerous when facing an advancing enemy or a charging wild animal (cf. Ps. 78:57). Because the people lacked the perspective to be obtained by giving the LORD his rightful place in their individual and national living, their decision-making had become erratic, and, just like arrows shot from a defective bow, it had also left them unable to counter an enemy attack.

Consequently, the leadership of the land would be swept away by the adversary. ***Their leaders*** (cf. 7:3) ***will fall*** in a violent death, just as had been happening to their kings in recent years (cf. 7:7). ***By the sword*** emphasises that this will occur in military conflict. ***Insolence*** is a term which denotes feelings of intense anger and the actions which result from that inner fury. In combination with ***their tongue*** it refers to uttering disparaging remarks (cf. 7:13) or even curses against God.

This will be their derision in the land of Egypt. At one level this reflects the scorn with which their attempts to reach an accommodation with Assyria will be viewed by the political realists in Egypt (cf. 7:11). But it conveys more than astute and insightful political comment. It is a matter of appropriate retribution falling on those who mocked the LORD that they will in turn be mocked. The outcome is doubly galling in that it is 'in the land of Egypt'. Possibly the reference is to refugees who have sought a safe haven there (cf. 9:6), but find there is no sympathy extended to them in their predicament (cf. Ezek. 36:20). It is also the case that it was from Egypt that the LORD had ransomed his people. By neglecting him they have doomed themselves to experience the reversal of that salvation.

REFLECTION

• True repentance is a gift from God in which he bestows a knowledge of the truth and brings an individual to his senses spiritually (2 Tim. 2:25-26). The conduct of the people of the north fell far short of this

30. It is unclear whether or not there are two roots *rāmâ* (as well as one meaning 'to throw'). BDB 941 distinguish *rāmâ* II 'to beguile, deal treacherously with' from a third stem meaning 'to be loose, slack'. Even if these are variants of one stem, it is probable that Hosea is playing on both senses.

because they were so absorbed in self. While they could see that all was not well with them, they were satisfied with imperfect remedial action. They failed to display gratitude to the LORD for his goodness (cf. Jer. 5:24), to recognise that they had offended him, and so to turn to him. Instead they nurtured wicked thoughts against him. As Jeremiah later advised Jerusalem, 'Wash your heart from evil that you may be saved' (Jer. 4:14), but in their blindness the people could not see that inner change was needed on their part. All they lamented was a lack of outward prosperity.

D. Reaping the Whirlwind (8:1-14)

Both this and the following section (8:1-14 and 9:1-9) have a similar structure, though here the speaker is the LORD while in 9:1-9 it is the prophet who is heard. Each section begins with an imperative and a general indictment of disloyalty (8:1-3; 9:1-3), and concludes with balancing announcements of judgement in 8:13 and 9:9.

A single theme does not stand out clearly, but as the life of the nation is surveyed, repeated mention is made in chapter 8 of their overreliance on their own resources and abilities. The emptiness of Israel's professions of religious loyalty (8:2), the frequent overthrow of their kings (8:4, 10), the indecision of their foreign policy (8:9-10), and their misplaced trust in military might (8:14) all combine to depict a nation whose affairs are out of control and which is therefore hurtling to its doom. This dire situation had arisen because of their violation of the LORD's covenant (8:1), their ill-conceived idolatry (8:4), particularly in connection with the bull-calf (8:5-6), and the misguided sacrifices of their worship (8:11-13). Inevitably they had drawn down divine judgement upon themselves (8:14).

It is possible to argue from 8:8-10 that Hosea relayed this message after of Tiglath-Pileser's success in the north of Israel in 733 B.C. and Hoshea's accession the following year (cf.; Wolff 1974:137 also *Introduction*, pg. 18). Though this is by no means certain, Hosea's message does fit in with the aftermath of a time of national upheaval when people would be reassessing their situation in the light of the reverses they had suffered at the hands of the Assyrians. There is, however, no explicit call for a return to the LORD. The people had first to realise how sinful their conduct was.

(1) The Broken Covenant (8:1-3)

The way back to God would only be found when the external threat facing the nation was interpreted as more than simply the outcome of international political forces. Their situation was under the control of the LORD, and he had decreed setbacks and disasters for Israel as judgement on their misconduct. They had violated the covenant (8:1), made empty professions of loyalty (8:2), and rejected the LORD's provision for them (8:3). Such religious infidelity was at the root of all their troubles. A tree which is rotten within is unable to withstand the blast of the storm.

8:1 To your mouth, a trumpet!
⌞One⌟ like an eagle ⌞is⌟ against the house of the LORD,
because they have transgressed my covenant
and have rebelled against my law.

The repeated 'my' in the last two lines of the verse shows that this is divine speech. ***To your mouth, a trumpet!*** employs a military metaphor in which an alarm is sounded to muster the local militia in the face of an impending attack (cf. 5:8). 'Your' is singular, but it is unclear whether the LORD issues the command to the nation in general or to the prophet himself. In either case the situation is one of a hitherto unrecognised threat from an enemy. This might correspond to the late 740s B.C. when the Assyrians first advanced into Syria-Palestine, or, more probably, after 733 B.C. when it seemed that the threat of an attack had subsided with Hoshea recognised by the Assyrians as the ruler of the enclave centred on the capital, Samaria.

The enemy is not explicitly named but is given the ominous description of ***one like an eagle*** or a 'vulture'. The same Hebrew word is used for both large birds of prey. The image of a vulture as a scavenger (cf. Prov. 30:17) circling overhead while waiting for the death of its prey yields the suitable corollary that the state of Israel was in its death throes. More probably, however, an eagle is intended here. As a predator swooping down on its hapless victim it was a recognised figure of strength and speed (cf. Job 9:26; 2 Sam. 1:23). It would point to Assyria since figures with an eagle's head or wings appear frequently in Assyrian art as guardian deities. However, ***against***/'over' strikes a negative note of menacing advance. The imagery probably also alludes to Deuteronomy 28:49 where, in a description of the LORD's curse coming upon the disobedient, it is said that 'he will bring a nation against you from far away, swooping down like an eagle'. Furthermore, this might well indicate that the covenant curse reversed the protective role of the LORD who had borne the people 'on eagles' wings' out of Egypt (Exod. 19:4; cf. Deut. 32:10-12).

In this context ***the house of the LORD*** is unlikely to refer to the

Temple in Jerusalem, as it generally does, or for that matter to one of the corrupt sites of worship in the northern kingdom (cf. 9:4). It embraces the whole of the land of promise (cf. 'house of Israel', 5:1), or rather its inhabitants, who as the LORD's household are the 'they' referred to in the second part of the verse. The threat which hung over them had not arisen from nothing: 'the curse causeless shall not come' (Prov. 26:2 AV). The people had set aside the terms of the union which bound them to the LORD and gave them access to his protection and to enjoyment of his favour. Their rebellion had to be penalised and reversed, and the LORD who controls the affairs of every nation was using the Assyrians to punish his errant people. ***Transgressed my covenant*** reflects the language of 6:7, but here it is specifically said that it is the LORD's covenant, undoubtedly that inaugurated at Sinai, whose terms have been violated, so that it is his prerogative to respond. He is the real suzerain, the true authority, and the fault is no longer Adam's (or mankind's in general), but Israel's. They ***have rebelled against my law*** (cf. 7:13), and such defiance cannot be tolerated. The parallelism between the last two lines shows that the 'law', a comprehensive term for the ordinances of the covenant king, sets out the behaviour he requires from his vassals. Defying his law is equivalent to violating his covenant. The repeated 'my' emphasises how directly and personally the LORD is affected by these breaches of his demands.

8:2 To me they cry out,
'My God, we—Israel—know you.'

The emphatic initial ***to me*** shows that the LORD continues to speak. ***They cry out*** (an imperfect verb of ongoing action) is a word with strong emotional content, often a cry for help (7:14). Here, however, the people are not represented as primarily interested in divine assistance, but in repudiating the allegations that Hosea had made against them: 'there is no knowledge of God in the land' (4:1); 'the LORD they do not know' (5:4). They repeatedly protested that they were being wrongly condemned because they were not disloyal as the prophet claimed. Who could deny that they were the LORD's people?

My God is difficult in view of the following 'we', but it expresses concisely the assertion that each individual made of a personal relationship with God (cf. 2:23).[31] The problem exposed here is not that

31. The NIV renders 'our God', but there is no textual basis for this. Quite possibly Garrett (1997:181) is correct in finding here fragments of three prayers, 'My God!', 'We know you', and 'Israel'.

they were Baal worshippers. Elijah's victory had banished outright Baal worship from the land (1 Kgs. 18:16-40). What had taken its place, however, was equally deadly, though less blatantly so. These people had been deluded into thinking they were loyal followers of the LORD when they were not. They focus on the name by which they were known. Did not the title ***Israel***, the people of God, establish their true identity? Can they not avow: ***We know you***? That represents a claim of covenant loyalty phrased in terms of Hosea's consistent focus on 'know', but rejecting his assessment that their profession was a sham. This is the speech of those who had been brainwashed by the syncretistic cult promoted by the state authorities in the north into thinking that they were true to the LORD, and so they had failed to realise that their idolatrous disobedience had sapped the vitality of the union between themselves and God, and jeopardised their relationship with him.

8:3 Israel has rejected good;
an enemy will pursue him.

That the people were mistaken in their self-assessment was revealed by their conduct. ***Israel has rejected good*** describes their attitude to the covenant, and to the King of the covenant. 'Reject'/'set as remote' (*zānaḥ*, cf. 8:5) echoes 'be promiscuous' (*zānâ*, cf. 1:2), with both words implying distance and estrangement from the LORD. 'Good' describes what he would provide for them, the totality of covenant blessing (cf. 3:5; Num. 10:24; Deut. 3:9, 15), but in their spiritual blindness they have spurned this by failing to respond to Moses' entreaty to choose life and good (Deut. 30:15). Enjoyment of the covenant is conditioned on obedience to the terms of the covenant, while Israel wanted to live as they fancied, not as the LORD directed. The inevitable consequence was that ***an enemy will pursue him*** (cf. Deut. 30:7; 32:30) as the LORD used other nations to chastise them. Those who despise the protection the covenant king offers are inevitably exposed to the hostility of their foes.

REFLECTION

- How tragic it is to be in the grip of spiritual self-delusion! How awesome the consequence to stand before the judgement seat and feel entitled to call Jesus 'Lord' and to claim to have acted in his name, only to be told 'I never knew you. Depart from me' (Matt. 7:21-23)! What is required for acceptance is doing the will of the Father who is in heaven (Matt. 7:21). 'Whoever says, "I know him," but does not keep his commandments is a liar and the truth is not in him' (1 John 2:4).

- Spiritual standing with God is not established by family or church connections. To claim the name 'Israel' or descent from Abraham (cf. John 8:39-40) does not ensure acceptance with God. 'It is not the one who commends himself who is approved, but the one whom the Lord commends' (2 Cor. 10:18), and his commendation is based on a committed faith which evidences itself by living as Abraham did. To profess to know God but to deny him by one's actions marks an individual as detestable, disobedient, and unfit for any good work (Tit. 1:16).

(2) Spurious Leadership (8:4a)

Israel's apostasy had become evident in the two interrelated spheres of politics and religion. The first part of 8:4 continues the LORD's indictment of the people by focusing on the inadequacy of their political arrangements. It does not involve an absolute rejection of kingship, for that after all had been envisaged as a possibility as early as Deuteronomy 17:14-20, and Hosea speaks positively of a David to come (3:5). What is repudiated and denounced is the way matters developed in the concluding years of the northern kingdom.

8:4a They themselves have made kings, but not from me;
they have made leaders, but I do not know ⌞them⌟.

They themselves points back to the nation of 8:3, and asserts that when they ***made kings*** they were acting on their own initiative. The dynasty of Jehu had been set up with prophetic accreditation (cf. 2 Kgs. 10:30), but that was not true of the chaotic conditions which prevailed after its overthrow with the murder of Zechariah (cf. 1:1). That coup and subsequent plots and assassinations were the product of human ambition, carried through without divine blessing. The regicidal usurpers were certainly not kings 'whom the LORD your God will choose' (Deut. 17:15), and ***but not from me*** points to the need for a legitimate king of the covenant people to be divinely appointed so that he could function as the LORD's representative, ruling in the fear of God (cf. 2 Sam. 23:3). ***Leaders*** probably here includes all the chief officers of state: kings and their appointed officials. ***I do not know them***[32] refers not to

32. The verb *yāda*ʿ, 'to know', is with other verbs of mental perception frequently treated as a quasi-stative verb, and the perfect is used to convey a present sense. Thus here, 'I know' rather than 'I knew' (cf. Joüon §111h, 112a).

mere cognition, but to approval of their persons and allegiance. Relying on their own wisdom and perception of what was expedient, the people had discarded the protocols of the covenant for choosing a king to rule over them—and the outcome had been disastrous.

REFLECTION

- Prophetic remonstrance with the rulers of the land is based on principles of justice and equity which should apply in every society. 'Act with justice and righteousness, and rescue one who has been robbed from the hand of the oppressor. Do no wrong and do no violence to the alien, the orphan, and the widow, and do not shed innocent blood in this place' (Jer. 22:3). How good it is to have rulers who punish those who do evil and praise those who do good (1 Pet. 2:14)! It is a great blessing for any land when its political system promotes to leadership positions those who recognise God and promote his ethical standards. 'When one rules righteously over mankind, when one rules in the fear of God, he is like the morning light when the sun rises, a morning without clouds, like the brightness after rain that makes grass to sprout from the earth' (2 Sam. 23:3-4).
- Due to the distinctive constitution of Israel as a theocratic nation under the Mosaic covenant where church and state were integrated, remarks about civil rulers have current application also in terms of the affairs of Christ's church. Those who have oversight of the flock are to do so willingly and with a shepherd's heart (Acts 20:28; 1 Pet. 5:2).

(3) The Bull-Calf of Samaria (8:4b-6)

To the political rebellion of Israel's mode of choosing a king there is next added condemnation of their religious practices. These charges are of course closely connected in that the king was responsible for the conduct of worship in the land, and throughout the existence of the northern kingdom the religion of the nation was state-controlled.

8:4b ⌊From⌋ their silver and their gold they have made
idols for themselves,
so that he will be cut off.

The manufacture of idols was the outcome of the religious policy of kings who did not rule in the fear of God. Idolatry in the worship of the LORD had originally been promoted by Jeroboam I, and reinstituted by the house of Jehu (2 Kgs. 10:29). Additionally, though ***they have made*** is quite a different term in Hebrew from the earlier 'made kings', there is the suggestion that they should be linked as equally human in their origin and equally useless to the nation. It was futile for the people to trust either idols or kings for deliverance from the looming threat posed by Assyrian expansionism.

Production of images misused the ***silver*** and ***gold*** (cf. 2:8) which the LORD had given Israel through the expansion of their territory and the ensuing economic prosperity. But, since they failed to recognise the true source of their affluence, they ***made idols for themselves*** (cf. 8:6, 14) from their new found wealth. This was motivated by their own ideas of what was appropriate, which had unfortunately been derived from the majority culture of the time. The term used for 'idols' describes them as objects shaped and fashioned for a purpose (cf. 4:17).[33] This fits in with the description given here: not of self-existent beings, but mere artefacts. Their production was in direct contravention of the requirements of the covenant (Exod. 20:4-6), and it was also an act of inherent irrationality quite apart from the covenant. The plural 'idols' may look back to the beginning of the northern kingdom when there were golden calves in Dan and Bethel, but more probably it includes a great number of other civic and personal images that were subsequently fabricated.

So that introduces the inevitable outcome of such activity. The words are spoken ironically, not of the direct intention of those who made the idols, but of the divine verdict on their activities: ***he will be cut off***. Though the people have been referred to in the plural (corresponding to the many idols they have made), the singular 'he' probably views the nation as one entity which experiences the imposition of the judicial verdict of their covenant King on its outrageous violation of his rights. The nation will no longer occupy the land of promise but will be dispossessed when the suzerain enforces the supreme penalty of eviction upon those who persist in disobeying him and have abused his property (cf. Ezek. 14:13-21).

8:5 He has rejected your bull-calf, Samaria.
My anger is kindled against them.
How long will they be incapable of purity?

Uncertainty surrounds the exact meaning of the first line of the verse. Even though the chapter largely consists of divine speech, there seems to occur one of those switches in grammatical person which are part of

33. Wolff (1974:139) notes that *ʿāṣāb*, 'idol', from the root *ʿṣb* I, 'to shape, form', always had negative, contemptuous overtones because of its similarity in sound to *ʿṣb* II, 'to hurt, cause pain or grief'.

Hosea's style (cf. 5:13) so that the third person ***he*** refers to the LORD.[34] The central feature of the line is the repetition of the verb ***reject***/'spurn' from 8:3. 'The word-play brings out the correspondence between the divine response and the sin that prompted it' (Chisholm 1987:45). Just as Israel had dismissed the good provided by the LORD, so he would dismiss what they had produced for themselves. They had put their trust in ***your bull-calf***, the symbol of Baal worship. 'Your' is in fact a second feminine singular form, presumably in reference to the 'city' (a feminine noun) of Samaria viewed as a corporate entity. However, there is no historical evidence of such an idol in Samaria (the bull calves were located at Bethel and Dan, 1 Kgs. 13:32), and so the capital city has named by synecdoche (interchange of a part and the whole of an entity) for the kingdom, or possibly by metonymy for the whole religious and political apparatus of the state run from the capital. 'Your' indicates that the calf was an unauthorised intrusion into the true worship of the LORD. The fact that only one calf is mentioned dates this saying in the period when Dan was no longer under Israelite control. We do not know precisely when that happened, but Amos talks about the 'god of Dan' (Amos 8:14), so presumably Dan had been lost to the advancing Assyrians after the close of his ministry.

The bull-calf, a prime young animal, was technically a piece of cultic furniture which was associated with the presence of the god who was envisaged as standing or sitting enthroned on the animal's back. It is doubtful, however, if the fine distinction between the calf and the god was maintained in popular thought, and the calves themselves came to be venerated. When a golden calf was produced by Aaron, it was identified with a god or gods (Exod. 32:4), and this precedent was no doubt part of what motivated Jeroboam I to reintroduce it (1 Kgs. 12:28). Additionally it would appeal to the Canaanites who continued to live in his realm (cf. 1 Kgs. 9:20-21). However, even if the bull-calves were identified as thrones for the LORD, their introduction violated his explicit command, and facilitated more extensive adoption of syncretistic ideology.

---

34. Translations vary in the way in which they deal with the change of person in this verse. Many render the first verb *zānaḥ* differently. For instance, the ESV has a first person form, 'I have spurned', and the NIV (following the LXX and early versions) reads an imperative, 'throw out'. The NRSV repoints the MT to yield a passive form, 'your calf is rejected'. Lundbom's suggestion that 'my anger' in the second line does double-duty, and is to be taken as the subject of the first line also, is not without plausibility (1975:229).

There is then a switch to direct speech (possibly to be indicated by supplying, 'saying' as in NASB, before the second line of the verse). It is the LORD's ***anger*** which ***is kindled against them,*** presumably the people of Samaria, who were the objects of his wrath for their attachment to the bull-calf.[35] The gravity of their misconduct and their obstinate refusal to return with penitence had left the LORD with no option but to act in judgement against them, just as had happened in the incident of the golden calf at Sinai (Exod. 32:10, 35).

How long? introduces a rhetorical question (cf. 6:4; 9:5) which springs from the LORD's sorrow and astonishment at the continuing misconduct of the people. ***Purity*** expresses the state of those who are innocent of cultic (cf. Ps. 26:6; 73:13) and moral (cf. Gen. 20:5) blemish. On both counts, however, Israel had repeatedly displayed improper behaviour, and so it would not be long before the LORD acted to cast them out of his presence.

8:6 For from Israel—
but as for it, a craftsman has made it,
and it is no god;
for it will be dashed to pieces,
the bull-calf of Samaria.

For from Israel is obscure, and has given rise to many suggestions. McComiskey (1992:125) argues plausibly that the last line of 8:5 is an interjection of the prophet, and that the sequence of thought moves from 'My anger is kindled against them' to 'for ⌊it is⌋ from Israel'. Certainly the LORD dismisses their bull-calf as something devised and introduced by the people themselves. Its continued existence and veneration proves that the people remain alienated from the LORD and in defiant rejection of his covenant.

Their bull-calf idol was a mere human contrivance, for ***a craftsman has made it.*** 'Craftsman' may here indicate a metal-worker (cf. 8:2). 'Made' recurs throughout the chapter ('have made idols', 8:4; 'his Maker', 8:14). The idol's human origin means that it has no reality beyond the material realm: ***it is no god***, or simply 'It is not God' (compare the title with 'not on high', 7:16). By countering precisely Jeroboam's declaration, 'Behold your gods, O Israel, who brought you up out of the land of Egypt' (1 Kgs. 12:28), which in turn had echoed that of Aaron (Exod. 32:8), this is a rebuttal of the confession of faith of the syncretistic north. The spiritual non-entity will be exposed as

35. The abandonment of the singular collective reference is similar to that which occurs in 6:4. There is also a change from second to third person.

such because ***it will be dashed to pieces*** (literally, 'fragments it will become')[36] and its shattered remains will testify to the impotence of the non-existent god to defend itself against the inroads of the enemy. And if that is so, what defence could it provide for the nation which claimed its protection? ***The bull-calf of Samaria***, the one worshipped by them or promoted by the regime (cf. 8:5), is postponed to the end of the saying to provide a climax. Only one calf is mentioned; the one at Dan no longer existed. Should that fact not have spoken to them?

REFLECTION

• The prophets frequently excoriated the folly of worshipping an artefact of human manufacture (cf. Isa. 2:8, 20; 40:18-20; 44:9-20; Jer. 10:1-16). Yet Israel refused to acknowledge the utter incongruity of human beings made in the image of God prostrating themselves before an inert statue they had constructed for themselves (Rom. 1:22-23). The essence of idolatry is to substitute for God that which is not God (cf. Col. 3:5). The propensity to do so arises from our fallen human nature because it provides us with a god whom we can control. Since our spiritual vision is now naturally obscured and distorted, adoption of idolatrous practices also arises from conformity to the prevailing culture, seeking human rather than divine approval.

(4) Ungodly Alliances (8:7-10)

Hosea varies his indictment of the land by introducing proverbial speech which bears some of the characteristics of wisdom teaching. As is so often the case, the thrust of the proverb is not immediately evident; so the hearer/reader must pause and reflect on what is being said. It is not until the mention of Assyria in 8:9 that the message is clearly spelled out: foreign alliances are fruitless and destructive.

8:7 Because a wind they sow,
  a whirlwind they will reap.
The standing grain has no ear;
  it will not produce meal.
Even if it were to produce ⌞meal⌟,
  strangers would swallow it.

---

36. *šəbābîm* occurs only here and its meaning is therefore uncertain, though the vast majority of interpreters associate it with the root *šābab* (I), 'to cut down'. The ESV margin 'go up in flames' suggests instead that the term is derived from *šābab* (II), 'to set fire to' (*HALOT* 4:1382; cf. also Job 18:5).

In this memorable verse (which is expressed in a proverbial fashion usually associated with wisdom writings) there are two thoughts: an inevitable correspondence between action and reaction, between misconduct and its consequences; and also the concept of intensification—the outcome will do more than reflect the original offence. The introductory word usually translated 'for', giving an explanation of what has preceded, here serves to introduce a link with what follows and is rendered ***because***. The transition to agricultural imagery is easily made because the Canaanite gods were primarily fertility deities. There is assonance between ***they sow*** (*yizrāʿû*) and ***they will reap*** (*yiqṣōrû*) which reinforces the message that actions inevitably bring consequences in their wake (cf. 8:5; 12:2). The proverb does not envisage those who sow *in* the wind. That might be quite a sensible course of action because a light breeze helps to disperse seed sown by hand. Rather what is pictured here is a sowing of wind, a common figure for what is insubstantial and fleeting, used particularly in Ecclesiastes' repeated assessment of how the outcome of human striving is unprofitable and ephemeral (e.g. 12:1; Prov. 11:29; Eccl. 1:14, 5:16).

Now the thought that you reap what you sow is fairly commonplace (cf. Job 4:8; Prov. 22:8; Gal. 6:7). Here, however, the outcome is intensified: those who sow worthless seed do not get no return from the harvest, but an overwhelmingly negative one. A ***whirlwind*** was a destructive force which could not be deflected (cf. Ps. 83:15). So what has started as folly will snowball in its consequences. What is in view are international alliances to resist Assyrian aggression. In themselves they were incapable of achieving their objectives. But they did not just simply fail. Deluding themselves as to the potential effectiveness of the arrangements they had entered into, the minor states of Syria-Palestine ventured into rebellion against Assyria, only to draw down upon themselves a whirlwind of reprisals and further suppression by the invincible forces of the empire.

In the second line the situation is further exposed through another word play, which, unusually for Hebrew, involves rhyme in that ***ear*** (*ṣemaḥ*, literally 'what sprouts') is echoed by ***meal*** (*qemaḥ*), grain that awaits final grounding into flour (cf. Isa. 47:2). Moreover, there is an additional sound play between 'meal' and ***standing*** (*qāmâ*). What has not been flatten by the gale is unable to produce anything that may be used for consumption.[37] The agricultural metaphors are to be applied to

37. There is an irregularity of gender because standing grain is feminine, whereas 'to it' is a masculine form.

the political and military situation. Even though they are able to muster some sort of coalition force, it would be incapable of stemming or reversing Assyrian inroads.

What is more, ***even if it were to produce meal***—which obviously it cannot[38]—that would not accrue to the benefit of Israel because it would be totally consumed by ***strangers*** (cf. 7:9; the Hebrew is *zārîm*, possibly intended as a play on 'will sow', *yizrāʿû*, at the beginning of the verse). If perhaps the coalition is not wiped out by the invading forces, there would still be the requirement to pay tribute to the Assyrians, as Menahem (2 Kgs. 15:9) and others found to their cost. Assyrian alliance or occupation would lead to the wealth of their land draining away, as economic strangulation stared them in the face.

8:8 Israel has been swallowed up.
Now they have become among the nations
like a vessel in which no one has pleasure.

Here Hosea sets out how the preceding riddle ought to be understood. The unwise foreign policy of ***Israel***, the northern kingdom, had failed with disastrous consequences. ***Swallowed up***[39] links to the previous line, but now it is not their crops but the nation itself which has been devoured by the enemy. Wolff (1974:142) associates this with the Assyrian annexation of Galilee and Gilead in 733 B.C., though it may also refer to an earlier loss of Israelite influence over territory within their zone of influence in the reign of Menahem.

Now may well indicate a logical rather than a temporal connection, that is, 'so now, as a consequence of their being swallowed up' (cf. 8:13) by Assyrian aggression Israel has lost the status which it enjoyed ***among the nations*** in Jeroboam II's reign. Through their imprudent international policy the territory and prosperity of the land had been diminished, and surrounding peoples had written them off as ineffective and without influence. The same vignette is later used by Jeremiah, ***a vessel in which no one has pleasure*** (cf. Jer. 22:28; 48:38), where

38. The figure of speech in which there is a claim that something will not occur only to be followed by an exploration of the negative consequences which would arise if it in fact did occur is known as *pseudosorites*. It is a technique employed by Hosea here as well as in 9:12, 16 and 13:15. See O'Connor (1987).

39. *HALOT* (1:135) identifies another homonymous root *bālaʿ* (III), 'be confused'. It is unlikely that this supplies the dominant sense of the passage, but Hosea could well be hinting at the bewilderment of the self-confident Israelites at what had happened to them.

the description is specifically of a broken and useless clay pot, rejected and consigned to the local rubbish heap.

8:9 For they themselves have gone up to Assyria.
A wild donkey ⌊lives⌋ alone, by itself;
⌊as for⌋ Ephraim, they have hired lovers.

For introduces the reason for the preceding statement about Israel, and so it too relates either to Menahem's payment of tribute (2 Kgs. 15:19) or to Hoshea's similar acceptance of subordinate status (2 Kgs. 17:3). ***They themselves*** emphasises that the course of action they embarked on is one which they devised and adopted on their own initiative. ***Have gone up*** indicates the direction of travel northwards, perhaps not all the way north to the Assyrian homeland but certainly until they reached the Assyrian forces as they pressed south.

There is a deliberate play between ***wild donkey*** (*pereʾ*) and ***Ephraim*** (*ʾeprayim*) in which the same three consonants are found in a different order (cf. also other word plays in 13:5; 14:8). Normally the thought is taken to be that they behaved 'like a wild donkey wandering alone' (NIV), and the description is of Israel's infatuated unfaithfulness which was like that of Judah a century later, who said, 'I love foreigners and after them I will go' (Jer. 2:25). However, more probably the thought here is that Ephraim's conduct is worse than that of a wild donkey. While the precise species of animal involved is a matter of conjecture, all the possibilities involve animals which are naturally gregarious. 'Wild donkey' is therefore used collectively to describe the behaviour of a herd which avoids contact with human settlements, as is clear in the extensive depiction of its natural habitat and conduct in Job 39:5-8. Wild donkeys which wish to elude being caught and used as pack animals have the sense to keep away from those who would catch them, but Ephraim's folly had been such that ***they have hired lovers***, or possibly 'paid for love affairs'. The verb 'hire' is connected with the nouns used for 'hire' in 2:14 and 9:11. They had negotiated a fee for the favours of outsiders, but they would find that purchased liaisons are superficial. When the money runs out, the attachment ends. In the same way Ephraim's attempts to buy security through political alliances would not work. Cooperation will not only be ineffective, but counter-productive by changing into something altogether more oppressive.

8:10 Even though they hire ⌊lovers⌋ among the nations,
now I will gather them.
And they will begin to become little because of the burden
of a king of leaders.

This verse develops the theme of the preceding one: the expedients Ephraim has employed will prove worthless. ***Even though they hire lovers among the nations***, bought help will do them no good as regards resisting the will of God. 'Among the nations' echoes 8:8. In ***now I will gather them*** 'them' might refer to 'the nations' (the immediate antecedent), who could possibly be gathered against Ephraim (cf. Ezek. 16:37). But more probably the pronoun refers to Ephraim. However, the thought of their being gathered to be restored to divine favour (a common expression, cf. Deut. 30:3; Jer. 31:8, 10; Ezek. 11:17) is quite out of place here. Rather the phrase is an ominous indication of the LORD's determination to summon Ephraim to an assembly where the nation will be judged and punished (cf. 9:6; Ps. 50:5-7; Ezek. 22:20; Joel 3:2; Mic. 4:12; Zeph. 3:8).

The second part of the verse is variously understood.[40] It expresses an aspect of the impending judgement in that Ephraim will be impoverished through ***the burden*** of tribute demanded from them. ***A king of leaders***/'rulers' (cf. 7:3) is probably an attempt to render the Assyrian royal title, 'king of kings', that is, a sovereign over petty rulers for whom the term 'king' was also used.[41] This is the outcome of going to Assyria: not a solution but intensified problems.

REFLECTION

- Life is a series of decisions of varying importance, but each ought to be made in the light of God's word (Pss. 43:3; 119:105), seeking the guidance of the Spirit through prayer (Ps. 143:10; Rom. 8:4; Gal. 5:16, 25), and aiming for the consolidation and advance of Christ's kingdom by conforming every act to his will (Rom. 12:11; Col. 3:23-24). If this attitude is not present, merely human decision making is liable to produce just 'wind' (8:7), which is incapable of providing satisfaction through securing what is desired. In the decades after

---

40. (1) Following the LXX rendering, it has been supposed that the verb was originally *ḥādal*, 'to cease'. The LXX, however, understands the line quite differently: 'they will cease from anointing king and princes' (cf. REB). (2) The verb has been taken as *ḥûl*, 'to writhe', and pointed as *waw* conjunctive followed by an imperfect form, *wəyāḥîlû*, 'they will writhe for a little', or 'in a little', that is, 'soon' (cf. NKJV, NRSV, ESV). (3) Retaining the verb as coming from the hiphil of *ḥālal*, 'to begin' (but pointed with conjunctive *waw*) and analysing *məʿāṭ* as a verbal infinitive form *məʿōṭ* yields the sense, 'they will begin to become little' (cf. NASB, NIV, NJPS, HCSB).

41. An alternative treatment is to read 'the king ⌞and⌟ princes' (ESV) following LXX, Peshitta, Vulgate, as well as some early Jewish sources.

Hosea, Isaiah had to combat a similar obtuseness among the people of the southern kingdom of Judah. 'Woe to the stubborn children,' declares the LORD, 'who execute a plan, but not mine, who enter into an alliance, but not by my Spirit, so that they add sin to sin! Who set out to go down to Egypt without asking my advice, to take refuge in the stronghold of Pharaoh and to find shelter in the shadow of Egypt!' (Isa. 30:1-2).

- We live in a structured universe. The laws which the Creator has imposed in the natural realm are generally obvious, such as the law of gravity or the principles of electro-magnetism. These have been acknowledged and explored by modern science, even though their divine origin is frequently denied. Equally, God has imposed a moral structure on the universe. Though its laws may not operate with the immediacy of physical laws, its principles are constant, being a reflection of the character of God himself. The rebellion of mankind against God obscures human perception of this reality, and we constantly need to be reminded of it. 'Do not be deceived: God is not mocked, for whatever an individual sows, that will he also reap. For whoever sows to his own flesh will from the flesh reap corruption, but whoever sows to the Spirit will from the Spirit reap eternal life' (Gal. 6:7-8; cf. 2 Cor. 9:6).

(5) Illicit Worship (8:11-13)

The repeated use of 'many'/'make many' throughout the concluding verses of the chapter heightens the portrayal of the scenes of intense activity. On the part of Israel it is religious activity, sacrificing (8:11), and military preparations, building fortress cities (8:14); on the part of the LORD it is possibly giving covenant direction to the people (8:12). None achieves its goal. The people do not gain acceptance with God or security from their enemies, and God does not induce the people to act responsibly by observing the terms of the covenant.

8:11 For Ephraim has made many altars for sin offering;
they have become for him altars for sin.

The introductory ***for*** seems to indicate a general connection in that a deeper analysis of their external policies reveals them not as isolated misguided acts but, at root, products of their aberrant religious outlook. The emphasis on altars and sacrifices picks up on earlier themes (cf. 4:8; 5:6). ***Has made many*** is repeated in 8:14, and forms an inclusion round the section.

The norm for the covenant people was that there would be one sanctuary where they would worship their one, unique God (Deut. 12:5-7). Having rejected the worship of the Temple in Jerusalem, the northern kingdom substituted the shrines of the bull-calves at Bethel and Dan, and Jeroboam I also erected temples on the high places throughout the land (1 Kgs. 12:31). These syncretistic shrines with a compromised priesthood continued to multiply. Ostensibly they provided ***altars for sin offering.***[42] The northern cult retained the rites and festivals of the south, though setting them in a significantly different religious context, and so deviating from Mosaic orthodoxy not only as regards the number of altars but also in the meaning attached to the sacrificial ritual. Consequently far from appeasing divine anger, their worship was a source of further provocation. ***They have become for him altars for sin,*** where 'sin' retains its basic sense of 'miss the mark' (cf. 4:8). The punishment for introducing cultic innovations was matched by their worship failing to achieve what was intended; indeed, offering unacceptable worship increased their guilt.

8:12 I kept writing for him ten thousand ⌊precepts⌋ of my law;
they have been regarded as something strange.

This word of divine complaint displays poignant awareness of what ought to have been, and of how perversely the people of God had reacted to the provision instituted for them. There is an element of hyperbole in the statement, ***I kept writing for him ten thousand precepts of my law,***[43] but it serves to emphasise the clarity and scope of the divine direction. Further, the fact that it had been written emphasises its accessibility and its permanence. All this exacerbates the culpability of Israel's conduct. Despite the comprehensive detail provided for them, they were not applying God's instructions to their

42. In both lines the MT reads *laḥăṭōʾ*, 'to sin ⌊against God⌋'. While this makes sense of the second occurrence, the first is implausible in that it makes the two lines tautologous (cf. ESV), though 'in his sin' (NEB) eases that difficulty somewhat. An alternative is to repoint the consonants in the first instance as *ləḥaṭṭēʾ*, 'to make a sin offering' (NIV, NRSV).

43. There are two variations in the MT. The phrase 'I kept writing for him' (a past frequentative imperfect) is spelled in the kethib as *ʾektôb lî*, whereas in the qere a maqqeph is present with consequential shortening of the vowel to read *ʾektob-lî*. The translation is not affected by this. Also, the kethib reads *ribbô*, 'ten thousand', but somewhat prosaically the Massoretes considered that there should be substituted *rubbê*, 'multitudes of', though such a plural form of *rōb* is not found elsewhere.

lives. Indeed, ***they have been regarded as something strange.*** What should have been familiar and treasured was held to be alien and intrusive (*zār*, cf. 8:7). In a strangely inverted sense of what was proper and fitting, they did not evaluate their alliances with foreign powers in that way, or other aspects of the cult, such as idols, as alien. Their perception was highly selective as they viewed the LORD's ordinances as antiquated and no longer of relevance to them while they sought to advance their religious life by conforming to the practices of the surrounding non-covenantal communities.

8:13 ⌊As for⌋ the sacrifices of my offerings
they keep sacrificing flesh and eat ⌊it⌋;
the LORD does not accept them.
Now he will remember their iniquity
and punish their sins:
they themselves will return to Egypt.

The beginning of the verse is difficult to understand, and has given rise to a number of emendations. ***Sacrifices*** (fronted for emphasis) and ***they sacrifice*** relate here to offerings part of which would be eaten at communal meals (fellowship offerings, traditionally peace offerings) with part dedicated to God. The term rendered ***my offerings***, which occurs only here, may be derived from a form of the usual Hebrew verb 'to love', with a sense such as 'offerings which I love', but more probably it comes from a root meaning 'to give' and signifies gifts or offerings either stipulated by God or made to him.[44] It would seem to mean that though outwardly they sacrifice according to the requirements of the law given to the people of God, and though they are ready—indeed eager—to ***eat***[45] the ***flesh*** of the fellowship offerings, there was no appreciation of the spiritual significance of sacrifice because there was no inward harmony between them and God. Their main concern was to relish a fine meal, and so their repeated religious endeavours amounted to nothing more than sitting down to a sumptuous repast. They were satisfied with their performance, but ***the LORD***

44. *habhābay* may be taken as a reduplicated form from a root *yāhab*, 'to give', or from *ʾāhēb*, 'to love', with the initial consonant suppressed in both instances. While use of the contracted form *hēbû* in 4:18 ('love', possibly a dialectal variant) favours the latter option here, the resultant sense is contrived, and the former derivation is much more plausible.

45. The form of 'eat' (a waw consecutive imperfect) is difficult; literally it is 'and they ate'. Possibly an ordinary waw should be read and the imperfect taken in a frequentative sense as is the initial imperfect, 'they keep sacrificing and eating'.

does not accept them,[46] an essential aspect of sacrificial ritual (cf. Lev. 1:4). That is his on-going and unchanging attitude, presumably to the sacrifices or those who sacrificed. Behaviour they considered acceptable, he regarded as obnoxious—the covenant relationship had been strained to breaking point.

Now points to the impending consequences of the situation (cf. 8:8) in that the LORD will take on the role of their accuser. ***Remember*** shows the LORD actively recalling their conduct and attitudes with a view to taking appropriate measures (cf. 7:2), and it is possibly a legal expression (cf. 9:9). ***Punish*** ('calls to account', cf. 1:4) indicates the outcome of the divine inspection of their behaviour. The LORD is personally involved in scrutinising Israel's religious activity, and it is the affront given to him which will determine the outcome for the nation. For ***iniquity*** see on 7:1, and for ***sins***, see on 4:8. This punishment will involve the people ***themselves*** in a ***return to Egypt*** (cf. 7:16).

This return can hardly be a matter of forming a political alliance with Egypt; Hosea has already been scathing in his assessment of such conduct (cf. 7:11, 16). Rather 'Egypt' recalls the oppression which the Israelites had formerly experienced there. Of the thirteen times Egypt is named in the prophecy, five look back to the time of the Exodus (2:17; 11:1; 12:10, 14; 13:4), and another five associate Egypt with Assyria as one of the two major powers of the time, of which Egypt was much the weaker (7:11; 9:3; 11:5, 11; 12:2). On the three remaining occasions (7:16; 8:13; 9:6) it still has sinister overtones. What is depicted here is reversal of the blessings of the covenant (cf. Deut. 28:68). The LORD who brought his people out of Egypt consigns them to return there (or to similar circumstances of bondage conjured up by the term Egypt) as a consequence of their sin and rebellion (cf. 9:3; 11:5). The redemption provided by the covenant is utterly reversed.

REFLECTION

- The reference to a written law (8:12) points to the covenantal heritage of Israel. Ancient monarchs fixed the terms of their treaties with subordinate nations by having them written. No less so did the heavenly King give a written law through Moses so that subsequent generations should be in no doubt about the LORD's requirements. The statement of 8:12 robustly challenges critical conceptions of a written law as being a later innovation in Israel's history.

---

46. The perfect *rāṣām*, 'he does not accept them' or 'he does not view them with favour', is to be analysed as stative.

- To regard divine precepts as strange or alien (8:12) is characteristic of those who have abandoned the love which they had at first (cf. Rev. 2:4). Love delights to please the one who is loved, and therefore is constantly seeking information regarding his or her likes and dislikes. That is why the psalmist loved God's commands (cf. Ps. 119:47-48, 127), not primarily as an end in itself, but as a means of becoming acquainted with what pleases him and so being in a position to express acceptable devotion to him. 'If you love me, you will keep my commandments' (John 14:15) is not therefore expressing an arbitrary association between love and obedience, but one which inevitably arises out of the attachment of love. When love to the Saviour sours and grows cold, then what pleases him becomes an object of criticism and a source of irritation, and is no longer a source of delight.

(6) The Divine Verdict (8:14)

8:14 Israel has forgotten his Maker,
and has built palaces,
and Judah has made many fortified cities;
so I will send fire on his cities,
and it will devour her citadels.

That ***Israel has forgotten*** (cf. 2:13; 13:6) ***his Maker*** stands in stark contrast to the way God remembers Israel's conduct (8:13). 'Maker' here refers not to God as creator of humanity, but to him as the one who formed the nation—a nation whose religion has now degenerated into the use of a craftsman making idols (cf. 8:6). In Deuteronomy 32:6 Moses had presented the LORD to the people as 'your father who created you, who made you and established you', and to whom therefore they owed allegiance ('It is he who made us and we are his,' Ps. 100:3). Forgetfulness of their Maker also implied suppression of the basis on which they occupied the land, and of the origin of the blessings they enjoyed.

So neglectful were they of all that the LORD had done for them that they ***built palaces***. (The word can also mean 'temples' but that seems unlikely in view of the following 'citadels'.) These great houses were the products of their wealth and constituted an ostentatious display of their affluence; they were also heavily fortified. Presumably this is an historical retrospect which looks back to the times of Jeroboam II, but the underlying attitude of trust in wealth and military security continued to be evident in the unsettled conditions of the 730s. Furthermore, just as the whole nation had been involved in the Exodus from Egypt, so ***Judah*** (cf. 1:7) in the south was not exempt from the trends evident in the north. Under Uzziah/Azariah they too had experienced territorial expansion and material prosperity (2 Chron. 26:1-15)—with the same attendant dangers. Whereas Ephraim had made many altars (8:11), those of the south had ***made many fortified cities***. Judah's defence policy was not based on trusting in the LORD as their protector, but involved the establishment of strategic garrisons throughout the land. Before much longer their inadequacy would be revealed; in 701 B.C. Sennacherib captured forty-six of them. Mention of palaces and fortified cities here is a distributed expression, a poetic device which does not imply one kingdom exclusively built one type of structure while construction activity in the other was of a different sort. Both were engaged in extensive building programmes undertaken for similar motives; and for neither would the results be what they desired.

In reverse order judgement is first pronounced on Judah: ***I will send fire on his cities.*** Again there is word-play with 'send' (*šālaḥ*) echoing 'forgot' (*šākaḥ*) and suggesting the response was fitting. As regards Israel, ***it will devour her citadels***, or 'strongholds', possibly the fortified section of a royal palace.[47] In the north too, military defensive measures had been undertaken which would prove ineffective. 'Devour' renders the same verb as 'eat' in 8:13 (cf. 7:7), and indicates the total destruction effected by the conflagration. Sayings involving 'fire' followed by 'devour' are also found in Amos 1:4, 7, 10, 14; 2:2, but that need not indicate any direct dependence of Hosea on the earlier prophet. A similar sequence is found much earlier in Numbers 16:35; 21:28 and Judges 9:15. Again, though the descriptions are distributed between north and south, they apply equally to both.

REFLECTION

• Origins are an important factor in our self-perception. Forgetting our Maker in a creational sense has debased western civilisation's perception of what constitutes true humanity. It makes all the difference to our assessment of our worth and destiny if we consider ourselves to be evolved blobs of mud or those animated by the breath of God (Gen. 2:7) and endowed with the potential and responsibilities of functioning as those in his image (Gen. 1:26). Similar considerations are operative as regards forgetting our Maker in terms of spiritual relationships. The

47. Ben Zvi (2005:173) takes 'his' as pointing to 'Israel and Judah' and 'her' to 'cities', but that hardly explains the switch from plural to singular. However, though Israel is usually masculine in references to the people as a whole, feminine forms do occur in 1 Sam. 17:21 and 2 Sam. 24:9.

'children of God' (Rom. 8:16; 1 John 3:1) are those who 'he caused to be born again' (1 Pet. 1:3). As they acknowledge their new relationship with him, so they are called on to 'be imitators of God, as beloved children' (Eph. 5:1) and are 'predestined to be conformed to the image of his Son, in order that he might be the firstborn among many brothers' (Rom. 8:29). When this is lost sight of, the life of faith falters and becomes 'sluggish' (Heb. 6:12).

E. Days of Reckoning, not Rejoicing (9:1-9)

This portion of the prophecy is a companion piece to the preceding section (see the introduction to 8:1-14), and consists of a two-part address by Hosea. (For the break after 9:9, see the introduction to 9:10–10:15.) Initially (9:1-6) there are words of prophetic warning based on the revelation of the preceding chapter. They may have been uttered at a time when there was a lull in Assyrian pressure, and the people, on the basis that their problems were merely a matter of politics, adopted the view that the worst was over. Hosea warns them against such complacency because Assyria was only an instrument in the LORD's hands. The real concern of the people should be God's verdict on them. The message was probably delivered in the course of a religious festival, and the impending exile is described as a time when such worship will inevitably cease (9:4-5). The concluding section (9:7-9) sheds light on how the people reacted to Hosea's ministry. They were misled by prophetic voices within the community which assured them that all would be well. Hosea, however, reiterates that the LORD will call the nation to account for its transgressions.

(1) Abandoned Festivals (9:1-6)

It has been plausibly proposed that Hosea uttered these verses at the time of a religious festival, most probably Sukkot, the feast of Booths, a variant of which had been established in the northern kingdom a month later than the LORD had directed. 'And Jeroboam ordained a feast in the eighth month on the fifteenth day of the month, like the feast which was in Judah, and he sacrificed on the altar [*or,* went up to the altar]. So he did in Bethel, to sacrifice to the calves which he had made' (1 Kgs. 12:32). As this was scheduled at the end of the summer, after the harvesting of the grapes and olives, it was intended to be a time of rejoicing and festivity (cf. Lev. 23:40; Deut. 16:14-15). Hosea re-evaluates the situation in the light of the LORD's condemnation of Israel, particularly as expressed in the preceding chapter, with which there are a number of verbal and thematic links: whoredom (8:9; 9:1);

grain and wine (8:7; 9:2); impending oppression and removal from the land (8:13; 9:3). So rejoicing was inappropriate because the festival which commemorated their sojourn in the wilderness after the Exodus (Lev. 23:43) will in fact prove to be a prelude to a return to similar circumstances.

9:1 Do not rejoice, Israel,
with exultation like the peoples,
for you have committed whoredom from beside your God;
you love a prostitute's wages
beside all threshing floors for grain.

After the climax reached in the final verses of the previous chapter, the direct imperatival address with which the verse begins confirms that this is the start of a new section (cf. 8:1). The prohibition, ***Do not rejoice***, suggests that this message was originally delivered at a time when that was precisely what the people were doing, probably on a feast day (cf. 2:11), and in such a context ***Israel*** reminds them of their status as the covenant community. The prophet's words would have cut across the general rejoicing.

The root behind ***exultation*** does not occur in several Biblical books (perhaps because of Canaanite overtones) but where it is used, the rejoicing in view is often before God and in response to his action (cf. Pss. 21:1; 31:7; 32:11; Isa. 41:16; 61:10; Joel 1:16; 2:21; Zech. 10:7). 'With exultation' is literally 'to exultation'—a somewhat difficult expression. While many translations take it as a further prohibition, e.g. 'do not be jubilant' (NIV)[48], it is preferable to treat it as an intensificatory use of the noun, forbidding rejoicing which degenerates into the uncontrolled excesses ***like the peoples***. In Canaanite and other fertility cults the worshippers were prone to indulge in uninhibited expressions of fervour, but different standards of behaviour should be evident in the covenant community. That should particularly apply when they have been clearly informed that the LORD has rejected their conduct as reprehensible and will shortly act against them.

48. A negative rendering of the second line, such as 'exult not' (cf. NIV, NRSV, ESV), involves changing the pointing of *ʾel*, 'to' to *ʾal*, 'not', and emending the noun *gîl* to a verb form such as *tāgēl* (because an imperfect/jussive form is required with that negative). This follows the example of the LXX and Vulgate, and establishes a parallel with the preceding prohibition. However, the phrase 'rejoice to exultation' also occurs in Job 3:22 where it seems to mean 'to the point of extreme exultation', and retaining it here is preferable to altering the consonantal text and revocalising it.

For shows that no matter how successful the harvest had been, the unresolved dispute between the nation and God had cast its shadow over all their affairs. The expression, ***You have committed whoredom*** (and still continue to do so) ***from beside your God***, is unusual in that the verb form is masculine, presumably indicating that it is here used metaphorically. 'Commit whoredom' constitutes the final occurrence in the book of a term derived from the root *zānâ* (last previous instance in 6:10) to describe Israel's misbehaviour in terms of the conduct of a promiscuous woman. The people's infidelity had ruptured their relationship with the one who was truly *your* God so that they were no longer living close to him as they ought to be.[49] Hence they can no longer expect to be the recipients of his favour.

You love a prostitute's wages (*ʾetnān*, 'a prostitute's wage', cf. *ʾetnâ*, 2:12). The perfect verb has a stative force: they had been attracted to what they thought accrued to them from their devotion to Canaanite gods, and their attitude remained the same—they continued to crave what they indulged in at the pagan shrines. By imitating the practices of their neighbours, they thought ***grain*** (cf. 2:9) had been given to them by Baal whom they accepted as the source of such agricultural fertility (cf. 2:5). What is being targeted here is ritual prostitution ***on all threshing floors for grain***.[50] Threshing floors were elevated areas for communal use, often located outside the city gates, where they also provided a suitable level area for public assemblies (cf. 1 Kgs. 22:10). The high places of the Baal shrines would be situated nearby. 'All' indicates that such corrupt practices were spread throughout the land.

9:2 Threshing floor and winepress will not feed them,
and the new wine will let her down.

Over against the expectations which informed the pagan ritual, it is declared that ***threshing floor and winepress will not feed them.*** The singular verb 'will feed' shows that the composite subject expresses, by metonymy, agricultural produce viewed as a whole. 'Feed' is a metaphor from shepherding and refers to the provision of adequate

49. One significant instance of the use of the compound preposition *mēʿal*, 'from beside', occurs in Gen. 17:22, 'When he had finished talking with him, God went up from beside Abraham.' The episode of familiar interaction had been concluded.

50. *kol-gānôt dāgān* is not pointed as a construct chain. English versions such as NIV and ESV do not explicitly render *dāgān*, 'grain'. Though the term is missing in the Peshitta, it was probably omitted to avoid redundancy.

supplies. The prediction of general famine involves the absence of such staple commodities, and this would also deprive them of an occasion for celebration at the autumn harvest festival, since the bounty they formerly rejoiced in would be replaced by barrenness as a result of the divine curse. A winepress was used for processing grapes (and also olives), whose juice flowed from an upper container, possibly hollowed out in the rock, where they were trampled, into a lower container for collection. In the first line the emphasis may well be on olives, whose oil constituted one of the basic goods traded in the land. These three staple items—corn, olive oil, and wine (2:8)—would be put to extensive use when the harvest was abundant, but the further the yield of these items fell short of expectations, the more the people would experience hardship.

Replenished supplies of ***new wine*** (cf. 2:8) would fail to materialise. The verb ***let down*** initially means 'to deny, keep secret, or delude', but it is also used in an extended sense of 'to fail' (cf. Hab. 3:17). ***Her*** shows that the prophet is viewing the nation as a harlot or an unfaithful wife[51] upon whom the curse of the broken covenant has come (cf. 2:8-13): a nation 'will not leave you corn, new wine or olive oil, the newborn of your herds or the young of your flock until it has caused you to perish' (Deut. 28:51).

9:3 They will not dwell in the LORD's land,
and Ephraim will return to Egypt,
and in Assyria they will eat what is unclean.

No matter how abundant the harvest, the people will not enjoy it because they will no longer be there to do so. Probably the underlying sequence of events is that crop failure imposed by the LORD through adverse climatic or other conditions will leave the land so weakened before its enemies that they will become subject to invasion and consequent deportation (cf. Deut. 28:38-41). ***They will not dwell in the LORD's land*** reminds them of who ultimately owned the land: 'the land is mine' (Lev. 25:23). As those who had compromised their allegiance to the LORD by turning to the worship of Baal, they would no longer enjoy rights of occupancy in the land. Their residence in it was conditioned on their remaining loyal, but they had not, and so ***Ephraim***

51. The MT reads *bāh*, 'in her', but the ancient versions presuppose *bām*, 'in them', which is indeed found in some Hebrew manuscripts. The translations may, however, be rendering according to sense rather than constituting a witness to a variation in the underlying text.

will return to Egypt.[52] Again (cf. 8:13) the reference is not primarily to a *physical* removal to Egypt (but note 8:6), but a reimposition of the conditions of oppression and hardship which had prevailed there, because those who had devoted themselves to pagan deities could no longer be permitted to defile the land of promise. 'Do none of these abominations ... lest the land vomit you out when you make it unclean' (Lev. 18:26-28).

The clause initial position of ***in Assyria*** indicates that this is a coordinate part of the same complex of events and not another curse which occurs later. ***Eat what is unclean*** refers to part of the LORD's directives for marking his people out as separate to himself, and the food laws of Leviticus 11 were a significant component of them. Unclean food might well have been all that was available to foreign deportees who would have no opportunity in exile to observe their national laws of ritual cleanness (cf. Ezek 4:13, Amos 7:17, Dan. 1). Having to eat such food would openly stigmatise them as alienated from God and experiencing his displeasure.

9:4 They will not pour out wine as a libation to the LORD,
and their sacrifices will not please him.
⌊They will be⌋ like bread of mourning to them;
all who eat it will make themselves unclean,
for their bread will be ⌊just⌋ for their lives—
it will not enter the house of the LORD.

Though this could describe future conditions in the promised land as it experienced crop failure, it probably continues the description of what will occur in the exile where there will be no sacrifices at all. ***They will not pour out wine as a libation to the LORD.*** Libations, drink offerings (cf. Exod. 29:38-41; Lev. 23:13; Num. 15:1-12), were a part, though in fact only a minor part, of the warranted worship of the LORD. In the constricted circumstances of exile there will be no opportunity even for libations. ***Their sacrifices will not please him.***[53] 'Be pleasing'/'be

---

52. There is another instance here of a play between *šûb*, 'to return' and *yāšab*, 'to dwell' (cf. 3:45; 11:5-11; 14:2-7). For the change in number in 'they will eat' after the singular collective noun 'Ephraim', compare 6:4.

53. The Massoretic accentuation favours reading 'and they will not please him. Their sacrifices will be like bread of mournings to them', but there is some early versional evidence for reading 'their sacrifices' with what precedes. Also, the verb *ye'erəbû* from the root *'rb* may have the meaning 'to offer' (IV) as Ugaritic evidence may suggest, rather than 'to be pleasing' (III) (cf. *HALOT* 877). This is found in GNB ('they will not give him sacrifices'), but it is not convincing or needed.

acceptable' is part of the technical vocabulary of sacrifice (cf. Jer. 6:20; Mal. 3:4). The thought, however, is probably not that their sacrifices will be unacceptable because they have been offered improperly (8:13) or were of poor quality (cf. Mal. 1:8), but that will be non-existent. Their captors will not permit them to offer any sacrifices at all to what they view as an alien deity.

⌞They will be⌟ like bread of mourning to them alludes to a gathering to mourn over the loss of the departed. The bread eaten at funeral meals was regarded as ***unclean*** (cf. 9:3) because the corpse defiled the house and all who came into contact with it for seven days (Num. 19:14; cf. also Deut. 26:12-15; Hag. 2:12-13). The supplement 'they' may refer to their sacrifices (cf. NIV, NRSV) or, more probably, to their bread as equivalent to food in general (RSV).

Their bread will be just for their lives in that it will simply be a source of physical nourishment—and probably none too bountiful for all that. Their food will also be deprived of spiritual significance in that ***it will not enter the house of the LORD***, since its origin would render it incapable of dedication to him. Hosea's reference may be to bread as used generally in temple worship (Lev. 23:17-18; 24:5-7), but mention of the house of the LORD in a northern context is problematic. It is also possible that by 'the house of the LORD' Hosea may be referring to the land as in 8:1 and 9:15. In that case it would be possible to translate 'he will not enter the house of the LORD', and find here a prediction that he (that is, any Israelite) would become so defiled by his contact with pagan uncleanness in Assyria that he would be ceremonially incapable of returning to the land and worshipping the LORD there.

9:5 What will you do on a day of an appointed festival
or on the day of the feast of the LORD?

The two-barrelled rhetorical question drives home the point (cf. 6:4). Hosea draws his hearers into exploring the outcome he predicts—an outcome which they of course rejected. In the exile they will be unable to celebrate the feasts of the LORD. ***Appointed festival*** and ***feast*** both designate celebrations appointed in the Mosaic law, though the latter term is more especially points to the joy associated with such an occasion.[54] Here the second expression, being definite, is more specific than the first. The 'festival of Yahweh' occurs in Leviticus 23:39 and Judges 21:19 for the harvest festival which was intended to be a time

54. *Waw* is taken here as introducing an alternative, 'or'. It may, however, be epexegetic, 'even on a day of a feast of the LORD'.

of rejoicing, and the phrase supports the idea that this speech was originally delivered at such a festival. In the difficult times that lay ahead the community will be unable to gather and celebrate those feasts—and certainly not in the corrupt fashion they had become accustomed to.

9:6 For when they have gone because of devastation,
Egypt will gather them,
Memphis will bury them;
their silver treasure—
weeds will possess them,
thornbushes ⌊will be⌋ in their tents.

For introduces two factors which will prevent the festival being held in the way they have become used to: the people will no longer be in the land; and they will no longer possess the resources (or the liturgical equipment) to support the celebration. ***When*** (literally, 'behold') sets out a set of circumstances envisaged as complete: 'in the event that they have gone'. As the Assyrians pressed further south, not everyone waited to be captured or killed. Many refugees had already fled to Judah and others would follow. Others yet again would go as far as Egypt ***because of*** (or, 'away from') ***devastation*** (cf. 7:13; 10:14) as the enemy spoiled the land and enslaved its inhabitants. But escape will not solve their problems. The prophet uses two instances of personification to portray the circumstances the people will be confronted with. ***Egypt will gather them*** (cf. the ominous use of 'gather' in 8:10) suggests more than 'provide them with asylum'. It pictures them as being taken into some form of confinement or detention. Egypt will not be a sanctuary, but a prison—indeed, it will become a cemetery. ***Memphis***, the former capital of the land, was situated in northern Egypt, on the west bank of the Nile, about thirteen miles (21 km) south of modern Cairo. It was known to have a vast cemetery which had already been in use for many centuries. Those who flee south will not enjoy freedom to celebrate the feasts of the LORD because they will be living in restricted circumstances until their deaths.

Further, they will no longer have the resources to maintain their traditional feasts.[55] The picture seems to be one of the refugees fleeing south and, as they go, discarding ***their silver treasure*** (literally, 'preciousness with reference to their silver'). Most probably this

55. It is unclear if the second part of the verse is to be understood as a bicolon ('Weeds will possess their silver treasure; thornbushes will be in their tents') or a tricolon. Stylistic considerations, particularly the tricolon in the first part of the verse, favour the latter option here also.

mention of part of their possessions is a synecdoche for all their wealth, including, but not exclusively consisting of, all the accoutrements of their idol worship. So intent are they on speedy escape that they cannot let themselves be held back by unnecessary encumbrances. ***Weeds will possess them***, overgrowing their chattels as they lie discarded at the roadside. ***Their tents*** may well be a traditional description for their family homes, now abandoned and dilapidated, with only ***thornbushes*** left growing there. If the silver is particularly cultic equipment, then tents may refer to their temporary shelters at cultic sites, but a more general scene is all that is required.

REFLECTION

• Who does not wish to enjoy happiness? It is especially unsettling to be told not to rejoice (9:1) at a time of celebration and gladness. Is not one who brings such a message just a killjoy? Hardly: if the volcano is about to erupt, if an explosive device has been detected, if a flood is going to sweep all before it, if a deadly germ had been released. No matter how intense the satisfaction of the moment, it is not true joy if it is not based on a secure foundation, if it is unable to cope with the shocks and disturbances of life—and of these the greatest is when God demands a reckoning. Then the folly of joy based on material prosperity or exploitation of others will be exposed as fraudulent. 'Look ⌞this is⌟ the man who would not make God his refuge, but trusted in the abundance of his riches and was strong by the destruction he caused' (Ps. 52:7; cf. Ps. 62:10). All such conduct can achieve is limited to this life (cf. Ps. 17:14; Luke 16:25), and joy derived from it shrivels up when confronted by the question, 'What will you do when …?' (9:5; cf. Luke 6:24; 12:20).

(2) Prophetic Misdirection (9:7-9)

The bracketing effect of 'punishment' (9:7) and 'punish' (9:9) indicates that these three verses form a unit whose overall theme is the certainty of the reckoning which is going to be required from the people for their behaviour. However, the details of what is described are far from unclear. There are two main approaches: either Hosea attacks a prophetic figure or the prophets as a whole in the community (cf. 4:5), or else his audience attacks Hosea as a fool and as mad, and the prophet rebuts their conclusion and charges them with being a snare to him, even in the sanctuary (9:8), and as committing an outrage similar to that in Gibeah in years gone by (9:9). Neither interpretation is implausible, though the former is somewhat more likely.

9:7 The days of punishment have come;
the days of retribution have come.
Let Israel know ⌊it⌋!
The prophet is a fool!
The man of the Spirit is mad!
because of the greatness of your iniquity
and ⌊because⌋ hostility ⌊is⌋ great.

The verse begins with a repeated assertion that divine judgement is inescapable. ***Punishment*** is 'visitation', the inspection by a superior who requires his subordinate to account for his actions (cf. 1:4; 8:13). The root in itself does not denote punishment but, if there is any malfeasance, then that would be the inevitable consequence. The way the root is repeated in 9:9 shows that imposition of penalty is in mind here. Both Yahweh and Tiglath-Pileser are marching against Israel. ***Retribution*** conveys the idea of complete payment for what has been done. Since the people of Israel have rebelled against their divine Overlord, he may justly impose a severe sentence.

But is this requital viewed as already present ('days … have come', e.g. ESV), or still future ('days … are coming', NIV)? Certainly the former rendering is more common in English translations, but a significant group of commentators take the verbs to be prophetic perfects ('shall come'), and understand the prediction of impending disaster to continue from 9:6. While that is grammatically possible, the deliberate repetition of ***have come*** suggests that Hosea is pointing to some catastrophe which has already struck the nation, though it may not yet be exhausted. Furthermore, ***the days***, rather than a singular 'day', probably points to the whole period of Assyrian pressure after 745 B.C.

In the Hebrew text the third line is associated with the words before it. If it is translated 'Israel will know ⌊it⌋' (cf. ESV), then 'this meaning is surprisingly banal for Hosea' (Irvine 1998:646), even when it is glossed as 'Soon Israel will know this all too well' (NLT). However, knowing and not knowing constitute one of the themes Hosea pursued throughout his ministry. The expression takes on a deeper significance when rendered as, ***Let Israel know ⌊it⌋.***[56] The use of 'know' without a

56. A frequently adopted alternative (e.g. 'Israel cries', NRSV) reads in place of *yēdəʿû*, 'they will know', *yārîʿû*, from *rwʿ*, 'to shout', supposing a scribal misreading in the MT of *daleth* instead of *resh*, and taking the phrase as introducing the following words. The verb *rwʿ*, however, means 'to raise a shout', and elsewhere it does not introduce direct speech. Moreover, the Massoretic accents associate 'Let Israel know!' with the preceding clauses.

stated object is also found in 7:9a, b; 8:4, and the reference has to be deduced from the context. What the prophet calls on Israel to recognise is not the fact of their suffering—they were well aware of that—but its source. They saw the hand of Tiglath-Pileser in all that had come upon them, but not that of the LORD. The prophet urges them even at this late stage to probe more deeply than political or military considerations and recognise that what they had experienced was the LORD's action against their rebellion.

The second part of the verse begins without any indication of a change of speaker. Such a signalled transition may not always be present in Hosea, and many interpreters take the words, ***The prophet is a fool! The man of the Spirit is mad!***, as the people's rejection of Hosea and his assessment of events (cf. the quotation marks in GNB, the reordering of the concluding lines in NIV, and the employment of both techniques, NLT). The reaction of the people would then indicate that they are so sure of themselves that they will simply shout down this individual who presents such a message of rejection to them, possibly by interrupting their festival (reading these verses in terms of the same scenario as 9:1-6). They characterise the prophet as 'a fool', one speaking nonsense (cf. Prov. 10:8). 'The man of the Spirit' as an alternative term for 'prophet' occurs only here. It is a suitable term for denoting the source of the prophet's message and ministry as being divinely originated and empowered (cf. Num. 11:25; Ezek. 2:2; 3:24; 13:3). This description had been employed of the prophets of the north (Elijah, 1 Kgs. 18:12; Micaiah, 1 Kgs. 22:21; Elisha, 2 Kgs. 2:9), but it would not be used here as a compliment. Rather they characterise him as 'mad', one who is crazed and not in his right mind, whose speech consists of demented ravings (cf. 2 Kgs. 9:11; Jer. 29:26).

However, elsewhere in the prophets when there is an interchange with the people, the presence of such a disputation is marked by words such as 'you say' (Mal. 1:2) or 'your people say' (Ezek. 33:17). It is therefore more probable that the prophet himself continues to speak here and criticises sharply either an individual who claims to be a prophet (cf. 4:5) or, if the singulars are collective, the whole class of such prophets.[57] They would be establishment figures present at the festival who themselves claimed to be endowed with the Spirit (1 Kgs. 22:24), but who promoted the syncretistic religion of the north and

57. This view was presented by several medieval Jewish commentators and taken up by Calvin (1986:323–327) and Keil (1977:122–123). For further details in relation to this passage, see Irvine 1998.

supported the official propaganda line regarding current events. So they would have rejected Hosea's message and encouraged the people to take no notice of it. Instead their argument would be that the ebb in national fortunes was only temporary and that all would indeed work out well.

Addressing the individual who has opposed him (or if the singular is collective, the group who opposed him) Hosea asserts that ***because of the greatness of your iniquity, hostility ⌞is⌟ great.***[58] 'Iniquity' (cf. 7:1) points to deviation from the standards of behaviour required by the LORD in that the prophets who claimed to be divine spokesmen were promoting the corrupt practices of the north (cf. 9:8). Their rejection of the LORD's message as brought by the true prophet Hosea is the culminating instance of their errors. The repetition of the root ***great***/'many' (used of number or extent, or both) links their rebellious behaviour with that of the people who adopted their outlook. ***Hostility*** expresses uncompromising antagonism. The term is found in the Old Testament only in Hosea (here and in the following verse), but it was later used in the Qumran Scrolls to describe the work of the enemies of God. The ministry of the false prophets who claimed to speak in the name of the LORD but who were actually impostors had contributed significantly to the spiritual animosity and blindness of Israel to the truth.

9:8 A watchman ⌞is⌟ Ephraim with my God;
a prophet; a fowler's snare on all his ways;
hostility ⌞is⌟ in the house of his God.

The rendering of this verse given above shows that it too is difficult to understand, and hence troublesome to translate. Any interpretation of these words, especially those in the first line, is tentative, and scholars frequently have recourse to emendation to obtain a satisfactory meaning. However, the variety of proposals brought forward indicates that none is convincing.[59]

---

58. The expression is terse and this rendering assumes that *ʿal* functions as a preposition and that the *waw* introduces an apodosis. Alternatively, *ʿal* is a conjunction and the following words are a non-verbal clause, 'because your iniquity is greatness'. This makes it easier to read *waw* as apodictic, though it requires the noun 'greatness' to be taken adjectivally.

59. A summary of the proposals for understanding 9:8 may be found in Dobbie (1955). It is difficult to determine the sense and function of *ṣōpeh*. Is it a noun or a participle? Does it convey the positive image of a 'watchman' (the expected sense of this word), or is it used negatively, 'to spy on, lie in wait for' (cf. Ps. 37:32)? How is it related to Ephraim? (To translate 'the watchman of Ephraim' is to ignore the Massoretic pointing which has an

One way of trying to make sense of the text as it has been transmitted to us is to assume that Hosea continues to criticise the religious spokesmen of the north and to reject their analysis of events, and that he does so by speaking sarcastically. This is something which he would have clearly conveyed to his original audience by his intonation, but which is difficult to indicate in writing. Sarcasm ostensibly says one thing, while the speaker's tone of the voice indicates that the opposite meaning is intended. It can therefore be difficult to detect when words are written down. Perhaps the sense of what Hosea said can be brought out in English by using questions or exclamations. '⌞So⌟ Ephraim ⌞is⌟ a watchman with my God? ⌞He is⌟ a prophet? A fowler's snare ⌞is⌟ on all his ways.' Or, '⌞So⌟ Ephraim ⌞is⌟ a watchman with my God! ⌞He is⌟ a prophet! A fowler's snare ⌞is⌟ on all his ways!'

Watchman is used metaphorically for a prophet (Jer. 6:17; Ezek. 3:17; 33:7; Mic. 7:4). The duty of the city watchman was to be constantly on the alert and to sound the alarm when danger threatened, and in a similar fashion the prophet was expected to be vigilant in detecting threats to the spiritual wellbeing of the community and to issue due warning. Hosea had performed that duty in view of the

---

absolute form and not a construct, *ṣōpēh*.) Is 'a prophet' to be taken with the first line or, as indicated by the Massoretic accents, with the second (cf. NKJV)? The latter is generally rejected in English translations (cf. NIV, NRSV).

Two recent attempts to resolve the matter are worthy of mention as a sample of the various options. Macintosh (1997:354–355) takes 'watch' in a hostile sense to refer to Ephraim's hostility towards the prophet. Also, even though 'a prophet' is represented in all the early versions, he regards it as a gloss which was introduced (wrongly) to indicate that 'watchman' should be understood as a legitimate prophet. In the remainder of the verse 'his' continues the references to Ephraim whose doom is portrayed because he 'stands in confrontation with my God'.

Stuart (1987:146) takes *ṣōpeh* in its ordinary sense, but includes 'a prophet' with the first line which he understands as consisting of two ironic questions with which Hosea rebuts the nation's attitude to himself by exposing their pretentious behaviour: 'Is Ephraim a watchman? Is God's people a prophet?' To do this he vocalises *ʿim*, 'with', as *ʿam*, 'people'—this is a commonly accepted emendation on the grounds that it provides a suitable parallel to Ephraim, whereas 'with' is difficult to interpret. He also reads *ʾĕlōhîm*, 'God' (with the LXX) rather than *ʾĕlōhāy*, 'my God'. Stuart's approach seems to be along the right lines, but the emendations he introduces are unnecessary. There is no difficulty in understanding Hosea to expostulate sarcastically with the people to the effect: 'So Ephraim ⌞is⌟ a watchman with my God! ⌞He is⌟ a prophet!'

impending crisis (cf. 5:8; 8:1), but he rejects the thought that Ephraim and its prophetic spokesmen were capable of acting in that way. ***With my God***[60] emphasises that the source of Hosea's message was quite distinct from wherever the spurious prophets may have derived what they said. Jeremiah was later to record the LORD's verdict: 'Among the prophets of Samaria I have seen a disgusting thing: they prophesied by Baal and they led astray my people Israel' (Jer. 23:13). So there could well be extended to Hosea's contemporaries the verdict given later against the false prophets in Jerusalem: 'they lead my people astray by their falsehoods and by their recklessness' (Jer. 23:32). Consequently in '⌊He is⌋ a prophet!' Hosea contemptuously denounces them as incapable of speaking as a genuine prophet should.

In talking about a ***fowler's snare*** (for 'fowler', see on 7:10; for 'snare', cf. Prov. 7:23), Hosea describes something which is concealed and intended to capture a bird for consumption. The precise sense of the line is determined by whether it is taken as one or two statements, and that depends on how verbal supplements are added in translation. But the snare points to the message brought by the false prophets. Its true significance is not obvious to those who hear it, and so they will be trapped and killed like unwary birds deceived by a fowler. ***On all his ways*** denotes every policy Ephraim adopts in the light of the deceptive message of the prophets will prove equally deadly.

The house of his God may refer to the land as a whole, but probably 'his God' (or 'his god') is a deliberate contrast with 'my God' in the first line. In the sacred precincts where they gather for worship there is ***hostility*** (cf. 9:7). Ephraim's attitude as fostered by his religious observances is one of total opposition to the truth, to the prophet who presents it, and so to the God who is truth and from whom truth comes. Hosea is asserting that there is an irreconcilable clash of religious systems, and a choice has to be made.

9:9 They have deeply corrupted ⌊themselves⌋
as in the days of Gibeah.
He will remember their iniquity;
he will punish their sins.

As well as making many their transgressions (cf. Amos 5:12), the people have also made them deep. ***They have deeply corrupted themselves*** is literally, 'they have gone deep' (cf. 5:2), 'they have corrupted/

60. It is unnecessary to repoint *ʿim-ʾĕlōhāy*, 'with my God', as *ʿam-ʾĕlōhāy*, 'people of my God' as in RSV, 'The prophet is the watchman of Ephraim, the people of my God.'

ruined', cf. 13:9). The expression shows that their misconduct was no trivial or passing matter, but entrenched in their hearts. The term 'corrupted' links back to the conduct of the pre-flood generation (Gen. 6:11-13), and threatens a similar outcome.

But Hosea's historical retrospect is not principally focused as far back as the flood. Though Gibeah had been as a base for Saul in the early days of the monarchy and Philistine invasion (1 Sam. 13:2, 15), ***as in the days of Gibeah*** (cf. 5:8; 10:9) points back to an incident earlier than that, during a low point in Israel's existence in the period of the judges. At Gibeah the Levite's concubine had been raped and murdered by the town's inhabitants (Judg. 19–21). It is noteworthy that the narrative also describes both the retribution that came upon Gibeah (Judg. 20) and a ribald dance in the vineyard at the yearly feast of the LORD at Shiloh (Judg 21:19)—which was probably not much different from what Hosea was having to confront in his own day. Hosea's point is that rebellious and scandalous behaviour was no innovation, but had been true of the nation for a long time, and such endemic misconduct will inevitably lead to retribution because of the character of God. He may not act immediately, but ***he will remember*** (cf. 7:2) ***their iniquity*** (cf. 7:1) and when he does he will take appropriate action. ***He will punish their sins***/'call their sins to account' (cf. 8:13; 9:7), as he scrutinises what they have done and reaches an appropriate verdict. After all, the incident at Gibeah had seen the tribe of Benjamin virtually annihilated at the LORD's command (Judg. 20:23, 28); what penalty would be imposed now?

REFLECTION

- False prophecy was not just an Old Testament phenomenon. Those who claim to be divine spokesmen, but are not, will continue to exist throughout the current age (cf. Matt. 7:15, 22; 24:11). Their plausible speech and even their power to work wonders will be such as 'to lead astray, if possible, even the elect' (Matt. 24:24). Consequently there is an on-going need 'to test the spirits to see whether they are from God' (1 John 4:1). There are some obvious criteria which may be applied, such as testing if their proclamation conforms to the gospel requirement of setting forth Jesus Christ come in the flesh (1 John 4:2), as well as promoting acceptance of all other doctrines of the gospel, and conformity in life-style to the example of Christ. But even such scrutiny may not detect every deceiver because of the skill with which false teachers may disguise their identity and purpose (cf. 2 Cor. 11:13-15). Ultimately spiritual discrimination is a gift of the

Holy Spirit who guides into all truth (John 16:27) both the individual whom he renews and the body of Christ collectively which, as God's temple, he indwells (1 Cor. 4:16). The Spirit who has inspired the Scriptures continues his work by assisting believers so that they may arrive at the correct interpretation of the message.

- Hosea does not mince his words in denouncing falsehood (9:7-8). Many times today the church has a false perception of what true love requires. The relativism of contemporary culture denies that there is absolute truth, and affirms the need for inclusivism and acceptance of all points of view. By implicitly adopting the politically correct view of being nice to all and offending none, the church has muted its criticism of those who deny the truth and has failed to expose the inadequacy of their views. But Christ was scathing in his critique of the scribes and Pharisees (Matt. 23), and Paul opposed Peter to his face because of his conduct (Gal. 2:11). When momentous issues are at stake, confrontation and plain speaking are unavoidable. Indeed, they are the expression of true love and concern for those who are being led astray eternally. Nehemiah was instrumental in keeping the post-exilic community in Jerusalem on the right tracks through his outspoken confrontation of those whose practices were undermining its well-being (Neh. 13:8, 11, 17, 25, 28).

F. Failed Prospects (9:10–10:15)

It is generally acknowledged that there is a significant thematic break in Hosea's material after 9:9, where a Massoretic division marker is also located. In this section the prophet has little new content, but re-presents topics he has already explored. Hosea again employs the technique of historical retrospect (cf. 6:7; 9:9), but now he does so more extensively as he examines the outworking of God's purposes. This is largely done by means of three images—grapes in the wilderness (9:10-17), a luxuriant vine (10:1-10), a trained heifer (10:11-15)—which incorporate nostalgic reflections on Israel's past relationship with the LORD. Each image embodies the theme of reversal, with early promise giving way to rebellion and so leading on to the tragedy of impending loss. However, these sections are not totally without mention of hope (10:12), though that awaits fuller development in the surprising intervention of divine grace set out in chapter 11. That display of God's love shines all the more brightly because of the sombre note of these three preceding sections.

(1) Grapes in the Wilderness (9:10-17)

This section begins with God's surprised delight with Israel when they left Egypt (9:10a,b). This positive presentation of the wilderness period occurs elsewhere in Hosea (2:15; 9:13a; 10:1a; 11:1, 3-4; 12:9). But the initial prospect did not last. Through their misconduct (9:10c) all that was left for the people was judgement and extinction. The consequences of Israel's sin at Baal-Peor are examined first (9:10-14), and then the similar aftermath of how they behaved at Gilgal (9:15-17). There is a thematic inclusion in which 9:10 matches 9:17, from wilderness wanderings to wandering among the nations.

The prevalence of divine speech in this section contrasts with 9:1-9, but 9:14 and 9:17 exhibit Hosea's personal reaction to the situation so that the prophecy almost becomes a conversation between the prophet and the LORD. There is development of agricultural imagery from the sowing and reaping of 8:7, and the nettles and thorns of desolation (9:6). The comparison may develop the idea of fruitfulness associated with the Feast of Tabernacles/Booths which is the probable background for the earlier part of chapter 9. The LORD is portrayed as a farmer who eagerly awaited the yield which would come from the crops he had planted, but who was frustrated and dismayed by the failure of the harvest and who would therefore take drastic steps to deal with the situation.

9:10 Like grapes in the wilderness
I found Israel;
like firstfruit on a fig tree in its beginning
I saw your fathers.
⌊But⌋ they came to Baal-Peor,
and dedicated themselves to 'the shame'
and became abhorrent like ⌊that which⌋ they loved.

The LORD speaks and presents the beginning of his dealings with Israel as a happy time in their relationship when the people, though far from perfect in their conduct, nevertheless responded positively to him (cf. Exod. 19:8; 24:3, 7; Deut. 5:27-29; Jer. 2:2-3). Moreover, God himself was delighted. ***Grapes in the wilderness*** is a picture of the unexpected—a wilderness is an unlikely spot for a vineyard—but the surprise is a pleasant one. Perhaps the image is of an oasis, a spot where a weary traveller would be sustained and refreshed even in such a harsh environment. ***I found Israel*** contains a note of tender reminiscence. 'He found him in a wilderness-land and in the howling waste of the desert; he surrounded him, he took care of him, he protected him like the apple of his eye' (Deut. 32:10). It may be significant that there is no hint that the divine pleasure in the covenant relationship was reciprocated by the people. The subsequent discussion of the conduct of 'your fathers' shows that Israel here refers to the early days of the entire nation, not just to the northern kingdom.

Firstfruit on a fig tree also conveys the idea of a delightful surprise (cf. Isa. 28:4; Jer. 24:2; Mic. 7:1). ***In its beginning*** is usually taken to point to early figs which ripen at the end of May (two months before the main crop) on sprouts formed in the preceding season, but it may refer to a fig tree coming to maturity in its first fruit-bearing season after five or six years of initial growth. In either case the figs would be a special treat. ***I saw your fathers*** reminds the people of how the LORD had regarded their forebears. 'See' is used in the sense of 'view favourably', not merely 'observe'. 'Your' (plural) is the only use in this passage of the second person (perhaps to include the prophet), and the speech reverts to impersonal third person references to Israel because their initial attitude did not last. In addition, this link with past generations opens the way for the thought that the children have repeated the mistakes of their fathers.

⌊But⌋ they expresses a strong disjunction from the preceding picture of delight.[61] Even in that early period, Israel spoiled its relationship with the LORD by its inexplicable and shameful behaviour. The place name ***Baal-Peor*** ('the Baal of Peor', cf. Num. 25:1-9; see also comments on 2:17) is an instance of localisation of the Canaanite deity Baal in a particular Moabite mountain, twelve miles (20 km) north-east of the inflow of the Jordan into the Dead Sea. From it Balaam had been asked to curse Israel (Num. 23:27-28), and there Israel had been induced to indulge in Canaanite practices through entanglement with Moabite women who 'invited the people to the sacrifices of their gods, and the people ate and bowed down to their gods. So Israel joined themselves to Baal of Peor' (Num. 25:2-3a). They ***dedicated themselves to 'the shame'*** describes participation in a religious ritual by which they professed their allegiance to Baal. 'Dedicated themselves' is not the word employed in Numbers ('joined themselves to'/'harnessed themselves to', Num. 25:3), but is a verb similar to that employed for the absolute dedication of the Nazirites (Num. 6:1-21), and also for priestly separation (Lev. 22:2). This inter-faith service was

61. The disjunction is expressed by the initial *hēmmâ*, 'they', which, because its sense is also conveyed by the following inflected verb form, functions antithetically (*IBHS* §16.3.2d).

not a neutral or lovingly inclusive act, but a disruptive violation of their covenant bond with the LORD (cf. Ps. 106:28-29).

'The shame' (*habbošet*) is an oblique reference to Baal. Later, it became a recognised scribal technique to substitute this term for Baal as a means of indicating aversion to the heathen god (cf. Jer. 3:24; 11:13), and so names such as Ishboseth (2 Sam. 7:8) or Mephiboseth (2 Sam. 21:8) are later respellings to avoid earlier forms such as Eshbaal (1 Chron. 8:33) which date from a more distant period when *baʿal* could still be legitimately used of the LORD himself (cf. 2:16).

Since the people's devotion to the LORD had waned and they had engaged in such unfaithfulness, the LORD's attitude towards them changed. They ***became abhorrent***/'abominated objects'. This is a term of utter reproach because of the detestable nature of their idolatrous conduct (cf. Jer. 4:1; 7:30; Ezek. 5:11; 7:20). It was not just the shrines or the idols which were abominated by the LORD, but those who worshipped in this way—and that led to the death of 24,000 (Num. 25:9). (Hosea is indirectly pointing out that the LORD's attitude and his condemnation back then had not altered in the intervening years.) ***Like ⌊that which⌋ they loved*** points to the pernicious nature of the influences to which they had exposed themselves.[62] Paganism is aggressive and seeks to subvert the loyalty of the people of the LORD. Toleration can easily overstep the mark and lead to contamination.

9:11 Ephraim—like a bird their glory will fly away:
no birth, and no pregnancy, and no conception.

There is a change of focus from past conduct to the consequences of the infidelity of the present generation of the covenant people. The fronting of ***Ephraim*** is a feature of Hosea's style (cf. 7:8; 9:13; 14:8) to concentrate on the contemporary northern kingdom. ***Their glory*** does not refer to the LORD's presence with them (cf. Ezek. 3:23; 8:4) or to Baal's (cf. 10:5), but to the size of their population and the consequent prosperity of the land (cf. 4:7; Isa. 5:13). 'Glory' was located at the opposite end of the spectrum of social prestige from 'shame'. The people had put their confidence in economic prosperity and increased

62. Hubbard (1989:165) adopts the view that the translation of *kəʾohŏbām* should be active, 'like Baal's love for them'. However, the third person plural pronominal suffix with the infinitive construct is in this instance ambiguous. Whereas *kə* used as a temporal indicator generally has a subjective suffix, it is here used comparatively, and contextual considerations determine whether a suffix is objective or subjective. English translations opt for the subjective use.

numbers to perpetuate the nation and to give it a solid foundation for survival and enhanced prestige. But, ***like a bird***, possibly a collective use evoking a picture of a flock of disturbed birds moving off in all directions and incapable of being turned back, population growth ***will fly away*** completely and swiftly (cf. Prov. 23:4-5). So it is predicted that those who have acted like birds (7:11-12) will experience the just and appropriate consequences of their behaviour (but note also 11:10-11).

This flight of their glory is expanded by three terse negative phrases in which 'no' represents the Hebrew preposition 'from' used privatively (cf. 6:6). Ephraim's plans will not come to fruition. Their futility is traced back through three stages of the process by which life begins. So there will be a reversal of the fertility which they had expected from the Baal cult because the LORD's intervention in judgement will involve the death of the community.

9:12 Even if they bring up their sons,
I will bereave them till none is left;
for also woe ⌞will be⌟ to them when I turn from them!

The disaster of the curse expressed in the previous verse is intensified. It is not stated that there will be surviving children, but even should there be, that would not reverse the curse (for this style of argument see 8:7; 9:16; 13:15). The collapse facing the nation will not be evaded through an improbable chain of events; there can be no escape. ***Even if they bring up their sons***/'children', then the LORD will act to ***bereave them till none is left*** (literally, 'bereave them from/without a human being').[63] This is the outcome of the imposition of the curse of the broken covenant (cf. Deut. 28:63).

The reason (***for***) for this drastic decline in their population is stated as ***also woe ⌞will be⌟ to them when I turn from them.***[64] 'Woe' (cf. 7:13) calls for an immediate expression of mourning in anticipation of the impending and inescapable catastrophe when God withdraws his gracious presence from them and no longer recognises them as his people. They will become Lo-Ammi (1:9) and so will have removed from them the blessings of the covenant, particularly increase in numbers (Gen. 17:6; 35:11).

---

63. 'From' is another instance of privative *min*, cf. 9:11.

64. The root *śûr* in *bəśûrî*, 'in my turning', is not attested elsewhere, but the rabbinic tradition that it is a dialectal variant of the standard form *sûr* is plausible.

9:13 Ephraim, as I have seen ⌞it⌟,
⌞is⌟ with respect to Tyre planted in a meadow,
but Ephraim must bring out his sons to the one who is slaughtering.

The verse has been variously understood. (1) Some follow LXX in finding hunting imagery: 'Ephraim, as I have seen, presented their children to be hunted'[65] (cf. RSV, NEB, GNB), referring to the risks of war into which the nation has plunged. (2) Another approach is adopted by the Vulgate which identifies here a reference to the city of Tyre, 'Ephraim, as I have seen that Tyre was founded in beauty' (cf. NASB, NIV, NKJV), where Tyre functions as a symbol of a proud, self-sufficient city, able to withstand aggression because of its island fortress, which Josephus records successfully withstood a five year siege by Shalmaneser V in this period (*Antiquities* 9.284–87). (3) A further technique is to retain the root meaning of Tyre (*ṣôr*), 'Ephraim planted on a rock', which could be an image of barrenness and lack of productivity (Theodotion, Coptic). (4) Again, another meaning may be proposed for *ṣôr*, this time based on an Arabic root. 'Ephraim, as I have seen, was like a young palm planted in a meadow' (ESV, cf. NRSV). A reference to a tree has the merit of cohering with 'plant'/'transplant', and would point to the advantageous beginning which had been accorded to Ephraim. (5) As a final possibility one might mention the identification of a specific idiom involving the verb 'to see' in the sense 'select something for a purpose' (cf. Gen. 22:8): 'Ephraim as I selected it for a Tyre planted in the valley', where Tyre is the flourishing commercial metropolis, and Ephraim being largely inland is instead described as 'planted in a meadow' (cf Keil 1977:126..; McComiskey 1992:150–152).[66]

The simplest view of the Hebrew words as found in the Massoretic

65. The LXX appears to have read the text as *ləṣayid šātû bānāyw*, with *ṣayid* having the sense 'hunting', 'game'. The LXX also seems to read the first two consonants of *šətûlâ*, 'planted' as a separate word (*šît*, 'to set'), and did not represent the remaining consonant in their translation (perhaps reading *lô*, 'for himself', as an ethic dative and disregarding it). Further for *bənāweh*, 'in a meadow' the LXX read *bānāyw*, 'his sons'.

66. To make his approach plausible McComiskey (1992:150–152) has to posit the prior existence of a body of prophetic material similar to Isa. 23:1-18 and Amos 1:9-10 which was already familiar to Hosea's audience so that they would readily supplement his saying to yield 'Ephraim—just as I have chosen [judgement] for Tyre, planted in [its] place, so [I have chosen for] Ephraim to lead forth its sons to the murderer.' The verb is considered to do double-duty in both parts of the saying.

text (though not without its difficulties, including the unexpected mention of Tyre, which does not arise from the immediate context) is ***Ephraim, as I have seen ⌊it⌋, ⌊is⌋ with respect to Tyre planted in a meadow.*** This would be a reference to the militarily strategic and agriculturally fruitful location of Ephraim which had contributed to its prosperity (cf. the description of the territory assigned to the Joseph tribes, Deut. 33:13-17). It may also reflect the extent to which the northern kingdom provided grain and other produce which was traded through the Phoenicians of Tyre. Possibly the idea is that Ephraim was even more advantageously situated than the prosperous maritime power of Tyre.

Yet despite its good fortune this self-same ***Ephraim*** 'is to bring out', that is, ***must bring out***[67] ***his sons to the one who is slaughtering.*** Mention of 'sons' presents Ephraim as a parent, and fits in with the theme of surrounding verses. This interpretation would be even more suasive if we knew of a recent bloodbath in the region surrounding Tyre as the Assyrians moved south. 'Slaughtering' mainly described violent killing of people; it is never used of sacrifice. This is a divine threat that their behaviour will lead to extermination.

9:14 Give to them, LORD —
what will you give?
Give to them a miscarrying womb
and dry breasts.

This verse is unusual in that the prophet speaks for himself, addressing the LORD in prayer.[68] Before the initial plea, ***Give to them, LORD***, is completed, it is interrupted by the question, ***what will you give?*** This expresses the prophet's uncertainty as to how to proceed. He displays an emotionally charged reaction which in measure matches that of the LORD himself (cf. 6:4; 11:8). He does not contest the LORD's right to act in judgement against the people, but he does recoil in horror from the prospect of the indiscriminate slaughter generated by an Assyrian invasion. Instead, perhaps with a view to mitigating the penalty, he suggests that the LORD imposes punishment not through enemy invasion, but directly: ***give to them a miscarrying womb and dry breasts.*** 'Miscarry' repeats the same root as 'bereave' (9:12). What Hosea asks

67. Literally, 'to bring out' with *lə* expressing compulsion GKC §114h, k.

68. 'Conscious of the fact that he is Yahweh's messenger, the prophet most often utilises the personal form of divine speech; he is the announcer of God's message' (Wolff 1974:xxiii). It is consequently all the more significant when the prophet does speak in his own name (9:14, 17).

should come upon those who have violated the covenant picks up the thought of 9:11 and seeks for a reversal of Jacob's blessing upon Joseph, the father of Ephraim, regarding 'Shaddai who will bless you ... with blessings of the breasts and womb' (Gen. 49:25). It is still judgement—that cannot be avoided—but less harsh. It is better that Ephraim's offspring never come into existence than that they suffer at the hands of the notoriously heartless and cruel Assyrians. Further, the imposition of barrenness would be an appropriate penalty to impose on a nation which had devoted itself to the fertility religion of Baal. Hosea is struggling to find a route between acquiescing in the divine revelation and compassion for his people.

9:15 All their evil ⌊is⌋ in Gilgal;
  indeed, there I have come to hate them.
On account of the evil of their deeds
  I will drive them from my house.
I will no longer love them;
  all their leaders are stubborn.

If this divine word came as a response to Hosea's intercession, then it bids the prophet to consider again what has happened in the past, and what was currently the case. The reference in ***their*** and ***them*** is not specified, but is clearly the people of the north, and ***Gilgal*** is selected as typical of their past and present behaviour. Gilgal ('a heap of stones') is the name of three, perhaps five, sites in the Old Testament. If it refers here to any of the others, such as the Gilgal south of Shechem, then the events alluded to can no longer be ascertained. However, the most probable reference is to the Gilgal which lay on the east bank of the Jordan, facing Baal-Peor and in the vicinity of Jericho. It was the site of the first encampment of Israel after they had crossed the Jordan, a place of rededication to the covenant (Josh. 4:19-20). Gilgal was also where the monarchy had begun with the recognition of Saul as king (1 Sam. 11:14-15), an allusion perhaps supported by the subsequent mention of leaders. But a contemporary reference seems probable. Gilgal was at the centre of the Baal cult in the north (cf. 4:15; 12:11; Amos 4:4; 5:5). It was there that ***all their evil*** which they practised in their perverted worship could be openly found, and it was representative of the whole land.

The connective *kî* usually rendered 'for' does not have a causative function here, and is probably to be translated as an asseverative, ***indeed***. What can be seen at Gilgal explains the LORD's reaction.

There I have come to hate them, an attitude that persists because ***the evil of their deeds*** remains the same. For 'deeds', see on 7:2. 'Hate' covers a range of emotions from mild distaste to utter revulsion. In this context it is at the latter end of the scale, in a way not dissimilar to its use in Deut. 22:13 and 24:4 of a husband who rejects his wife and wishes to divorce her. ***I will drive them from my house*** employs the analogy of an unfaithful wife being put out of the family home. The verb described Hagar's expulsion from Abraham's camp (Gen. 21:10). The thought then is that the LORD's covenant partner will be no longer be allowed to stay in his land but will be deported from it. At the Exodus the LORD had promised to drive out the Canaanites from the land (Exod. 23:28-30; 33:2; 34:11); now that blessing is reversed because the Israelites have become virtual Canaanites (cf. 12:7).

For 'love', see on 11:1, and for the behaviour which characterises love, see on 3:1. In saying ***I will no longer love them*** God does not annul the basic relationship which in his love he has instituted between himself and the nation. Rather, in the face of the repeated provocation of Israel's behaviour God withdraws the affection and provision which his love would have extended to them. Even although Israel had not reciprocated the love he had extended to her and had therefore to be treated as Lo-Ruchama (Not-Shown-Compassion, 1:6), the LORD's corrective discipline would function in love to recall her and to restore a completely meaningful and fulfilled relationship between them.

Hosea again employs the device of homophony, a play on the similarity in sound between ***leaders*** (*śārêhem*; cf. 7:3) and ***stubborn*** (*sōrərîm*). 'Stubborn' is not a political term (as say 'rebel' is, cf. 7:13), but one appropriate to individual conduct in the family circle (4:16; Deut. 21:18, 20; Ps. 78:8). The political leadership of the land should have encouraged observance of the covenant. Their failure in their duties meant that there was no hope of reformation being sponsored by them. They obstinately and rebelliously refused to respond to God's entreaties because they were totally committed to the mixed worship of the north.

9:16 Ephraim has been smitten;
their root has dried up;
they will not produce fruit.
Even if they give birth,
I will put to death the treasured ones of their womb.

In the prevailing situation the punishment has already begun. ***Ephraim has been smitten*** uses a metaphor drawn from a tree struck with an axe. As a result, ***their root has dried up.***[69] The well-watered meadow of 9:13 no longer exists: the tree has been chopped down, and its roots are drying up. Contrary to the picture found in Job 14:7-9 of new shoots springing up round the stump of a felled tree, this was a blow from which the land would not recover. So Ephraim (*ʾeprayim*) ***will not***[70] ***produce fruit*** (*pərî*). The name which had once been a hopeful token (possibly 'doubly fruitful', Gen. 41:52) has its significance reversed. 'Ephraim the "doubly fruitful" ... is now Ephraim the completely fruitless' (Stuart 1987:154). Population growth will stall (cf. 9:11).

Again (cf. 9:12) a possibility which has already been rejected is further explored: ***if they give birth***. But that prospect is no sooner mooted than it is squashed by the dire announcement, ***I will put to death the treasured ones of their womb.*** 'Treasured' is the same word as is used in 9:6 for Israel's silver, but here there is something truly valuable being lost: their children. This is the dire curse which would fall on the disobedient community (cf. Deut. 28:62).

9:17 My God will reject them,
 for they have not listened to him,
 and they will be wanderers among the nations.

As in 9:14, Hosea speaks personally and summarises the situation into which the people have brought themselves.[71] He does not attempt to demur from the inevitable consequences he perceives, but completely acquiesces in the divine will. ***My God*** indicates the prophet's relationship with the LORD, possibly in distinction from what has become the nation's relationship. Hosea has no doubt that God ***will reject them*** (cf. 4:6) because in their intransigence ***they have not***

---

69. For the switch from a singular collective to a plural pronoun, compare 6:4.

70. For the negative the kethibh reads the less common form *bəlî* whereas the qere recommends *bal*. The change does not affect the meaning and is unnecessary in that Hosea has already used *bəlî* to negate a verb (8:7; cf. also 4:6; 7:8). The less common form may have been used here to rhyme with the preceding *pərî*, 'fruit'.

71. In the MT 9:17 is marked as constituting a unit in its own right, probably to ensure that the distinction between the first person references in 9:16 and 9:17 is clearly maintained. A second section marker points to a distinct body of material beginning with 10:1.

listened to him.[72] There is a play on the sound of the two verbs, *šāmaʿ*, 'to listen' and *māʾas*, 'to reject'. 'Listen' or 'hear' is the response the people should accord their King (Deut. 4:1, 30, 36; 5:1), or his messenger. If they failed to act in obedience to the warnings conveyed to them, then that would seal their fate. So the people are going to be expelled from the land and become ***wanderers among the nations.*** Those who had strayed from the LORD (7:13) will reap the full outcome of their defection, being left to rove rootlessly like rejected Cain ('you will be a fugitive and wanderer', Gen. 4:14),[73] and no longer enjoying the protection and blessings of the covenant. They would be scattered among the nations and even there find no resting place for the soles of their feet (Deut. 28:64-65).

REFLECTION

- 'They have become abhorrent like that which they loved' (9:10) alerts us to the dangers posed by our spiritual environment. Exposure to moral depravity appeals to our baser instincts. Repeated exposure desensitises us to its vileness, dampens our recoil from it, and lowers our defences against being polluted by it. 'Do not be deceived. "Bad company corrupts good morals" ' (1 Cor. 15:33). How much greater is the danger when we wilfully indulge in dalliance with the immoral and the apostate. 'They walked after the worthless one, and became worthless themselves' (Jer. 2:5). We therefore need to pay heed to the injunction: 'Detest what is evil; cling to what is good' (Rom. 12:9). By clinging to what is good, however, and exposing ourselves to the truth our tendency to absorb and reflect what surrounds us may be employed beneficially. Beholding the glory of the Lord promotes transformation from glory to glory (2 Cor. 3:18). Thinking about what is pure and true, and practising such virtues, leads to the blessing of the presence of the God of peace (Phil. 4:8-9).

---

72. Again it is not easy to understand the verb forms in this verse. The imperfect *yimʾāsēm* may have jussive force 'Let him reject them'. If so, this would explain the ordinary *waw* and imperfect of *wəyihyû* as introducing a consequence 'so that they will become wanderers'. Alternatively, Macintosh (1997:380) argues that the first imperfect expresses a perceived obligation, 'he must reject them' and the construction of the last line also expresses consequence.

73. Chisholm suggests that Israel's 'wandering' (*nādədû*) in 7:13 is later punished by the people being made into 'wanderers' (*nōdədîm*) in 9:17: 'Since Israel was so determined to wander from the Lord, He would make wandering their way of life' (1987:47).

- Hosea's pause in his prayer and the reflecting question he poses (9:14) indicate the difficulty he had in formulating a petition which was appropriate to the circumstances. There could be no doubt that God passes over transgression for the remnant of his inheritance (cf. Mic. 7:18). He does not desire that any should perish (cf. Ezek. 18:23, 32; 2 Pet. 3:9). But mercy had been displayed, and God's patience had been misconstrued as unbounded toleration (cf. Matt. 23:37; John 5:40). The prophet accepted that the situation could not continue unchecked (cf. Amos 8:2). To extend the period of grace further would not remedy matters since their sinful propensities had been evident for centuries, right back to Baal-Peor. Even so, Hosea was emboldened to ask that the penalty be mitigated to the extent that the numbers involved be limited. If the LORD caused the birth-rate to decline, there would be fewer individuals in the land to undergo the suffering which would inevitably imposed on it.
- Though the prophecy of 9:17 in the first instance concerns Ephraim rather than Judah, the words of this verse have often given rise to questions as to whether the Jews will ever lose their wandering status among the nations. Undoubtedly the penalty imposed on them was severe (and reimposed after their rejection of Christ, cf. Matt. 23:38; Rom. 11:20-21), but it is contrary to the whole thrust of Hosea's message to assume that this outcome is utterly irremediable. One might think of the name reversals of chapter 2 and the vision of chapter 14. The intent of punishment is eventual reclamation and restoration. But this renewed favour shown to the Jews will not exist apart from their acknowledgement of Christ and reincorporation as branches into the olive tree from which they have been snapped off. 'I tell you, you will not see me again until you say, "Blessed is he who comes in the name of the Lord." ' (Matt. 23:39; cf. Rom. 11:23).

(2) A Luxuriant Vine (10:1-8)

This section again begins by looking back to an earlier stage of Israel's history, not now to the journey through the wilderness after the Exodus (9:10) but to the period when the people were settled in their divinely bestowed inheritance of the land flowing with milk and honey. Instead of being compared to 'grapes in the wilderness' (9:10), by that stage they had become a vine spreading throughout Canaan (cf. Ps. 80:8-11; Isa. 5:1-7; Jer. 2:21; Ezek. 17:5-6). Once more, however, a favourable initial prospect is marred because there had been no change in Israel's innate propensity to rebel against the LORD and engage in pagan practices. Therefore Hosea again depicts all that is wrong in the land: idolatrous worship (10:1-2; cf. 8:11-13); empty oaths (10:4; cf. 4:2, 15); the bull-calf of Beth-Awen (10:5; cf. 8:5-6); impending defeat by Assyria (10:6; cf. 9:7); loss of their king (10:7; cf. 7:7, 16); and desolation such that even idol worship is abandoned (10:8; cf. 9:6).

Van Leeuwen (2003) argues that it is possible to detect a chiastic structure which holds this prophetic denunciation together as a literary unit:

(a) prosperity of Israel, v. 1a
  (b) 'many' altars and *maṣṣēbôt*, vv. 1b-2
    (c) powerless king(s) indicted, vv. 3-4
      (d) Bethel's calf-statue deplored and derided, v. 5
      (d') the calf-statue carried away in exile, v. 6
    (c') Samaria's king swept away, v. 7
  (b') high places and altars destroyed, v. 8a
(a') adversity and despair among the Israelites, v. 8b.

By adroit dividing and labelling a text there is a danger of imposing a chiastic structure where one does not exist in the first place. The value of such an analysis depends on whether or not it aids interpretation of a passage, and this one does seem to clarify some interpretative conundrums in these verses (cf. 10:7, 8).[74]

10:1 Israel ⌊was⌋ a luxuriant vine;
  he kept producing fruit for himself.
According to the abundance of his fruit,
  he has multiplied the altars;
according to the goodness of his land,
  they adorned standing-stones.

Hosea's switch from the immediately preceding depiction of the people as wanderers among the nations (9:17) is not signalled by any textual

74. 'The structure can help us to offer a more certain interpretation of the verses which, until now, have been explained differently by various scholars. So some scholars have held the view that the king spoken of in v. 7 would not be Israel's king but the calf-statue of Bethel, represented here as a king, shattered and its remains sprinkled on water, just like the calf in the desert destroyed by Moses (Exod. xxxii 20). Our structure shows that this explanation is not correct. In the scheme c' (v. 7) must correspond with c and so the king of c' must represent a real king of Israel. In the same way, the words of v. 8b cannot be spoken by the altars of v. 8a (so Ibn Ezra) for v. 8b (a' in the scheme) must correspond with a, speaking of Israel/the Israelites' (Van Leeuwen 2003:377).

indicator, and so he jolts the reader into pondering why Israel's affairs developed in the way they did. Once more the prophet stresses the promising start which they made after they settled in the land. ***Vine***, which is usually a feminine noun, is here treated as a masculine one, possibly because Hosea's focus is on the people of Israel, not the vine with which they are compared. Hence the rendering 'he kept producing fruit for himself' rather than 'it kept producing fruit for itself'.

However, this self-gratifying focus was contrary to the LORD's intention. The vine was an appropriate symbol for Israel not just because it grows prolifically there and reflects the agricultural productivity of the land. The vine also functioned as a reminder of how the LORD had taken care in preparing the land to receive his people, of how he had transplanted them there as a vine of choice stock, and of how he continued to protect them (cf. Ps. 80:8-11; Isa. 5:1-2; Jer. 2:21; Ezek. 17:10-11). As the owner and keeper of the vineyard, the LORD had the right to look for the vintage it would yield, and, considering all the advantages he had bestowed on it, the vine could reasonably be expected to produce an abundant harvest.

Luxuriant is literally 'emptying'. The expression might at first convey the thought of a damaged vine, but that is quickly corrected to the picture of one emptying itself of its potential in an abundant and prolific growth.[75] ***Fruit*** points to agricultural produce and economic prosperity. ***He kept producing*** is literally 'setting' or 'fixing' fruit on his branches,[76] and does so ***for himself***, for his own ends and to his own advantage: this constitutes the inherent flaw in their situation.

---

75. The root can hardly be identified as the more common *bāqaq* (I), 'to lay waste', 'to ruin'. The idea of barrenness is adopted in the AV, and also the NJPS rendering (following medieval Jewish commentators), 'Israel is a ravaged vine and its fruit is like it' (cf. Nah. 2:2). Grammatically this is possible — and it may to an extent have been intended to be heard — but it does not fit well with what follows which reflects a time of prosperity, and so the dominant root is almost certainly *bāqaq* (II), 'to be luxuriant', 'to proliferate'. Acceptance of this may be noted in the REB's reversion to 'a spreading vine' from the NEB's 'rank vine'.

76. The verb 'produces' is taken to be from *šāwâ* (II), 'to place, set', rather than *šāwâ* (I), 'to make like' (cf. NJPS), or 'to even off, settle or soothe'. Still it is very close in form and sound to *šāwʾ*, 'emptiness, vanity' (cf. 10:4; 12:11). 'Such seditious word-play conspires to subvert the outwardly positive meanings of 10:1 in what we might characterize as a metonym of Hosea 4–14's wider message: Israel's prosperity is only skin-deep, within lie the seeds of emptiness and waste' (Moughtin-Mumby 2008:60).

Hosea does not state—he had done so often before—that the affluence Israel enjoyed was from the LORD. Instead he elaborates on how Israel misused their wealth. The second reference to ***fruit*** marks the change from the metaphor to the reality of Israel's agriculture-based prosperity, a prosperity which had reached new heights in the reign of Jeroboam II. Again there is a wordplay between ***abundance*** and ***multiplied***/'made abundant' which are both derived from the root *rbb*, 'to be numerous'. This root is repeatedly used in various forms to express the immense scale on which everything was happening. It is used of the LORD's gifts in 2:8; 12:10; of Israel's increase in 4:7; and of the people's rebellion in 8:11, 14; 9:7; 10:13; 12:1. What they did when their population and produce increased is expressed ambiguously. ***He multiplied the altars*** might indicate more altars dedicated to the LORD, which could perhaps have been a sign of increased devotion.[77] It is not till the final line that it becomes clear that what they did with their wealth was to misapply it in increasing the number of paganised altars.

Hosea then restates and heightens his indictment. Israel acted ***according to the goodness of the land***, that is, according to what their covenant Overlord provided for them (cf. 3:5). But, not recognising the true origin of the corn, wine and olive oil (2:8), the people had perverted their wealth when they ***adorned***/'made good' ***standing-stones*** (cf. 3:4), no longer innocent memorials of the past, but paganised symbols of their male deity. The increase in the material wellbeing of the land was matched by a corresponding growth in expenditure on the accoutrements of idol worship. Both 'altars' and 'standing-stones' provide links with the following verse.

10:2 Their heart is deceitful;
  now they will suffer for their guilt.
He himself will break their altars;
  he will devastate their standing-stones.

The statement contained in the first two lines is highlighted by being at the centre of the preceding and succeeding references to 'altars' and 'standing stones'. What had gone wrong in Israel was primarily

---

77. The phrase that is used is literally, 'he made many with respect to altars'. It may indicate 'made many pillars at their altars' (Hubbard 1989:171), or the use of *lə* to mark an accusative may be influenced by Aramaic. Possibly the *lə* is syntactically redundant and included to effect a sound sequence similar to the foregoing *kərōb ləpiryô*, 'according to the abundance of his fruit'.

spiritual. ***Their heart is deceitful*** introduces another term for Israel's perfidious conduct. For 'heart', see on 4:11. 'Deceitful' is a metaphor drawn from what is 'smooth' or 'slippery'.[78] In their inner thinking and disposition they deliberately maintained a smooth, hypocritical stance in which they convinced themselves they were genuine worshippers of the LORD, who remained true to him, yet all the while they spent the wealth he had given them on Canaanite worship. They had deluded themselves into thinking that such conduct was not perverse. ***Now***, as a consequence of this, ***they will suffer for their guilt*** (*'āšam*). The verb may indicate either the guilty status of those who have done what is wrong or the consequences they will have to endure (cf. 13:16).

He himself is a reference to God, who will take action against the proliferation of altars dedicated to the worship of Baal. It is improbable that this is a prediction of Josiah's reform programme in 2 Kings 23:14-15, though both that passage and this one reflect the teaching of Deuteronomy (cf. Deut. 7:5). God ***will break*** their altars. The verb used is elsewhere employed of breaking the neck of animals (Exod. 13:13; 34:20; Deut. 21:4, 6; Isa, 66:3), and here it graphically refers to snapping the horns off the corners of the altars and so desecrating them (Amos 3:14). ***Devastate*** (cf. 7:13; 9:6; 10:14) refers to total destruction of all the paraphernalia of their cultic sites, for which the ***standing-stones*** (cf. 10:1) are mentioned as a representative item. This prophecy relates to the impending destruction of Israel's sacred sites and to the ensuing desertion of them foretold in 3:4.

10:3 For now they are saying,
'We have no king,
for we do not fear the LORD,
and ⌞as for⌟ the king, what could he do for us?'

There is uncertainty about the import of ***for now***. It may point to the circumstances which will prevail in the impending judgement ('then', NIV) with the verb translated as a future (cf. NRSV, ESV). Absence of any king would then be again reminiscent of Hosea's earlier prophecy (cf. 3:4), and the verse might point to a hopeful change of outlook on their part. However, it is more probable that their words are spoken in tones of resignation and disillusionment. In that case 'for' would only link in a general way with preceding verses, in effect indicating that

78. Again it is possible to derive the verb from one of two homonymous roots, *ḥālaq* (I), 'to be smooth, slippery' or *ḥālaq* (II), 'to divide, apportion, share' (cf. AV). The latter root would seem to require repointing to a pual form, *ḥullaq*.

what follows is further evidence of the present degenerate condition of the people, which will lead to the destruction of the nation. ***They are saying*** takes the imperfect aspect of the verb as describing existing, on-going attitudes. ***We have no king*** refers not to God, but to the realities of their political situation. If these words originated around 733 B.C., then they reflect a popular assessment that they do not have a real king because Hoshea was just a puppet in the hands of Assyria. Or, the passage may relate to what happened in the closing months of the northern kingdom when Hoshea was imprisoned by the Assyrians before Samaria itself fell, and it was then literally true that they had no king (2 Kgs. 17:4). Most probably, however, the sentiment just echoes the disillusionment of the period after Jeroboam II when a succession of assassinations and fragile regimes deprived whichever ruler was currently in power of any legitimacy or respect.

More significantly, the people are envisaged as tracing this reversal in their national fortunes to the fact that ***we do not fear the LORD***. They realised that they had offended him, and that because of their disobedience they had no reason to expect help from him. It is only here that Hosea uses the verb 'to fear', a common expression in the Old Testament for true reverence for God, characterised by a respectful awe and submission to his will, though a similar thought may be found in 3:5. After experiencing the many years of turmoil which had engulfed the land, the people felt let down by kings and rulers, and wondered, ***As for the king, what could he do for us?*** Time and again their kings and leaders had proved inadequate to the challenges to be surmounted, and nothing they could do now would avert total disaster (cf. 10:7, 15; 13:10). This rhetorical question (cf. 6:4) forcefully expresses the people's conviction regarding the uselessness of their kings. Indeed, the expression is virtually a form of pseudo-sorites (cf. 8:7) because of the immediately preceding assertion that they have no king.

10:4 They have spoken words,
sworn falsely,
made a covenant.
And justice has sprouted like wormwood
in furrows of a field.

Taken on its own the portrait of 10:4 might further describe the deceitful heart of the people (10:2), but, despite the singular reference with which the previous verse ends, the content of the verse indicates that the plural ***they*** focuses primarily on the kings of Israel in its final, tumultuous years. ***They have spoken words*** (a durative perfect), nothing more. Fine-sounding promises have not been accompanied by successful implementation. Indeed it is not a matter of inability, rather they have ***sworn falsely***, that is, they solemnly committed themselves to what was empty and insubstantial, amounting to nothing (*šāwʾ*, cf. 12:11). It was not just that their treaties were designed to so the impossible—keep Assyria at bay. The pacts were worthless because there had no intention of keeping them if they could find a better way to survive.[79] They ***made a covenant***, not with the LORD, but with allies or, more probably, the Assyrian emperor. In doing so, an Israelite king inevitably compromised his standing with the LORD because of the role accorded to heathen deities in the ratification of such treaties where they were invoked as witnesses to what was agreed. Royal policy had been formulated in response to pressures of the moment, and today's solemn agreement soon became yesterday's policy.

Such a disregard for truth and solemn pledges filtered down from the top of a society to affect all levels of administration in it. ***Justice has sprouted like poisonous weeds.*** The term 'justice' (cf. 2:19; 12:6) includes the thought of appropriate judicial verdicts (5:1, 11), but goes well beyond that to the good order which prevails in a society where all the administrative processes of government are characterised by equity and where people conduct their day to day relationships in a similarly upright and fair manner. What Hosea has in view here is not divine justice, but the whole moral tenor of the land. ***Sprouted*** describes the growth of a plant (cf. 14:5, 7), and ***poisonous weeds*** refers to an unknown plant, often associated with the bitter, but not toxic, wormwood (Deut. 29:18; Jer. 9:15; 23:15; Lam. 3:19; Amos 6:12). Its growth and effect is compared to the harmful and corrupt way things were run in the land (cf. Amos 6:12). ***In furrows of a field***[80] where the grain should be (cf. 12:11), there could only be found noxious, wasteful growth, which must be weeded out. Israel has lost sight of the true purpose which should inform and structure her collective life.

---

79. The form *ʾālôt* could be the plural of *ʾālâ*, 'an oath' (cf. ESV, NRSV) functioning exegetically in apposition to 'words'. However, in view of the following infinitive absolute (*kārōt*, 'cutting'), it too is probably an infinitive absolute, with an unusual spelling (cf. NKJV, NIV). The infinitives give closer specification to the verb 'have spoken'. The list is somewhat reminiscent of that found in 4:2.

80. *śādāy*, 'field', may be an archaic form which had been retained in northern speech (cf. 12:12).

10:5 With respect to the heifers of Beth-Awen,
the residents of Samaria will be fearful,
for its people shall mourn over it,
and its priests will rejoice over it—
over its glory,
for it will have departed from it.

In this and the following verse Hosea utters a prophecy describing the removal to Assyria of the bull-calf idol of ***Beth-Awen***, his derisive term for Bethel (cf. 4:15). It lies at the centre of the chiastic structure of 10:1-8 and is its main thematic focus. ***Heifers*** is a feminine plural word, and in this respect it is difficult to see why it is used instead of the masculine singular word ordinarily employed for the bull-calf. While it may be an abstract plural formation indicating the cult of calf worship[81], or the spelling may just be a northern variant, it is more probable that this is a plural of majesty, used sarcastically by Hosea: 'this great calf'. Indeed sarcasm pervades this verse.

The residents is a singular form and may be a mock-honorific title for the idol. There are six singular references to 'it' in the remainder of the verse. However, a collective usage seems more probable because the verb ***will be fearful*** is plural. Use of ***Samaria*** may imply that this saying was uttered when all that remained of the northern kingdom was the capital and surrounding area. It is not awe that the nation will display with respect to the bull-calf, but anxious concern about what would become of their cherished idol—not the sort of worry one would expect in connection with the worship of a true deity.

For points out what has led to this state of affairs. ***Its people*** probably refers to the devotees of the bull-calf throughout the northern kingdom. Here and in ***over it*** there is a change to a masculine singular form in reference to the idol. ***Shall mourn*** is a prophetic perfect emphasising the certainty of this outcome. It is unlikely to be a reference to some cultic ceremony of wailing in connection with the worship of the calf; it predicts Samaria's sorrow because of their devastating sense of loss when their idol is carried off as plunder.

Priests is not the ordinary term employed for legitimate priests, but one taken over from Phoenician and Aramaic, which is used to refer to pagan priests (2 Kgs. 23:5; Zeph. 1:4). Their livelihood and careers would be undermined by the removal of the object of their veneration, but Hosea sarcastically urges them to ***rejoice***, a term for the intense joy

81. Van Leeuwen (2003:374) suggests, 'Perhaps the feminine plural indicates an ironic abstract sense of the word, something like "calf-business".'

(cf. 'exultation' 9:1), which they would ordinarily have associated with the worship of their idol.[82] Was that not what priests of such a great and illustrious god were supposed to do? They made much of ***its glory*** or splendour. Why should the devotees of such a god ever be silent or become anything less than jubilant? But there is the closing dash of cold water: ***it will have departed from it***. The words are somewhat ambiguous. They may mean that when the captured idol is carted off by the enemy, it will no longer possess magnificence or distinction. More probably, the verb 'depart' has the narrower sense of 'go into exile' and the final 'it' is a reference to the people themselves: 'their idol will have gone into exile from them.' There is a word play between 'cry out' (*yāgîlû*) and 'gone into exile' (*gālâ*). Since both words additionally contain two of the consonants of 'calf' (*ʿeglâ*), the sounds reinforce the fitness and inevitability of the outcome.

10:6 Moreover, it itself will be carried to Assyria,
 a present to king Jareb.
Ephraim will receive shame,
 and Israel will be ashamed because of his counsel.

Moreover adds a further set of details to the preceding predictions of the LORD's judgement and the nation's loss of wealth and prestige. Special prominence is given to ***it***,[83] that is, the bull-calf, viewed as a mere object which required to be carried—an emphasis which heightens the portrayal of its impotence. No longer will the idol be found in the magnificence of its own temple. ***Be carried*** is often used in the sense 'be taken as tribute' (12:2; Ps. 68:30; Isa. 18:7). The practice of the time would be for the idol of a conquered nation to be placed in the temple of the conqueror's god as an indication of the superiority of the latter (cf. the ark in the temple of Dagon, 1 Sam. 5:2). The place of exile is clearly stated to be ***Assyria***, where it will constitute ***a present***, in fact tribute, ***to king Jareb.*** For this name, see on 5:13. The king at the time of the assault on Samaria (and possibly also at its fall) was

82. *yāgîlû*, 'they will rejoice', is sometimes given a more general sense of 'they will cry out' probably in anguish. Another proposal is to emend the text to *yəlēlîlû*, 'they will lament' (cf. NRSV, NLT). The Massoretic accents take 'rejoice' with the words which precede it, and this yields a satisfactory sense if the whole utterance is interpreted as sarcastic.

83. *ʾōtô* is placed first for emphasis, but the verb is passive 'it will be carried', so *ʾet* is probably being used as an emphatic particle rather than as an object marker. No longer is a feminine form used for the calf; it has reverted to the expected masculine.

Shalmaneser V, but by the time any booty reached Assyria Sargon II would have been on the throne (see *Introduction*, pp. 14-15).

With the exposure of the inadequacy of their aspirations and their worship, the people will be brought to realise the utter falsity of their vision of life, and they will experience ***shame.***[84] ***Because of his counsel*** may also be heard and read as 'because of his wood' (cf. 4:12; Jer. 6:6), after all, that was all that the idol was. The variation in English translations shows that it is difficult to know which understanding would have been uppermost to Hosea's audience. Since the next verse develops the theme of the fate of the king, the main reference was possibly to the advice which lay behind the policies of the nation as a whole. 'Shame' and ***be ashamed*** do not in the first instance point to feelings of embarrassment and dismay, but to outward circumstances of public disgrace and humiliation as others perceive their failure.

10:7 ⌞As for⌟ Samaria, her king is being destroyed
like a twig on the face of the water.

There is one verb in this verse, a participial form from a root which denotes 'to perish', 'to cease from existence', 'to be ruined'. However, there are two uncoordinated nouns, 'Samaria' and 'her king', which are possible subjects for the verb, and some device has to be used to cope with this. To translate, ***⌞As for⌟ Samaria, her king is being destroyed*** is awkward because this is not a simple instance of fronting in that Samaria is not the first, but the second word in the sentence. On the other hand, 'Samaria is being destroyed' is an unlikely rendering in that the participle is a masculine form and Samaria is generally treated as a feminine noun. Furthermore, some commentators have taken 'her king' to be not the monarch, but the idol. Van Leeuwen's argument (2003:374) that the reference is to Israel's monarch because in the chiastic structure of the passage it balances the statement made in 10:3 is of significance in resolving the matter. There is a switch from the idol, and the theme reverts to that of the king who sponsored the idol worship.

The king's powerlessness is brought out by the simile ***like a twig on the face of the water.*** 'Twig' may also suggest instead 'splinter' or 'chip' (or possibly 'foam', as in the Vulgate), and 'water' points to the current found in a river. The piece of wood is borne helplessly

---

84. The noun *bošnâ* occurs only here. While it is difficult to account for the presence of the *nun*, there is little doubt that the word is derived from *bôš*, 'to be ashamed'.

downstream by the force of the water. The swirling and rushing affairs of international politics at this time left Israel's king with no control over events and unable to resist the overwhelming pressure which swept him and his nation to their doom.

10:8 And the high places of Awen will be wiped out,
 the sin of Israel;
thorn and thistle will come up
 on their altars.
And they will say to the mountains, 'Cover us!',
 and to the hills, 'Fall on us!'

In Van Leeuwen's chiastic analysis this verse is treated in two parts (cf. introductory comments to this section). The first part, consisting of the first four lines (which are also taken together by the Massoretic accents), describes the devastation which will come upon the sacred sites frequented by Israel. ***Wiped out*** is a strong word, implying that they will be catastrophically overthrown and left utterly unusable. The reference in ***Awen*** (literally, 'wickedness') is to Bethel (cf. 4:15; 5:8; 10:5), rather than to misconduct in general, and specifically in view are its ***high places***, sites associated with Canaanite worship clustered round the temple there. Hosea has no hesitation in describing them as ***the sin of Israel***. These were places where it was glaringly evident that Israel had abandoned the true worship of the LORD and adherence to his standards, and substituted for them a corrupt amalgam of ideas largely derived from Canaanite practices and beliefs.

Thorn and thistle is a combination found in Genesis 3:18 as part of the curse consequent on the Fall, and presents Israel's misbehaviour as of similar gravity and with a similar long-term impact. ***Their altars***, those associated with various Baal shrines, are going to fall into desuetude and lie deserted, overgrown with weeds (cf. 9:6).

The final two lines of the verse correspond to the first part of 10:1, not now describing the recent prosperity of Israel but the reversal of their circumstances as devastation and adversity engulf them. As their land is dominated by their Assyrian conquerors, the people will give up in despair and ***say to the mountains, 'Cover us,' and to the hills, 'Fall on us'***. This foreshadows Revelation 6:15-16 (cf. Luke 23:30). In an area which is seismically unstable the impact of a severe earthquake and its associated landslides would be well known. In their agony the people wish for such sudden death and devastation rather than enduring the long drawn-out horrors which await them.

REFLECTION

- In John 15 Jesus appropriates for himself the image of the vine. In saying 'I am the true vine' (John 15:1) he presents himself as the ultimate and genuine realisation of all that Israel should have been. It is only in union with him that an individual may be fruitful before God (John 15:4-5). However, the Father is the vinedresser, the one who is responsible for sending Jesus, and the one who expects fruitfulness from those who are branches in his vine. If a branch does not bear fruit it is cut off, and even those branches which do produce a crop are subject to pruning to increase their fruitfulness (John 15:2). This process of spiritual discipline is essentially one with the LORD's action towards his people in Hosea's day, and with what Paul describes as still occurring in the church. He reminds us that 'it is not you who support the root, but the root supports you' (Rom. 11:18), and that we should 'stand fast through faith ... If God did not spare the natural branches, neither will he spare you' (Rom. 11:20-21).
- The theme of judgement to come is one which we often shy away from considering, but Hosea would not let his contemporaries do so because it was what would shape their immediate—and their eternal—future. The relevance of the message of impending judgement has not diminished in New Testament times, 'for we must all appear before the judgement seat of Christ' (2 Cor. 5:10). The citation of 10:8 in Rev. 6:15-16 (cf. Luke 23:30) shows that features of the judgement which befell the nation of Israel foreshadow what will prevail on the Great Day. It will bring shame and confusion (10:6) to those who have not committed their lives to Christ (Rom. 9:33; 1 John 2:28). It will reverse the status enjoyed in this world by the powerful and the rich who remain impenitent (10:7) when they will receive their just reward from the Lord (Luke 6:24; 16:25; Rev. 18:9-10; 19:17-21). It will involve wiping out (10:8) all that opposes Christ and his kingdom (1 Cor. 15:25). It will evoke a despairing desire for annihilation in those who are not reconciled to the Lord (10:8) rather than undergo the dire penalty of eternal separation and utter meaninglessness apart from him (Matt. 8:11; 25:30; 2 Thess. 1:9; Rev. 9:6).

(3) A Trained Heifer (10:9-15)

The structure of the prophecy is not as clear at this point as it was in the two preceding sections. Indeed, it is difficult to know if the transitional verses (10:9-10) are associated more with what has gone before or what follows.[85] On balance, starting a new unit at 10:9 is favoured by the direct address to Israel found there, which also forms a sort of inclusion with the mention of Israel in 10:15. In addition a further historical reminiscence in connection with Gibeah (10:9) is introduced, and it too is matched in 10:15 by mention of another town, Bethel. Identification of a structural transition here is also reinforced by the clear departure from direct prophetic speech in 10:10, and the change of topic from the religious dimension of Israel's rebellious behaviour to its inevitable repercussions on the fortunes of the nation.

A threefold division is appropriate (10:9-10; 10:11-12; 10:13-15), with the initial and concluding paragraphs focusing on Israel's misconduct and over-reliance on military power, and on the judgement the LORD will bring upon them through enemy invasion and warfare. The central paragraph shows that Israel's situation had not arisen from lack of opportunity or from divine harshness (10:11a), but now intervention is required (10:11b). Even so the exhortation of 10:12 shows that there is still opportunity for them to amend their ways. To some extent this call for a return to covenant standards anticipates the more positive future set out in chapter 11.

(a) Awaiting Punishment (10:9-10)

10:9 From the days of Gibeah
  you have sinned, Israel.
There they stood.
Will not war against the sons of wickedness
  overtake them in Gibeah?

Since the next verse is divine speech, it is probably the LORD who here directly addresses Israel, using an example drawn from four centuries before to alert the current generation to the gravity of their persistent wrongdoing. ***Gibeah*** has already been mentioned in connection with the incidents recorded in Judges 19–21 when all Israel engaged in war against the tribe of Benjamin because of the violent outrage which had been perpetrated by the men of Gibeah (cf. 5:8; 9:9).[86] ***From the days***

85. In the MT a paragraph break is present after 10:8, but not after 10:10, indicating a preference for taking the verses with what follows.

86. Another interpretation is that Hosea's references to Gibeah are inherently anti-monarchical and allude to events connected with Saul's elevation to kingship in 1 Sam. 11–13, but as Arnold (1989:448–450) points out, Gibeah is not central to those narratives, and Hosea is inimical to current royal failures, not the institution of the monarchy in itself.

of takes that incident as a starting point for a pattern of behaviour which has been endemic ever since. ***You have sinned*** comes from the same root as 'sin' (10:8). Repeatedly, though not necessarily always in the same way, ***Israel***, the people of the covenant, had acted in heinous defiance of its standards, and so had given offence to the LORD. Implicit in this observation is a tribute to the LORD's patience in dealing with them that he had not swept them away sooner.

The LORD next speaks about Israel rather than to them, but the thrust of the words is uncertain. ***There*** (i.e. at Gibeah) ***they stood*** seems to indicate that whereas Israel, supposing material prosperity to be the only index of advancement, had thought that the nation had progressed over the intervening centuries, the LORD's verdict is that morally and spiritually they had stayed at the same level as in the days of the judges. Possibly there is an allusion to the recent internecine squabbling known as the Syro-Ephraimite war (cf. *Introduction*, pg. 17). This was a blatant exposed the extent to which covenant loyalty and awareness had become corrupt.

Although there is no formal indicator of an interrogative (hence the rendering of the NKJV), the conclusion of the verse is generally treated as a rhetorical question which dramatically envisages a threat (cf. 6:4).[87] There will be ***war against the sons of wickedness,***[88] an expression which points to the disgraceful behaviour of the past as repeated now by those who had morally stayed ***in Gibeah***, that is, they displayed conduct matching that which had been witnessed at Gibeah in former years. That being so, the LORD announces a similar outcome for the current generation. They too will be reduced to the point of extinction just as the tribe of Benjamin had formerly been (cf. Judg. 20:46-48).

---

87. A similar reading may be obtained by emending the negative *lōʾ* into an asseverative particle, *lə*. (Andersen, et al. 1980:565; Hubbard 1989:177) Because the question is not explicitly marked, others take this as a statement (cf. 'The battle in Gibeah against the children of iniquity did not overtake them', NKJV), but that is awkward in that shocking retribution had been imposed in the past (cf. Judg. 20). The NIV has a rhetorical question relating to the past, 'Did not war overtake ...?', but it is difficult to see how this comes from the imperfect verb *taśśîgēm*, 'it will overtake them'.

88. The spelling *ʿalwâ* involves a metathesis from *ʿawlâ*, 'malice, injustice'. Quite possibly this pronunciation reflects Hosea's northern dialect. The expression 'the sons of wickedness' (with the expected spelling) occurs in 2 Sam. 3:34; 7:10.

10:10 When I please, I will discipline them,
and peoples will be assembled against them
when they bind ⌞them⌟ for their two iniquities.

The LORD asserts that retribution will come on the timescale he chooses. ***When I please*** (literally, 'at my desire'[89]) indicates that the resolution of Israel's present violation of the covenant will be determined by divine preference and control. ***I will discipline them*** might at first seem to refer to educational chastisement (cf. 5:2), but more than that is in view. The next clause makes clear this correction will be effected through the instrumentality of foreign nations: ***peoples will be assembled against them.*** The passive indicates that God is the unspecified agent who will act to gather them, just as Israel had formerly gathered against Benjamin. ***When they bind them***[90] refers to their enemies taking Israelites captive and shackling them ready to lead them off into exile and slavery. It is in God's, not the nations', evaluation that ***their two iniquities***[91] exist, but what is specifically referred to is unclear. The use of 'two of' suggests a combination of factors. An obvious possibility is Gibeah past and Gibeah present, or perhaps the joint crime of forsaking the LORD and turning to idols (cf. Jer. 2:13). Less likely is the idea that it refers to the two calves, at Dan and Bethel. Though that provides a lead into the following verse, the idol at Dan was no longer there by this later stage in Hosea's ministry.

REFLECTION

• 'When I please' (10:10) does not indicate that God derives pleasure from disciplining his people or punishing sinners (cf. Ezek. 28:23, 32). 'He does not willingly [literally, 'from his heart'] afflict or grieve the children of men' (Lam. 3:33). His wrath does not have equal ultimacy

---

89. Rather than being taken as the preposition *bə* with *ʾawwâ*, 'desire', the word is also read as a verb form, either as a perfect of *bôʾ*, 'I have come' (REB), or as the preposition *bə* followed by a Hebrew-Aramaic root *ʾth*, also meaning 'to come', e.g. 'I will come against' (NRSV, following LXX).

90. *bəʾosrām* is a qal infinitive construct from *ʾāsar*, 'to bind', which would mean 'when they bind', that is, it is the nations who bind. An alternative approach is to follow the LXX and identify the verb as *yāsar*, 'to chasten or discipline' (NRSV).

91. The kethib reads *ʿênōtām*, 'their eyes', but the qere indicates *ʿônōtām*, 'their iniquities', and this is also found in the early versions (cf. LXX, Peshitta, Vulgate), giving the sense 'on account of their double iniquity'. McComiskey suggests that despite the unusual use of the plural (rather than the dual) of *ʿayin*, 'eye', the sense is 'before their two eyes' (1992:173–174).

with his love. Nevertheless his wrath is real and cannot be evaded. It is, however, completely under his control. 'When I please' points to his sovereign determination of his treatment of his people. Neither they nor those ranged against them are able to delay or deflect the penalty which he has resolved to impose.

(b) The Docile Heifer (10:11-12)

It is at this point that the sequence of metaphors drawn from nature and agriculture, which had begun with the grapes (9:10) and the vine (10:1), is concluded with the trained heifer (10:11).

10:11 Now Ephraim ⌊was⌋ a trained heifer
which loved to thresh,
while I for my part passed over on the beauty of her neck.
I will harness Ephraim,
Judah will plough,
Jacob will harrow for himself.

The introductory 'and' is rendered ***now*** because, followed by a noun rather than a verb, it functions to effect a transition in the LORD's discourse as a third metaphor for ***Ephraim***, the northern kingdom, is taken up. The time frame of the first part of the verse is not specified, but the previous metaphors suggest that it describes the early conduct of the people in the land. 'Trained' is the opposite of 'stubborn' (cf. 4:16), and so ***a trained heifer*** indicates a docile animal which has learned how to perform various tasks and responds readily to instructions conveyed to it (cf. the opposite image in Jer. 31:18). Cattle were often used to thresh grain either by treading on it or, more probably, by pulling a threshing sledge over it. In either case the animal doing this enjoyed a measure of freedom. It was employed alone, not yoked to another and so not compelled to coordinate its efforts. Furthermore it was unmuzzled and permitted to eat while working (Deut. 25:4). Hence it is said that the heifer ***loved to thresh***.[92] This encapsulates Israel's willingness to serve the LORD in the land which he had allotted to them and to enjoy its fruits.

I for my part passed over on the beauty of her neck may be interpreted negatively as the LORD's resolve to disregard the beauty he had once seen in the people (the verb is used in the sense 'overlook' in Prov. 19:11 and Mic. 7:18; cf. McComiskey 1992:176), and to proceed to punish them. More probably, however, the sense is that in the past

92. The verb *ʾōhabtî*, 'loving'/'loved' is a feminine participial form in the construct with a paragogic vowel (cf. Joüon §93n).

the LORD had spared Israel from any further imposition during those early years.[93]

Now, however, as the second part of the verse reveals, this favourable treatment is going to end—and not just in the north. ***I will harness*** refers to fitting the animal with a yoke so that it could plough. From threshing which it enjoyed Ephraim is going to be required to engage in harder work. Furthermore, ***Judah will plough.*** This would refer to breaking up the ground with a plough consisting of a wooden shaft and probably an iron ploughshare. But why is Judah included here?[94] Probably because the south too was slipping away from covenant standards under Ahaz, though the defection was perhaps not yet as widespread there. ***Jacob will harrow for himself.*** A wooden board with iron teeth was pulled over the ground to break up clods after ploughing, or to cover seed that had been broadcast on the surface of the ground. Jacob seems here to be used to refer to the nation north and south (cf. 12:2). It is overly pedantic to take it as significant that it is Ephraim which is harnessed while Judah actually does the ploughing. The division of labour is a poetic device to present the one message of the hard times that are going to come on the people who had not appreciated God's previous gentleness and goodness towards them. No longer is any hint given of enjoying the fruits of their labours. 'For himself' is an idiom indicating the one who benefits (or not) from an action. The same idiom is repeated in 10:12, and it seems to indicate a contrast. The thought here is that for Jacob the harrowing is tedious and causes discomfort.

10:12 Sow to yourselves with respect to righteousness;
reap according to the measure of steadfast love;
break up for yourselves your fallow ground.
Now ⌊it is⌋ time to seek the LORD
until he comes and rains
righteousness for you.

A case can be made that, although in this verse the LORD is referred to in the third person, divine speech continues to the end of the chapter

93. The NIV, 'I will put a yoke on her fair neck' reads *heʿĕbartî ʿōl ʿal* for the MT *ʿābartî ʿal*, 'I passed by (spared) her fair neck', and assumes a prophetic perfect. While the *waw* disjunctive may be an adversative use, 'but', in a verse with two triplets a coordinating use is more probable, setting out a further feature of the previous situation. This accords with the Massoretic reading of the passage as indicated by the *athnach* which associates the clause with what precedes.

94. For the view that Judah is a redactional insertion, see on 1:7.

(cf. 1:2). It is, however, more probable that these words convey Hosea's exhortations to the people. The fact that this message is positive need not imply that he felt his advice would be acted on and the impending disaster averted. But these things needed to be said even if only a few responded. Furthermore, this record would make clear when disaster had came that the nation had needlessly brought it on themselves through their refusal to repent.

Agricultural imagery continues to be used, but the people are now viewed as farmers, and are addressed in three imperatives. ***Sow to yourselves*** is a plural, possibly reflecting Ephraim and Judah in the previous verse, or showing the need for this advice to be followed individually. 'To yourselves' employs the same idiom as 'for himself' (10:11), but now the reference is positive. This course of action will be profitable and lead to a beneficial outcome. The sowing which is in view is their lifestyle in general, which should be shaped and governed by ***righteousness***, conformity to the norms of the covenant (2:19). If they sow in accordance with the LORD's standards, then in due season they will ***reap*** not merely physical crops but a divine reward for their loyal behaviour ***according to the measure of steadfast love*** (cf. 4:1). The proportionality of the LORD's response is applied to his blessing as well as to his punishment. If their conduct is characterised by the consideration and compassion of those who truly acknowledge their Overlord, then he will respond with 'good measure, pressed down, shaken together, running over' (Luke 6:38).

Even so, it is not implied that covenant loyalty is an easy option. It takes effort to ***break up for yourselves*** ('in your own interests') ***your fallow ground.*** 'Fallow ground' refers to soil which has not previously been under cultivation, or which has been left untilled for a lengthy period so that work on it must start from scratch again (cf. Jer. 4:3). The corruption in their national life, both political and religious, had become like deeply rooted weeds and rough growth which could not be easily eradicated. But that was the task to which they had to set themselves. Only by rigorous, possibly painful, action would the ground be prepared for healthy crops and a bountiful harvest.

Not only was their response to be thorough going; it was to be immediate. ***It is time to seek the LORD*** (cf. a synonymous verb in 3:5; 5:6). They were to become reacquainted with the LORD's requirements regarding their conduct, and to live in prayerful trust on him. ***Until he comes and rains righteousness for you*** (cf. Isa. 45:8) does not specify when this refreshing experience will occur (cf. Joel 2:23). But, though the outcome is left open in an unspecified future, there should be no doubt that LORD will respond.

Hosea uses two nouns from the same root to express 'righteousness' in this verse: first *ṣədāqâ* and then *ṣedeq*. Is there any difference between them? Though the terms frequently overlap in their significance, one approach is to suggest that in Hosea the latter term is more theological in its orientation, relating to the people's conduct towards the LORD, whereas *ṣədāqâ* relates to relationships within the covenant community (*NIDOTTE* 3:763). Alternatively, the variation here may occur because in the second instance what is in view is the product of divine righteousness. To those who seek him the LORD graciously extends all the covenant Overlord can bestow on his people. In conformity with his promises he protects and provides for his own. Moreover, 'the LORD will give what is good, and our land will yield its harvest. Righteousness (*ṣedeq*) will go before him and prepare the way for his steps' (Ps. 85:12-13).

REFLECTION

- The instructions given to 'sow', to 'reap', and to 'break up' (10:12) were not devoid of value because the people had repeatedly proved themselves incapable of responding in this way. The criteria of God's law provide the unchanging norm for human conduct, and it is never inappropriate to advise individuals to structure their lives in accordance with their Creator's standards. But these injunctions ought not to exhaust the advice that is given. Recognition of divine norms and attempts to follow them, if genuinely and self-critically attempted, quickly reveal to any person seeking to live in accordance with them that we are incapable of fully implementing them. 'I have the desire to do what is excellent, but not the ability to carry it out. For I do not do the good I want, but the evil I do not want I keep on doing' (Rom. 7:18-19). It is with such awareness that the cogency of the subsequent advice—'It is time to seek the LORD'—becomes apparent. What the sinner requires is not a repackaged or a recycled heart, but a new heart, and it is only through divine grace and blessing that it is imparted (cf. Ezek. 11:19; 18:31; 36:26).
- 'Break up your fallow ground' (10:12) indicates that life in submission to God's will involves effort and perseverance. The deep hold that sin has taken on an individual's heart and the alluring prevalence of evil on all sides calls for intense, unremitting and costly endeavour. 'If anyone would come after me, let him deny himself and take

up his cross daily and follow me' (Luke 9:23). 'I press on towards the goal for the prize of the upward call of God in Christ Jesus' (Phil. 3:14).

(c) Impending Devastation (10:13-15)

10:13a You have ploughed wickedness,
you have reaped injustice,
you have eaten the fruit of lies.

In contrast to the prospect that awaits obedience, Hosea calls Ephraim to realistic self-appraisal by setting out bluntly the nature of their conduct and its consequences. ***You have ploughed wickedness.*** Sowing and ploughing would often occur together in ancient agriculture, as the seed was first broadcast on untilled ground and then covered over by being ploughed in. 'Wickedness' is the opposite of righteousness, and describes violent behaviour contrary to justice and the norms of the covenant. This ill-conceived and rebellious conduct is compared to seed which in due course yields a crop: ***you have reaped injustice***. This term also points to wrongdoing effected by violent means (cf. 10:9), and so what they have done serves only to produce more of the same. ***You have eaten the fruit of lies.*** That is, they had been taken in by the distortion of God's teaching which was promoted by the syncretistic outlook of the times (for 'lies', cf. 7:3; 11:12), and, though Baal worship had promised much, the outcome was not prosperity, but the dire circumstances they were already enduring.

10:13b Because you trusted in your ⌊own⌋ way,
in the multitude of your warriors,
10:14 so a tumult will arise among your people,
and all your fortresses will be devastated,
like the devastation of Shalman ⌊at⌋ Beth-Arbel in the day of battle—
a mother dashed to pulp along with ⌊her⌋ sons.

The reason for their current calamity is then clearly spelled out. The last clause in 10:13 should probably be construed with what follows in 10:14 (cf. ESV, NIV), a proposal supported by the change from 'you' plural to 'you' singular at this point and maintained in 10:14. While the singular pronoun may refer to the nation as a whole, it is probably a reference to the last Israelite king, Hoshea, and the policies which he pursued. ***You trusted in your own way*** rather than in the way that the LORD had laid down as appropriate for the covenant people and their king.[95] National security was based on worldly strategies, not on reliance on the divine King. Their strategy focused on military measures: ***in the multitude of your warriors*** (cf. Ps. 33:16-17). 'Multitude' is another instance of the root *rbb* (cf. 4:7; 8:11; 10:1). 'Warriors' were trained soldiers, not the less reliable conscripts raised by a levy from the population as a whole. High hopes were entertained of their success in battle (cf. Amos 6:13).

But it is predicted that developments will confound their expectations. There will indeed be ***a tumult***, a term which describes in the first instance the roar of water, and then the din of armies engaged in combat on the battlefield (cf. Amos 2:2). However, the surprising aspect of the situation is that this ***will arise***[96] ***among your people***. That implies that despite all the defensive measures which they had put in place the enemy has made inroads deep into their territory. ***All your fortresses will be devastated*** (for the verb, cf. 7:13; 10:2). 'Fortresses' or 'fortified cities' is probably a military term for a site with a garrison (cf. 8:14). Generally they were situated at the frontiers of the land or at strategic points within it. Once they had fallen, the land would lie helpless before an invading army.

The severity of the impending destruction is emphasised by a comparison with that effected by ***Shalman at Beth-Arbel in the day of battle.*** There can be no doubt that the atrocity committed there was vividly remembered by Hosea's contemporaries, but perpetrator, site and event can no longer be identified with any degree of certainty. The name Shalman is not attested elsewhere. In form it is close to Shalmaneser, and it may be a reference to Shalmaneser V (727–722 B.C.), or, less probably, to the inroads of Shalmaneser III (859–825 B.C.) who campaigned a number of times in Aram and Israel. Another possibility is a Moabite king Salamanu, mentioned in Tiglath-Pileser's tribute list (*ANET* 282) from around 728 B.C., who may have attacked the Ammonites living in this area of Gilead. Beth-Arbel is generally

---

95. Because 'your way' does not closely parallel 'the multitude of your warriors', alternatives have been proposed. (1) Assuming the consonants of *bədarkəkā*, 'your way', have been misread, *BHS* proposes *bərikbəkā*, 'your chariot forces' (cf. RSV, GNB). (2) It has also been argued on the basis of Ugaritic evidence that the root *drk* 'way' may also have the sense 'strength' or 'power' (cf. *HALOT* 1:232), and this has been adopted by some translations (NIV, NRSV, NLT). Neither proposal seems necessary: the second line may simply specify more closely what their own way consisted of.

96. The form *qā'm* has an *aleph* as a vowel letter, as is frequent in Aramaic.

identified as a site in Transjordan, around 20 miles (30 km) south-east of the Sea of Galilee and at about the same latitude as Bethshean on the west of the Jordan valley. An alternative, smaller site lies just west of the Sea of Galilee (1 Macc. 9:2). However, no information survives about brutalities perpetrated at either. The only thing which is incontestable is that neither Assyria (cf. Nah. 3:10) nor Moab (cf. Amos 2:1-3) would have held back from such an atrocity as ***a mother dashed to pulp along with her sons***/'children' (cf. 1:10). (For the verb, cf. 13:16; 2 Kgs. 8:12; Isa. 13:16; Nah. 3:10).

10:15 Thus he shall do to you, O Bethel,
because of your utter wickedness;
at dawn the king of Israel
shall be utterly destroyed.

Thus (a somewhat emphatic form, 'precisely this') refers back to the atrocities committed at Beth-Arbel, described in the previous verse. The verb ***shall do*** is a prophetic perfect, whose subject 'he' has been variously identified. The vocative rendering, ***O Bethel***, with Bethel being a metonymy for those who resided or worshipped there, is by no means certain.[97] For instance, 'at Bethel' is grammatically feasible and found in the NASB. One older approach was to take Bethel as the subject of the verb to yield the sense that Bethel, standing for the religious aberrations promoted at the sanctuary there, would be responsible for bringing on you (plural), that is, Ephraim, a fate similar to that recounted in 10:14 (cf. Vulgate, AV, NJPS), but it is then difficult to account for the phrase 'because of your utter wickedness'. If Shalman is correctly identified as Shalmaneser, he could possibly be the one who also acts against Bethel. Most probably, however, the construction is impersonal with ***he*** = 'one'. Even so there should be no doubt that the LORD is behind this doom coming on the people ('you' is plural) from whatever quarter it is imposed. Ultimately he is the one who is against Bethel, the religious centre of the kingdom, ***because of your utter wickedness*** (literally, 'the wickedness of your (plural) wickedness').

While ***at dawn*** might be a remembered feature of Shalman's attack on Beth-Arbel, it is more probable that it indicates right at the start of a battle when troops first engage. Dawn comes quickly in the east so that this implies that a major loss will be inflicted early and swiftly. ***The king of Israel***, an official title focusing on the status of the ruler rather

97. 'O house of Israel' (RSV) follows the LXX. The only factor in its favour is the way Hosea generally avoids using the name Bethel (but cf. 12:4).

than his person, was the monarch whose demise was anticipated in 10:3 (cf. 10:7, 13b-14). In fact Hoshea was captured before the siege of Samaria began, early on in Shalmaneser's campaign against the remnant of the northern kingdom (2 Kgs. 17:4). We do not know if he was subsequently executed or if he died in captivity, but ***utterly destroyed***[98] (cf. 4:5, 6; 10:7) shows he shared the same fate as the people: ruined and wiped out. The loss of their king would have removed the last element of coordination from the resistance of the nation.

REFLECTION

'You trusted in your own way' (10:13) encapsulates the folly of mankind in their rebellion against God as they attempt to dislodge him from his rightful place as the one who rules their hearts and lives. The ways Israel preferred were principally those of political scheming and idolatrous worship, and in both alike 'claiming to be wise, they became fools' (Rom. 1:22). The same attitudes are still prevalent. To substitute our wisdom or resources for the light of God's truth is to condemn ourselves to frustration and eventual despair, because forsaking the right way inevitably leads us astray (cf. 2 Pet. 2:15). Rather than relying on self, we should develop dependence on the LORD, rely upon the salvation he provides, and approve what he delights in (cf. Jer. 9:23-24; 1 Cor. 1:31; 2 Cor. 10:14).

G. Restoration (11:1-11)

In the final section of this division of his prophecy, Hosea discloses the intensity and tenacity of the LORD's love for his people. The prophet continues his technique of historical retrospect to contrast past beginnings, so full of potential and hope, with the subsequent reality of misconduct and impending doom. On this occasion, however, Hosea varies his approach by extending the timeline through from looming judgement to an envisaged climax of restoration. This reflects the divine perspective on history, which is not a mere retelling of the past to illumine the present or the immediate future. Rather, God's dealings with his people, and with mankind as a whole, are unbounded by our temporal limitations and develop coherently to bring his purposes of grace to completion. So in closing this portion of his work the prophet is guided to end with a note of deliverance which crowns God's

98. 'Utterly' renders an infinitive absolute before a perfect (taken as a prophetic perfect) niphal from the root *dmh* III, 'to destroy'.

salvation. It is, however, made clear that this salvation will not occur in place of judgement; instead it is salvation after, indeed through, judgement.

In this section the LORD is no longer portrayed as a farmer surveying crops or animals which have not lived up to his expectations; he is now the fond father whose hopes for his child have been frustrated by the child's rebellious behaviour. The prophet who has himself known the depths of rejected love is privileged to portray the unfathomable depth of the love of God who will not relinquish those whom he has acknowledged as his own. Though their conduct has rendered punishment inevitable, God will work to achieve his objectives even through the imposition of penalty. No longer can exile be avoided, but the prospect of return after exile is presented. The concluding words of hope in 11:10-11 mirror what is expressed in 3:5. There are always two sides to a relationship, and that is true also of the bond which unites the parties to the covenant. Despite the rebellion of his people, the LORD remains committed, and he will have the final say on their relationship.

The unity of the section is indicated by the presence of inclusion with the repetition of 'out from Egypt' (11:1, 11; note also the occurrence of Egypt in 11:5), the mention of 'my son' (11:1) and 'sons' (11:10), and the contrasting references of the verb in 'they went'/'they will go' (11:2, 10). This presentation of Israel's history, past and future, points to a reversal of the tragic defections of the past, and to eventual reinstatement because of the LORD's tenacious grasp of the people.

In accordance with the concluding phrase in 11:11, God is the main speaker throughout 11:1-11, but he addresses the people directly only in 11:8-9.

(1) A Father Remembers (11:1-4)

In this section it is father-son imagery which is used to illumine the Yahweh-Israel relationship. However, since Israel is depicted as a youth, the LORD is clearly the dominant partner who authoritatively structures the union and who provides needed support for the people. But this is not done in an overbearing, authoritarian fashion; all the LORD's actions are motivated by loving tenderness and concern. Even so, the relationship was not one on which Israel should presume. The LORD was not naturally bound to treat them in this way. His sovereign choice had designated them as his sons by adoption, and they ought to respond with grateful obedience to all that had been bestowed on them.

11:1 When Israel was a youth, I loved him,
and out from Egypt I called my son.

The nostalgic tone which pervades 9:10-10:15 continues here. ***When Israel was a youth*** looks back to the founding of the nation at the time of the Exodus and their formative years (2:15; Jer. 2:2; Ezek. 16:22, 43, 60). As a term for age, 'youth' may apply from infancy (cf. Exod. 2:6; 1 Sam. 4:21) through to late adolescence (cf. Gen. 37:2) and beyond (Gen. 41:12 when Joseph is 30 years old), but the picture here is of the early years when the people were still vulnerable and helpless, incapable of extricating themselves from the oppression of their situation in Egypt, and consequently also unable to bear the responsibilities placed on them (cf. 11:3). In this connection Solomon's words are significant: 'I am a mere youth: I do not know how to go out or come in' (1 Kgs. 3:7). 'Youth' implies a lack of experience which requires guidance to make correct decisions or intervene effectively in public affairs (cf. Jer. 1:6-7). It is also possible that the word 'youth' is employed here because it sometimes has the sense 'servant' or 'attendant' (cf. Gen. 22:3; Neh. 4:16). In Egypt Israel had been not only immature but also enslaved.

I loved him points to the intimate and fond relationship which the LORD instituted (and continued to maintain) between himself and the people (cf. 3:1-2; 9:15; 14:4) by setting his love on them (cf. Deut. 7:7; 10:15). 'Love' at a human level denotes the positive emotional attachment of one person to another, primarily in a family relationship. It gives rise to a special concern for the well-being of the individual who is loved. So, at a time when their situation was desperate and there was nothing to commend the Israelites to the LORD, he gave evidence of his love for them by sovereignly intervening to deliver them from oppression and to constitute them his own by taking them ***out from Egypt***.[99]

I called my son issues not an invitation but a command. Moreover, it goes beyond a directive to the people to leave Egypt. It is the sovereign summons of the LORD to those he has called by which he designates them to a special role in his service (cf. Isa. 41:9; 43:1; 51:2). Furthermore, what is in view here is not merely dutiful obedience, but the grateful response of those who now enjoy the privileged status of a

99. Whereas in 12:15 and 13:5 the Hebrew preposition *min* is used temporally with 'the land of Egypt' to indicate what has occurred in the period after their departure from Egypt, here the preposition retains its locative sense to point to what the LORD's electing love had delivered his people from.

new, elevated relationship with the LORD. 'My son' formally bestowed this on the nation when it was announced in Exodus 4:22-23, 'And you will say to Pharaoh, "Thus says the LORD, Israel is my firstborn son, and I say to you, 'Let my son go so that he may serve me.' " ' It is this relationship which underpins the LORD's action with respect to Israel at the Exodus and subsequently (cf. Deut. 4:37-39; 7:8, 13; 32:6, 10-14). It was this relationship which should have informed and motivated Israel's response.

Matthew's Use of Hosea 11:1.

It has often been felt that Matthew's citation of Hosea 11:1, 'so that there might be fulfilled what was spoken by the Lord through the prophet, saying, "Out of Egypt I have called my son" ' (Matt. 2:15), is inappropriate and that he misunderstood the prophet's meaning because the next verse (11:2) clearly shows that Hosea was concerned with the historical experience of Israel at the time of the Exodus when the LORD had rescued his people from Egypt. It is therefore argued that to suggest that this was a prophecy of Christ which required to be fulfilled is to read into the text something that was never there.

Kaiser in his treatment (1985:47–53) points out that the text comes in one of the bright passages in Hosea's prophecy where, despite the people's persistent rejection of the LORD, he manifests his persevering love for them and does not utterly reject them despite their misconduct. In the same way in Matthew's narrative there is highlighted God's preserving love in the early years of Jesus' life.

But more than that is involved. 'My son' is a designation of the covenant community, first found in Exodus 4:22-23, but finally and completely realised in the incarnation of the Messiah, and so it warrants Matthew connecting the essential theme of the two passages. Howard calls this 'analogical correspondence' and views it as a refinement of traditional typological analysis which has often been marred by supposing that the passage and the events described in Hosea were intend to prefigure the Messiah either to the prophet himself or to his contemporaries. It is only in the light of events as they actually transpired that Matthew and those who are later than him occupy the privileged stance of being able to look back and detect analogies in the Lord's way of working on the two occasions. 'Even as the nation was taken into Egypt and brought out, so also the Messiah was taken into Egypt and brought out.'[100] Also, on both occasions there was a

100. Howard 1986:321. This article contains extensive details about vari-

background of persecution. Matthew's use of 'fulfil' does not apply only to actualisation of specific predictions; it may equally describe part of a process in which a later event of a similar nature occurs in the outworking of God's purpose.

Furthermore, Kaiser (1985:51) emphasises that Matthew does not introduce this quotation into chapter 2 of the gospel after verse 20 or even after verse 22, but after verse 15. Its location before the narrative of the return from Egypt signals the fact that the essential point being made is not a recapitulation of the Exodus, but the permanence of God's preserving love for his son, whether that is a reference to the people as a whole or to the Son *par eminence*. Hosea was concerned not just with the past fact of history, but with the spiritual significance of what was exemplified there, and the whole context culminating in 11:10-11 of the prophecy shows that he expects further displays of that same paternal love. That this was also in Matthew's mind can be inferred from the way in which in place of the Septuagint rendering, 'Out of Egypt I called his children', he maintains the Hebrew reading, 'Out of Egypt I called my son'.

11:2 ⌊As⌋ they called to them,
so they went from them;
to the Baals they kept sacrificing,
and to images they kept burning incense.

However, because of the disobedience of the people, the relationship between the LORD and Israel did not progress smoothly. The existence of a comparison in the first half of the verse is indicated by ***so*** which introduces the second clause. The ground of the comparison is generally taken to be the correlated frequency with which the actions occurred, but the precise nature of what is described is not totally clear. 'They' in ***they called to them***[101] is not specified. It may be an indefinite plural so that the construction is equivalent to a passive, 'they were called', but the following 'from them' makes that improbable. Others suggest in the light of the rest of the verse that what is in view is a competing call from the Canaanites in general, in which case 'from

---

ous interpretations of the passage.

101. The first verb is often emended to 'I called to them' on the basis of the LXX and Peshitta (cf. NIV, GNB, REB, NRSV). This is accompanied by reading, 'so they went from me' in which *mippənêhem*, 'from their face' is redivided into *mippənay* 'from me' and *hēm* is taken with the next line as an emphatic use of the pronoun. This procedure results in a sense similar to taking 'they' as the prophets.

them' may have the sense 'because of them' (cf. Gen. 6:13; Exod. 3:7; Judg. 6:6). Indeed, some interpreters find a reference to the seductive voices of the Moabite women in the incident at Baal-Peor (cf. 9:10; Num. 25:1-2; Andersen, et al. 1980:578). However, the most probable interpretation is that already found in the Targum and the Vulgate, and explicitly represented in the ASV, '⌞the prophets⌟ called to them'. The LORD did not call his people to himself only once, but did so on a series of occasions through his messengers (cf. 6:15; 9:8; 12:10; 2 Kgs. 17:13; Jer. 7:25; 25:4-7; Zech. 1:4). Nevertheless as often as he called in this way, ***so they went from them***/'away from their faces/presence'. The verb 'go' may be used of a spiritual response (cf. 2:13). Here it is that of the people in their perversity rejecting prophetic warnings and invitations to return.[102]

Heedless of the LORD's entreaties, they persisted in their erroneous ways, and ***to the Baals they kept sacrificing.*** The verbs are now imperfects which denote repeated action in the past. 'Baals' (2:13) stands for the multiplicity of heathen deities. Right from the incident of the golden calf at the foot of Sinai (Exod. 32:1-10), the allure of Canaanite worship proved too much for the people to resist, and it influenced their conduct in other matters as well. For 'sacrificing', see 4:13-14; 8:13. ***Images*** (the precise term is used only here in Hosea) are objects produced by the skill of a craftsman, whether hewn from stone or carved from wood, or possibly cast from metal. For ***burning incense***, see on 2:13. Rejecting the LORD did not leave a spiritual vacuum, but led to embracing all that he hated and had prohibited.

11:3 But I ⌞was the one who⌟ taught Ephraim to walk;
he took them on his arms,
but they did not know that I healed them.

---

102. Another possibility which retains the MT is that proposed by Macintosh (1997:439–440). He takes 'they' in the first clause as the Israelites and, alluding to 7:11 ('they called to Egypt, they went to Assyria'), he argues that Hosea then describes the people's deviant response. They did not call on the LORD in response to his call to them, but they called in what they reckoned were their own best interests to Egypt (the thought of which would be readily supplied from the mention in the previous verse), and then in a similar fashion they (Ephraim) abandoned their alliance with them. The second part of the verse presents a separate aspect of their disobedience. The plausibility of this approach, as of that adopted, depends on how readily one considers the various references would have been supplied.

The verse begins by refocussing attention on the LORD.[103] The ingratitude and spiritual incomprehension of Ephraim is contrasted with the care which the LORD bestowed on them and the attention with which he had advanced their interests. ***I taught Ephraim to walk.*** Ephraim is here the whole of the northern kingdom in its best days. The picture is most probably that of a father teaching a young child to walk. If, however, the term 'youth' (11:1) still controls the metaphorical imagery, since a youth would usually have progressed beyond the toddler stage, the phrase might be understood as 'I walked in front of Ephraim' to guide him.[104]

The second line may be a prophetic expansion of the description, or it may be another instance of a switch of person in reference to the LORD in a divine speech (cf. 11:11, 12). Also, the alternation of plural and singular in 'them' and 'his' is not out of line with Hosea's style elsewhere. ***He took them***[105] ***on his arms*** is usually interpreted as the LORD lifting up and carrying the young child, possibly when it became too tired to go any further. The verb, however, is not the most natural one for conveying this idea and the arms referred to may be Ephraim's: 'he grasped them on his [Ephraim's] arms' to guide and protect them.

Despite this care Israel did not perceive or acknowledge the activity of the LORD on their behalf. ***They did not know that I healed them.***

---

103. For a similar use of *wə*, 'and', with *ʾānōkî*, 'I', followed by a finite verb, functioning disjunctively, see 7:13.

104. The word *tirgaltî* occurs only here. It has been generally taken as a tiphel form (equivalent to a hiphil) and associated with *regel*, 'foot'. This yields the sense 'cause to walk', 'teach to walk'. For the interpretation 'walk in front of', see, Andersen, et al. 1980:579 adopted by Hubbard 1989:188. The alternative explanation does account for the preposition *lə*, 'to', 'with respect to', but it is difficult in any event. McComiskey (1992:185) favours the idea of moving oneself about for the purposes of close observation, being attentive — a picture of parental care.

105. It is difficult to account for the form *qāḥām*, though it is generally derived from *lāqaḥ*, 'to take', possibly with a third person plural suffix (cf. the form found in Ezek. 17:5). If it is a third person masculine singular perfect form, then the subject would seem to be the LORD, but it is difficult to understand how a child could be taught to walk by lifting them upon the arms. Alternatively, it might be an infinitive absolute form (though a pronominal suffix makes that improbable), which could be rendered 'taking them upon his arms', but again 'his arms' causes difficulty, and the early versions read 'my arms'. Many modern scholars emend the text in some way to yield an acceptable sense.

For 'did not know', see on 2:8. They obtusely refused to acknowledge how the LORD had dealt with them and provided for them. His benevolence is described under the imagery of healing, with an obvious play on the words 'Ephraim' (*ʾeprayim*) and 'I healed them' (*rəpāʾtîm*). 'Heal' (cf. 5:13; 6:1; 7:1; 14:4) is used in a wider sense of 'restore, make whole', particularly here in respect of their relationship with God. 'I am the LORD who heals you' (Exod. 15:26) connects his restorative power not primarily with physical disease as such, but with covenant obedience and maintenance of a right relationship with him. Here it would refer to all that the LORD had done by way of forgiving their breaches of the covenant and restoring their national fortunes. However, the people had wilfully refused to admit what was obvious in the history of the LORD's dealings with them because they had been blinded by the allure of Canaan.

11:4 With cords of a man I kept pulling them,
with bands of love;
and I became to them like those who raise a yoke on their jaws,
and I stretched out to him, I made ⌞him⌟ eat.

Interpretation of this verse depends on whether the father-child metaphor continues (at least in part), or whether it changes to one of farmer/trainer-animal. Decisions regarding this focus on the Hebrew word *ʿōl*, 'yoke' in the third line, which has the same consonants as *ʿul*, 'a young child' (cf. NRSV, cf. Isa. 49:15; 65:20, where the word is spelled in full). This would give rise to a translation such as, 'I became to them like those who raise an infant against their jaws/cheeks, and I stretched out to him, I made him eat' (cf. REB, NRSV). The plural in 'those who raise' suggests that this is not a simple extension of the father-child metaphor. It is more probable that there is a switch from the imagery of the previous verse, and that language similar to that of 10:11 is again used.[106]

'Cords' and 'bands' suggest pieces of harness to control an animal, though it is possible mothers did use light cords to keep their toddlers from straying too far. ***With cords of a man***/'human being' (*ʾādām*) may indicate restraints imposed by the LORD on the people through the human instrumentality (cf. 'rod of men' and 'stripes of the sons of men', 2 Sam. 7:14, NIV, HCSB), or it may just suggest humane and

106. Another view is that after the lack of knowledge displayed by the people, this verse is to be read harshly of the chastisement that the LORD inflicted on them (Smith 1994:45–46).

sensitive treatment. ***I kept pulling them*** points to their repeated attempts to go off on their own, and the LORD's restraining influence as he educated them in the way that was right. The verb denotes grasping something with a view to pulling it or drawing it along (cf. 'With everlasting love I have loved you, accordingly I have drawn you with steadfast love', Jer. 31:3), but there was no harsh treatment since all was done ***with bands of love*** (cf. 11:1).

Raise a yoke on their jaws does not describe cruel, insensitive action, but a considerate, humane attitude, lifting the yoke to change its position so that it lay more easily on the animal ('jaws' seemingly is used for 'neck', cf. NIV). Alternatively, if this clause is in sequence with the following line it may picture the removal of the yoke so that the animal may feed unimpeded (cf. 10:11), but a break between the lines seems more likely because of the switch from plural to singular. It is unclear whether the first word of the last line is an adjective 'gently' (so Laetsch 1956:87; McComiskey 1992:185) or a verb ***I stretched out to him***,[107] indicating an action of tender care, stooping down of father to the child, possibly to listen to something which has been said. ***I made ⌊him⌋ eat*** completes the picture of God's loving provision for the needs of his people.

REFLECTION

- Use of 'Father' as a metaphor to describe God is restrained throughout the Old Testament probably because the ideological influence of pagan cults was liable to cause it to be misunderstood in a grossly physical sense. In the Old Testament the fatherhood of God does not even relate to his giving life to all peoples or to his sustaining them in his providence. The conception is reserved for the LORD's unique relationship with Israel as his people whom he has adopted and to whom he has given the special status of 'firstborn son' (Exod. 4:22). He is the Father who created Israel not by natural birth, but by electing them to their special role in the outworking of his saving purpose (cf. Deut. 32:6; Ps. 100:3).
- The basis of God's electing love is not open to human inspection. 'I will be gracious to whom I will be gracious, and will show mercy to

---

107. As a verb, *wǝʾaṭ* is pointed as an ordinary *waw* followed by a short-form imperfect from *nāṭâ*, 'to reach out', rather than a *waw* consecutive imperfect form as might have been expected (cf. 6:1). It is difficult to account for this form (cf. GKC §109k), but poetic variation (or possibly a northern mode of expression) may be relevant factors behind a preterite rather than a future translation.

whom I will show mercy' (Exod. 33:19). Omitting several subordinate clauses brings out the circularity of the argument in 'it was not because … that the LORD set his love on you and chose you … but it is because the LORD loves you' (Deut. 7:7-8). The LORD's love is explained by the LORD's love, grounded in his secret counsel, and consequently not dependent on human character or achievement. Equally, therefore, the sovereign determination of God is irrevocable since it originates solely in his good pleasure. That, however, does not mean that no response is required from those whom he loves. Rather the overwhelming magnitude of the gift bestowed should impel to every effort.

- As Father, God displays tender and compassionate care towards his children. 'Like an eagle which stirs up its nest, which hovers over its young, spreading out its wings, catching them, bearing them on its pinions, the LORD alone guided him' (Deut. 32:10-11). His provision for them was consistent and comprehensive: freedom from oppression, warning against error, training in action, restoration, guidance in conduct, alleviation of hardship, provision of physical nourishment. How perverse their ingratitude in the face of such benevolence!
- The LORD's punishment of sin is not a contradiction of his love, but an expression of it. This had been clearly stated by Amos when he relayed the divine message to the people of Israel, 'Only you do I know of all the families of the earth; therefore I will punish you for all your iniquities' (Amos 3:2). There 'know' refers not to mere cognition, but to the electing love which constituted them 'my people'. Special privilege is accompanied by heightened responsibility (cf. Rom. 2:9; 1 Pet. 4:17), and also by the overtures and discipline of reclaiming love (cf. Heb. 12:5-7).

(2) The Punishment Imposed (11:5-7)

As the Father of his people, the LORD had dealt with them in a patient and kindly manner, but he still had expectations regarding their behaviour, expectations which he was not prepared to modify. Because they persistently continued to defy him and disregard his directions regarding their conduct, he could not allow the existing state of affairs to continue indefinitely and would have to take disciplinary action against their intransigence. The LORD's verdict against his people would be effected through foreign domination (11:5) which would involve destruction of their land (11:6).

11:5 He will not return to the land of Egypt,
but Assyria—it ⌊will be⌋ his king,
for they have refused to return.

He in the first line of the verse is not a reference to Hoshea, the last king in Samaria, and the way he sought Egyptian help (cf. 12:1), but continues Ephraim as the subject as in previous verses. However, this line has caused much perplexity in view of its seeming contradiction of statements such as, 'They themselves will return to Egypt' (8:13) and 'Ephraim will return to Egypt' (9:3; cf. 9:6; 11:11). The NRSV deals with this problem by translating, 'They shall return to Egypt', which treats the initial term in the sentence not as the Hebrew word 'not', but as a homonym with an asseverative function (cf. 'surely', ESV footnote). The NIV takes the same word as carrying interrogative overtones, and translates, 'Will they not return to Egypt?'[108] It is more probable that while on other occasions Hosea uses Egypt as a metaphorical description of conditions of oppression and domination such as those which the people had once experienced there (cf. 8:13), here it is the country itself which is in view. While there will be refugees who escape to Egypt (9:6), it is explicitly ruled out that Egypt is going to control the people; instead they will fall under the domination of ***Assyria***, which at this point in history would a far harsher taskmaster. ***It*** (possibly 'it alone') is emphatically expressed to exclude alternatives and misunderstanding. Ephraim's own leadership had collapsed (10:3, 15), and so he will be compelled to have a foreign overlord as ***his king***. This loss of national sovereignty will come about because ***they have refused to return*** in repentance to the LORD. The problem was not lack of an invitation to do so, but the fact that they stubbornly and deliberately said no. For 'return' (*šûb*), see on 3:5. The repetition of the 'return' in different senses points to the pivotal role of repentance. The verb is employed again in 11:7 and 9.

11:6 And a sword will swirl against his cities,
and it will finish off the bars of his ⌊gates⌋,
and it will devour because of their plans.

108. The LXX construed the ending of 11:4 and the start of 11:5 quite differently. The translation 'I will prevail with him. Ephraim dwelt in Egypt' was obtained by reading *lô*, 'to him', rather than the negative, and taking it with the verb at the end of the previous verse, and also by identifying that verb as a form of *yākōl*, 'to be able, prevail', rather than as a form of *ʾākal*, 'to eat'. Furthermore the first verb in 11:5 was read as a form of *yāšab*, 'to dwell', rather than of *šûb*, 'to return'.

This verse describes three aspects of enemy aggression which will be the outcome of Ephraim's refusal to repent. While the first and third lines are fairly clear, the second line is problematic. ***A sword*** indicates that the damage will not occur from a natural disaster, but that devastation and death will come as a consequence of military action (cf. 7:16). ***Swirl*** (from a root meaning 'to go round' or 'to dance') catches the dashing blows of the advancing enemy forces as they clash with the armies of Israel. Mention of ***his cities*** reflects their strategic importance as fortified centres of resistance (8:14; 10:14), situated at key locations throughout the land, where they would also serve as hubs for the life of surrounding communities, including their religious life. The translation ***against*** is not quite certain; it might also be 'in'. The decision depends in part on how the following line is understood.

The second line of the verse provides further detail regarding the havoc caused by the sword, which stands by metonymy for military action in general. But what is it that it ***will finish off***? The word rendered ***the bars of his ⌞gates⌟*** may be understood in various ways, such as 'districts' (NKJV), 'limbs' (NJPS), 'oracle-priests' (NRSV; cf. REB), or even 'boasting' (Garrett 1997:226). None of these is without some lexical warrant, but many English translations favour a reference to the city defences (NIV, ESV, HCSB).[109] The gate functioned to block unauthorised entry into the city, and it was the weakest part of its fortification. If there was no bar to hold the gate firm against enemy pressure, then the strength of the city walls was irrelevant, and other forms of defences were worthless. Once the gate has succumbed to enemy action, the city lay open to its attackers.

There is a third reference to the impact of the military invasion in ***it will devour*** (from the root *ʾākal*, 'to eat'), which echoes the preceding 'it will finish off' (from the root *kālâ*), and which also forms a sombre

109. The Hebrew word in question is *bad*, for which *HALOT* (1:108-109) lists five roots. *bad* (I) occurs in the sense of a 'part' or 'portion', as well as in the plural 'limbs' (Job 41:4). *bad* (II) describes the poles used to carry the ark and sacred objects (e.g. Exod. 25:14), and that is extended to the similarly shaped object used to close the city gates. *bad* (V) is identified as having the meaning 'oracle priest' (Isa. 44:25; Jer. 50:36), while 'boasting' is associated with *bad* (IV) (cf. Isa. 16:6; Jer. 48:30). These last two options favour reading this line with the final line as descriptive of the misguided policies which were pursued in the land. Whereas in Jer. 50:36 association with other classes of people such as 'wise men' gives plausibility to identifying *bad* (IV) there, despite Hubbard's arguments to the contrary (1989:191), the context here favours a more military rendering.

contrast with the previous divinely imposed eating (11:4). ***Their plans*** refers to the frantic attempts to work out a strategy to counter Assyrian pressure, all of which proved unavailing because they were not conceived in submission to God. What they devised led not to safety, but drew them into further peril and eventual destruction.

11:7 But my people are hung on backsliding from me,
and upwards they call on him;
he will not raise them up together.

The one who says ***my people*** must be taken to be the LORD, and not the prophet, because of the following reference to 'backsliding from me', which cannot refer to Hosea. 'My people' shows that despite all their deviance the LORD still recognised his relationship to them, something which the people themselves were perversely not prepared to do. Rather they ***are hung on backsliding from me.*** The verb embodies a metaphor of something being hung up on hooks, possibly exposed to public disgrace (cf. 2 Sam. 21:12), or else caught dangling in a state of suspense (cf. Deut. 28:66). Either way, the people are viewed disparagingly as they are helpless in the grip of their hankering after pagan gods. 'Backsliding' is derived from the same root as 'return', which may be used positively of moving back in repentance to God. Literally the phrase is 'my backsliding'/'my return', but the backwards movement is that of the people as they spiritually regress from adherence to the LORD and his covenant standards into the pagan ways of Canaan (cf. Jer. 2:19; Ezek. 37:33).

The second line of the verse poses yet another interpretational conundrum. The overall sense seems clear: despite entreaties for help, the people will not be able to extricate themselves from their predicament. But to whom are their cries directed? Literally the line reads, 'and to up (*ʿal*) they will call him.' Hosea has already used 'up' (*ʿal*) in a similar context in 7:16, where it might be taken adverbially 'upwards' or as a reference to deity. Some translations do take this as a call to God as 'the Most High' (NIV, ESV), a call which he rejects, but that fails to account for the twofold reference which then occurs in 'to the Most High they call on him'. Possibly the sense is simply ***upwards***, that is, heavenwards, ***they call on him.***

Another approach to the second line notes that the initial ***and*** followed by a non-verb indicates that the line is to be read as describing a coordinated aspect of the people's backsliding. In that case the one on whom they call using this unconventional title would be

Baal.[110] Possibly ***call*** is an ironic reference back to the divine call of 11:1, not echoing that of the LORD, but addressed in a different direction altogether. Though the people recognise their need of assistance, they turn their backs on Yahweh and instead implore Baal. The third line may then be understood as exposing how futile their efforts will be as Baal is incapable of helping them.

More probably, the third line of the verse records that, because the people have refused to repent, the LORD will not grant their requests for relief (cf. Isa. 59:2; Zech. 1:4, 7:11-13). ***He will not raise them up together.*** 'Raise up'/'lift up' may be used in the sense of elevating to a safe place and so effecting a rescue (cf. 'lift high on a rock', Ps. 27:5). 'Together' indicates 'totally' or 'entirely' (cf. 11:8; Ps. 33:15), and so, accompanied by a negative, the sense would be: 'he will not rescue them at all' .

REFLECTION

- 'Hung on backsliding' (11:7) graphically pictures the incapacity of those who were trapped by their own spiritual perversity. They refused to respond to God's entreaties (11:5), and instead relied on their own plans (11:6), considering them to be superior to his. As individuals, they were self-deluded and self-harming, like addicts unable to acknowledge the grip their addiction had on them and so helpless in its grasp. As a nation, they had so prided themselves in their own acumen that they despised the counsel God gave them. Such self-reliance springs from the rebellion of fallen humanity, and its debasing influence is still evident when a nation or civilisation turns away from its Christian heritage and succumbs to forces which inflate its self-esteem so that it considers itself wiser than God.
- 'He will not raise them up' (11:7) shows that the LORD will be unresponsive to Israel's belated entreaties. Prayer to him is based on relationship with him, and those whose inner alienation from him is such that their hearts are turned away from him and they do not respond to what he says cannot expect their prayers to be heard or answered. They cannot act on the basis of the promise, 'If you abide in me, and my words abide in you, ask whatever you wish, and it will

---

110. Many commentators indeed accept the emendation proposed by *BHS* and read *wəʾel-ʿal*, 'and to up', as *wəʾel baʿal*, 'and to Baal'. However, it is possible to treat *ʿal* as a divine epithet related to the word *ʿelyôn*, 'most high' (cf. Andersen, et al. 1980:586; Wolff 1974:192–193). Another reading of the text is to vocalise *ʿal*, 'height, upwards, up', as *ʿōl*, 'yoke' (cf. GNB, RSV, following Vulgate).

be done for you' (John 15:7). Instead those who have defected from the LORD will find fasting, sacrifice and other rituals unavailing (cf. Jer. 14:12) because their iniquities have become a divide between them and God, and their sins have hidden his face from them (Isa. 59:2).

(3) Divine Reluctance (11:8-9)

The enduring nature of the LORD's commitment had already been indicated when, despite the gross misconduct of the nation, he continued to regard them as 'my people' (11:7). Now he directly addresses them, and reveals the intensity of his attachment to them. Even though he has unsparingly exposed their deep-seated disposition to rebel and to offend him, there still wells up within him love and tender compassion. On the verge of destroying them utterly he draws back. This provides the ultimate context within which previous statements announcing doom have to be understood (cf. 5:6; 8:13; 9:3, 6, 17).

11:8 How can I give you up, Ephraim?
⌞How⌟ can I hand you over, Israel?
How can I give you up like Admah?
⌞How⌟ can I set you like Zeboyim?
My heart is in turmoil within me;
my compassions are aroused altogether.

Distraught, the LORD reflects on Israel's unrepentant behaviour, which dooms the whole nation to destruction. They have thoughtlessly given up on him, but his commitment is stronger and he cannot just leave them to the dire outcome of their wilful defiance. ***Ephraim*** and ***Israel*** must be synonymous in this context (cf. 11:1, 3), and both refer to the entire northern kingdom, with the latter term particularly considering them as the covenant people of the LORD.

The two expressed uses of ***how?*** each do double duty, and are to be understood with the following line also. 'How?' is a word of lamentation (cf. 2 Sam. 1:19; Mic. 2:4), which here articulates deep concern at their intransigence rather than being a rhetorical question asked of others for dramatic effect. Instead, God addresses himself, and in this soliloquy Hosea's audience—and subsequent readers—are permitted to overhear that inner communing and so have access to the mind of God. This profound questioning of anguished disappointment is, of course, an anthropomorphic presentation, but it is not on that account to be reckoned as unreal or contrived. ***Give you up*** and ***hand you over*** require a potential scenario involving more than a single enemy incursion against the nation, no matter how savage. What is envisaged is the

LORD completely surrendering the people to their foes to do with them as they please.

The argument is illustrated by examples from the past. Previously such backward glances had been to incidents involving Israel, but now they are to ***Admah*** and ***Zeboyim***, two of the five cities of the plain which may well have been located under what is now the southern end of the Dead Sea (Gen. 14:2). Along with the better known Sodom and Gomorrah they were utterly destroyed by the LORD (Gen. 19:24-29), though they are not specifically identified in that narrative. But later these four cities are named by Moses when he says of them that their land had been turned into 'a scorching waste of brimstone and salt; nothing could be sown; nothing could grow; no vegetation could spring up in it' because of the LORD's anger and wrath (Deut. 29:23). Here these two more obscure cities, and not their more notorious associates, Sodom and Gomorrah, are probably mentioned because of the sound of their names,[111] and also to recall the description Moses gave of their fate (though Hosea doubtless also enjoyed puzzling his hearers into reflecting more deeply on what he said). The misconduct of the cities of the plain had justly exposed them to the unabated indignation of God, and it was the same penalty which awaited the people of the north. Because they had abandoned the LORD's covenant and become virtual heathen (cf. Deut. 29:24-28), as the righteous Judge this was the only verdict he could deliver. ***Set*** is probably not just 'destine' you to such an end, but actually 'impose' it on you.

But the questions posed by God do not reveal him as a cold, heartless dispenser of justice. The two concluding lines make further reference to his inner feelings. Although 'heart' may describe an individual's thought and determination (cf. 4:11), it can also indicate emotion and that seems appropriate here in view of the parallel expression. ***My heart*** speaks of the sorrow God experiences when he contemplates the unmitigated imposition of the verdict demanded by justice. ***Is in turmoil*** (from *hāpak*) perhaps pictures a process of inwardly turning over one option after another to see if there is a more acceptable way forwards. The same root (*hāpak*) was used of the LORD 'overthrowing' those cities (Gen. 19:25, 29; Deut. 29:23), but the prospect of such a judgement on his people impacts on the LORD himself, causing intense

111. Ben Zvi suggests that reference to these particular cities 'is related to the presence of the א, and even better, an initial א — as is the case in most words in this series — in the word Admah' (2005:229). The stylistic desire to repeat the sound determined which places were named.

inner perturbation (cf. Lam. 1:20), even before disaster engulfs the people. ***Within me*** is literally 'upon me' and pictures the emotionally fraught situation pressing down on the spirit of the individual involved.

My compassions (cf. Isa. 57:18; Zech. 1:13) refer to God's desire to comfort and console, and not to execute judgement. The verb ***are aroused*** occurs with a similar term denoting compassion in Gen. 43:30 and 1 Kgs. 3:26.[112] 'Aroused' describes deep emotional stirring, with associated warmth and fervency of feeling, to which ***altogether*** (cf. 11:7) adds a note of the intensity and completeness of the reaction. Justice demands that Israel's misbehaviour be punished, but the prospect is so horrific that God recoils from its full impact. This is a highly anthropomorphic presentation of the divine tension which arises in this situation. A new initiative of love is required, as in chapter 3, to alleviate the full measure of what was due.

11:9 I will not execute the fierceness of my anger;
  I will not return to ruin Ephraim,
for I ⌞am⌟ God and not man,
  in your midst the Holy One;
  and I will not come into a city.

The tensions exposed in the divine self-disclosure of the previous verse are now resolved by a decided rejection of the option to impose the utter extermination which justice on its own demands. Instead God determines not to ***execute*** / 'do, make, carry out' ***the fierceness of my anger*** (cf. Jer. 4:26; 12:13). This double expression for God's wrath may well reflect the use of the two roots in Deuteronomy 29:23, 26. There is no denying the existence of divine wrath against Israel's sin, and that, if it were the only factor in the situation and if it were allowed to run its course unmitigated, then sheer ruin would ensue. But the reality of divine anger against the bull-calf of Samaria (cf. 8:5) and the associated misconduct of his people are balanced by other considerations arising from within the character of God himself. His restraint in the situation is marked by the fourfold negative ***not***, indicating that the seemingly inevitable and logical outcome of the scenario does not eventuate. Lines 3 and 4 of the verse explain why this is so, but nowhere is there any indication of how God will resolve this inner dissonance between love and justice without compromising his integrity.

---

112. Both verbs in 11:8c are niphal forms which indicate internal turmoil in Yahweh rather than an external overthrowing of the fortunes of the people.

The significance of ***I will not return to ruin Ephraim*** depends upon when it is envisaged that the divine word is spoken—before or after the fall of Samaria? For 'ruin', see on 9:9; 13:9. After the fall of the city it is possible to take the verb *šûb*, 'to return', in an auxiliary sense as equivalent to 'do again' (cf. *HALOT* 4:1430): 'I will not again destroy Ephraim'. These words would then anticipate the scenes of restorative return in 11:10-11. However, a setting before the fall of the city is much more probable, and in that case retaining the sense of 'return' for the verb would fit in with the previous intimation of the LORD's withdrawal from the people (5:15). The character of his renewed intervention in the affairs of the north, severe though it would be, would not have as its final outcome the sweeping ruin which had been imposed on the cities of the plain. This thought is apparently taken up again in the last line of the verse.

For sets out why the LORD determines to act in this way and maintain his commitment to the covenant relationship. ***I am God and not man*** (*ʾîš*). 'God' (*ʾēl*, cf. 1:10) emphasises his true deity. As such, he is different from his creation (cf. Num. 23:19; 1 Sam. 15:29). It is doubtful if the focus here is merely on mankind as sinful, so that what is being said is that his response is worthy of God and not patterned after the corrupt and degraded behaviour of Adam's fallen descendants. It looks further than that to the intrinsic difference between the eternal and uncreated God and a created being. There are ways of operating that are available to God which lie beyond humankind.[113] It is perhaps relevant that the passage in Deuteronomy 29 which forms the interpretative background for these verses finishes by reminding us that 'the secret things belong to the LORD our God' (Deut. 29:29). This is an occasion not for explanation but for worshipful wonder.[114]

Holiness in the Old Testament characterises that which is separate, and ***the Holy One*** as a divine title points to God as unique, the one who stands apart from his creation, perfect (cf. Matt. 5:48) and good

---

113. Radical feminism has taken this text to mean that God as mother rejects the male (*ʾîš*) behaviour patterns of destruction in favour of female attitudes and actions. The text does not, however, posit a male-female disjunction. At most it might be argued that God is here presented simply as 'parent' in relation to 'child'.

114. 'If I were a man, I would in my sorely provoked anger let them have it! They deserve nothing else! But I am not a man, nor am I a prisoner to human passions and grudges; I am God—the compassionate, loving, and faithful God, whose purpose is not to destroy, but to forgive and redeem' (Bright 1977:93).

(cf. Luke 18:19).[115] His action and responses are not conditioned by finitude; they are incomparable. But the wonder of his covenant relationship with his people is that he is ***in your midst*** (cf. Isa. 12:6; Zeph. 3:15-17). His is not an arms-length commitment but is one in which he is present and active in the community of the faithful and also within their lives as individuals (cf. Isa. 57:15). God's otherness works itself out not by compromising his uniqueness (and inherent purity) but by manifesting itself in a love which will so change his people that his goals will be accomplished.

The last clause of the verse is generally regarded as obscure. The Hebrew text reads, ***and I will not come into a city*** (cf. LXX, AV, TNIV), but it is not immediately apparent what this can mean. It may look back to 'cities' (11:6) to form an inclusion round this passage, in which case it is coming in judgement that is under consideration. However, the LORD recoils from such an outcome and resolves not to act in anger. Since many have felt that this and other interpretations which retain the sense 'city' are forced and artificial, other options have been proposed. One is to keep the consonants of 'into a city' and identify a form of a verb, 'to burn, consume' (cf. 7:4, 6) or a related term 'to remove, destroy' ('I will not come to destroy', RSV). Many English translations (e.g. NIV, ESV) retain a prepositional phrase, but, less convincingly, take the noun as meaning 'agitation, wrath' (cf. Jer. 15:8): 'I will not come in wrath'. The right approach may well be to find here yet another allusion to the destruction of the cities of the plain when the LORD came down to investigate what was occurring (Gen. 18:20-21) and the two angels entered Sodom (Gen. 19:1). If the LORD enters a city to take close cognisance of what is perpetrated there, the enormity of what he finds would readily precipitate sweeping judgement, 'as Sodom and Gomorrah and the cities around them, since they in the same way as these committed sexual immorality and practised perversions, are set out as an example of undergoing the punishment of eternal fire' (Jude 7). It is a token of moderation in the sentence he imposed that he stopped short of this step in the case of Samaria.

REFLECTION

- The rhetorical questions posed in 11:8 (cf. 6:4) are designed to heighten the people's awareness of the 'dilemma' in which their

---

115. There is no article with the adjective *qādôš*, 'holy', and it is therefore possible to render this line as, 'in your midst ⌊I am⌋ holy'. However, the adjective may be used substantivally and the rendering 'the Holy One' is generally accepted here (cf. Job 6:10; Isa. 40:25; Hab. 3:13).

perverse and ungrateful rebellion has placed the LORD. They needed to perceive this so that they would not undervalue the solution which divine love would provide to enable justice and compassion to co-exist. The offensiveness of sin had not to be played down, and forgiveness and acceptance were not to be taken for granted. Hosea's generation, and ours too, have to realise that grace is not cheap, though at this juncture in the cumulative process of divine revelation the cost of the ransom price is not spelled out. Now, however, we know that it took nothing less than the incarnation and atoning death of the Son of God (cf. 1 Cor. 6:20; 7:23; Phil. 2:6-8).

- In addressing the northern kingdom, the LORD enunciates principles which are foundational to his dealings with his covenant people. His actions spring from who he is in himself, 'God and not man' (11:9). Yet, because mankind are created in his image, we must not suppose that God is totally unlike man. Where Scriptural warrant exists, it is legitimate to argue by analogy, though we have always to be conscious of the inadequacy of any verbal formula or metaphorical description in connection with God. The problem is acute as regards divine emotion. The concept of a God who is not touched by our infirmities and who is impassive before human suffering must be assessed as quite at variance with the Old Testament (and Biblical) presentation of God. 'In all their affliction he was afflicted' (Isa. 63:9). But divine emotion does not sweep God off his feet into an unthinking, impulsive response, as if his emotions were automatic reflexes over which he has no real control. God is not the hapless victim of any external stimulus. Indeed, not only is he in control of his own actions; he is also the one who controls and originates the stimulus. His feeling is real, but it exists in harmony with every attribute of his being, so that every aspect of the response that he displays expresses his total character.
- God created and endowed mankind so that true communication and fellowship might exist between him and them. That harmonious relationship which was originally constituted in Eden was shattered by mankind's sin, and it will not be fully restored till the consummation of redemption in the new heavens and the new earth when God will again dwell with his people without constraint (Rev. 21:3). In Old Testament times this reality was foreshadowed by the glory presence in the tabernacle and temple. It was fully present, though veiled, in the incarnation of the Son: 'the Word became flesh and tabernacled among us' (John 1:14; cf. John 2:21), and God's presence is still in the midst of his people through the indwelling of the Holy Spirit (cf.

1 Cor. 3:16-17), though even so our vision is dim (1 Cor. 13:12).

- 'I will not come into a city' (11:9), but did not Samaria fall? As far as human perception is concerned her fate seems indistinguishable from that of the cities of the plain. The land was annexed, its people deported, and others were settled there (2 Kgs. 17:6, 24). But the all-seeing eye of God penetrates further than human vision. He displays his power by achieving his purposes in face of the seemingly impossible. A remnant, preserved against all outward probability, will be preserved by him to fulfil his commitment. After all, was not Samaria accorded a prominent place in the initial programme of gospel proclamation (Acts 1:9; 8:5, 14)?

(4) Restoration Envisaged (11:10-11)

By divine enabling the prophet is permitted to vault over intervening years and ages to view the circumstances under which the LORD will restore his people. The presentation has a humorous quality to it in that the people are compared to a flock of birds which have been startled by the roar of a lion. There is, however, a serious message behind the picture: that of God's dignity and effective command, and of the compliance of his people, no matter how surprised they are. Although it is often asserted that these verses are the product of later redactional activity, there is no evidence to warrant taking them as something other than Hosea's expectation of what will happen when the final stage of God's determination to save his people is activated. The process of dealing with those who have 'refused to return' (11:5) and 'are hung on backsliding' (11:7) does not terminate in annihilating punishment, but after they have passed through harrowing judgement, there is scope for restoration. Again, the prophet seems unaware of how this outcome will be achieved; he is satisfied with the knowledge that the LORD has guaranteed that this is what he will bring to pass.

11:10 After the LORD they will go,
like a lion he will roar;
for he himself will roar,
and so sons will tremble from the west.

They refers to the Israelites, as does ***sons*** at the end of the verse. Now they are pictured as walking ***after the LORD*** (cf. 1:2; 2:5) rather than away from his messengers (cf. 11:2), at last acting in obedience to his summons rather than wilfully disregarding his commands. ***Like a lion he will roar*** is a clear, resounding declaration of the authority of the LORD (cf. Jer. 25:30; Amos 1:2). Though never without an element of menace, the lion's roar is also employed to reveal its presence and claim its territory. So here the simile does not focus on ferocity (cf. 5:14; 13:7-8; Mic. 5:8), but on the sovereign majesty of the one whose word cannot be ignored. As a result of divine intervention, the people of God will reverse their conduct and no longer rush headlong along a path of their own choosing, but will respectfully respond to the summons of their God.

For introduces a further explication of the scenario set out in the previous line. It is emphasised that the LORD's action will be personal and overwhelming: ***he himself will roar.*** As a consequence[116] those who are ***sons*** (cf. 11:1) ***will tremble***, or 'will come trembling', where the idea of movement is implied by the preposition 'from' (cf. 'to', 3:5). Their fearfulness will not lead to disobedience, but to an awestruck response. ***From the west*** is literally 'from the sea', a term which, given the orientation of Israel, is equivalent to the west. The reference to the area around the Mediterranean (rather than Assyria to the north or Egypt to the south) does not originate directly from anything said so far in the prophecy, but seems to reflect Hosea's general awareness of the far flung nature of the people's dispersal.

11:11 They will tremble like birds from Egypt,
and like a dove from the land of Assyria;
and I will make them dwell in their houses,
declares the LORD.

The significant aspect of the response of the people is accentuated by the repetition of the verb 'tremble' from the preceding verse. If 11:10 picks up the lion imagery found elsewhere, in this verse it is Hosea's use of birds that is brought to its conclusion (cf. 7:12). ***They will tremble like birds*** pictures the people as a flock of disturbed birds, fluttering in perturbation, and yet moving overall away ***from Egypt*** (corresponding to an initial deliverance from there, 11:1) and ***from the land of Assyria***. The invasion of their land would have dispersed some to Egypt as refugees and led to others being deported as captives to Assyria. Wherever they went, they would have experienced dislocation and oppression, which the LORD now acts to reverse.

The comparison with ***a dove*** does not here focus on its gullibility (cf. 7:11), but on how easily it may be frightened and panicked. But this panic is unusual in that it leads into a movement away from these places of exploitation and slavery. Though the people will shortly

116. The idea of consequence is implied by the use of ordinary *waw* with the imperfect verb in *wәyeḥrәdû*, 'and they tremble'.

experience the imposition of judgement (cf. 11:5), that will not be the last episode in their national history.

Furthermore, their movement will consist of more than mere return. Divine initiative will ensure complete restoration: ***I will make them dwell in their houses***, as the ravaged cities (11:6) are restored. The scope of this promise extends to all their territory, both that of individuals and of the nation as a whole. In an echo of the pledge in 2:23, there will be a new settlement in the land as their God-given inheritance and the locus of their fellowship with him.

This whole scene comes with the divine guarantee of ***declares the LORD.*** This formula of attestation occurs frequently in other prophets, but rarely in Hosea (elsewhere only in 2:13, 16, 21). Here it adds a note of security to the immediately foregoing pledge of restoration, and in terms of the structure of Hosea's written prophecy it also marks the conclusion of a major section of his presentation. He has once more traversed the route from sin through punishment to future restoration. Whether viewed as an adulterous wife (chapters 1–3) or as a disobedient son (11:2, 7), the people enjoy true peace by the initiative and achievement of their committed God.

REFLECTION

- Different views are held as to how and when the restoration described in 11:10-11 will occur. The catastrophe which was about to engulf the nation was that of exile, and the reversal of that threat inevitably involved returning to the land. After the exile the LORD recalled his people from all the places to which they had been scattered (cf. Ps. 107:3), and that undoubtedly constituted a partial fulfilment of what is envisaged here. However, the return from Babylon fell far short of consummating the extensive blessing associated with the LORD assembling the banished of Israel and gathering the dispersed of Judah from the four corners of the earth (Isa. 11:12; cf. Jer. 29:14; Ezek. 20:34).

  The LORD's aim in restoring the fortunes of his people, though pictured in geographical and territorial terms, is not ultimately about occupation of real estate, but about fellowship with himself. This is clearly set out in Deuteronomy 30:4-10, where return to the land from the uttermost parts of heaven is not the end of the process of restoration but the means through which the people will be drawn into a dedicated, loving and obedient relationship with the LORD. When the symbols of Old Testament times are more than actualised in the New Testament, a renewed relationship with God is uniquely achieved by faith in Christ, and full participation in fellowship with God is accomplished in the new and heavenly Jerusalem. This is not to subvert the terms of the original promises, as some suppose, but to more than fulfil them, surpassing the merely external dress in which they were once presented and revealing the sublime and glorious reality of the heavenly inheritance secured by Christ. Occupying a prepared room in the Father's house (cf. John 14:2-3) gives effect to and transcends any earthly dwelling used to envisage the promised blessing in 11:11.

- Restoration is solely a divine achievement to which the only proper response is respectful acceptance.

IV. The Final Resolution

(11:12–14:9)

OUTLINE

A. Children of Jacob (11:12–12:14)

1. The LORD's Dispute (11:12–12:2)
2. Family Resemblance (12:3-6)
3. Ephraim's Greed (12:7-8)
4. The LORD's Testimony (12:9-14)

B. The Guilt of Ephraim (13:1-16)

1. Ephraim's Past, Present and Future (13:1-3)
2. Savage Judgement (13:4-8)
3. Instability (13:9-11)
4. Grappling with Sheol (13:12-14)
5. Samaria's Doom (13:15-16)

C. Restoration (14:1-9)

1. The Plea of the Repentant (14:1-3)
2. The Divine Response (14:4-8)
3. Concluding Advice (14:9)

In this final division of his prophecy, Hosea once more sets out the core themes of his message, structured round the heinousness of Israel's sin (chapter 12), the LORD's determination to punish them for their persistent rebellion (chapter 13), and the counter-intuitive promise of the LORD's gracious resolve to restore his people to fellowship with himself (chapter 14). This sequence continues the basic pattern of Hosea's presentation where the reality of impending judgement is asserted along with the LORD's ultimate aim of bringing his people to repentance through the imposition of his sentence on their sin and so to restore them to his favour and reinstate them in the blessings of the covenant. There are precursors of this final hope in 12:6, 9—and arguably in 13:14—before it is fully displayed in chapter 14.

Major breaks within this division of the prophecy are provided by the evident thematic change between 11:11 and 11:12, which is also indicated by a Massoretic paragraph marker. The break at the end of 12:14 is determined more by the inclusion to be detected between 13:1 and 13:16, both of which deal with the doom of Ephraim/Samaria. The final verse (14:9) is obviously a concluding device for the book as a whole, and so is not linked directly to the immediately preceding verses (14:1-8) which are consequently identified as a separate section. This is also reflected in the positive tone of these verses which contain a closing plea for repentance and a vision of what God will eventually achieve in and for his people.

Those who view the book as the product of later redactional activity stress that the prophecy lacks unequivocal historical settings, a feature which contrasts with much in Isaiah 1–39 or Jeremiah. So they argue that the primary intention of the book is to communicate hope to a much later, probably exilic or post-exilic, audience. While it is correct to identify hope as a substantive theme of this division of the prophecy—indeed, of the book as a whole—there is no need to assign the origin of these chapters to a date later than Hosea. In general terms this division fits in well with the concluding years of Hosea's ministry during the reign of Hoshea, the last monarch of what remained of the northern kingdom (cf. 12:1). Blinded to the true significance of the events which engulfed them, the community as a whole was lurching towards its doom. Words of hope for a time beyond the inevitable catastrophe would have immediately sustained those who shared Hosea's outlook. Moreover his message regarding why the LORD's judgement had fallen on the land and how he was determined to restore his people made provision for those who would survive the impending calamity by giving them an inducement to persevere through the difficulties they would encounter and a framework within which to set their lives. In this way Hosea as a writing prophet extended his ministry beyond his immediate contemporaries and laid up a legacy for future generations.

A. Children of Jacob (11:12–12:14)

This section consists of a prophetic sermon which is mainly concerned with applying what had been recorded in Genesis regarding Jacob to the character and circumstances of his descendants many centuries later. Hosea's presentation presupposes that his contemporaries acknowledged their ancestry and were familiar with the patriarchal narratives which set out Jacob's life story. This provided a further opportunity to draw lessons from the past, though now recalling people rather than places from history.

Thematic links throughout the section are found in the repeated references to Jacob (12:2-4, 12), to Egypt (12:9, 13), and the use of the root *ʾwn* in a variety of senses (12:3, 8, 11). A further interconnection is provided by the term 'deceit' (*mirmâ*) which forms one element of the initial dispute the LORD has with his people (11:12). Also, in looking back to the behaviour of Jacob in 12:3-6 mention is made of the deceitful way in which he treated his brother. Although 'deceit' does not occur in these verses, in the underlying narrative in Genesis it is found in Isaac's declaration to Esau, 'Your brother came with deceit/deceitfully and has taken your blessing' (Gen. 27:35). Such deceitful behaviour continued to characterise Ephraim in their economic and social relationships (12:7-8).

Then over against their misconduct the LORD reminds the people of how he had treated them in saving them from Egypt (12:9) and in issuing through the prophets repeated warnings as to how they should behave (12:10). The concluding verses of the chapter (12:11-14) probably provide samples of such ministry, designed to alert the people to their danger and to direct them back to trusting in the LORD alone.

(1) The LORD's Dispute (11:12–12:2)

Hosea's presentation of a time of future restoration in 11:1-11 is now followed by confrontation with the current behaviour of the covenant people. A noteworthy feature of these verses is the fact that Judah is included in the scope of the LORD's denunciation (cf. 1:7; 5:14; 6:11). The two nations were in reality one in terms of the spiritual privileges which had been extended to them, and, alas, they were also one in their failure to live up to the status divinely accorded to them. Therefore neither would escape the LORD's just and proportionate response to their lack of faithfulness.

11:12[1] Ephraim has encircled me with lies,
  and the house of Israel with deceit,
and Judah is continually wandering about with El,
  and being loyal with ones ⌞he counts⌟ holy.

Carrying on from the thought of God being 'in their midst' (11:9) as the Holy One, the speaker, ***me***, is the LORD rather than the prophet. This verse summarises the LORD's perception of the nation's present conduct, on which the prophet subsequently elaborates. Since this section originates after the accession of Pekah in 740 B.C. (indeed, most probably at least a decade later during Hoshea's reign), ***Ephraim*** and ***the house of Israel*** do not refer to different parts of the north (cf. 5:5) but are here synonymous terms for the rump of the kingdom. The charge levelled by the LORD against them concerns their duplicitous behaviour primarily in their religious activities, though in 12:7 their social and commercial conduct is also scrutinised.

Lies (*kaḥaš*, cf. 4:2; 7:3; 10:13) relates to dealing falsely with someone by presenting as true that which is not. The underlying Hebrew root substantially overlaps in meaning with the term 'falsehood' (12:1), though that may point more towards the act of deception whereas 'lies' describes a whole set of circumstances in which what is false is deliberately and knowingly maintained to be true. These 'lies' cover both their false protestations of loyalty to the LORD (cf. 5:7; 6:7) and their inconstant and devious dealings with others. ***Deceit*** (*mirmâ*) refers to underhand dealings and speech which treacherously corrupt a relationship. The use of the term here opens up the way for the description of 12:7 (cf. Jer. 5:27; 9:6; Amos 8:5). As regards their attitude towards their covenant King, it is equivalent to treason. Furthermore, it is not an isolated misdemeanour which is in view. The LORD describes

1. The Massoretic chapter break occurs at this point so that 11:12 is 12:1 in the Hebrew text, with subsequent verses of chapter 12 numbered one greater than in English translations. The English chapter break is derived from LXX and Vulgate. However, since a different theme is taken up in 11:12, the Hebrew chapter break is situated more appropriately. The alternative tradition probably arose from understanding 11:12b as portraying the present faithfulness of Judah and a consequent desire to separate it from the indictment of 12:2a.

himself as ***encircled*** with such false behaviour. This may well envisage the mixed rituals they performed at their sanctuaries.

Interpretation of the second part of the verse is complicated by uncertainty as regards its translation. One form of literal rendering is, 'but Judah is still roaming about with El, and is established with holy ones'. English versions vary in their understanding of the initial conjunction. Either Judah is commended for remaining loyal to the LORD ('But Judah still walks with God and is faithful to the Holy One', ESV; cf. NJKV, NRSV), or condemned for being disloyal to him ('And Judah is unruly against God, even against the faithful Holy One', NIV). 'Roaming about' may indicate freedom of movement in the sphere of fellowship with God, or, more probably, unrestrained behaviour (Jer. 2:31; cf. also Gen. 27:40; Ps. 55:3).[2] 'Still' basically connotes 'continuingness', and here conveys the notion that Judah's behaviour is ongoing. 'Is established' denotes a fixed relationship which is on a stable footing; indeed, the verb may be rendered 'remains faithful'.

Neither style of translation of the verb, however, reveals the main difficulty which is determining whether *ʾēl*, 'god' or 'God', and 'holy ones' refer to the LORD or to the Canaanite cult. The term 'holy ones' may be taken as a plural of majesty descriptive of the one true God (cf. Prov. 9:10; 30:3), in the same way as the plural term Elohim is the standard Hebrew idiom for God. Moreover, there is a similar connection in 11:9 between 'God' (*ʾēl*) and 'Holy One' (*qādôš*, a singular form). Even so, it is a grammatically singular noun (*ʾēl*) which would be rendered here as 'God', and that would make the following plural description somewhat artificial. The more obvious translation 'holy ones' might refer to angels, loyal worshippers (Ps. 34:9), male cult prostitutes, or the many deities of the Canaanite pantheon which constituted El's court. A plausible simpler approach is to take the term as grammatically neuter, and as a reference to the 'holy things' or idols of Canaanite worship. This can be combined with either understanding of the term *ʾēl*, as in 'and Judah is still restive under God, still loyal to the idols he counts holy' (REB), or 'Judah still wanders with El and is

2. The verb may be understood as the perfect or participle of *rûd*, 'to wander about', 'to be unruly' (cf. Gen. 27:40; Jer. 2:31; cf. NIV, NASB), though a more neutral understanding of the verb as 'go to and fro' or 'walks with' may be possible (NKJV, NRSV, ESV). The presence of *ʿôd*, 'continually', favours analysis of the verb as a participle rather than a perfect. The rendering 'rules with God' (cf. AV, ASV) takes the verb as *rādâ*, 'to rule', but this requires that a syllable has been wrongly omitted, and is unlikely. The RSV translation, 'is still known by God', is derived from the LXX.

faithful to holy ones' (HCSB). Perhaps to combine these two renderings is as close as we can get: ***And Judah is continually wandering about with El, and being loyal with ones ⌞he counts⌟ holy.*** Following Garrett (1997:230), the two lines may then be interpreted as intentionally ambiguous so as to denote the wavering devotion of Judah, in that terms which might conceivably apply to Yahweh are used to cloak a disloyal hankering after the gods of Canaan.

Judah is thus charged with displaying the same perverse character traits as her northern neighbour, and this would fit in with the contemporary turn of events in Judah under Ahaz. 'He walked in the way of the kings of Israel and even caused his son to pass through the fire according to the abominable practices of the nations whom the LORD had driven out from before the sons of Israel. And he sacrificed and burned incense on the high places and under every green tree' (2 Kgs. 16:3-4). Ahaz also introduced a specially built foreign-style altar into the Temple and removed the bronze altar to an obscure site (2 Kgs. 16:10-15). Well might Hosea, though a prophet to the north, take cognisance of the precipitate decline in the religious state of the south.

12:1 Ephraim is feeding on wind
and pursuing the east wind all the day.
He multiplies falsehood and devastation,
and they make a covenant with Assyria
and oil is carried to Egypt.

But Hosea did not have to look south to find practices to criticise; they were obvious throughout the north. Ephraim was not only knowingly disloyal towards the LORD, but the nation also exhibited crass stupidity in its international policies. ***Feeding***/'grazing' ***on wind*** refers to a foolish, futile endeavour. Who can derive nourishment from mere wind? Or, it may be that the thought is who can 'shepherd it', that is, trap the wind and make it do what one wants. What is more, misguidedly ***pursuing the east wind*** as if it could be controlled (cf. Hosea's earlier use of 'sowing the wind', 8:7) was worse than fruitless because the east wind, blowing in from the desert, was renowned for its withering and drying effect (13:15; Ezek. 17:10; 19:12). Hunting it down and capturing it would be positively destructive. Such aberrant conduct was not occasional, but occurred ***all the day***[3] as a matter of accepted policy. Mention here of both 'the wind' and 'the east wind' anticipates their recurrence in 13:15, and this forms an inclusion which serves to

3. The Massoretic accents may indicate that 'all the day' is to be taken with what follows, but the LXX and Peshitta read it with what precedes.

bracket together the material in these two chapters.

Both the domestic and the international policies promoted by Ephraim come under censure in the following three clauses which list the actions that lay behind the preceding metaphorical description. In the first clause, ***multiplies*** resumes an earlier theme (cf. 4:7; 8:11; 10:1), emphasising that this behaviour is endemic. For ***falsehood*** (*kāzāb*), see comments on 11:12. Here it is coupled with ***devastation*** (cf. 7:13 for both terms). The combination portrays the inevitable consequence of practising deception. The social and economic life of the land disintegrates in the absence of integrity of word and conduct, and all that remains is mutual hostility and havoc.

The final two lines of the verse describe Ephraim's foreign policy. ***They make*** (literally, 'cut', the standard term for the solemn process by which a covenant was sealed, cf. Jer. 34:18-19) ***a covenant with Assyria*** presumably points to the treaty arrangements under which they had committed themselves to be loyal subjects of the Assyrians (cf. 2:18; 5:13; 6:7; 7:11), most recently at the installation of Hoshea (2 Kgs. 17:3). However, when they think it will be to their advantage, ***oil is carried to Egypt.*** The oil in view is olive oil (cf. 2:5), a major commodity in international trade and abundantly available in Israel (cf. Deut. 8:8), but the thought here goes beyond trading arrangements. This oil was being sent as a bribe to induce the Egyptians to support an alliance against Assyria. The nation was trying to ride two horses at the same time—a strategy which inevitably leads to disaster. Possibly the description reflects various factions within the court at Samaria, with now one side, now another, gaining the upper hand and directing the policy of the nation. It is highly probable that there is a reference to the events described in 2 Kings 17. 'And the king of Assyria found a conspiracy in Hoshea in that he had sent messengers to So, king of Egypt, and had not brought up tribute to the king of Assyria as ⌊he had done⌋ year by year' (2 Kgs. 17:4a). Confronting the might of the Assyrians was unwise at a worldly level. Relying on international alliances to remedy their situation was also an affront to the LORD whose help they persisted in ignoring.

12:2 And ⌊there is⌋ a complaint the LORD has with Judah
and ⌊that is⌋ to call Jacob to account according to his ways—
according to his deeds he will repay him.

Particularly when the references to Judah in 11:12 are interpreted positively, commentators have found the mention of ***Judah*** surprising, and have consequently advocated substituting 'Israel' for 'Judah', though there is no textual evidence to support this (cf. 1:7). The whole people had inherited the one set of national failings, even though the decline of the two kingdoms had not progressed at quite the same rate. They had a common father in ***Jacob***, and so the conduct first of the north and then of the south comes under review at this point.

And ⌞there is⌟ a complaint reminds Judah also that there is a far more serious crisis facing them than coping with the pressures of Assyrian aggression. The LORD was outraged by their behaviour and confronts them with his 'complaint'/ 'accusation' (cf. 4:1) because they have infringed his prerogatives as their King. The action of their Overlord ***to call Jacob to account*** (cf. 1:4; 8:13) was obviously a serious matter which could not be sidestepped. The threatened penalty is expressed in terms very similar to those of 4:9, except that here it is the proportionality of the response which is stressed by using ***according to***. ***Ways*** (cf. 4:9) refers to the lifestyle which they have rebelliously selected for themselves, and which has been outlined in 11:12. ***His deeds*** points to all the particular acts of rebellion they have engaged in (4:9; 5:4; 7:2; 9:15). ***Repay*** (from the root *šûb*, cf. 3:5) signifies 'to cause to return', and forms an inclusion between this line and 12:14. The concluding lines of the verse are expressed in concentric fashion with the outer terms 'call to account' and 'repay' having the major emphasis, rather than the inner repeated terms, 'his ways' and 'his deeds'. There should be no doubt about the impending reality of the LORD's intervention, even though it is not stated precisely what he will impose.

REFLECTION

- Mention of Judah in 11:12 and 12:2 demonstrates that the LORD judges impartially in his dealings with mankind (cf. Rom. 2:11; Col. 3:25). There is no exemption from his exposure of wrongdoing whoever it is that perpetrated it. To plead that our offence is not as great as that of others does not deflect his scrutiny, for 'all must render an account' (Rom. 2:6). We ought therefore to pay attention to Peter's admonition: 'And if you call on him as Father who judges impartially according to each one's deeds, conduct yourselves with fear throughout your time on earth' (1 Pet. 1:17).
- 'According to his ways ... his deeds' (12:2) establishes that the LORD acts equitably in his administration of justice. 'He will repay to each according to his works' (Rom. 2:6; cf. Ps. 62:12; Matt. 16:27; Gal. 6:7).
- Ephraim's dealings with Assyria and Egypt provide a clear instance

of the incompatibility of serving two masters simultaneously (cf. Luke 16:13). If such folly is so evident at a political level, how much more so spiritually!

(2) Family Resemblance (12:3-6)

In these verses the mention of Jacob as a designation for the whole nation in 12:2 is pursued further as Hosea explores the conduct of the nation's revered ancestor. The prophet's use of the personal history of Jacob shows that both he and his contemporaries knew the Genesis narratives, even though the allusions are not in the same order. Just as Hosea's use of the Decalogue in 4:2 in a different sequence from that found in Exodus 20 does not imply that something other than the traditional order was prevalent in Israel, so the variations from the Genesis narrative in this passage do not indicate a variant textual tradition. Hosea's intention was not to retell the story, but to apply significant aspects of it to the situation in his own day. By adapting the material to suit his own purpose, he uses it to remind the nation—particularly the north—that they have inherited the character weaknesses of their forefather, and are still displaying behaviour like his. If, however, they repent, then they can like Jacob know divine acceptance (12:6).

12:3 In the womb he grasped his brother by the heel,
and in his manly vigour he strove with God.

The lack of any transitional formula indicates that the subject of this verse remains the same as in 12:2, namely Jacob, though now it is the patriarch himself who is in view rather than his descendants. ***In the womb*** considers Jacob's behaviour even before his birth when ***he grasped his brother by the heel*** (cf. Gen. 25:26). His twin brother Esau was born first, but with Jacob holding his heel. It was from this incident that Jacob received his name. Although long before Jacob's birth names similar to his are attested throughout the Semitic world, their verbal component came from a root *ʿāqab* meaning 'to watch', 'to protect', so that the sense conveyed was 'May God protect' (*HALOT* 422). There is, however, a homonymous verb *ʿāqab*, derived from the word for 'heel', which means 'to cheat'. Apparently the idea is that of going behind someone so as to act deceitfully because you cannot grasp their heel if you are in front of them. Hearing the name as the 'heel grasper' would remind Hosea's audience of Jacob's character as a trickster, always out to get an advantage for himself.

The second half of the verse incorporates a reference to the name which the patriarch was given when he was much older. The verb ***he***

strove has the same root (*śārâ*) as that incorporated in the name Israel, and the incident alluded to is Jacob's encounter with the angel at Peniel as a consequence of which he was called Israel, meaning either 'he strives with God' or 'may God strive ⌞for him⌟' (Gen. 32:28). At the beginning of the second line the root *ʾwn* occurs (cf. 12:8, 11). Its meaning here seems to be determined by its use in Genesis 49:3 where Jacob employs it to describe Reuben as 'the firstfruits of my strength/manhood (*ʾwn*)'. The term would additionally recommend itself to Hosea because it echoes *ʾāwen*, 'wickedness' (cf. 12:11; and Beth-Awen, 4:15). As in the first part of the line 'in the womb' denotes a stage in Jacob's life, so here ***in his manly vigour*** points to this later incident when he was an adult.

But are these references to Jacob positive or negative? Is their ancestor's behaviour being commended to the people as an example to be followed? Is Jacob viewed as exerting himself even before his birth to receive the blessing God bestowed on the firstborn? If so, Israel is being admonished to give the same priority to being in a right relationship with God. Alternatively, the thought may be that after such self-assertive and misguided behaviour Jacob received divine blessing gratuitously, and that his descendants ought therefore to live in obedient gratitude for the covenant bond which has subsequently been extended to them and not seek to establish themselves by worldly means and alliances.

It seems evident that both actions are here viewed negatively by Hosea. They are signs of Jacob's impulsive and competitive nature which led him to overstep the bounds of what was proper. He may have received blessing at Peniel, but he was left with his hip out of joint, limping to meet his brother Esau (Gen. 32:25, 31).

12:4 And he strove with an angel and prevailed;
he wept and pled with him for favour.
⌞At⌟ Bethel he would find him,
and there he would speak with us.

Several difficulties arise in connection with this verse. As no change of subject is indicated, it appears to be Jacob who is still being described. ***Angel*** is used to refer to the individual who is simply called 'a man' in Genesis 32:24, 25, but who in some sense is also God ('I have seen God face to face', Gen. 32:30). Probably the initial ***and*** introduces an expanded version of what has just been described, rather subsequent stages of the story. The repeated verb ***strove*** involves a word-play with a similar root which would convey the thought 'he lorded it over'.[4] 'With an angel' is literally 'to an angel', where the preposition 'to' (not 'with' as in preceding line) presents something of a difficulty. ***Prevailed***, however, reflects the language of Genesis 32:28.

He wept and pled with him for favour. This is not recorded in connection with the incident of Jacob's wrestling with the man at the brook Jabbok in Genesis 32. While this may be explained by supposing that Hosea had access to information not contained in Genesis, it is much more probable that this résumé of Jacob's life is constructed chiastically (Holladay 1966) with the second line of 12:4 echoing the first line of 12:3, both describing the relationship between Jacob and Esau. Certainly, in the next stage of Jacob's interaction with his brother, they both wept (Gen. 33:4) and Jacob sought to find favour with him (Gen. 33:8, 10; 'favour' coming from the same root as is employed here).

It is therefore possible to set out the lines as below with Jacob the subject of each line:

(a) In the womb he grasped his brother by the heel,
  (b) and in his manhood he strove with God.
  (b') And he strove with an angel and prevailed;
(a') he wept and pled with him [that is, his brother] for favour.

The series of verbs with only 'he' for a subject continues in the last two lines of verse 4, but the presence of 'Bethel' at the beginning of the third line of 12:4 leaves open the possibility that Jacob is no longer the subject of subsequent verbs. English translations usually render the two verbs as past tenses, 'he found' and 'he spoke', but the Hebrew here changes to imperfect forms which are of broader temporal application. As well as being used in poetry for a simple past tense, the imperfect may indicate repeated past occurrences or what is presently true. At any rate the change in tense indicates that Hosea is not looking at matters from the same stance as that of preceding lines.

Indeed, Holladay argues strongly that 'what we have here is a

---

4. It is difficult to determine which verb is represented by *wāyyāśar*. It may be an imperfect qal form of the root *śûr*, which would mean 'to see', but most English translations understand it as a form of the preceding verb *śārâ*, 'to strive'. The confusion has probably arisen from the various levels of word-play involved. If the root is identified as *śrr*, then the sense to 'lord it over' is possible (cf. AV, ASV). The combined presence of the consonants *sin* and *resh* would additionally suggest a reference to 'Israel' and 'leaders', both terms where these consonants also occur.

complete change of tone, outlook, color in the oracle. There has been a great reversal. The tables have been turned. We are now looking at Jacob-Israel from a new angle altogether. This change Hosea has accomplished subtly but unmistakably' (Holladay 1966:58). One way in which this is signalled in the clause is the initial position of ***Bethel***, with its abandonment of the derogatory use of Beth-Awen to refer to the town. What Hosea is now pointing to involves Bethel in its rightful role, and the significance of Bethel for what he has to say is also indicated by the repetition involved in ***there***. The historical references are to the LORD's encounters with Jacob at Bethel as recorded in Genesis 28:10-22, when he was en route to Haran, and in Genesis 35:1-15, after his return.

The verb ***find*** may be used in the sense 'meet accidentally' and that might fit in with Jacob being the subject (more neatly in reference to Gen. 28:10-22 than Gen. 35:1-15, but still possible). However, as Kaiser points out (1985:42), in several contexts (Deut. 32:10; Ps. 89:21; Jer. 2:2) 'find' is a technical term for God's election as he deliberately looks for one whom he has chosen. It therefore is probable that the subject changes at this point to 'God' and the way in which he conveyed his blessing to Jacob quite apart from—even despite—Jacob's own striving for success in whatever way he thought he could achieve it.

What then of the next clause, ***and there he would speak with us***?[5] There are good grounds for thinking that Hosea here applies the lesson to be learned from Jacob to his own contemporaries and challenges them as to whether they could say the same regarding what occurred in Bethel in their own day. 'Speak with us' indicates that the covenant arrangements the LORD made with Jacob still extend to Israel as his descendants (cf Kaiser 1985.). Both readings bring out Jacob's inability to handle his crisis situation through deception; only by acceptance of the LORD's gracious provision could he survive. Similarly Hosea's

5. *ʿimmānû* might be a variant form for *ʿimmo*, 'with him', but it would normally mean 'with us'. It seems to have arisen through scribal confusion over the force of the pronominal suffix on the verb in the previous clause, when they understood *yimṣāʾennû* as 'he finds us'. However, the suffix is not first person plural, but third person masculine singular, 'he finds him'. The LXX and Peshitta read a third person masculine singular suffix on the preposition here, and that is followed by most English versions, but, as Kaiser (1985:42–43) contends, 'with us' is the more difficult reading which should be retained. It is not impossible that Hosea deliberately used an ambiguous form to convey both meanings.

contemporaries ought to make getting right with God their priority by humbly accepting what he graciously held out to them. In that was they could share in the hope that Jacob had come to know.

12:5 And the LORD, the God of hosts—
the LORD ⌊is⌋ his memorial name.

This hymn-like verse breaks into the prophet's sermon from history to remind the people of the character of the God with whom they have to do (cf. Amos 4:13; 5:8-9; 9:6). Naming the LORD clarifies the unspecified references in the previous verse, and also indicates the awe with which the people should conduct themselves before him. The full title, ***the LORD, the God of hosts***, which Hosea uses only in this passage, changes the perspective from a specific locality (Bethel) to the universal sovereignty of the LORD (cf. 2 Sam. 5:10). The 'hosts' are the angelic armies through whom the LORD effects his purposes on earth. While 'the LORD' or Yahweh reminds of the covenant closeness of God, the other term speaks of his unlimited power and majesty. Furthermore it is not the ordinary word for 'name' (*šēm*; contrast Amos 4:13; 5:8; 9:6) that is employed in this verse, but ***memorial name*** (*zēker*, 'remembrance'; cf. 14:7; Exod. 3:15), pointing to the importance of keeping in mind the unique character of Yahweh, his unchanging commitment, and the effectiveness of his intervention.

12:6 And ⌊as for⌋ you, you should return in your God.
Keep steadfast love and justice,
and wait on your God continually.

The prophet then turns to the people with an emphatic ***⌊as for⌋ you***, a collective singular, which switches the focus to Ephraim. He urges them to follow through on the practical application of the theological confession they make regarding the LORD. For similar admonitions in connection with complaints, see 10:12 and Micah 6:8. Hosea teaches that there should be renewed personal commitment, The exhortation, ***you should return***, calls for recognition of their false conduct, particularly their addiction to the religion of Canaan, which they are urges to abandon so that they might come back in repentance to the LORD.[6] If they are truly Jacob's children, they should respond spiritually just as

---

6. Contrary to the view of Macintosh (1997:491), although *tāšûb* is imperfect and not jussive in form, the fact that it introduces imperative forms indicates that here the verb does not predict what will happen, 'you will return', but rather, what ought to occur, 'you should/ought to return' (cf. Gen. 20:9; Exod. 4:15; *IBHS* §31.4g).

he had done when the LORD commanded him 'Return to the land of your fathers and to your relatives, and I will be with you' (Gen. 31:3). The phrase ***in your God*** (cf. 1:7) is not the 'to your God' (cf. NIV, NRSV) which might have been expected (14:1-2; Joel 2:12-13). It may well indicate 'by the help of your God' (an idiom similar to that found in 1:7; cf. NKJV, ESV), or 'with respect to your God', and refer to the divine promise to Jacob: 'Behold, I am with you and will keep you wherever you go, and will bring you back to this land; for I will not leave you until I have done what I have spoken to you' (Gen. 28:15).

Renewed personal commitment to the covenant King would be evidenced by maintenance of the sort of conduct he stipulated in his law. There were two aspects to this: their behaviour towards God and towards their fellows (cf. Micah 6:8). ***Steadfast love*** (cf. 2:19; 4:1; 6:4, 6) probably points more to their basic heart attachment to the LORD while ***justice***/'judgement' requires a well-ordered society where due regard is paid to the rights of others (cf. 2:19). Jacob was one whose grasping character needed to be reminded of this. He had been led to put his trust in the divine promise, and his descendants should do so also.

Furthermore, a return to a true relationship with the LORD was not to be some passing outburst of religious enthusiasm, but an ongoing dependence on him and an uninterrupted acceptance of his timescale, ***wait on your God continually.*** This describes a positive, eager experience (cf. 'door of hope', 2:15), but not a merely passive one. 'Wait for the LORD and keep his ways' (Ps. 37:34) expresses the two-sided nature of loyal expectancy.

REFLECTION

- Hosea has no hesitation in using the historical narratives of Genesis to teach spiritual lessons. Here he focuses on the need for spiritual transformation such as is recorded in the story of Jacob. He had started his life by trusting his own wits and acumen, but it was not human striving or manipulation which brought him lasting blessing. Rather this came by the divine initiative of the God who found him (12:4). This is the essence of the message of 'the grace of God which was given to you in Christ Jesus' (1 Cor. 1:4). 'By grace you have been saved through faith. And this is not from yourselves; it is the gift of God, not from works, so that no one may boast' (Eph. 2:8-9).
- God's 'memorial name' (12:5) is revealed to counter human forgetfulness. We need constantly to be reminded so that we 'forget not all his benefits' (Ps. 103:2), but more especially that we do not ignore

the one who bestows those gifts. The name, 'the LORD', reminds us of his covenant commitment to his people (cf. Isa. 49:15), and 'God of hosts' points to his unlimited power and authority which ensure that he possesses the ability to carry out his promises. Each name of God is a succinct revelation of his character and a pledge of his favour.

- Human impatience and lack of perspective on how and when God is working are to be remedied by waiting (12:6). 'The LORD is good to those waiting for him, to the soul that seeks him' (Lam. 3:25), even when outwardly the prospect is gloomy and there is no immediate respite. Such waiting recognises the sovereign purpose and goodness of God, and so is an attitude of anticipation and tense eagerness, even though 'we groan inwardly as we wait eagerly' (Rom. 8:23; cf. Heb. 9:28). Faith gives rise to patience because it is certain that the realisation of the promise is worth waiting for (Tit. 2:13). Furthermore, this waiting is not a passive exercise, but spurs on to present spiritual diligence to be ready for the Lord's return (2 Pet. 3:14).

(3) Ephraim's Greed (12:7-8)

Hosea continues to set before the people of the north God's perspective on their behaviour. Despite the lessons which have been presented to Israel from the career of their venerable ancestor and in spite of the LORD's invitation to return in repentance, their conduct has remained brazenly defiant. In everyday life they had adopted the economic ethos of Canaan, and their business dealings were characterised by sharp practice. They were proud of how smartly they made the most of every opportunity, and repudiated any suggestion that they were acting unjustly or oppressively. Possibly in the background there is still the figure of the earlier Jacob who was quite unscrupulous in his dealings with others (cf. Gen. 25:29-34; 27:35).

12:7 Canaan! In his hand ⌞are⌟ deceitful scales;
he loves to exploit.

Canaan is ambiguous in Hebrew. While it can refer to the whole area once known as Palestine, it is more properly a reference to the coastal zone of Phoenicia and to settlements in the Jordan valley (cf. Num. 13:29; Isa. 23:11). Moreover, though it can refer to the country or its inhabitants, the same word is also a common noun for 'merchant' or 'trader' (cf. Zeph. 1:11). Certainly here Hosea begins by directing his audience's attention away from themselves, either to the original inhabitants of the land or to their principal occupation. It is the next verse which reveals the full scope of his message: Ephraim is acting like the Canaanites. The people's conduct is at variance with their covenant status and commitment so that the dividing line between them and their heathen neighbours has become blurred. As virtual Canaanites will they now become liable to the same treatment meted out to the original inhabitants of the land (Gen. 15:16)?

Deceitful scales gives a particular instance of unscrupulous conduct (Prov. 11:1; 20:23; Amos 8:5-6). 'Deceitful' recalls the use of the term in 11:12, and also Isaac's verdict on Jacob's conduct in Genesis 27:35. Here the picture is of a set of scales, consisting of a centrally poised crossbar from either end of which were hung two containers. In one of them stones of known weight were placed, and in the other the object to be weighed. In ancient times it was difficult to standardise the weights employed, and cheating was rife.

The second line of the verse states a more general allegation regarding their misconduct. ***He loves*** points to the fact that these actions are deliberate; indeed, they are a matter of self-congratulation. ***To exploit*** or 'oppress' (cf. 5:11) describes menacing harassment of those who lack the ability or resources to maintain their own rights.[7] The LORD did not tolerate such behaviour among his people, whether towards a fellow Israelite or a resident alien. 'You shall not exploit a hired labourer who is poor and needy, whether one of your brethren or one of your resident aliens who is in your land within your gates' (Deut. 24:14). The prevalence of such extortion towards the disadvantaged (cf. Jer. 7:6; Zech. 7:10) was symptomatic of disloyalty to the LORD because of the underlying rejection of the covenant lifestyle which pleased him.

12:8 And Ephraim said, 'Surely I have become rich;
 I have found wealth for myself;
⌊in⌋ all my labours they will not find in me
 any iniquity, which ⌊is⌋ sin.'

Now the true identity of the one being described is revealed, and Hosea does so dramatically by imaginatively portraying Ephraim's own description of his conduct. Others do not need to condemn him; he

---

7. Hubbard (1989:207) provides an alternative reading of the text by arguing that *ʾāhēb* should not be translated as a finite verb, 'he loves', but as a participle which expresses the object of the infinitive, 'to exploit a loved one'. Ephraim then has no scruples regarding cheating even those with whom he enjoyed friendly relationships, perhaps a reference to the southern kingdom.

does so himself by his foolish boasting. ***Surely I have become rich*** reflects the self-confident attitude of a nation enjoying affluence. ***I have found*** repeats the verb of 12:4, but unlike the spiritual encounter mentioned there here it is material ***wealth*** (from the root *ʾwn*, cf. 12:3) that is the focus. The outlook of Ephraimite society is encapsulated in the little addition ***for myself***, which claims their prosperity is their own achievement and selfishly appropriates it for their own enjoyment (cf. 2:5). Such an attitude was in direct contravention of Moses' warning that when the people entered the land and thrived in it that they should 'beware lest you say in your heart "My power and the might of my hand have made for me this property" ' (Deut. 8:17; cf. 8:11-20). They failed to recognise God's role in their national success and well-being.

Ephraim's boasting continues.[8] ***In all my labours*** points to the wearisome exertions of the community who consider their accomplishments to be merely the products of their own hard work. The repetition of the verb from 'I have found wealth for myself' in ***they will not find in me*** is another telling instance of Hosea's use of this rhetorical device to highlight a contrast. ***Any iniquity which is sin*** seems to be the careful evasion of a legalist. 'Iniquity' is deviation from a standard, crookedness (cf. 7:1). Ephraim asserts that he has 'wealth' (*ʾôn*) not 'iniquity' (*ʿāwōn*), but Ephraim does not say that others will not find any iniquity at all in his practices. Rather he qualifies his assertion by adding ***which is sin***, or 'which is a sin'. Hosea frequently uses the root (cf. 4:7), but not this exact form. Ephraim protests against too harsh a description being applied to his behaviour. He had taken every advantage in the situation, but it was unjustifiable to label his conduct 'sin'. Misconduct is relabelled to minimise its significance and deny that it constitutes any real offence at all.

REFLECTION

- The covenant created and regulated complementary relationships: on the one hand between an individual and the LORD, and on the other hand between an individual and all those in the covenant community who professed their loyalty to the same Overlord. It was a gross violation of the bonds of covenant love to abuse one's social status, power, or wealth in order to exploit others who were less favourably placed. Such extortion was an affront to the King himself. 'Whoever exploits a poor ⌊person⌋ shows contempt for his Maker, but whoever

---

8. Though the RSV breaks off the quote in the middle of the verse, this requires emendation of subsequent first person references, an approach which most English translations avoid.

is gracious to the needy honours him [i.e. God]' (Prov. 14:31). The same social and economic obligations are no less obligatory in New Testament times (cf. Jas. 5:1-6).

- Personal wealth attracts admiration, but care must be exercised as to how riches have been accumulated and how they are used. An individual may congratulate himself on his achievements and others will join the chorus which praises him, but all must reckon with the impermanence of any worldly fortune because no one can take it with them at death (Ps. 49:16-20). What is more, after death there follows the scrutiny of the one who knows the heart, and 'what people regard highly is an abomination in the sight of God' (Luke 16:14-15). It requires spiritual understanding to perceive one's own needs and to lay up treasure in heaven (cf. Matt. 19:21; Luke 12:33; 18:22). There are many who, like Ephraim, have been spiritually blinded by affluence, including the church in Laodicea (Rev. 3:17). Economic prosperity may not be interpreted as a sign of divine endorsement of the lifestyle of an individual or a nation in the absence of heart submission to God and obedience to his word.

(4) The LORD's Testimony (12:9-14)

The structure of Hosea's material in the remainder of the chapter has been analysed in various ways. As robust an approach as any is to find here a sample of the arguments presented by the prophets—and particularly by Hosea himself—to counter the complacent delusions of the self-satisfied community. He begins by citing the LORD's claim on their obedience and the way he will discipline them (12:9). Next he points out how the LORD had not left the northern kingdom without prophetic ministry to remind them of what was required from them (12:10). The transition at 12:11 is somewhat abrupt, and Hubbard (1989:209) suggests that it may be eased by treating 12:11-13 as specific illustrations of how the prophets fulfilled their mission described in 12:10 by presenting their message in terms of current events (12:11) and the lessons to be drawn from Jacob (12:12) and the Exodus (12:13), but ending with a solemn warning of impending doom (12:14).

(a) Faithful Conduct (12:9-10)

Those whose lives unmask their practical forgetfulness of the LORD need to be reminded of who he is and the claims he has on them. Over against Ephraim's introverted self-satisfaction Hosea presents the LORD's own declaration of his sovereignty. Ephraim must recall that all they are and all they possess originated in his saving intervention at the time of the Exodus (12:9) and that since then he has faithfully sent prophets to keep setting before them their obligations under the covenant (12:10).

12:9 But I ⌊am⌋ the LORD your God
  from the land of Egypt;
I will again make you dwell in tents
  as in days of an appointed feast.

The verse begins with ***but*** to introduce the other side of the covenant relationship.[9] Hosea cites the words of the LORD as he makes the fundamental claim: ***I am the LORD your God.*** The expression is reminiscent of the preamble to the covenant which establishes the basis of the LORD's right to rule over the people ('I ⌊am⌋ the LORD your God who brought you from the land of Egypt, from the house of slavery', Exod. 20:2; cf. Deut. 5:6; Ps. 81:10). The Israelites may congratulate themselves on their shrewdness and success, but this reminds them that it is divine scrutiny that they have to face. The phrase ***from the land of Egypt*** (cf. 2:15) is effectively a temporal expression (cf. Num. 14:19), which also asserts his sovereign right to demand appropriate behaviour from them because he is the one who redeemed them from the oppression of Egypt and has established his covenant with them. But the omission of the 'who brought you' found in Exodus 20:2 extends the thought from a compressed reminder of all that had happened in the distant past to a declaration of the constancy of the LORD's provision throughout subsequent centuries up to the present. No matter how variable their conduct had been over time, his had not, and he had not compromised his claim over them.

Again in the second part of the verse shows that it too seeks to draw lessons from past events. ***As in the days of an appointed feast*** (cf. 2:11) probably refers to the celebration of the feast of Tabernacles/ Booths (cf. 9:1) when the Israelites erected and lived in rough shelters in remembrance of their stay in the wilderness (Lev. 23:39-43). Though this festival was a time of rejoicing (Lev. 23:40; Deut. 16:14-15), this statement is not a direct promise of a return to times of prosperity, or of the continuation of the annual cycle of their feasts. The focus is on ***I will again make you dwell in tents***, where the LORD uses the comparison to illustrate the judgement he will impose on

---

9. Though modern translations (e.g. NIV, ESV) have no conjunction at the start of 12:9, it is appropriate to take the *waw* followed by a non-verb in *wəʾānōkî* as an instance of *waw* disjunctive introducing a contrasting statement (NASB, NKJV, NLT).

them. Dwelling in tents points to a reversal of the prosperity and affluence on which they congratulated themselves. Instead they would be forced out of the land and back to wilderness conditions of deprivation and hardship. But there is also implicit here, as there was in the earlier mention of the wilderness in 2:14, the thought of recovery. The tents at the feast were a symbol of their acknowledged dependence on God during their residence in the wilderness and, though the LORD's treatment of them might seem harsh, it would instil in them a renewed reliance upon him, not on their commercial acumen and scheming ways.

12:10 And I have spoken to the prophets,
and I ⌞was the one who⌟ multiplied vision
and through the prophets have kept speaking in parables.

In three co-ordinated clauses the Lord of the covenant sets out before the community who had reneged on their commitment how he had faithfully asserted his right to their obedience. In the period after the Exodus he had not been silent, leaving the people to work out what to believe and how to act as best they could for themselves. Instead he had been communicating with them and unceasingly reminded them of their obligations (cf. 2 Chron. 36:15; Jer. 7:25). ***I have spoken to the prophets.***[10] As Hosea was himself numbered among those prophets, this section implicitly sets out his claim to be heard as a divine spokesman. 'To' is an unexpected choice of preposition, but it emphasises the divine transmission of their message to the prophets as recipients, whereas the later ***through the prophets***/'by the hand/agency of the prophets' directs attention to them as the channel through which the message flowed to the people (cf. 6:5). Even though such revelation exposed the nation's shortcomings and though its challenges to renewed faithfulness disturbed their mood of self-satisfaction, such warnings were evidence of God's continuing concern for them, and it was a privilege for them to receive them.

What is more there was no stinting on God's part as regards his self-revelation. ***I*** (emphatic 'I', cf. 2:8) ***multiplied vision*** may refer to divine disclosures which consisted just of words (cf. 2 Sam. 7:17), but probably also of inner presentations to the prophets of essentially

10. It is technically possible to render *wədibbartî* as a waw consecutive perfect, 'and I will speak', but it is then difficult to construe the following perfect form *hirbêtî*, 'I multiplied'. Possibly both perfects are to be taken as past frequentative forms, and the following imperfect, 'I kept speaking in parables', may be understood in a similar fashion.

visual material whose content they then had to verbalise and relay to the people. The feature which is stressed is that the content originated with God and did not arise from mere human initiative. ***Have kept speaking in parables***/'comparisons'[11] points to the variety of forms in which the divine message came. It may imply that the prophets used enigmatic, puzzling speech, but it is more probable that the thought is that of using illustrations and figures of speech to attract attention and ease understanding.

REFLECTION

• God does not leave mankind without notice of his claim to their obedience and worship. To those who have not the privilege of hearing his word, he testifies through the natural realm which he has created and which he governs. 'Yet he did not leave himself without witness, ⌞in that⌟ he did good by giving you rains from heaven and fruitful seasons, satisfying your hearts with food and gladness' (Acts 14:17; cf. Acts 17:27; Rom. 1:19-20). In lands and societies where the word of God has reached this witness is mediated through the proclamation of the truth. It is the special privilege given to the covenant community that the testimony of the word and the gospel invitation of salvation is preserved and presented in their midst. It was true as regards the Old Testament people of God that they were 'entrusted with the very words of God' (Rom. 3:2), and that birthright extends unchanged in New Testament times, with the proclamation of the word being entrusted to ministers of the gospel (cf. 1 Tim. 5:17; 2 Tim. 4:2; 1 Pet. 1:12).

(b) Prophetic Ministry (12:11-14)

The connection of thought at this juncture is less than clear, and Hubbard's suggestion mentioned above (page 331) is as feasible an approach as any. These verses provide typical examples of the prophets' messages which the LORD has mentioned in 12:10. Certainly in this unit there is a change from direct divine speech to prophetic presentation of the truth. But if these are indeed samples of prophetic speech, that adds to the difficulty of interpreting their message because it is presented in isolation from a specific context.

12:11 ⌞Was⌟ wickedness ⌞in⌟ Gilead?
Surely they have become nothing.

---

11. 'I will bring destruction' (NRSV) takes the verb *'ădammeh* not as an instance of *dāmâ* (I), 'to be like, resemble' but from *dāmâ* (III), 'to destroy'. Possibly the double meaning was intended to be heard as Hosea had already referred to the negative effects of the prophetic ministry in 6:5.

In Gilgal they have sacrificed oxen,
even their altars ⌊will be⌋ like heaps of stones
beside furrows of the field.

Two places are named as representative of the nation as a whole. For details of their respective location, see on 6:8 and 4:15. The selection of ***Gilead*** and ***Gilgal*** was motivated both by the alliterative effect of their names and by their geographical spread. Gilead was in Transjordan, whereas Gilgal was near the southern border of the northern kingdom. What was true of them would tell the story of the nation as a whole.

The structure of the verse has been variously analysed. The first clause may be a condition, 'if there is deception in Gilead' (ESV), or a question (NASB; NIV), though there is little difference in meaning between them. A rhetorical question (cf. 6:4) would strongly assert that wickedness was in Gilead. The verb in the second clause would normally indicate an action in the past ('they have become nothing'), or it may be a description of their present character ('they are worthless'), though it might also be a prophetic perfect, which is used to make an emphatic assertion, 'they shall come to nothing'. Taking this verse as uttered by Hosea in the closing period of his ministry, Gilead was already occupied by the Assyrians, and so it is appropriate to take the reference in both clauses as being to the past—the very recent past.

Hosea has previously mentioned the ***wickedness*** (*ʾāwen*, cf. 6:8) of Gilead, where it involved the murderous conduct of its inhabitants. In the light of the remainder of the verse it may refer here to idolatry (it is used in connection with false worship in 1 Sam. 15:23; Isa. 66:3; Zech. 10:2). Additionally *ʾāwen* is employed for rhetorical effect as it repeats the consonants of 'manly vigour' (12:3) and 'wealth' (12:8). ***Surely*** asserts the certainty of the link between their previous behaviour and the fact that ***they have become nothing*** (*šāwʾ*; cf. 5:11; 10:4). The latter term conveys the ideas of ineffectiveness and falsehood (*NIDOTTE* 4:53) whether in connection with false speech (Exod. 20:7) or idolatry (Ps. 24:4; 31:6). It is linked with 'wickedness' in Isaiah 1:13 in a description of empty, unacceptable worship. Hosea urged his audience to learn the lesson of current events by considering the calamity which had already overtaken Gilead. The ruined state of the territory east of the Jordan was the consequence of their debased religious practices.

Hosea then invites his hearers to focus on what is still happening ***in Gilgal.*** Possibly the second part of the verse continues with another rhetorical question, 'Have they sacrificed oxen in Gilead?' At any rate what is described is a debased ritual, probably as part of syncretistic worship supposedly of the LORD. Consequently the threat is uttered that ***their altars ⌞will be⌟ like heaps of stones beside furrows of the field.*** This description permits a further word-play through the repetition of the consonants *gl* in Gilead, Gilgal, and 'heaps of stones' (*gallîm*, cf. Andersen, et al. 1980:620). Farmers gathered the stones from the soil they cultivated and placed them in heaps at the edge of the field; so the picture is of a worthless mound of stones. Possibly there are here overtones of destruction as the sites used for empty rituals meet their deserved fate. More significant, however, is the fact that Gilead echoes the name Galeed ('heap of stones as a witness') which Jacob used in Genesis 31:46, and that leads in to the following verse.

12:12 And Jacob fled to the district of Aram,
and Israel worked for a wife
and for a wife he kept ⌞sheep⌟.

While there may be a link with the history of Jacob given in 12:3-4, it is better to treat the prophetic message in 12:12-13 as an independent of the earlier passage, though still developing the behavioural similarity between the people and their ancestor to bring out another lesson to be learned. ***Jacob*** and ***Israel*** are two names for the patriarch (cf. 12:3). ***Fled*** denotes hurried movement from one location to another through pressure of circumstances. Here Hosea alludes to how Jacob's wrongdoing had rebounded on him when his brother Esau threatened his life (Gen. 27:41), and Jacob had to leave home in a hurry. ***District of Aram*** is literally 'field of Aram' (the area in the western curve of the Euphrates), and so picks up on the mention of the furrows of the field in the preceding line. The reference is to Jacob's stay with Laban for whom he worked so as to pay the bride-price for marrying Rachel—and getting Leah as well (Gen. 29:15-30). Laban put him in charge of his flocks. The verb 'keep' or 'watch' provides a link between this verse and the following (cf. Mays 1969:169), between the way Jacob obtained his bride(s) and the way in which Yahweh obtained his (12:13).

12:13 But by a prophet the LORD brought Israel up from Egypt,
and by a prophet he was kept.

The behaviour of Jacob and the LORD do not constitute complete parallels. Jacob's actions led to a life of fear, exile and virtual slavery as a result of his deception of Esau. The LORD's intervention achieved quite the opposite—he delivered the people from slavery, fear and exile in Egypt. ***But*** functions adversatively to show that what Jacob had to do for himself, the LORD achieved ***by a prophet.***[12] The prophets designated by this phrase were presumably Moses in the first line, and in the second line, Samuel, who at a later period was used mightily by the LORD when the nation was on the verge of being overwhelmed by foreign threat (1 Sam. 7:13). However, precise identification of the prophets in view is not the point at issue, rather it is that the LORD was at work through them. The use of ***Israel*** extends from Jacob as an individual to his descendants. In this way Israel ***was kept***, watched over and preserved by the LORD (the same word as in the previous verse).

The message is conveyed that whereas Jacob's reliance on his own acumen and trickery only brought him drudgery and virtual slavery, the LORD's treatment of his people led to deliverance and preservation. The community is being urged not to copy Jacob's mistakes but to take advantage of the LORD's provision for Israel.

12:14 Ephraim has provoked ⌊with⌋ bitternesses,
and he will leave his blood ⌊guilt⌋ on him,
and his Lord will repay his reproach to him.

Unfortunately Ephraim was incapable of learning the lessons of history, whether recent or more distant. The people spurned prophetic ministry which warned them of the calamitous outcome of their disobedience. It was not just Hosea who was disappointed by their conduct. The absolute use of the verb ***provoke*** without a direct object suggests that the impact was on both Hosea and the LORD. Hosea had endured much because of his prophetic calling—and had been rejected. But the key to the LORD's response was not the people's attitude to his prophet, but their attitude to himself. The LORD had blessed them abundantly—and had been rebuffed. It is that repudiation of his authority and the reproach which it brought on his name that is the primary aspect of the LORD's response. The verb 'provoke' is used repeatedly in 1 and 2 Kings for the impact of the people's misconduct in idol worship on the LORD and his furious reaction to them (e.g. 1 Kgs. 14:9). ***Bitternesses*** (cf. Jer. 6:26; 31:15) is a modal accusative with a plural of intensity which describes how deeply their misconduct affected the LORD.

His blood guilt/'bloods' refers to crimes which incurred the death penalty, especially murders which have been committed (cf. 1:4; 4:2;

12. The repeated phrases 'for a wife' (12:12) and 'by a prophet' (12:13) use the same preposition *bə* (first of price, then of instrument) as a way of contrasting Jacob himself working to achieve a goal and the LORD using another party to effect his purpose in connection with his people.

6:8). There is no relief promised; no prospect of forgiveness is held out. The nation has to pay the penalty for the whole of their misconduct. Deliberately avoiding the personal covenant name the LORD, Hosea delays mention of ***his Lord*** (*ʾădōnāyw*) until the very end of the verse where it functions as the subject of both preceding verbs. It is only here that Hosea uses the term Adonai, but it clearly points out who was the superior in the situation. It is Ephraim's Sovereign who judicially ***leaves his blood guilt on him***. His guilt is established and the sentence will be imposed. ***Will repay*** or 'make to return' establishes the equity of the divine verdict. ***His reproach*** refers to Ephraim's shameful conduct and the contempt he had exhibited towards the LORD (cf. Jer. 6:10). It will be turned back on his own head when he undergoes divine punishment and is treated with contempt by the nations (cf. Ps. 79:12; Neh. 3:36; Dan. 11:18).

REFLECTION

- Discussion of Gilead's downfall (12:11) is an instance of a recent event being used as an example of a fundamental Scriptural principle: the certainty of divine punishment coming on those who flout God's requirements. Current events may still provide many illustrations of basic spiritual truths, but there is a need for caution in employing them because wrong inferences may be readily drawn (cf. Luke 13:1-5).
- The incidents from Jacob's life referred to in 12:12 act as a warning against spiritual hero worship by reminding us of how ignominiously he had to flee from his home and how he was exploited by Laban. Just as the Jews of our Lord's day felt that their standing with God was secure because they could say, 'Abraham is our father' (John 8:39), so many have thought their ancestry or appreciation of another's faith constituted an adequate basis for their personal standing with God. But no mere individual has been able to solve his own problems or those of his generation, especially when it comes to securing acceptance with God. How different is the provision made for those who 'by God's power are being guarded through faith for a salvation ready to be revealed in the last time' (1 Pet. 1:5).

B. The Guilt of Ephraim (13:1-16)

This chapter brings Hosea's condemnation of Ephraim's conduct to a climax. The inclusion formed by 'he became guilty' (13:1) and 'she will suffer for her guilt' (13:16), both forms of the same verb, sets the focus firmly on the culpability of the nation, firstly on its origin and finally on its consequences. That the chapter ends with an address to Samaria probably indicates that this message originated during the final phase of Hosea's ministry when all that was left of the land was the capital and its surrounding enclave. While there is no evidence that these words were spoken while the city was actually under siege, they are certainly to be located in the years immediately before Shalmaneser 'invaded all the land and came to Samaria' (2 Kgs. 17:5).

(1) Ephraim's Past, Present and Future (13:1-3)

In three successive pictures Hosea portrays the past, the present and the future of the northern kingdom. Its decline had started with Baal worship (13:1); it was currently characterised by increasing reliance on gross idolatry (13:2); and this would inevitably lead to its utter disappearance (13:3).

13:1 When Ephraim spoke, ⌞there was⌟ trembling;
he ⌞was the one who⌟ lifted up ⌞his face⌟ in Israel,
and he became guilty through Baal and died.

Ephraim here refers to the tribe, though in the closing years of Hosea's ministry the territory which was associated with that tribe was virtually all that was left of the kingdom of Israel (cf. 2 Kgs. 15:29). Hosea begins, however, by looking back to earlier days when Ephraim had enjoyed a dominant role in the north. Though Joshua was from the tribe of Ephraim (Num. 13:8, 16; 1 Chron. 7:27), it is unlikely that the period in view is as early as that. Rather it starts at the division of the united kingdom when another Ephraimite, Jeroboam I (1 Kgs. 11:26), led the revolt from the south. Consequently the tribe was at the centre of the nation geographically and politically, and when it ***spoke***, the reaction of those who heard was one of ***trembling*** (possibly 'horror', a meaning found for this term in the Qumran scrolls and also here in the Vulgate here). ***He ⌞was the one who⌟ lifted up ⌞his face⌟ in Israel.***[13] There had been a time, particularly during the dynasties of Omri and Jehu, when Ephraim had been proudly self-sufficient (cf. 12:8).

13. The terse expression 'he lifted up in Israel' is awkward and enigmatic. To insert 'himself' ('he exalted himself', NKJV) yields a decidedly unHebraic construction, but 'to lift up the face' or 'to lift up the head' are standard idioms for a positive, assured attitude. Such an ellipsis is assumed here. Alternatively the verb may be used intransitively, 'he was lifted up' (cf. Ps. 89:10; Nah. 1:5; Hab. 1:3, cited in BDB 670, but with reservations). Commentators frequently point the verb as a niphal, *niśśāʾ*, 'he was exalted', an approach which seems to adopted in English translations (cf. ESV, NIV, NRSV).

But matters did not stop with politics and economics. ***He became guilty through Baal*** (*'āšam*, cf. 13:16). Though 'through Baal' may also be rendered 'at Baal', in which case it would stand for Baal-Peor (cf. 9:10), the prophet is at this point considering events in subsequent centuries. The reference is unlikely to be only to the syncretistic religion introduced by Jeroboam I (1 Kgs. 12:16, 26-30), though the state promotion of that amalgam undoubtedly paved the way for further religious decline by desensitising the people to the truth. Jeroboam's bull-calves misrepresented God and led Israel into pagan modes of thought. The culmination of this degeneracy occurred under Ahab who 'set up an altar for Baal in the house of Baal which he built in Samaria' and also made an Asherah (cf. 4:12; 1 Kgs. 16:32-33). Though Elijah purged the land of open Baal worship, the damage had been done. The next dynasty founded by Jehu did not revert to true worship of the LORD but retained the bull-calves (2 Kgs. 10:28-31), and so the nation slipped, in a spiritual muddle, further and further away from God.

Consequently Hosea concludes that in all this Ephraim ***died***. This does not refer to the economic or military vitality of the nation, but to its life as the covenant people to whom the LORD had assigned the special role of being his witnesses upon earth. Through persistent violation of the demands of the covenant their apostasy with the Baal cult left them, spiritually speaking, as the living dead (cf. Deut. 30:15-20; Wijngaards 1967:238).

13:2 And now they sin more and more,
  and make for themselves a metal image,
idols from silver according to their understanding,
  craftsmen's work, all of them.
With respect to them they are saying,
  'Let people who sacrifice kiss the calves.'

And now refers to the contemporary situation in the north in Hosea's day. The spiritually dead nation did not grasp the serious impact of its conduct, and so heedlessly engaged in further iniquity. This intensified the downward spiral in the land and hastened its inevitable doom as ***they sin more and more*** (literally 'they add with respect to sinning'), particularly as regards idolatry. Often this involved making ***a metal image*** by pouring molten ore into a mould (cf. Exod. 32:4, 8), whereas ***idols*** is a general term for artefacts made from various materials (4:17; 8:4). The use of ***silver*** may indicate that that metal was more highly prized than gold in Hosea's day (cf. 2:8; 8:4). More was involved than

Jeroboam I's bull-calves; the picture is of a land where idol manufacture was rife (cf. Amos 8:14).

Understanding goes beyond the acquisition of factual knowledge; it relates to perception gained through observation. This may describe their religious insights as they worked in a way unlike that of Moses who had constructed everything according to the pattern shown him on Sinai (Exod. 25:40; Heb. 8:5). Instead they were guided by their own ideas of how to worship God. Alternatively, 'understanding' may relate to the technical and artistic skill that was embodied in what they produced. Either way, the idols were ***craftsmen's work*** (cf. 8:6)—and only that. ***All of them***, whether singly or combined, were merely items limited by human horizons and imagination. No matter their cost or beauty, these products of the prevailing spiritual climate promoted by the ruling elite and accepted by the nation were justly the subjects of ridicule.

It is such ridicule that Hosea embodies in the third, obscure part of the verse. The initial ***with respect to them*** most naturally refers to the idols rather than indicating that the words are addressed to their worshippers. ***They are saying*** describes the on-going speech of the people as they venerate the pagan idols, or more probably the instructions of the priests who supervised the ceremonies. The next phrase is literally 'ones sacrificing of mankind'. While this might be taken in apposition to the 'they' who are speaking, and so characterise the worshippers as engaging in human sacrifice (cf. LXX, NIV, REB, ESV), it is more probable that the Hebrew expression signifies those individuals of mankind who engage in sacrifice (cf. AV, NASB).[14] Part of the awkwardness of the expression probably derives from Hosea in his presentation of their ritual juxtaposing 'people'/'mankind' (*ʾādām*) and 'calves' to highlight the absurdity and irrationality of what was being practised. For the calf worship, see on 8:5-6. Sacrifice was a major component of the rites which were prevalent at Israel's shrines, but there was the additional ritual requirement that any who came to sacrifice should ***kiss the calves,*** an act of adoration and devotion performed with the bull-calf idols (cf. 'every mouth that has not kissed him', 1 Kgs. 19:18). To reverence a lifeless object they themselves had brought into existence was clear evidence of their crass moral and religious insensitivity.

---

14. 'Ones sacrificing' renders *zōbəḥê*, a construct plural form, used in a partitive sense. LXX and Vulgate pointed these consonants as a plural imperative, *zibḥû*, 'sacrifice!' (NLT, NRSV).

13:3 Therefore they will be like a morning cloud,
and like the early dew ⌊which⌋ goes away,
like chaff ⌊which⌋ is blown away from the threshing floor,
and like smoke from an opening.

Therefore introduces the impending outcome of such a course of irrational folly and covenant perversity. Hosea's description is of the future awaiting not the idols, but those who worship them. He uses four similes which individually and cumulatively are a skilful reinforcement of his message that the idolaters are doomed to vanish without trace. ***Like a morning cloud*** and ***like the early dew which goes away*** recall the description of Ephraim's behaviour in 6:4. Previously the people had been characterised as those whose love kept vanishing; now it is asserted that they themselves will themselves vanish. Hosea does not just repeat a pleasing literary effect; there is an underlying theological truth. Fickle love leads to fickle fortunes. But we ought also to be alert to the fact that the prophet's thematic development of the figure of dew is not yet complete (cf. 14:5).

Chaff which is blown away from the threshing floor is another image for the light and worthless (cf. 9:1-2; Ps. 1:4). 'Blown away' does not envisage a light breeze leaving traces of the chaff, but a tempestuous gale after which nothing can be seen (cf. Ps. 103:16). It is anachronistic to translate ***an opening*** as 'a chimney' (NKJV, NLT, REB). It refers to a lattice window, or a loosely covered hole in the ceiling of a building. Either way, when there is a strong gust of wind it disperses ***smoke*** from a fire or from oil lamps burning within a building. Similarly not only their wealth, but the people themselves will disappear—utterly.

REFLECTION

- When an individual or a nation fails to recognise God as he truly is, there may continue to be physical life, but there is no spiritual life. The individual and societal consequences of continuing in such a living death lead to further disintegration. 'Those who are dead in trespasses and sins' (cf. Eph. 2:1) do not exist in some morally neutral fashion, securing for themselves the future to which they aspire. Instead they are 'following the course of this world, following the prince of the power of the air, the spirit which is now at work in the sons of disobedience' (Eph. 2:2). Unless God in his grace intervenes to arrest its downward course, living death leads inexorably to eternal death under the curse of the offended God.

(2) Savage Judgement (13:4-8)

The divine speech which begins here continues to 13:14. Initially it involves a contrast between the LORD's character and commitment (13:4-5) and the arrogant ingratitude and forgetfulness of his covenant partners (13:6). Though they had been liberally and bountifully provided for, their uncomprehending denial of his goodness leads to a restatement of judgement in which the LORD who would have saved them instead turns against those who have persistently spurned him. The imagery of being mauled by various wild animals (13:7-8) presents a picture of ferocious and unrestrained attack which warrants the epithet 'savage'.

The divine reaction to Israel's intransigence reminds us that God is not mocked, and no nation, civilisation, church, or individual can deny him with impunity. We naturally shrink from the reality of divine judgement which is starkly presented here, because we know that we too are sinners and failures. But these inescapable facts are set before us to make clear the urgency with which we should seek the unique escape route which God has provided from the condemnation which is his fully justified verdict on us and our behaviour.

13:4 But I ⌊am⌋ the LORD your God,
from the land of Egypt,
and gods besides me you should not know,
and there is no saviour except me.

The words by which the LORD declares who he is are expanded from 12:9, but to make the same point—the reality of the LORD and his power over against the folly of the people who reject him and are infatuated with pagan substitutes for him. ***I ⌊am⌋ the LORD your God*** is an abbreviated form of the covenantal prologue found in Exodus 20:1, which asserts his dignity and his claim on them as their Redeemer. Either the words 'who brought you from the land of Egypt, from the house of slavery' are shortened to ***from the land of Egypt***, or, more probably, these words point to the perpetuation of the relationship ever since that time (cf. 12:9), emphasising to the people that the LORD on his part had continued to extend his covenant goodness to them over the intervening years.

However, unlike the earlier passage (12:9), there is added here a reminder of Israel's obligations by a reference to the first commandment: 'You shall not have other gods before me' (Exod. 20:3). It has been plausibly argued that Hosea's insistence on the LORD being the God of the Exodus (cf. 11:1-3) may not simply be a reaffirmation of the fundamental covenant basis of genuine Israelite faith; it may also assert that faith as a corrective to the distorting theology perpetuated in the syncretism of the official cult of the north (cf. Chalmers 2006). The bull-calf at Bethel was not some innocent or neutral adornment of a sanctuary which, it could be claimed, remained in reality dedicated to the LORD. It was a highly subversive and insidious reintroduction of Canaanite ideology. After all, it had been Aaron who, when he presented the Golden Calf to the Israelites at the foot of mount Sinai, said, 'These ⌊are⌋ your gods, O Israel, who brought you up out of the land of Egypt' (Exod. 32:4, 8), and the same terms were deliberately used by Jeroboam I when he inaugurated the state-religion of the northern kingdom: 'Behold your gods, O Israel, who brought you up out of the land of Egypt' (1 Kgs. 14:28).

Hosea is then not simply restating what had been forgotten, but is countering a false theology promoted by attempting to worship God using idols. This inculcated a debased conception of the LORD and corrupted Israel's perception of the exclusive bond which should exist between them themselves and the LORD who had rescued them from Egypt, carried them on eagles' wings, and brought them to himself (Exod. 19:4). The use of the term ***know*** (rather than 'have' as in Exod. 20:3) stresses not only that they should acknowledge in word and deed the sovereign claims of the LORD but that there should also be a close, trusting relationship between the people and their King (cf. 2:20; 4:1, 6; 6:6). Israel claimed that they still lived in terms of the bond to which they had pledged themselves (5:5; 6:3; 8:2), but the LORD rejected their claim as false. The evidence of their idol worship substantiated his indictment.

The redemptive implications of the covenant relationship are further emphasised by ***there is no saviour except me.*** The root 'to save' is used of deliverance from danger or distress of any sort (cf. 1:7). It is applied to the LORD as the one who acts on behalf of his people when they fall into dire circumstances—and what could be more dire than the peril that then menaced the nation? Here it is stressed that God alone is competent to reverse their circumstances. It was therefore folly to turn from his unique assistance and substitute reliance on other gods or on human alliances where their partners were liable to renege on their promises or find that they were unable to implement their commitments.

13:5 I ⌊am the one who⌋ knew you in the wilderness,
in a land of extreme drought.

The emphatic ***I*** at the beginning of the verse marks not only the LORD's personal involvement in all that occurred after the Exodus from Egypt, but also the initiative he displayed throughout. ***You*** is singular and views the people of God collectively as the LORD briefly addresses them in fond reminiscence. There is a play on the use of the verb 'know' in the previous verse, contrasting the LORD's conduct and their unresponsiveness. ***Knew***[15] brings out not only his initiative in forming the covenant bond (cf. Amos 3:2) but also his ongoing acknowledgement of the relationship as evidenced by his effective provision for them. ***Wilderness*** (cf. 9:10) and ***land of extreme drought*** (literally, 'droughts', a plural of intensity) show that the support had been given when they were enduring adverse circumstances. The abundance of the physical supply could not be explained away as arising from natural causes; it was sovereignly gifted by the LORD in his grace. The outcome should have been unending gratitude on the part of the people.

13:6 According to their pasturage they became full;
they became full and their heart was lifted up.
On account of this they have forgotten me.

There was, however, a stark contrast between the generous provision of God and the response of the people. Those who had been taken from the land of Egypt (13:4) and preserved through the land of extreme drought (13:5) had been brought to a 'place of abundance' (Ps. 66:12). ***According to their pasturage*** focuses on the resources God gave them. 'Pasturage' was grazing land for their flocks and, by synecdoche (part for the whole), points to all the bounty God bestowed. Indeed the figure may be more extensive than that with the LORD as the divine shepherd lavishing his care on the people as his flock ('when they had grazed', ESV).[16] So abundantly did the LORD supply their needs that ***they became full***. In terms of material prosperity, they lacked nothing, but this did not lead to spiritual well-being. The repetition of the thought ***they became full*** brings out how complete this provision was so that there is a sharp contrast to their

---

15. The MT reads *yəda'tîkā*, 'I knew you' (cf. AV, NKJV, ESV), but the LXX and the Peshitta reflect a text which reads *rə'îtîkā*, 'I shepherded you'. Many recent English translations (including NASB, NIV, NRSV) adopt this reading, but in the light of Hosea's extensive use of 'to know' the change seems unnecessary, and probably arose from conformity to the following verses.

16. The MT *kəmar'îtām* is often read as *kəmô rə'îtîm*, 'as often as I shepherded/pastured them' (cf. NIV).

ungrateful reaction in that ***their heart was lifted up.*** This expression is different from that of 'lifting up the heart/soul' in praise or in dependence (as in Ps. 25:1; Lam. 3:41). Rather the reality was that their thoughts and emotions became characterised by haughtiness. The verb is connected with that of 11:7, and also occurs in the Deuteronomic warning that their hearts should not be lifted up lest they become forgetful (Deut. 8:14; cf. Deut. 17:20; Ps. 131:1). But that warning had gone unheeded, and ***on account of this*** (cf. 4:3) points to the consequence that has resulted from their complacent self-esteem, ***they have forgotten me*** (cf. 2:13; 8:14).

13:7 So I have become to them like a lion;
like a leopard by the path I am lying in wait.

The conjunction 'and' is rendered ***so*** because what follows is the outcome of the course of folly which the people had pursued. The spurned and forgotten Shepherd has turned into a ravaging threat against the sheep.[17] ***I have become*** indicates that the people have already experienced the LORD's punishment in part, but more still awaits them. The ferocity of divine judgement on their ungrateful and rebellious conduct is expressed using four comparisons with wild animals. ***Like a lion*** recalls the LORD's description of himself in 5:14. 'Lion' is one of a number of Hebrew words for the animal, and its reference is fairly certain—a male lion just reaching its prime, and so capable of launching a savage, merciless attack. For attacks by animals as a covenant curse, see *Introduction*, pg. 30.

There is a further aspect to the judgement awaiting the people since the LORD also compares himself to ***a leopard by the path.*** This comparison stresses the sudden, unexpected nature of the attack (cf. 'swifter than leopards', Hab. 1:8). ***I am lying in wait*** renders a verb which emphasises paying careful attention. When his judgement on the people is reversed, the same word is used of the LORD's care in 14:8, but here it describes a lurking predator assessing the right moment to spring from its ambush. The verb *ʾāšûr*, 'I am lying in wait', is very close in sound and spelling to the Hebrew noun for Assyria, *ʾaššûr*. Indeed, the early Greek, Syriac and Latin versions read 'Assyria' here,

17. 'So I have become' (*wāʾěhî*) is a waw consecutive imperfect, which more naturally carries a past sense, though a present perfect rendering is possible: 'I have become and so continue to be' (cf. ESV). The following verb is an imperfect, which probably does not describe something exclusively future, 'I will lie in wait', but instead describes God's ongoing attitude towards the people.

but that is unlikely to be original. Doubtless, however, the implication was heard by Hosea's contemporaries: the LORD was waiting to bring Assyria against them once more.

13:8 I will pounce on them like a bear bereaved ⌞of its cubs⌟,
and I will tear the enclosure of their heart,
and I will devour them there like a lion;
wild animals will rip them up.

I will pounce on them portrays a confrontational situation with a formidable opponent, ***a bear bereaved of its cubs***. The adjective 'bereaved' is from a root found earlier (9:12, 14). There is no indication of the precise form of the calamity which has led to the untimely loss or death of the young animals. It is probably overinterpretation to see the cubs as a reference to future generations of Israelites of whose love and loyalty the LORD has been deprived. The essential fact is that the bear is in a frenzied state, and ready to lash out at anyone. Indeed the analogy in Amos 5:19 where meeting a bear intensifies the threat from encountering a lion probably reflects the unpredictability of an enraged bear (cf. 2 Sam. 17:8; Prov. 17:12). ***I will tear the enclosure of their heart.*** The LORD compares the action he will take to the ferocity of the animal distracted by its loss. So the LORD will strike at the nation, not just to maim but to inflict mortal injury. Mention of the heart indicates that the punishment matches the offence of those who had haughtily lifted up their hearts (13:6).

The savagery of the scene is intensified by use of another term for ***a lion***, which conveys the thought of 'a roarer'.[18] The prey has been seized and the animal is devouring ('eating' cf. 2:12) its prey ***there***, presumably right at the spot where the kill occurred, not bothering to take it off to its lair. Similarly the LORD will act to wipe the people out completely. This is emphasised by the final clause: ***wild animals will rip them up.*** This may refer to scavengers disposing of the remains of the carcass, or it may sum up the description of these two verses.

REFLECTION

- When the LORD 'knows' us by his sovereign election, then even the barren wilderness is transformed through his providential care. 'I am the LORD your God who brought you up out of the land of Egypt. Open your mouth wide, and I will fill it' (Ps. 81:10).
- Material prosperity crowds out spiritual desire. When we have eaten

18. The term *lābîʾ* is sometimes rendered 'lioness' (e.g. NASB, NLT). The word may refer to a male or female animal.

and are full, then forgetfulness becomes a real danger (cf. Deut. 8:11-20). The remedy for such a spiritual malady is to be found in careful remembrance of who the LORD himself is, and of all that he has done. 'Bless the LORD, O my soul, and forget not all his benefits' (Ps. 103:2). The extent of divine benevolence is now supremely seen in the self-offering of the Son, and it is with his knowledge of our propensity to forget that he instituted the Lord's Supper. 'Do this in remembrance of me' (1 Cor. 11:24). Our thankfulness for daily mercies should never be allowed to obscure our gratitude for the greatest gift of all.

- The fierce violence of how the LORD treats his errant people may well leave us uncomfortable, but it is nonetheless an important Scriptural truth that 'it is a fearful thing to fall into the hands of the living God' (Heb. 10:31) whether that refers to his judgement on the unbeliever or to his disciplining of his wandering people. It is significant that while Hosea portrays the intensity of God's love, he does not shirk the need for a frank statement of the impact of his wrath when God's righteous judgement against sin is revealed (cf. Rom. 2:5). It is only by acceptance of the provision of divine love to resolve the problem of our sin that any human being can escape the wrath of God. This calls for faith in Jesus, the Son sent by the Father to be the propitiation for our sins (1 John 4:10); that is, his offering of himself as a sacrifice turns aside God's wrath from the sinner onto himself as their substitute (Rom. 3:25; Heb. 2:17).

(3) Instability (13:9-11)

Verse 9 may be understood as a transitional verse in that it both looks back to the result of Israel's reliance on false gods and also anticipates her reliance on inadequate leadership as contributing to her downfall (13:10-11). These two features of her national conduct alike focused on something other than the LORD himself as the one who would assist and defend them. But neither substitute—a false god or a human king—was able to provide what could come from the LORD alone.

While these verses upbraid Israel for their unthinking rejection of the LORD and their trust in others to solve their difficulties, the tone is not one of harsh reprimand, but of sorrow and pathos. To think that after all had been done for them, the people in their obstinacy had persisted in acting in this way! But even Christ's tears over Jerusalem did not turn the city from its folly (Luke 19:41-44).

13:9 It has ruined you, Israel,
that ⌞you are⌟ against me, against your helper.

This verse has been variously reworked by commentators, but it does seem possible to interpret it as it stands.[19] The verb ***has ruined*** (cf. 9:9; 11:9) may refer to various aspects of corruption, destruction, or decay, but it is significant that it is used in connection with the annihilating destruction of the flood (cf. Gen. 6:17; 9:15) and also of the overthrow of the cities of the plain (cf. Gen. 13:10; 19:13, 29). It therefore points to the utter devastation imposed by divine judgement rather than the outworking of some impersonal force.

But who is the subject of the verb here? 'It' might point to an unspecified agent, and so the expression would be equivalent to a passive (cf. 'you are destroyed', NIV). However, the following clause may be understood not as expressing a reason ('It has ruined you because you are against me'), but as a noun clause which would then provide the subject for the verb.[20] The people had set themselves ***against me*** through their self-reliance (13:4-8) as epitomised by their manmade idols and the accompanying belief system (13:1-2). In this way ***Israel***, the people of the covenant who should have know better, had acted perversely ***against your helper***, for the LORD had solemnly engaged to assist them against their adversaries (cf. Deut. 33:7, 28, 29), and his intervention was often celebrated in the Psalms (e.g. Ps. 33:20; 70:6; 115:9-10; 121:1-2; 124:8). When because of their disobedience the LORD withdrew his aid from them, then the people are without any saviour (13:4) and helplessly exposed to their doom. Yet this need not have been the outcome. When the Egyptian pharaoh, Shishak, had invaded Judah shortly after the break up of the united kingdom, the people had humbled themselves, and the LORD had pledged in response, 'I will not ruin them but will soon give them deliverance. My wrath will not be poured out on Jerusalem through Shishak' (2 Chron. 12:7). For Jerusalem read Samaria, and for Shishak

19. The verb *šiḥetkā* is a third person singular perfect piel form, 'he/it has ruined you'. Insertion of a *yodh* yields *šiḥattîkā*, 'I have ruined you'. When this is understood as a prophetic perfect, it yields 'I will ruin you' (cf. NRSV; ESV margin). While this makes good sense, there is no manuscript or versional support and it remains conjectural. The NIV rendering 'you are destroyed' takes the third person reference as being to an unspecified subject, and therefore equivalent to a passive.

20. The NRSV accepts an emendation of the text from *kî-bî* ('that/for against me') to *kî-mî* ('that/for who?'). This reading has the support of the LXX and the Peshitta. It yields a good sense, especially if the previous emendation is also adopted: 'I will ruin you, Israel; who then can be your helper?' However, the changes involved are not required.

read Shalmaneser, but the key difference remains: not humility before the LORD, but opposition to his ways.

13:10 Where is your king? Where?
And ⌊where is one who⌋ would save you in all your cities?
and your judges of whom you said,
'Give me a king and leaders'?

The LORD continues with a taunt in which he challenges the people with the consequences of their folly. Since they had turned from him, there was no one else able to provide effective leadership in the turmoil of the closing years of the northern kingdom. Certainly their king could not. ***Where***[21] ***is your king? Where?*** are two rhetorical questions (cf. 6:4) which are sarcastically couched in terms reminiscent of Israel's first request for a king, 'Appoint for us a king to judge us like all the nations. ... Give us a king to judge us' (1 Sam. 8:5-6). The quest for ***one who would save you*** may imply that the Assyrians had already captured Hoshea, an event which occurred three years before the fall of the city (2 Kgs. 17:4-5), or it may simply assert that whoever claimed to be their king was ineffective. The name of Hoshea, the last king of Israel, incorporates the root 'save', and so is obviously in view here. However, the LORD had a proven track record (13:4) which showed that he was the only one who could effectively realise the promise of the name Hoshea, that is, 'salvation'.

In all your cities points to the key role these fortified settlements played in the security and defence of the land (cf. 11:6). But even when the people were behind the protection of the city walls on which their political leaders had expended so much effort, they were not exempt from Assyrian aggression. They could undergo siege, one of the most brutal aspects of ancient conflicts. ***Judges*** (cf. 7:7) points to those in administrative as well as judicial office in the land; ***leaders*** (cf. 7:3) were those who constituted the king's advisers. The mention of these officials as well as the king shows that the deficiencies of the

---

21. The first occurrence of 'where?' renders the word *ʾěhî*, but it may also be analysed as a verb form, 'I will be'. This gives rise to the rendering 'I will be your king' (cf. AV, NKJV). However, the word recurs twice in 13:14, and there the sense 'where?' is secure (cf. the quotation of 13:14 in 1 Cor. 15:55). It is unlikely that the threefold occurrence of the form in this passage is a result of scribal error. It is more probable that it represents a northern form of the more common *ʾayyēh*, 'where?' This conclusion is reinforced by the fact that *ʾēpôh*, 'where?' is also used in 13:10 for the second occurrence of 'where?'

government of the land had been cruelly exposed at every level of administration by the current crisis.

13:11 I kept giving you a king in my anger,
and kept taking ⌊him⌋ away in my indignation.

The verbs ***kept giving*** and ***kept taking … away*** apparently look back on a sequence of events associated with kingship.[22] It is not a statement regarding one particular transition in the monarchy, but something which could be discerned as recurring. The pattern went back to the inauguration of Saul as king in Israel at the request of the people and despite the warnings of Samuel (1 Sam. 8). The people had not been prepared to see the dangers which their preference for a human ruler posed for their perception of the LORD's sovereignty over them. Saul proved to be a failure, and so had the succession of kings and dynasties throughout the history of the northern kingdom. The instability of the regime in its closing years was an aspect of the LORD's judgement on the nation. For ***anger***, see on 8:5 and 11:9. ***Indignation*** (cf. 5:10) refers to the intense displeasure of the LORD, which was displayed in a fierce reaction.

REFLECTION

The tragic impact of sin on humanity is intensified when those who become aware of their need for assistance resolutely reject that offered by the only One who is 'a very present help in trouble' (Ps. 46:1). Even the most intense affliction may fail to eradicate our perverse desire to be independent and autonomous. Pride asserts itself and will not accept help from another, and especially not from him who had compassion on the crowds because they were harassed and helpless (Matt. 9:36). Instead of accepting his cure and submitting to his rule, in haughty self-sufficiency we seek solace, if not a solution, for our difficulties elsewhere. Politicians and secular counsellors cannot grapple with our deepest spiritual needs, 'for helpless is man's aid' (Ps. 108:12, *Scottish Metrical Version*). The delusive relief of alcohol or drugs creates a dependency which aggravates the situation. The only true relief is to be found in the work of the good shepherd (John 10:11) who enables us to say with Paul, 'Our sufficiency is from God' (2 Cor. 3:5).

---

22. It is possible to retain a future force for the imperfect verbs if the references are taken as ironic: 'I will give you a king, but in my anger it will be the king of Assyria who will rule over you; and I will take in my indignation the king you have appointed for yourselves.'

(4) Grappling with Sheol (13:12-14)

The Massoretic text marks a major transition in the prophecy at this point. While the change may not merit quite so significant a status, a shift in emphasis undoubtedly occurs, from cause to consequence, from historical retrospect to current circumstances, from the inability of human leadership and the resources of the Baal cult to the punishment which awaits Israel. Only secondarily do these verses reflect on the behaviour which has incurred that verdict.

13:12 Wrapped up is the iniquity of Ephraim;
stored up is his sin.

The verse consists of five Hebrew words, with Ephraim occupying central position, and flanked on either side by his iniquity. The passive participles ***wrapped up*** and ***stored up*** each begin with the same sharp ṣ sound, which intensifies the sense of enclosure as well as making the saying memorable. It is possible that this verse accuses Ephraim of being so addicted to his wrongdoing that he has deliberately taken steps to wrap it up and prevent it from being exposed to view, with the following verse declaring the divine verdict on such behaviour (Hubbard 1989:220). More probably 'wrapped up' uses the illustration of a scroll carefully covered for protection and tightly knotted to keep it for future consultation (cf. Deut. 32:34). 'Stored up' might picture treasure securely concealed, but here it is far from treasure that is involved. The LORD has kept a detailed record of ***the iniquity of Ephraim*** (cf. 7:1) and ***his sin*** (cf. 12:8). It is a mistake to suppose that these infringements of the covenant, which were nothing less than violations of the majesty of the LORD, have his escaped notice because there had been no immediate reprisal. An account had been carefully kept, and payment for every offence which had been committed would be required in due course. There is a dark day of reckoning ahead of the land.

13:13 The sorrows of a woman giving birth will come on him;
he is a son who is not wise,
for ⌞it is⌟ time that he should not be inactive
at the breaking forth of sons.

There can be no doubt that this verse foreshadows the dire calamities which awaited Ephraim, but the imagery is developed in an unusual fashion. At first the situation of Ephraim is compared to that of ***a woman giving birth*** (a feminine participle). ***Sorrows***/'birth pangs' are frequently used as an analogy for sudden, unavoidable, dominating agony associated with divine punishment (cf. Isa. 13:8; Jer. 13:23). Paul uses the same figure for the suddenness of the destruction which the day of the Lord will bring on the complacent when they think they are enjoying inviolable peace and security (1 Thess. 5:3). That final reckoning is here foreshadowed in the Assyrian invasion and siege of Samaria.

However, the second part of the verse elaborates on the theme of giving birth and being born, and this suggests that there might be more to the illustration than is at first apparent. Ephraim is no longer compared to a woman, but becomes a ***son*** at the ***time*** of his being born. However, the child is not moving towards birth as he ought to be. ***Should not be inactive***/'stand' indicates that there had occurred a delay which should have been avoided. In some respects the thought is reminiscent of Hezekiah's complaint as he lamented over the weakness of Judah, 'sons have come to point of birth and there is no strength to give birth' (2 Kgs. 19:3; Isa. 37:3). Yet here the problem is not the mother's lack of strength, but the fact that ***he is a son who is not wise*** (cf. 4:11, 14; 7:11). He is unable to recognise the critical nature of the moment and act appropriately. Hankering to be left with what he had enjoyed in the past, he fails to make the right decision as to his own conduct and well-being, and so his future rests in the balance. The scene is one of life ebbing away (cf. Moughtin-Mumby 2008:51), but the metaphor is not fully worked out. We are not told if the mother dies, or if the child is stillborn. So the references to giving birth may leave open the possibility that somewhere in the background there is the potential for new life to come into existence. It is not implied that the people necessarily desire this, but that the LORD may sovereignly providing it. What form this new life might take or how it will be achieved is not stated, but the following verse may be intended to shed some light on the matter.

13:14 From the grasp of Sheol I will ransom them;
  from death I will redeem them.
Where ⌞are⌟ your plagues, O death?
  Where ⌞is⌟ your sting, O Sheol?
Relenting will be hidden from my eyes.

The LORD continues to speak, but interpreters are divided on the significance of what he says. The nation has been brought in 13:13 to the point of birth, of coming alive, but it still remains threatened with death through its own inability to commit itself to life. In this highly charged statement, does God deal a death blow or does he extend life?

Before consideration of the overall meaning of the verse, it is worthwhile to examine three specific terms in it. ***Ransom*** (*pādâ*, cf. 7:13) describes a process in which ownership or control is transferred from one individual to another by means of an appropriate payment. When a person is ransomed, it is assumed that they have been previously deprived of their freedom, for example, by being kidnapped or enslaved, and the ransom payment effects their deliverance.

When the same transfer is undertaken specifically because of the responsibilities of kinship, then the appropriate term is ***redeem*** (*gāʾal*, used only here in Hosea). It is the concept of relational obligation, rather than that of payment, which dominates when the LORD is described as the Redeemer of his people who have fallen of hard times (cf. Exod. 6:6; 15:13).[23] A redeemer is one who is legally entitled to intervene, who must possess sufficient resources to meet the obligation that is due, and who is willing to act in this capacity (cf. Ruth 4:6). Only the LORD matches up to these requirements as regards fallen humanity.

Like 'redeem', ***Sheol*** seems to have been an exclusively Hebrew term, and not part of the general Semitic vocabulary of the times. Because of this, Sheol was able to express the particular view of life after death that had been disclosed to Israel at that stage of the progressive revelation of God. Unlike the elaborate mythical portrayals of the afterlife found in surrounding religions, Israel's beliefs were austerely stated, being confined to what had been explicitly communicated by God. Much had to await the resurrection of Christ which provided a fuller framework for understanding what is involved. However, despite almost unanimous scholarly claims to the contrary, Israel in faith accepted that the believer goes to be with God after death (cf. Ps. 49:15; 73:23-26). The term 'Sheol' is now usually transliterated rather than translated, though 'grave' as used in the NIV is generally an adequate understanding.[24]

Returning to consideration of the verse as a whole, it is evident that there are three styles of translation for its first four lines. (1) They may be rendered as four affirmations (AV, NKJV). This involves taking *ʾěhî* at the beginning of lines 3 and 4 not as 'where?' but in its more usual

---

23. Leon Morris (1955) is an excellent source of information regarding 'ransom' and 'redeem'.

24. For information on Israelite views on Sheol and life after death, see Harris (1987) and Johnston (2002).

sense of 'I will be'[25] to yield 'I will be your plagues, O death! I will be your sting, O Sheol!' However, the interrogative sense of *ʾĕhî* has just occurred in 13:10, and this approach introduces an unnecessary tension with Paul's allusion to the passage in 1 Corinthians 15:55 where he has two interrogatives. So this understanding is better avoided.

(2) Many modern exegetes translate the four lines as questions (cf. RSV, NASB, REB, NLT, ESV). It is accepted that the first two lines assume that God has the power to act in compassion but, interpreting them as rhetorical questions demanding a negative response, it is supposed that in asking, 'Will I ransom them from the power of Sheol? Will I redeem them from death?', God poses the questions only to reject such a course of action. Treating these lines as interrogatives is grammatically possible because, as we have seen, questions in Hebrew need not be marked as such (cf. 2:2). The following two lines are then treated as in effect a summons for death and Sheol to come and inflict their worst on Israel. Some translations even abandon an interrogative form for a statement of intense desire: 'Oh, for your plagues, O death! Oh, for your sting, Sheol!' (NEB, cf. GNB). Death and Sheol are personified as alien powers operating through plague and sting as a means of inflicting death. ***Plagues*** refers to outbreaks of the dreaded bubonic plague (cf. Lev. 26:25, as a covenant curse; 1 Sam. 5–6; Ps. 91:3, 6). The precise nature of ***sting*** is less clear; it may be a destructive plague in general (cf. Deut. 32:34).

It is argued that such a negative reading alone does justice to the context in Hosea which is concerned with the deserved judgement that is coming on the people. On this basis the fifth line of the verse is translated as 'Compassion will be hidden from my eyes.' While a related noun *niḥûmîm* is translated 'compassions' in 11:8, the word here rendered 'compassion' (*nōḥam*) occurs only in this passage. However, the root from which it is derived is well attested, though with two senses. It may convey the idea of a 'change of mind', or alternatively of 'comfort' or 'consolation', and so be rendered 'compassion' (cf. ESV, HCSB; NIV, though the line is taken with the next verse). Paul's use of the passage can then be understood by way of reversal. Taking the lines interrogatively, 'Shall I ransom them from the power of the grave, redeem them from death?' Geerhardus Vos commented: 'Observe the magnificent manner in which Paul has turned this question into its triumphant opposite in 1 Cor. 15.55' (1975:290).

25. Some of the Greek versions later than the LXX, and the Vulgate also decide in favour of a form of the verb 'to be'.

(3) However, there is also room for a third approach, which notes the absence of explicit interrogative markers in the first two lines, and takes them as two statements, followed by two questions. This understanding of the passage is found as early as the Septuagint, and is retained in NIV, NJPS, HCSB. The positive statements constitute a promise that, no matter what may come on the current generation because of the extent of their rebellion, the LORD will again act as an Exodus-style redeemer and preserve a remnant of the people by rescuing them from the full impact of what is coming on Israel.[26] The two questions, ***Where ⌞are⌟ your plagues, O death? Where ⌞is⌟ your sting, O Sheol?***, may then be understood as the LORD's sovereign dismissal of Sheol and death (cf. the use of 'where?' in the taunt of 13:10). They and their weaponry are impotent when he has decided to the contrary. In that case, the fifth line of the verse may be translated by following the other possible sense of *nōḥam* (cf. the use of the verb in Ps. 110:4), as ***Relenting will be hidden from my eyes***, an assertion that there will be no change in the divine resolve on the matter.[27] The main objection to such an approach is that it leaves 13:14 unconnected to what precedes or follows it. That may be answered by saying that there are often such inexplicable transitions in Hosea, and that the move from 13:13 may not be as abrupt as it is often presented to be. Furthermore, Hosea is bringing his prophecy to its conclusion on a note of divine intervention to save, and he may well be anticipating that here.

In Hosea's day the believing community did possess an awareness, albeit one that was incomplete and blurred as to its details, of the reality of new life for the faithful, but in the first instance the divine assertions made here do not relate to ***them*** as individuals, but as Ephraim. The death that was in view was the loss of their existence as a covenant nation (church and state), which would be swept from the

---

26. Though it is not commonly done, it is possible to treat the first two lines as questions in which the LORD muses over the fate of the people, and answers the questions positively. Such a reading affirms the same truths as are found by taking the first two lines as statements, though in a less direct fashion. On this understanding little is gained by reading the two interrogatives into the text.

27. If the other translation 'compassion' is adopted, then the remarks of Kidner are pertinent: 'The "compassion" which God withholds in the final line is, of course, withheld not from the victims of death and the grave, but from this pair of tyrants themselves. *Cf.* the personifying of them in Revelation 20:14, "Then Death and Hades were thrown into the lake of fire." ' (1981:119).

geopolitical scene as completely as 13:3 foretold. The promise given is of corporate resurrection, and is similar to that found in Ezekiel 37:1-14 in connection with the exilic community because the LORD had not given up on his plan. From that revelation of their corporate destiny the people were in a position to deduce something of what was true at an individual level, but it awaited the coming of Christ and the fulfilment of his work for the disclosure of the details of how these promises would be finally fulfilled.

REFLECTION

- Hosea's message in the first instance concerned the fate of the citizens of the north. The record of their wrongdoing was conclusive evidence against them (13:12). Furthermore, when they endured divinely imposed affliction designed to bring about new life through repentance, they refused to respond (13:13). Their lack of wisdom ensured that the disaster coming on the nation would not be averted. But even so the LORD looked beyond the immediate catastrophe, and out of his grace pledged himself to redeem even from Israel a remnant who would truly be his people, and of this we see one instance in the case of Anna of the tribe of Asher (Luke 2:36).
- But in discussing the destiny of the northern tribes there is invoked a potent principle of far reaching significance. The LORD will not permit death and Sheol to have the last say on the outworking of his purposes. What is said about these malign forces applies to far more than the preservation of a remnant from Ephraim. In 1 Corinthians 15:55 Paul alludes to it in connection with his citation of 'Death is swallowed up in victory' (Isa. 25:8[28]) to show how it also governs the implications of Christ's ransoming and redemptive work and the reality and extent of the resurrection. There the triumph of God's plan is reached in the impotence of death and its banishment through the victory of Christ.
- Despite the failings of his people and the aggression of hostile forces, God's plan is sure to succeed and to do so irreversibly. 'The gifts and the calling of God are irrevocable' (Rom. 11:29). While our deficiencies may cause us to be despondent, we are called on to have hope and confidence in him. Even in the face of known contraventions of the covenant by those called to be parties to it, the LORD affirms, 'I will not violate my covenant or change what went forth from my lips' (Ps. 89:34).

28. For further discussion of this verse, see Mackay 2008:531.

(5) Samaria's Doom (13:15-16)

These words in which the LORD is spoken of in the third person are a prophetic commentary on the foregoing. The prophet accepts the inevitability of the impending judgement. Probably there is a polemic here against Baalism by asserting its inability to control the forces of nature when they are summoned by the LORD against his people. Though the worship of the Baals promised fertility, it would in fact lead to famine and death. The conclusion in many respects parallels what has been said in 11:12–12:1.

13:15 Though he himself will be fruitful among his brothers,
an east wind will come,
the wind of the LORD coming up from the wilderness,
and it will dry up his spring
and his fountain will be parched.
He ⌊is the one who⌋ will plunder treasure,
every desirable object.

There is a further play on the name Ephraim (*ʾeprayim*, 'doubly fruitful'; cf. 9:16) in the verb ***will be fruitful*** (*yaprîʾ*; cf. Gen. 41:52).[29] This metaphor drawn from plant life refers to the growth of the nation, particularly the population increase which had been experienced (cf. Gen. 1:28). ***Among his brothers*** recalls Ephraim's traditional position of influence among the northern tribes (cf. 13:1)[30] rather than expressing an international comparison.

But Hosea once more explores a scenario which has been effectively ruled out (cf. 8:7). The idea that the plant will continue to flourish has already been negated by divine decree, and even if Ephraim were to prosper, it would not avert disaster. ***An east wind*** recalls Ephraim's pursuit of the east wind (12:1) in trying to enter into a treaty with Assyria; now those efforts will recoil on him in destruction. This will happen not just because of the inherent folly of the policies they pursued, but because of the LORD's intervention to ensure this

29. Probably there is a deliberate misspelling of the normal form of the verb *prh*, 'to bear fruit', as *prʾ* so as to repeat the three consonants of Ephraim's name.

30. There is no need to follow translations such as NASB and NRSV by changing *ʾāḥ*, 'brother', to the rarer term *ʾāḥû*, 'reed, reed-bed' (cf. Gen. 41:2, 18; Job 8:11), and taking the final *nun* with the following word. While 'son of brothers' is an odd expression, it is possible that *bēn* is here an alternative (northern?) spelling of *bên*, 'between, among' (cf. LXX, AV, NIV, ESV), which is found in the Aleppo Codex of the MT.

outcome. ***The wind of the LORD coming up from the wilderness*** emphasises his role in bringing the armies of Assyria. ***It will dry up his spring***[31] points to the desiccating effect of the dry desert wind on the water resources of the land. ***His fountain will be parched*** reinforces the picture of the desolation of the land through lack of water. Behind the picture of natural disaster lies the impact of invading armies as the closing two lines make clear.

The emphatic ***he*** (a masculine term, not a feminine one referring to 'the wind' as in HCSB) marks the transition from metaphor to reality. What is threatened is not primarily natural disaster in the form of a drought, but enemy incursion. Assyria will conquer what remains of the land and ***will plunder treasure,*** the physical resources and accumulated wealth, on which Ephraim relied and take ***every desirable object*** away as booty.

13:16[32] Samaria will suffer for her guilt,
for she has rebelled against her God.
By the sword they will fall:
their youngsters will be dashed in pieces,
and their pregnant women will be ripped open.

Ephraim, having turned its backs on the LORD, will experience the full imposition of the curse of the broken covenant. In particular the impact on the population is singled out to intensify the horrors of invasion and pillage. Mention of ***Samaria*** is not just an instance of synecdoche (part for whole) in which the capital represents the whole nation. In the decade after 733 B.C. it had virtually become the nation because of the extent to which the Assyrians had taken control of the territory. For a while the enclave round the city had been exempt from the full impact of the invasion, but that will not be allowed to continue indefinitely.

---

31. The MT points the verb as *yēbôš*, 'it will be ashamed', which is contextually inappropriate. More probably, as in the early versions and English translations (including the AV), the form should be read as *yōbîš* (a hiphil form from *yābēš*), 'it will be dried up'. This and the following verb are linked by ordinary waw to indicate that the three verbs describe not successive features of the scene, but three simultaneous aspects of it.

32. 13:16 is taken as 14:1 in the Hebrew text with subsequent verse numbers of chapter 14 being one greater than those in English translations. The Hebrew chapter division is less appropriate than that of English versions. Indeed a Qumran manuscript of Hosea (4QXIIc) has a blank line after 13:16 [14:1 in the Hebrew text], and the Massoretic paragraph marker also occurs at the same point.

Samaria will suffer for her guilt (*ʾāšam*, cf. 4:15; 5:15; 10:2; 13:1)[33] emphasises that it must not be forgotten why she will be engulfed by this disaster: ***she has rebelled against her God***. 'Rebelled' is a term for defiant obstinacy which intentionally contravenes a superior's known requirements (cf. Num. 20:24; Ps. 107:11). The use of the verb 'suffer for guilt' closes the thematic bracketing begun by 'became guilty' (13:1). Samaria's wilful violation of the covenant will have inescapable consequences in that her guilty status will be matched by the imposition of an appropriate penalty.

The chapter concludes with the horrific annihilation of Samaria's population in the atrocities of war. The covenantal death of the nation is not a constitutional nicety; it is a grim and unmitigated catastrophe. This is what comes from abandoning the LORD for the seeming advantages of worshipping Baal. What had held out the prospect of fertility and life had instead brought the opposite: death and disaster. ***By the sword they will fall*** is probably not confined to the fate of the fighting men: the whole community will suffer, with no exemption for the weak and vulnerable. ***Their youngsters will be dashed in pieces*** (cf. 10:14). ***Their pregnant women will be ripped open*** (cf. 13:8; 2 Kgs. 8:12; Amos 1:13). That was warfare back then; now the only real difference is in the scale on which it happens. There is nothing left for the north but to await their land being overwhelmed and looted, and the community being decimated so that there will be no prospect of anyone left to restart life in the ruins.

REFLECTION

- 'Guilt' (13:1, 16) is not to be understood simply as a subjective experience of guilt feelings. In Scripture the term is primarily objective, and guilt exists whether or not it is felt or acknowledged. A person who is guilty has incurred personal legal or moral liability to penalty. Punishment, however, need not ensue immediately, but there should be no doubt that if an offender is arraigned and convicted, the appropriate penalty will be imposed. If the offence is against God, then exposure is inevitable, and due reparation will be required. The only way to avoid personally suffering for rebellious conduct against God is through the work of the Servant of the LORD who is constituted, or constitutes himself, 'an offering for guilt' (Isa.

---

33. The LXX reads 'Samaria will be desolated' taking the verb as *tēšam* from *šāmam*, 'to be deserted', rather than as *tēʾšam* from *ʾāšam*, 'to be guilty, to pay for one's guilt', but the link with 13:12 argues against this.

53:10), and so is in a position to 'make the many to be accounted as righteous in that their iniquities he himself will carry' for them (Isa. 53:11).

- Our instinct is to recoil from horrific portrayals of divine judgement such as those found in 13:7-8, 16, but that does not lessen or mitigate what the LORD has warned he will impose on those who are intransigent in their rejection of his overtures of mercy. It is not possible to conceive how dreadful and appalling will be the experience of those who will cry out 'to the mountains and rocks, "Fall on us and hide us from the face of him who is seated on the throne, and from the wrath of the Lamb, for the great day of their wrath has come, and who can stand?" ' (Rev. 6:16-17). The wrath of the Lamb reminds us that there is no escaping this reality by supposing that the love of God overrides the requirements of his justice. Those requirements have been met by the Lamb of God who 'takes away the sin of the world' (John 1:29), and if his offer of salvation is spurned, then his wrath will ensue. Such dire presentations of judgement are intended to cause the unthinking to reassess their eternal destiny and those who are already reconciled by his blood to redouble their efforts to snatch out of the fire (Jude 23) those who heedless of their danger.

C. Restoration (14:1-9)

For the last time in the prophecy Hosea switches from describing the dire fate which awaits the intransigent community to the wonder of divine persistence in grace. Devastation is not to be the last act in the drama. Though the people had wilfully played false in their relationship with the LORD, he remained 'your God' (14:1) and had not totally given up on them. As Hosea uttered these words, he was still holding out the possibility of personal repentance to individuals in the beleaguered community. He was also permitted to see beyond the ominous storm clouds which presently surrounded Samaria, beyond even the destruction and deportation which would shortly engulf her. By means of the harsh discipline of invasion and the atrocities associated with ruthless conquest by their enemies, the LORD was creating conditions for heart change which would lead to a general return in prayerful submission (14:1-3). The LORD assures those who repent that he will respond with overwhelming compassion and liberality to them, and that they will enjoy renewed vitality (14:4-8). The prophet concludes by affirming that those who ponder these matters will gain deep insight into the character and purposes of God (14:9).

(1) The Plea of the Repentant (14:1-3)

Hosea carefully teaches Israel how they should respond to the LORD's dealings with them so that the way may be opened up for divine mercy to flow. Previously they had refused to return (cf. 11:5), but in his providence God has so shaped their affairs that the time will come when they will be brought to acknowledge the error of their ways and to approach him with sincere penitence and an eager desire to commit themselves to him.

14:1 Return, O Israel, to the LORD your God,
for you have stumbled in your iniquity.

Return is the basic spiritual movement which is required of those who have departed from the ways of the covenant (cf. 3:5; 6:1; 12:6). It is expressed using a form of the root *šûb*, which occurs five times in the chapter (14:1, 2, 4 *twice*, 7). The basic physical movement behind the spiritual metaphor is to 'turn around' so as to face in the opposite direction. The prophetic entreaty calls on the people to confess that they had turned from the LORD—how can one come back without first having departed?—and it also looks for clear thinking leading to a decision which motivates resolute action. Essential to successfully moving in a new direction is selection of an appropriate destination, and about that there should be no doubt. Their movement must be ***to the LORD your God*** (cf. 12:9; 13:4). The preposition *ʿad*, 'to', conveys the thought of 'right up to', not merely 'in the general direction of'. It is a picture of close fellowship and loving embrace, without any scope for further wandering. Furthermore, it is a tribute to the LORD's gracious and persevering commitment to the covenant that he still allows himself to be called, 'your God'. So the people have not been utterly written off, but are addressed as ***Israel***, the covenant community. Though, as the mention of Ephraim in 14:8 shows, Hosea's initial audience came from the northern tribes, by using this covenant name the prophet indicates that his exhortation is of relevance to all whom the LORD recognises as being in such a bond with himself.

The people's repentance is needed because they ***have stumbled*** (cf. 4:5) ***in your iniquity*** (cf. 7:1). The phrase used here, as in 5:5, denotes the judgement they had brought on themselves through their obstinate perversity in following unsuitable paths of their own devising. It was thus no wonder that in their economic, political and religious life they had found the going rough and had encountered obstacles which caused them to lose their footing. At root it had been their disregard of the norms of the covenant which had brought about their downfall. So now they must abandon their rebellion and permit themselves to be regulated and guided by the LORD.

14:2 Take with you words,
  and return to the LORD.
Say to him, 'Completely forgive iniquity,
  and receive good,
  and so we will render ⌞as⌟ bulls our lips.'

Hosea turns from addressing the community as a single entity and uses three plural imperatives to urge each member of his audience (present and future) to respond with appropriate action. As they draw near to the LORD, they are to ***take words***. The prophet does not have in mind glib words, easily uttered and signifying little. Instead what he is recommending is to be understood in contrast with the mere ritual with which the people had been previously satisfied (cf. 6:6). What he is advocating is a thoughtful, not a thoughtless, approach. The injunction 'take' implies that due consideration has been given beforehand to what they will say on the solemn occasion when they ***return to the LORD*** (cf. 14:1) in repentance. An example of what the prophet considers appropriate is to be found in the concluding part of this verse and in 14:3.

In the initial part of his model prayer Hosea commends to his listeners the use of three positive petitions. The first of these begins with the word 'all', but, as it is exceptionally placed at the beginning of its clause, coming even before the verb and not before the noun 'iniquity', the translation ***completely*** is appropriate. This word order stresses the need for a radically reconstituted relationship with the removal of every trace of guilt and liability to punishment arising from ***iniquity*** (cf. 14:1). 'It involves the profound recognition, not merely of sin, but sinfulness' (Vos 1975:291). ***Forgive*** employs the usual Hebrew idiom of 'to lift, to take off' (cf. Exod. 34:7; Mic. 7:18), as though a burden would be raised from their shoulders, and any barrier in the way of their acceptance by their King removed by him. They are to implore God to do this as he is the only one who can achieve the desired outcome.

Then Hosea urges the people to plead that the LORD ***receive good.*** It is unclear whether 'good' is used as a title for God, that is, 'receive ⌞us⌟, O Good One', or whether 'good' is the equivalent of an adverb to describe the manner in which the LORD is implored to receive, that is, 'receive ⌞us⌟ graciously' (cf. NKJV, NASB, NIV, NLT), or whether 'good' is a description of the confession they are presenting to him, as if to say, 'accept our genuine and sincere confession because it is good' (cf. NJPS, NRSV, ESV, HCSB). The weakness of the first two approaches is the need for the supplement 'us', which is a major component of what is being expressed. Possibly the third approach is to be preferred. It would incorporate the advice given in 6:6 that first place in approaching God is to be given to steadfast love and heartfelt acknowledgement of him rather than to lavish but empty sacrifices (cf. Mic. 6:6-8).

Thirdly, there is set out how they should commit themselves to respond to divine forgiveness and acceptance.[34] ***We will render*** employs a term that may be associated with a payment made to compensate for a loss (cf. Exod. 21:36; 22:3-6), or to fulfil a vow by means of an appropriate thankoffering (cf. Deut. 23:21; Ps. 22:25; 50:14). The speakers acknowledge that the payment in view is one that they are obligated to make. But what is that payment? There are two words without any grammatical connection indicated between them: 'bulls' and 'our lips'.[35] ***Bulls*** were appropriate animals for sacrifice, and by combining the words as 'bulls ⌞of⌟ our lips' the thought 'bulls in accordance with the vows of our lips' may be obtained. A frequent alternative is to read the phrase 'bulls of our lips' as 'fruit of our lips' by reassessing the significance of one letter.[36] But most probably the second word is in apposition to the first and serves to clarify it. They will present not offerings of animal sacrifices but instead offerings from their lips as they sincerely confess, pray to, and praise the LORD in adoration and thanksgiving (cf. Ps. 51:14-17). They now recognise that is what he truly desires (contrast 5:6).

---

34. The use of ordinary *waw* with the cohortative (*nəšalləmâ*) after an imperative probably expresses the consequence or intended result of the imperative being carried out.

35. The MT reads *pārîm śəpātênû*, 'bulls our lips', but the first noun is in the absolute and not the construct, which makes the expression intelligible only with the help of a considerable supplement. Alternatively it is proposed that the final *mem* on the first word be treated as an enclitic *mem* and the word itself read as *pərî*, 'fruit of', as in LXX (so NRSV, NIV, NASB). The ESV 'vows' may come from understanding this 'fruit' as the implication of the initial 'words'.

36. There are a number of plays involved in this chapter on the name Ephraim. In verse 2 there is *pārîm*, 'bulls', (or *pərî*, 'fruit'); in verse 6 *yipraḥ*, 'blossom'; and in verse 8 *peryəka*, 'your fruit'.

14:3 'Assyria cannot save us;
 on a horse we will not ride;
and we will not again say, "Our gods",
 to the work of our hands—
because ⌊it is⌋ in you the fatherless is shown compassion.'

The changed outlook which is embodied in this proposed prayer is now set out in three negative declarations which the prophet proposes that the people employ as they repudiate the remedies they had previously resorted to. No longer will they rely on international alliances, military might, or paganism and idolatry for protection and blessing. As they turn to the LORD as their true provider, they admit that their past conduct had been futile and wrong.

Assyria (preposed for emphasis) ***cannot save us*** (for 'save' see on 13:4) is more than a statement of political reality that 'Assyria will not save us'.[37] It represents the people coming to their senses in respect of the world of political intrigue and alliances on which they had formerly based their hopes (8:9; 12:1), and realising that it was incapable of delivering what it promised. Assyria might seem an unlikely candidate for an ally because its expansionism had totally unsettled the nations at the east of the Mediterranean. But one possible way of coping with the challenge of the aggressor had been to collaborate with them. Now it is seen that such an approach simply entailed a slow death because unremitting Assyrian demands for tribute undermined the economic and military strength of its satellite states. Peace and security were paid for by impoverishment and oppression. So the people admit the folly of a merely political deliverance, and recognise the LORD as the only true Saviour.

Secondly, they undertake not to ***ride on a horse***. The primary significance of the horse was as a military animal (cf. 1:7; Joel 2:4). This is a repudiation of their former policy of relying on their own military strategies and resources to guarantee their national security (Hos. 8:14; 10:13-14). Additionally it may suggest avoidance of seeking help from Egypt which was a major player in the international arms trade of the day through its being a source of horses (cf. Deut. 17:6; Isa. 31:1-3). Now in faith they commit themselves to God, not armaments, for their security. 'Some trust in chariots and some in horses, but we trust in the name of the LORD our God' (Ps. 20:7; cf. Ps. 33:17-18).

---

37. The imperfect is taken as having potential force (cf. *IBHS* §31.4b).

Furthermore, they relinquish paganism and idolatry. ***We will not again say, 'Our gods',***[38] ***to the work of our hands.*** They do not deny that they had made idols (cf. 8:6; 13:2) and worshipped them. Now, however, the LORD had brought them to acknowledge that their infatuation with all things Canaanite had precluded true fellowship with him. So they concede the utter impropriety of such conduct and, realising the damage it had done to their relationship with God, they renounce it so that they may enjoy divine blessing once more.

Ultimately, however, the foundation of their prayer is not to be their resolution to amend their behaviour but their perception through faith of the character of the God they approach: ***because in you the fatherless is shown compassion.*** 'Is shown compassion' or 'receives compassion' (HCSB) are preferable to the usual 'finds compassion' which suggests that this may be a reward bestowed on their activity. 'Fatherless' describes one who is bereft of family connections, and so vulnerable, helpless and with a compromised future. But whereas such individuals might well be exploited by their fellows, their reception from the LORD was quite different. Just as when the prodigal son came to his senses he felt himself no longer worthy to be called the son of his father (Luke 15:19), so when Israel comes to a true perception of where their rebellious rejection of their Father's care has left them in relation to God (11:1-7), they recognise that they had effectively orphaned themselves. Lo-Ruchama (1:6) sees that only by divine grace can she become Ruchama, the recipient of divine compassion (2:1, 23), and so she casts herself unreservedly on the 'helper of the fatherless' (Ps. 10:8; cf. Ps. 27:10; 68:5).

REFLECTION

- Two entreaties echo throughout the pages of Scripture: 'come' (cf. Matt. 11:28) and 'return' (cf. Deut. 4:30; 30:1-2; Lam. 3:40. Joel 2:12; Amos 4:6, 8, 10, 11). The latter exhortation is extended particularly to those who, though they have heard of the LORD's goodness and experienced something of his favour, have still turned their

38. There is an inherent ambiguity in the ascription *ʾĕlōhênû*. It may be an instance of the standard idiom of the plural *ʾĕlōhîm* being used of the one true God, and simply mean 'Our God' (NRSV, ESV). In that case what is being repudiated is the syncretistic introduction of idolatry into the worship of the LORD. But *ʾĕlōhîm* is also used as a true plural in reference to the gods of the nations, and in view of the religious situation Hosea has been describing that seems more likely here: 'our gods' (NIV, HCSB). In that case it is both idolatry and polytheistic worship which are being renounced.

backs on him and wandered off into ways that seemed right to them, but whose end is in fact death (cf. Prov. 14:12). It is a reflection of God's love that he does not give over on those who are errant and out of the way, but continues to view them with compassion and to entreat them to reconsider and repent. Just as the father looked eagerly for his profligate son to return and went eagerly to meet him on his return (Luke 15:20), so the Father awaits the return of those who are his backslidden children. Just as the father in the parable did not wait for his son to finish his prepared speech before clothing him and making ready to celebrate his return, so the Father shows compassion to those who fear him and recognises our frailty (cf. Ps. 103:13-14).

- Compromise with a relentless aggressor such as Assyria could at best afford only temporary respite. The adversary had not changed his character or abandoned his ultimate goal, and it was to live in a fool's paradise to suppose otherwise. Similarly the Christian is still engaged in spiritual warfare with a devious and implacable foe who attempts to outwit the unwary (2 Cor. 2:11). To compromise with Satan and his allies is to court disaster and to risk making shipwreck of our faith (1 Tim. 1:19). The Scriptural command is to 'stand against the schemes of the devil' (Eph. 6:11) and to 'resist the devil', and then it is promised that 'he will flee from you' (James 4:7). However, success will only follow if there is true submission to the Saviour who sends the Holy Spirit to provide his followers with the resources that are needed.
- God's compassion towards the fatherless finds its ultimate expression in Christ's promise: 'I will not leave you orphans' (John 14:18), unpitied, unprotected, unprovided for. He never leaves or forsakes his flock, but constantly provides them with comfort and with every resource that they require to face and overcome the challenges which confront them. 'It is no longer I who live, but Christ lives in me' (Gal. 2:20).

(2) The Divine Response (14:4-8)

The speaker in this passage is clearly God, who pledges himself to respond compassionately to the repentant prayer which his people will utter (14:1-3). He will cure them and reinstate them into enjoyment of his love (14:4), lavishly providing for all their needs (14:5-7). In 14:8 there is a final description of the LORD's favour towards restored Ephraim. No longer in thrall to his idolatry, he is perpetually provided for by the one who displays real concern for him.

14:4 I will heal their backsliding;
I will love them spontaneously,
for my anger has turned from him.

Divine chastisement had been described as wounding (5:12-14; 13:7-8), and so it is appropriate that its reversal is presented as ***I will heal*** (cf. 5:13; 6:1; 7:1; 11:3). Furthermore the divine Physician's treatment goes beyond healing of the physical scars and losses inflicted on the land, restoring the years which the locusts have eaten (Joel 2:25). He addresses the fundamental, spiritual problem, ***their backsliding*** (cf. 11:7). This term also derives from the root *šûb*, 'to return' (cf. 14:1), but here it describes their turning away in apostasy and rebellion from God. He, however, now deals with their persistent propensity to stray (cf. 5:4; 7:2; 11:5) and all the woes that had drawn down upon them.

There is reversal of the sentence imposed on them earlier: 'I will no longer love them' (9:15). In saying, ***I will love them*** (cf. 11:1), God demonstrates that his restored relationship with his people would not be cold and distant, but personal and cordial, fully restored without any reservations. Although he had punished them, that too was an action of his love which he had never totally withdrawn (cf. 3:1; Ps. 89:33). So what is principally in view is a time when the people will again enjoy unrestricted access to him and to the blessings he bestows. Furthermore, God's action occurs ***spontaneously.*** The term may describe a freewill offering (cf. Lev. 7:16), and is used adverbially to characterise the voluntary and unfeigned nature of God's action. He is not coerced by any external pressure or stimulus, nor is his love prompted by any worthiness on their part (not even their repentance). Its origin is, as it had always been, in the unfathomable determination of God (cf. Deut. 7:7-10).

This change in outlook towards the people will occur ***for my anger has turned from him.*** 'My anger' is the LORD's indignant response to the affront to his majesty given by their disloyalty and misbehaviour (cf. Deut. 7:3-4; 29:19). The verb 'has turned' is again *šûb*, the same root as is used to denote 'to return' in repentance (14:1). The LORD's anger is no longer 'kindled against them' (8:5) but, having accomplished its purpose in punishing them and bringing about their change of heart, it subsides.

14:5 I will be like the dew to Israel:
he will sprout like the lily,
and he will strike his roots like Lebanon.

The extravagant language used to portray the restored spiritual relationship employs metaphors drawn from the physical prosperity and fertility of the promised land (cf. Joel 3:18; Amos 9:13-14; Mic. 7:14). In ***I will be*** the LORD quietly asserts that he alone is the source of this revival in their fortunes. He will no longer come upon them like a lion or bear (13:7-8), but ***like the dew*** as it silently and gently provides the moisture required for life and growth during the rainless dry season. Earlier the metaphor of dew had pointed to how transient Israel's faithfulness was (6:4), and also to how completely they would be removed in judgement (13:3). Here the same imagery is developed to portray gracious reversal with a focus on the daily renewed refreshing and sustaining properties of dew, as found in Isaac's blessing of Jacob, 'May God give you of the dew of heaven' (Gen. 27:28; cf. Deut. 33:28). ***To Israel***, the people of the covenant promise, the LORD will bring every reinvigorating influence needed to promote newness of life.

As a result, the people ***will sprout***, the same verb as had been used of judgement 'springing up' like a noxious plant in 10:4, but here the image is used positively, of the development and blossoming of a plant (cf. Isa. 35:1). Most probably the flower referred to is ***the lily***, which grew in Galilee and on mount Carmel (King 1988:121), and which was noted for its rapid growth and for its beauty (cf. Matt. 6:28-29). Moreover, they will experience not the barrenness of judgement in which their root would dry up (9:16). Instead, ***he will strike his roots.*** This unusual, almost violent, phrase describes forceful growth, which is compared to that of the trees of Lebanon whose roots will penetrate deeply into the soil—a picture of stability and permanence.

Three successive verses end by mentioning ***Lebanon***. This was not a nation state in Biblical times, but a geographical term for the mountainous zone which stretched northwards from Galilee, parallel to the Mediterranean coast, for 100 miles. There were two mountain ranges facing each other with a long, fertile valley running between them. The area was renowned for it fertility, and especially for its forests and the quality of the timber they produced (cf. Ps. 72:16; 92:12; Isa. 35:2).

14:6 His shoots will go out,
and his beauty will be like the olive tree,
and his fragrance like Lebanon.

Three further statements extend in hyperbolic terms the picture of the lush growth of a tree which depicts how the restored people will prosper, especially symbolising how they will flourish spiritually. The term

shoots occurs only six times in the Old Testament, describing a twig (Ezek. 17:22), the second growth from the base of a tree (Job 14:7) or the tendrils of a vine (Ps. 80:11). The picture may continue to be that of the cedar from 14:5.[39] As its roots take firm hold of the ground, so new branches sprout and grow. Alternatively, ***like the olive tree*** may also be taken with the first line of the verse. Either way, the metaphor depicts new life springing forth abundantly, resulting in the ***beauty***—there might even be regal tones of 'majesty'—of the fruitful tree (cf. Ps. 52:8; Jer. 11:16). Olive oil was one of the major crops in the land (cf. 2:5, 22), and the abundant foliage of the tree also provided much needed shade. The desirability of the scene is completed by mention of ***his fragrance***, probably likened to the scent of all the flowers and shrubs found in ***Lebanon*** (cf. Song 4:11).

14:7 Those who dwell under his shade will return;
  they will give life to corn.
They will sprout like the vine;
  his fame ⌊will be⌋ like the wine of Lebanon.

In the first line of this verse there is a word play between 'will return' (*yāšubû*) and 'those who dwell' (*yōšəbê*), the one action leading to the other. 'Return' renders *šûb*, 'to turn back', but there are two ways in which the verb may be translated. It could be understood as employed in its auxiliary function (cf. 3:5; 11:9), which indicates repetition of the action of an accompanying verb: 'they [that is, the restored people] will again dwell beneath my shade' (cf. NIV, NRSV). If the emendation 'my shade' is adopted,[40] then this is a prediction that the covenant community will again enjoy the favourable environment of shade provided by God as he protects them and causes them to flourish (cf. Ps. 91:1; 121:5). Further the LORD as the tree providing shade naturally leads in to the thought of 14:8.

However, two factors militate against this interpretation. 'Those who dwell' is a participle rather than a finite form which the auxiliary use of *šûb* would normally require. Further, in the preceding verses it has

39. Another approach is to take the first line of 14:6 as concluding the thought of 14:5 (cf NEB, NIV), which may then be understood as having the usual bicolonic structure. But two triplets in 14:5 and 14:6 is just as feasible a pattern in Hosea.

40. Emending *bəṣillô*, 'his shade', to *bəṣillî*, 'my shade', is frequently advocated (cf. *BHS*), and has a measure of inherent plausibility in that the two Hebrew letters involved were frequently confused. However, the change has no manuscript or versional support, and ought therefore to be avoided.

been Israel which is compared to a tree or a plant, not the LORD. It is therefore preferable to take ***those who dwell under his shade*** as a description of individuals who have in faith aligned themselves with God's people and enjoy the 'shade'/'protection' provided by the covenant community of Israel (= 'his'). Because of their acceptance of what Israel truly stands for, they too ***will return***. This would be a reference to the spiritual reorientation of repentance (return from exile, picking up on 11:11, is possible, but less likely) of this group also. It is feasible to argue that this looks forward to the incorporation of the Gentiles into the new Israelite community.

The verb in ***they will give life to corn*** does not suggest that the restored community will live or flourish like corn as many translations favour, but that they impart life to it. It seems to be a picture of the revitalised people invigorating every aspect of their existence. ***They will sprout*** (cf. 14:5) ***like the vine***, a frequent symbol for Israel (cf. 10:1). Though judgement was going to deprive Israel of her vines (2:12), in the renewed land the LORD will ensure prolific growth. ***His fame***, the reputation by which he (= Israel) is remembered (cf. 12:5), will be divinely established. We do not hear elsewhere of ***the wine of Lebanon***, but the implication of the verse is that it was a renowned vintage. The comparison is somewhat unusual, but seems to be drawn from the preceding simile of the vine and to echo the references to Lebanon at the end of the previous two verses.

14:8 O Ephraim, what have I to do any more with idols?
I ⌞am the one who⌟ has answered and I will care for him.
I ⌞am⌟ like an evergreen cypress;
from me is your fruit found.

Mention of ***Ephraim*** shifts the focus of the divine speech from the more distant future to the prevailing situation of the remaining enclave in the northern kingdom. The first line of the verse may be understood in two ways. Following a Jewish tradition, Ephraim may be taken as the one who utters the following words: 'Ephraim ⌞will say⌟, "What have I to do any more with idols?" ' (cf. NKJV, NJPS). This projects the words into the future, and reads them as an aspect of Ephraim's repentant response as they renounce their idolatry (cf. 14:3). However, the supplement is not inconsiderable, and the connection with the following lines is not smooth. It would seem preferable to take Ephraim as a vocative, and to understand the words as uttered by the LORD (NASB, NIV, NRSV, ESV).[41]

This rhetorical question (cf. 6:4) incorporates the LORD's final plea to the rebellious nation: ***What have I to do any more with idols?*** The idiom does not imply that there had been some way in which the LORD and idols (for the term, cf. 4:17) could legitimately have been associated. It is rather an emphatic repudiation of what he had so far put up with in his longsuffering. In effect the LORD declares, 'I will have nothing more to do with idols' (cf. HCSB); my patience is exhausted. This interpretation does justice to the term 'any more' (*ʿôd*), rather than translating simply as 'What have I to do with idols?' (ESV) and taking the expression only as a repudiation of idolatry.

Over against the impotence of the idols, the LORD asserts: ***I am the one who has answered.*** The use of emphatic 'I' (cf. 2:8) separates the LORD from any other supposed deity to whom the people had prayed. He alone could 'answer' (the same term as 'respond', 2:21-22). This he has done and will continue to do for, as their covenant God, he has given the commitment, ***I will care for him.***[42] This is a reversal of the previous threat involving the same term, no longer lying in wait to pounce (13:7), but in a detailed and solicitous fashion watching their situation and meeting every need they have.[43]

The startling impact of what is said in ***I am like an evergreen***

---

41. A similar interpretation may also be achieved by taking 'Ephraim' as a further instance of fronting, bringing forward a word from its usual position in the word order of a sentence to flag it up as the theme of what is said: '⌊Regarding⌋ Ephraim'. This would then be taken up in the following 'him' and 'me'. Another approach which reads the verse antiphonally, with lines 1 and 3 spoken by Ephraim, and lines 2 and 4 by the LORD, is improbable being too involved without further indication of the speakers being given.

42. The pointing *wa* rather than *wā* indicates that the verb is not understood as a waw consecutive, 'and I cared for him', but as a true imperfect, 'I do and will care'.

43. The first *ʾănî*, 'I', before the finite verb 'I have answered' is undoubtedly emphatic. Though the second *ʾănî* is needed in the non-verbal clause 'I ⌊am⌋ like an evergreen cypress', which otherwise lacks a subject, the repetition of the pronoun still conveys a measure of emphasis in this passage, directing attention to the LORD. The Hebrew for 'It is I who have answered and I will care for him' (*ʾănî ʿānîtî waʾăšûrennû*) is very close to 'I am his Anat and his Asherah', an even more astounding assertion which Wellhausen famously adopted as the true reading (cf. Wolff 1974:233.). That was certainly not what Hosea said, but such a skilled wordsmith would not be unaware of what he almost said.

cypress is now largely lost. However, comparing God to a tree occurs only here in the Old Testament, because it could too readily be misinterpreted as giving validity to the worship of the fertility cults where evergreen trees represented the goddess Asherah. Though identification of the particular tree involved is uncertain (it might also be a fir, a juniper or a pine), it is the fact of its being evergreen that is significant as a symbol of unceasing life and vigour. This bold appropriation of heathen symbolism asserts that what was mistakenly sought in the perverse worship of heathen gods is genuinely found in the LORD himself.

The final line adds the assurance of fruitfulness. ***From me is your fruit found.*** Though evergreen trees were suitable as an image of life, they do not bear fruit and so this comparison has to be supplemented with the promise of fruit. 'From me' echoes contrastively with 'not from me' (8:4), and stresses that the LORD is the true source of his people's vitality and prosperity. This includes both the provision he makes for them and how they use his gifts to honour him. In 'fruit' there is another punning allusion to Ephraim's name (cf. the note to 14:2); in God he has at last achieved his full potential for life and blessing.

REFLECTION

- 'My anger has turned from him' (14:4) states the reality on which the outpouring of divine blessing is based, but it does not explain how this can be. It is not the consequence of some divine whim, nor for that matter does it spring from the changed attitude of the people. It is based on the abiding reality of God's electing love which sovereignly designates those whom he calls to be his own, and on his provision of salvation in Jesus Christ the righteous who 'is the propitiation for our sins' (1 John 2:2). 'In this is love, not that we have come to love God but that he loved us and sent his Son to be the propitiation for our sins' (1 John 4:10). It is at the cross that the spontaneous (14:4) and unconstrained love of God is fully revealed.
- Reliant upon God Ephraim will produce all that God desires from his people. The same requirement of fruitfulness still applies to those who trust God. 'By this my Father is glorified, that you bear much fruit. ... I chose you and appointed you that you should go and bear fruit and that your fruit should last' (John 15:8, 16). This can only be achieved by remembering 'from me' and so seeking the fruit of the Spirit which he produces in renewed hearts and lives (Gal. 5:22-23).

(3) Concluding Advice (14:9)

The concluding verse shares many expressions with language considered to be typical of wisdom literature: wise, understand, discerning (from the same root), know, ways, straight. However, similar ideas are also to be found in Deuteronomy, and are indeed part of the general vocabulary of Israel. For instance, the frequency with which the phrase 'walking in the ways of the LORD' occurs in Deuteronomy (Deut. 8:6; 10:12; 11:22; 19:9; 26:17; 28:9; 30:16) means that it can hardly taken as exclusively characteristic of wisdom.

While 14:9 stands apart from what precedes it, there are still links with the book in general.[44] For instance, reference to the 'wise' contrasts with the folly displayed by Israel in the past (cf. 13:13, and the stupidity of the people). So, though many have assigned this postscript to a later, possibly post-exilic, redactor, the text itself provides no compelling reason for this assessment. The verse displays none of the features of a scribal colophon, a concluding technical note appended with information regarding matters such as the origin or transmission of the text. It may be readily understood as a device with which Hosea concluded his prophetic memoirs, commending them to the attention of readers, present and future, and reminding them of the momentous issues at stake in their reaction to the word which he had conveyed from the LORD.

14:9 Whoever is wise, let him understand these things;
⌞whoever⌟ possesses understanding, let him know them;
for the ways of the LORD are straight
and the righteous will walk in them,
but the rebellious will stumble in them.

The exhortation to study this message and gain insight into it is similar to Psalm 107:43. ***These things*** are the declarations and teaching contained in the prophecy. When Israel obediently followed the LORD, they were characterised as 'wise' and 'possessing understanding' (Deut. 4:6). ***Understand*** (cf. 4:14) goes beyond collection of information to the ability to assess the practical significance of what is observed. It is not a matter of reading or hearing his prophecy that Hosea has in mind, but perception of the message contained in it. That will enable those who possess understanding to ***know***. This is the final

44. Seow announced his agenda in studying this verse in these terms: 'I seek to demonstrate that the language and ideas of this textual unit are not at all incongruent with the rest of the book' (1982:213).

occurrence of one of Hosea's key terms. It too looks beyond factual knowledge to an inner acknowledgement of the truth and dependence on it, and especially on the one who stands behind the truth, the LORD of the covenant himself (cf. 4:1).

The reason why it is important to have the perception which results in practical recognition of the LORD is the blessing that ensues. ***The ways of the LORD*** define the conduct and attitudes he requires from his people, and they constitute the sole mode of living to attract his protection and approval. 'So you shall keep the commandments of the LORD your God, to walk in his ways and to fear him' (Deut. 8:6). In other words, the LORD's ways are defined by the commands of the law, and so, when Israel's conduct was at variance with the covenant, their ways (4:9; 9:8; 10:13; 12:3) became subject to divine condemnation. The LORD whose own conduct is ***straight***/'upright' (Deut. 32:4) is the one who prescribes similar ways for his followers.

In consequence of this the commands of the LORD divide mankind. ***The righteous***, those whose behaviour conforms to the norm instituted by God, ***walk***, that is, 'conduct their lives', with success because they follow what God expects and blesses. But over against the righteous there are set ***the rebellious*** (cf. 7:13; 8:1). In wisdom literature the antithesis to 'righteous' is ordinarily 'wicked' (Stuart 1987:219), but here the use of 'rebellious' suggests a covenantal background. Confronted with the demand to walk in obedience to the LORD, they reject his ways, and so ***stumble***. This reference forms an inclusion round this chapter by echoing 'have stumbled' in 14:1, as well as reflecting earlier passages (4:5; 5:5). Those who wrongheadedly ignore their Overlord's directions are unable to negotiate successfully the route that lies before them in life, and so doom themselves to failure.

REFLECTION

- God demands that we choose. Scripture sets before us the terms of that choice, often in terms of travelling to a destination. One route is prescribed by the LORD. There may be features of the way that is 'straight' which are unwelcome or even inexplicable to us. But there is this guarantee: it is the way which 'leads to life' (Matt. 7:13).
- The only alternative is to follow the 'way that seems right to a man', but we are assured that its end is 'death' (Prov. 14:12). We are also told that 'the way of a fool is right in his own eyes, but a wise man listens to advice' (Prov. 12:15). Here we have the advice given through Hosea. Have we listened?

ABBREVIATIONS

ABD	*Anchor Bible Dictionary.* D. N. Freedman (ed.). 6 volumes. New York: Doubleday, 1992.
ANET	*Ancient Near Eastern Texts Relating to the Old Testament.* J. B. Pritchard (ed.) 3rd edition. Princeton: Princeton University Press, 1969.
AV	Authorised Version (King James) (1611).
BDB	F. Brown, S. R. Driver and C. A. Briggs (eds.), *A Hebrew and English Lexicon of the Old Testament.* Oxford: Clarendon Press, 1907.
BHS	*Biblica Hebraica Stuttgartensia.* K. Elliger and W. Rudolph (eds.). Stuttgart: Deutsche Bibelstiftung, 1977.
ESV	*English Standard Version.* (Anglicized edition) London: Collins, 2002.
GKC	W. Gesenius, E. Kautzsch and A. E. Cowley, *Gesenius Hebrew Grammar.* Oxford: Clarendon Press, 1910 (second edition).
GNB	Good News Bible (= Today's English Version). Glasgow: Collins/Fontana, 1976.
HALOT	*The Hebrew and Aramaic Lexicon of the Old Testament.* L. Koehler, W. Baumgartner and J. J. Stamm. 5 volumes. Brill: Leiden, 1994-1999.
HCSB	The Holman Christian Standard Bible. Nashville: Holman Bible Publishers, 2003.
IBHS	*An Introduction to Biblical Hebrew Syntax.* B. K. Waltke and M. O'Connor. Winona Lake, Indiana: Eisenbrauns, 1990.
Joüon	Joüon, P. *A Grammar of Biblical Hebrew.* Translated and revised by T. Muraoka. Rome: Editrice Pontificio Istituto Biblico, 1991.
LXX	Septuagint, according to *Septuaginta II*, ed. A. Rahlfs. Deutsche Bibelgesellschaft: Stuttgart, 1982.
MT	Massoretic Text (as in *BHS* above).
NASB	New American Standard Bible. LaHabra, California: The Lockman Foundation, 1995.
NEB	The New English Bible: Old Testament. Oxford University Press and Cambridge University Press, 1970.
NIDOTTE	*New International Dictionary of Old Testament Theology and Exegesis.* W. A. VanGemeren (ed.). 5 volumes. Grand Rapids: Zondervan, 1997.

NIV New International Version. (Anglicised edition). London: Hodder and Stoughton, 1984.

NJPS *Tanakh: The Holy Scriptures: The New JPS Translation according to the Traditional Hebrew Text*. Philadelphia: The Jewish Publication Society, 1985.

NKJV New King James Version. Nashville: Thomas Nelson, 1982.

NLT New Living Translation. Wheaton, Illinois: Tyndale House, 1997.

NRSV New Revised Standard Version. New York and Oxford: Oxford University Press, 1989.

REB Revised English Bible. Oxford University Press and Cambridge University Press, 1989.

RSV Revised Standard Version. London: Oxford University Press, 1963.

TDOT *Theological Dictionary of the Old Testament*. G. J. Botterweck, H. Ringgren and H-J. Fabry (eds.) continuing. Grand Rapids: Eerdmans, 1974-.

TLOT *Theological Lexicon of the Old Testament*. E. Jenni and C. Westermann. Peabody: Hendrickson, 1997.

TNIV Today's New International Version. Grand Rapids: Zondervan, 2005.

TWOT *Theological Wordbook of the Old Testament*. R. L. Harris and G. L. Archer (eds.). Chicago: Moody Press, 1980.

WORKS CITED

Adams, Karin. "Metaphor and Dissonance: A Reinterpretation of Hosea 4:13–14." *Journal of Biblical Literature* 127 (2008): 291–305.

Andersen, Francis I., and David N. Freedman. *Hosea*. Anchor Bible. New York: Doubleday, 1980.

Anderson, G. W. "Hosea and Yahweh: God's Love Story (Hosea 1–3)." *Review and Expositor* 72 (1975): 425.

Arnold, Patrick M. "Hosea and the Sin of Gibeah." *Catholic Biblical Quarterly* 51 (1989): 447–60.

Ben Zvi, Ehud. *Hosea*. The Forms of the Old Testament Literature. Grand Rapids: Eerdmans, 2005.

Bergen, Robert D. "Calling Forth Yahweh's Curses: Hosea's Judgment of Israel in 8:1–10:15." *Criswell Theological Review* 7 (1993): 39–50.

Bosma, Carl J. "Creation in Jeopardy: A Warning to Priests (Hosea 4:1–3)." *Calvin Theological Journal* 34 (1999): 64–116.

Bowman, Craig. "Reading the Twelve as One: Hosea 1–3 as an Introduction to the Book of the Twelve (the Minor Prophets)." *Stone-Campbell Journal* 9, no. 1 (2006).

Bright, John. *Covenant and Promise: The Future in the Preaching of the Pre-Exilic Prophets*. London: SCM, 1977.

Calvin, John. *Hosea*. Vol. I of *Commentaries on the Twelve Minor Prophets*. Translated by John Owen. 1846. Repr.. Edinburgh: Banner of Truth, 1986.

Carew, M. Douglas. "To Know or Not to Know: Hosea's Use of *Yd'/D't*." Pages 73–85 in *The Old Testament in the Life of God's People: Essays in Honor of Elmer A. Martens*. Edited by Jon Isaak. Winona Lake, Indiana: Eisenbrauns, 2009.

Chalmers, R. Scott. "Who Is the Real El? A Reconstruction of the Prophet's Polemic in Hosea 12:5a." *Catholic Biblical Quarterly* 68 (2006).

Cheyne, T. K. *Hosea with Notes and Introduction*. The Cambridge Bible for Schools and Colleges. Cambridge: University Press, 1884.

Chisholm, Robert B. Jr. *Handbook on the Prophets*. Grand Rapids: Baker, 2002.

———. "Wordplay in the Eighth-Century Prophets." *Bibliotheca Sacra* 144 (1987): 44–52.

Clines, David J. A. "Hosea 2: Structure and Interpretation." Pages 83–103 in *Studia Biblica 1*. Edited by E. A. Livingstone. Sheffield: SAP, 1978.

Davies, Graham I. *Hosea*. Old Testament Guides. Sheffield: JSOT Press, 1993.

DeRoche, Michael. "The Reversal of Creation in Hosea." *Vetus Testamentum* 31 (1981): 400–409.

———. "Structure, Rhetoric, and Meaning in Hosea IV 4–10." *Vetus Testamentum* 33 (1983): 185–98.

———. "Yahweh's *Rîb* Against Israel: A Reassessment of the So-Called 'Prophetic Lawsuit' in the Preexilic Prophets." *Journal of Biblical Literature* 102 (1983): 563–74.

Dobbie, Robert. "The Text of Hosea IX 8." *Vetus Testamentum* 5 (1955): 199–203.

Fairbairn, Patrick. *The Interpretation of Prophecy*. 1865. Repr.. Second Edition; London: Banner of Truth, 1964.

Fensham, F. Charles. "The Marriage Metaphor in Hosea for the Covenant Relationship Between the Lord and His People (Hos. 1:2–9)." *Journal of Northwest Semitic Languages* 12 (1984): 71–78.

Garrett, Duane A. *Hosea, Joel*. The New American Commentary. Nashville: Broadman and Holman, 1997.

———. "An Introduction to Hosea." *Criswell Theological Review* 7 (1993): 1–14.

Good, Edwin M. "Hosea 5:8–6:6: An Alternative to Alt." *Journal of Biblical Literature* 85 (1966): 273–86.

Harper, William R. *A Critical and Exegetical Commentary on Amos and Hosea*. International Critical Commentary. Edinburgh: T & T Clark, 1905.

Harris, R. Laird. "Why Hebrew *She'ol* Was Translated 'Grave'." Pages 75–92 in *The Making of a Contemporary Translation: New International Version*. Edited by Kenneth L. Barker. London: Hodder and Stoughton, 1987.

Harrison, R. K. *Introduction to the Old Testament*. Leicester, England: Inter-Varsity Press, 1969.

Holladay, William L. "Chiasmus, the Key to Hosea XII 3–6." *Vetus Testamentum* 16 (1966): 53–64.

Howard, Tracy L. "The Use of Hosea 11:1 in Matthew 2:15: An Alternative Solution." *Bibliotheca Sacra* 143 (1986): 314–25.

Hubbard, David Allan. *Hosea: An Introduction and Commentary*. Tyndale Old Testament Commentaries. Leicester: Inter-Varsity Press, 1989.

Irvine, Stuart A. "Enmity in the House of God (Hosea 9:7–9)." *Journal of Biblical Literature* 117 (1998): 645–53.

———. "The Threat of Jezreel." *Catholic Biblical Quarterly* 57 (1995): 494–503.

Johnston, Philip S. *Shades of Sheol: Death and Afterlife in the Old Testament*. Leicester: Inter-Varsity Press, 2002.

Kaiser, Walter C. Jr. "Inner Biblical Exegesis as a Model for Bridging the 'Then' and 'Now' Gap: Hos. 12:1–6." *Journal of the Evangelical Theological Society* 28 (1985): 33–46.

———. *Toward an Old Testament Theology*. Grand Rapids: Zondervan, 1978.

———. *The Uses of the Old Testament in the New*. Chicago: Moody, 1985.

Kaufman, Ivan T. "The Samaria Ostraca: An Early Witness to Hebrew Writing." *Biblical Archaeologist* 45 (1982): 229–39.

Keil, C. F. *The Twelve Minor Prophets*. J. Martin. 1878. Repr.. Grand Rapids: Eerdmans, 1977.

Kelle, Brad E. "Hosea 1–3 in Twentieth-Century Scholarship." *Currents in Biblical Research* 7 (2009): 179–216.

Kidner, Derek. *Love to the Loveless: The Message of Hosea*. The Bible Speaks Today. Leicester: IVP, 1981.

King, Philip J. *Amos, Hosea, Micah: An Archaeological Commentary*. Philadelphia, Pa.: Westminster, 1988.

Laetsch, Theo. *The Minor Prophets*. Saint Louis, Mo.: Concordia, 1956.

Landy, Francis. *Hosea*. Sheffield: Academic Press, 1995.

Liang, Wang-Huei. "Is She Not My Wife, and Am I Not Her Husband?" *Horizons in Biblical Theology* 31 (2009): 1–11.

Lundbom, Jack R. "Contentious Priests and Contentious People in Hosea IV 1–10." *Vetus Testamentum* 36 (1986): 52–70.

———. "Double-Duty Subject in Hosea VIII 5." *Vetus Testamentum* 25 (1975): 228–30.

———. "Poetic Structure and Prophetic Rhetoric in Hosea." *Vetus Testamentum* 29 (1979): 300–308.

Macintosh, A. A. *A Critical and Exegetical Commentary on Hosea*. International Critical Commentary. Edinburgh: T & T Clark, 1997.

Mackay, John L. *A Study Commentary on Isaiah. Volume 1: Chapters 1–39*. Darlington: Evangelical Press, 2008.

Mays, James Luther. *Hosea: A Commentary*. Old Testament Library. London: SCM, 1969.

McComiskey, Thomas E. "Hosea." Pages 1–237 in *The Minor Prophets: An Exegetical and Expository Commentary*. Ed. T. E. McComiskey. Grand Rapids: Baker, 1992.

———. "Prophetic Irony in Hosea 1.4? A Study of the Collocation פקד על and Its Implications for the Fall of Jehu's Dynasty." *Journal for the Study of the Old Testament* 58 (1993): 93–101.

McFall, Leslie. "A Translation Guide to the Chronological Data in Kings and Chronicles." *Bibliotheca Sacra* 148 (1991): 3–45.

Morris, Leon. *The Apostolic Preaching of the Cross*. London: Tyndale, 1955.

———. *Testaments of Love: A Study of Love in the Bible*. Grand Rapids: Eerdmans, 1981.

Moughtin-Mumby, Sharon. *Sexual and Marital Metaphors in Hosea, Jeremiah, Isaiah, and Ezekiel*. Oxford: University Press, 2008.

O'Connor, M. "The Pseudosorites: A Type of Paradox in Hebrew Verse." *JSOTSup* 40 (1987): 161–72.

Ortlund, Raymond C. Jr. *Whoredom: God's Unfaithful Wife in Biblical Theology*. New Studies in Biblical Theology. Leicester: Apollos, 1996.

Paul, Shalom M. "The Image of the Oven and the Cake in Hosea VII 4–10." *Vetus Testamentum* 18 (1968): 114–20.

Pusey, E. B. *The Minor Prophets, with a Commentary, Explanatory and Practical*. New York: Funk and Wagnalls, 1885.

Rooker, Mark F. "The Use of the Old Testament in Hosea." *Criswell Theological Review* 7 (1993): 51–66.

Rowley, H. H. "The Marriage of Hosea." Pages 66–97 in *Men of God*. London: Nelson, 1963.

Scanlin, Harold P. "The Emergence of the Writing Prophets in Israel in the Mid-Eighth Century." *Journal of the Evangelical Theological Society* 21 (1978): 303–13.

Seow, C.L. "Hosea 14:10 and the Foolish People Motif." *Catholic Biblical Quarterly* 44 (1982): 212–24.

Shea, William H. "The Date and Significance of the Samaria Ostraca." *Israel Exploration Journal* 27 (1977): 16–27.

Smith, Duane A. "Kinship and Covenant in Hosea 11:1–4." *Horizons in Biblical Theology* 16 (1994): 41–53.

Stuart, Douglas. *Hosea–Jonah*. Word Biblical Commentary. Waco, Texas: Word, 1987.

Thiele, Edwin R. *The Mysterious Numbers of the Hebrew Kings*. Rev. ed. Grand Rapids: Zondervan, 1983.

Van Leeuwen, Cornelis. "Meaning and Structure of Hosea X 1–8." *Vetus Testamentum* 53 (2003): 367–78.

Van Groningen, Gerard. *From Creation to Consummation*. Vol. II. Sioux Centre, Iowa: Dordt College Press, 2003.

Vos, Geerhardus. *Biblical Theology: Old and New Testaments*. 1948. Repr.. Edinburgh: Banner of Truth, 1975.

Walker, Peter W. L. "The Land and Jesus Himself." Pages 100–120 in *The Land of Promise: Biblical, Theological and Contemporary Perspectives*. Edited by Philip Johnston. Peter Walker. Leicester: Apollos, 2000.

Wijngaards, J. "Death and Resurrection in Covenantal Context (Hos VI 2)." *Vetus Testamentum* 17 (1967): 226–39.

Willis, John T. "The Expression *Be 'Acharith Hayyamin* in the Old Testament." *Restoration Quarterly* 22 (1979): 54–71.

Wolff, Hans Walter. *Hosea: A Commentary on the Book of the Prophet Hosea*. Hermeneia. Philadelphia: Fortress, 1974.

Wyrtzen, David B. "The Theological Center of the Book of Hosea." *Bibliotheca Sacra* 141 (1984): 315–29.

Yee, Gale A. "Hosea.". In *The New Interpreter's Bible*, vol. 7. Edited by Leander E. Keck. Et al. Nashville: Abingdon, 1996.

Young, Edward J. *An Introduction to the Old Testament*. 1949. Repr.. Grand Rapids, Michigan: Eerdmans, 1984.

———. *Old Testament Prophecy*. Toronto: Gospel Witness, 1965.

Young, Rodger C. "Tables of Reign Lengths from the Hebrew Court Recorders." *Journal of the Evangelical Theological Society* 48 (2005): 225–48.

———. "When Was Samaria Captured? The Need for Precision in Biblical Chronologies." *Journal of the Evangelical Theological Society* 47 (2004): 577–95.

SUBJECT INDEX

Achor 97
Adam 196
Adonai 338
adoption 292
adultery 51, 113
Ahab 340
Alt, Albrecht 169
altar 236, 270
Amaziah, priest of Bethel 143
Amos 12, 18, 143
Aram 14–15, 17, 173, 200, 287, 336
Asherah 148
Assyria 15–18, 121, 167, 173, 214, 223, 246, 299, 310, 320, 365
Baal 33, 81, 85, 89, 100, 340
  love of 114
Baal-Peor 258
Baals 93, 101, 294
Beth-Arbel 287
Beth-Awen 153, 168, 274
Bethel 143, 153, 288, 325
betrothal 104
Booths, feast of 92, 242, 257, 332
bull-calf 228–29, 231, 340–41
Canaan 328
  ideology 34, 87, 92, 148
  religion 33
  worship 50, 93, 119, 149, 219, 243, 270, 318, 341
chiasm 43, 268, 277
cities of the plain 304
covenant
  curse 31
  divine 30, 103, 196, 224
  lawsuit 127
cult prostitute 33, 50, 150
David 120
Decalogue 130, 343
divorce 75
Egypt 98, 214, 239, 246, 248, 291–92, 299, 310, 332, 336, 343
Elijah 8, 82, 340
Elohim 63
Ephraim 161, 339, 358
Esau 322
Exodus 217, 291, 336, 343
Gibeah 168, 255, 279
Gilead 197, 335
Gilgal 152, 263, 335
God
  anger of 230, 305, 368
  compassion of 63, 80, 305
  in control of history 31
  election 35
  Holy One 306
  love of 96, 113, 368
  wrath of 305
Gomer 50, 54, 110
Gomorrah 304
guilt 360
heal 296, 368
Hezekiah 68
Hosea 45
  marriage 19
  ministry, dates of 10
  from the north 18–19
  support for 20–21
  use of history 31, 316
Hoshea 14, 46, 204, 216, 272, 315, 320
idolatry 154, 228, 340, 372

Israel
early history of................52, 98
restoration of 38–40, 66, 68, 120, 309, 367
Jacob
the nation.............................283
the patriarch.................322, 336
Jareb 174, 275
Jehu 9, 57
Jeroboam I................................8
Jeroboam II 11, 47, 56, 126
Jezreel 56, 58–59, 71–72, 108
Josiah......................................68
Judah ...19, 62, 70, 152, 170, 173, 199, 283, 318–19
knowledge of the LORD........105, 130, 138–39, 184, 193, 295, 344, 374
Lebanon.................................369
Living God 70
love.......................................116
marriage 48
Massoretic Text........................23
paragraph marker...................23
vocalised..............................23
Menahem........14, 161, 163, 173, 208, 233
Messiah 39, 71, 120
Mizpah 158
Nathan 74
Omri, dynasty of......................57
Pekah.......14, 161, 163, 173, 197, 204, 208
Pekahiah..........................14, 204
Peniel....................................323
people of God..........................65
Peshitta 23
priests 136, 142, 198, 274
prophets.....8, 137, 192, 251, 294, 333, 337
Ramah 168
remember.............................. 203
repentance...................... 181, 362
resurrection............................ 184
Salamanu 287
Samaria.. 202, 229, 231, 276, 360
date of fall of......................... 15
Ostraca............................... 208
Samirina 15
sarcasm 253
Sargon II............................... 276
Septuagint................................ 21
Shalman................................ 287
Shalmaneser III..................... 287
Shalmaneser V.............. 276, 287
shame (Baal).......................... 259
Shechem 198
Sheol.................................... 354
Shittim 160n41
Sodom.................................. 304
steadfast love 105, 129, 191, 193, 284, 327
structure of the prophecy....... 43, 125, 189, 315
stumble 163, 362
Tabor 159
Targum 23
Thiele, Edwin R.
chronology 10
third day.......................... 183–84
Tiglath-Pileser III 15, 167
treaty, international........ 273, 320
Tyre 261
Vulgate 23
whoredom... 50, 80, 145, 147–48, 161–62, 244
wilderness........ 79, 96, 257, 333, 345, 359
Yahweh 63, 65
Zechariah................................ 13

SCRIPTURE QUOTATIONS

GENESIS
2:23-24 48
2:24 112
3:6 152
4:12 66
4:14 266
4:19 50
8:1 203
22:17 69
27:28 369
27:35 316
28:15 327
32:28 323
32:30 323
41:52 265
49:3 323
49:25 263
EXODUS
3:14 65
3:15 ....111n46
4:6 ....111n46
4:22 297
4:22-23 292
6:7 65
10:25 89
19:4 223
19:6 139
20:2 332
20:3 ....83, 114, 343
20:8 203
20:14 48
20:24 101
21:10 79
22:28 140
23:13 101
24:3 98
24:7 ....98, 191
32:4, 8 344
33:19 ....35, 298
34:6-7 ....61, 129n4
34:15 48
LEVITICUS
18:26-28 246
19:17 136
23:1 91
25:23 245
NUMBERS
12:2 49
25:2-3 258
DEUTERONOMY
4:6 374
4:29-30 179
4:30 86
4:35 ....34, 83
5:12 203
7:7-8 298
7:8 217
8:6 375
8:17 330
11:1 116
11:12, 14-15 88
11:17 116
17:12 136
17:15 226
24:4 75
24:14 329
27:17 170
28:47-48 79
28:49 223
28:51 245
29:23 304
29:29 306
30:19 31
32:6 240
32:10 258
32:10-11 298

32:35 ... 163
32:39 ... 183
JOSHUA
24:14 ... 52
1 SAMUEL
8:5-6 ... 350
15:22 ... 166
2 SAMUEL
2:8 ... 100n42
23:3-4 ... 227
1 KINGS
3:7 ... 291
3:8 ... 70
12:28 ... 230
12:32 ... 242
14:28 ... 344
18:19 ... 137
18:21 ... 9
19:18 ... 341
2 KINGS
10:30 ... 57
14:25 ... 11
14:25-27 ... 201
15:19 ... 14, 173
15:29 ... 176
16:3-4 ... 319
17:4 ... 320
17:5 ... 339
17:6 ... 176
17:13-14 ... 192
19:3 ... 353
1 CHRONICLES
8:33 ... 100
8:34 ... 100
9:3 ... 39
14:7 ... 100
2 CHRONICLES
12:5 ... 145
28:20-21 ... 177
28:22 ... 176
32:8 ... 64
EZRA
8:35 ... 68
JOB
17:6 ... 79
PSALMS
10:8 ... 366
11:4 ... 161
18:47 ... 148
20:7 ... 101, 365
27:5 ... 302
31:6 ... 146
33:16-17 ... 63
37:34 ... 327
46:1 ... 351
50:15 ... 209
52:7 ... 249
81:3 ... 168
81:10 ... 347
81:11-12 ... 179
85:12-13 ... 285
89:34 ... 357
100:3 ... 100, 240
103:2 ... 327, 348
106:35 ... 211
108:14 ... 351
PROVERBS
9:9 ... 217
9:17 ... 152
11:3 ... 146
12:4 ... 173
12:15 ... 375
13:15 ... 86
14:12 ... 375
14:31 ... 331
20:1 ... 209
26:2 ... 224
31:4-5 ... 209
ECCLESIASTES
10:16-17 ... 209
SONG OF SOLOMON
8:7 ... 112

ISAIAH
1:18 75
7:3 55
7:4, 5 .... 14n4
8:3 55
9:5 137
25:8 357
26:16 180
30:1-2 236
46:10 194
50:1 75
53:10 360
53:11 361
63:9 308
JEREMIAH
2:2-3 98
2:5 266
3:1 112
3:20 112
4:14 222
6:16 99
14:10 204
15:3 57
22:3 227
23:13 254
23:32 254
31:12, 14 121
LAMENTATIONS
3:25 328
3:33 281
EZEKIEL
33:17 251
DANIEL
2:21 59
4:17 59
AMOS
2:6 12
3:2 298
5:5 153
5:7 12
5:11-12 12
5:13 136
5:24 105
6:7 155
JONAH
2:8 217
ZECHARIAH
10:9 59
11:15 .... 111n46
MALACHI
1:2 251
MATTHEW
2:15 292
6:33 95
7:13 375
7:21-23 225
9:13 195
10:16 217
10:25 .... 100n42
12:8 195
12:34 102
15:14 157
21:30 194
23:39 267
24:12 141
24:24 255
27:46 109
LUKE
6:38 284
8:18 134
9:23 286
12:19 146
12:48 31
16:14-15 331
JOHN
1:14 308
1:29 361
8:39 338
10:10 98
10:16 40
14:15 240
14:18 367

15:1 ... 278
15:7 ... 303
15:8, 16 ... 373
17:3 ... 186

ACTS
14:17 ... 334
20:35 ... 146
26:14 ... 86

ROMANS
1:22 ... 289
2:4 ... 189
2:6 ... 321
3:2 ... 334
6:19 ... 141
7:18-19 ... 285
8:23 ... 328
8:29 ... 242
11:18 ... 278
11:20-21 ... 118, 278
11:29 ... 357
12:9 ... 266

1 CORINTHIANS
1:4 ... 327
10:6 ... 47
10:12 ... 200
11:24 ... 348
15:4 ... 184
15:33 ... 157, 266
15:55 ... 355

2 CORINTHIANS
1:12 ... 217
3:5 ... 351
4:6 ... 140
5:10 ... 278
5:20 ... 194
7:1 ... 106
10:18 ... 226
11:3 ... 55

GALATIANS
2:20 ... 367
3:5 ... 200
5:15 ... 176
5:25 ... 106
6:7-8 ... 236

EPHESIANS
2:2 ... 342
2:8-9 ... 327
2:14-15 ... 109
5:1 ... 242
5:2 ... 105
5:26 ... 55
5:27 ... 55
6:11 ... 367

PHILIPPIANS
2:8 ... 109
3:14 ... 286

COLOSSIANS
2:10 ... 140

1 TIMOTHY
1:20 ... 179
6:17 ... 82

TITUS
1:1 ... 140

HEBREWS
6:12 ... 242
10:31 ... 348

JAMES
4:7 ... 367

1 PETER
1:3 ... 242
1:5 ... 338
1:17 ... 321
1:18-19 ... 218

1 JOHN
2:2 ... 373
2:4 ... 226
3:1 ... 73
3:4 ... 141
4:1 ... 255
4:10 ... 117, 373

JUDE
7 ... 307

REVELATION

3:17....................................146
6:16-17 361
19:16......................................59
21:27....................................106

HEBREW WORDS

ʾādām 341
ʾāhēb 112
ʾāwen 153
ʾĕmet 129n4
ʾên 129
ʾwn 330
ʾôn 330
ʾāpâ 206
ʾîš 85
ʾāšam 152, 178, 360
ʾāšûr 346
ʾetnān 244
ʾetnâ 92n36, 244
baʿal 100
bošet 259
gāʾal 354
gûr 219n26
zēker 326
zānâ 244
zônâ 51
zənûnîm 50
ḥesed 105, 129, 191, 193
yākaḥ 169n48
yāsar 169n48
lûṣ 207n16
nāʾap 206
nablût 90
nōḥam 355
sûr 219
ʿôd 111n46
ʿāwōn 202, 330
pādâ 217, 354
pāqad 56
rîb 76, 128
šûb 85, 120, 178, 181, 219, 362, 368, 370
šēm 326

Other Commentaries from John L. Mackay

mentor
Exodus
A MENTOR COMMENTARY
John L. Mackay

Exodus:

A Mentor Commentary

John L. Mackay

The book of Exodus is about a journey: a journey out of Egypt, but more particularly a journey from a land where God's power, sovereignty and continuing interest in his people could be easily questioned, to a place where God dwelt in the midst of his people. Exodus describes God's power, his redemption of his people, his covenant requirements at Sinai, and the rules of his worship.

John L. Mackay interacts with other scholars in either text or footnotes. In addition to exploring the meaning of the text he examines the chonology, authorship, composition and structure of Exodus. In addition, at the end of each section he provides a reflective comment.

'Professor Mackay has produced a strong commentary on the Book of Exodus. It is filled with excellent material for the pastor and the serious-minded Bible student. I especially appreciate the work on application that is normally so difficult to draw out of historical literature. I recommend this work highly. It is a valuable tool for the study of this most important period in Israel's history.'

John D. Currid,
Professor of Old Testament,
Reformed Theological Seminary, Charlotte, North Carolina

'A tour de force of conservative evangelical exposition. Massively researched, painstakingly explained, theologically nuanced, reliably expounded, simply expressed and sensitivly applied; this volume will be of considerable value to all preachers and Bible students. For accessible and scholarly comment Mackay's work should quickly become the standard evangelical work on the Book of Exodus.'

Stephen Dray,
Minister, Ferndale Baptist Church, Southend-on-Sea

ISBN 978-1-85792-614-9

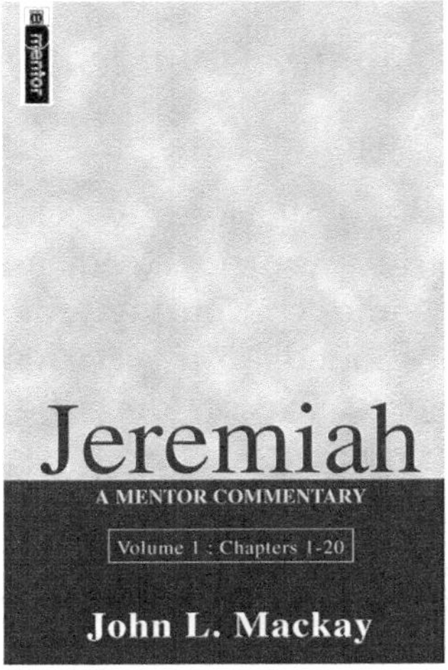
mentor
Jeremiah
A MENTOR COMMENTARY
Volume 1 : Chapters 1-20
John L. Mackay

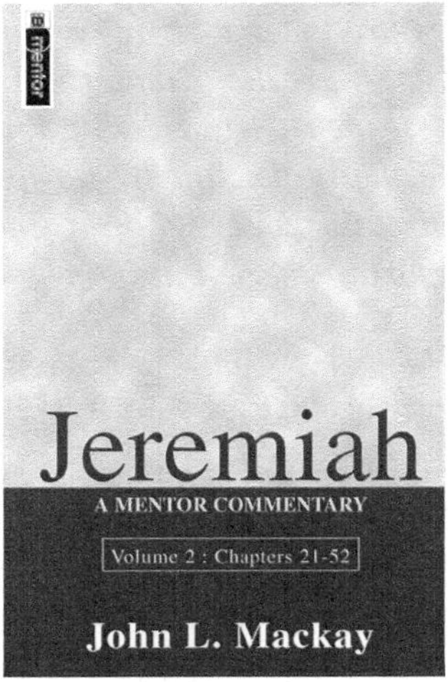
mentor
Jeremiah
A MENTOR COMMENTARY
Volume 2 : Chapters 21-52
John L. Mackay

Jeremiah Vol. 1 & 2

A Mentor Commentary

John L. Mackay

Professor Mackay's commentary on Jeremiah is trebly welcome: first, from his earlier work on Exodus (in this series) we know that he will take the highest view of Scripture as the Word of God, ...secondly, he argues cogently for Jeremiah as author of the whole, contending that the book as we have it represents written records contemporary with the prophet's preaching... Thirdly, from the start he is concerned to handle the book of Jeremiah, not as an anthology, but as unfolding a unified message. Lovers of Hebrew will find a kindred spirit in Professor Mackay. Those without Hebrew will find a patient teacher leaving no stone unturned to make the word of God plain.

ALEC MOTYER

This eagerly awaited commentary on one of the longest and most taxing books of the Old Testament fulfils every expectation... The message of Jeremiah's forty-year ministry is here firmly rooted in the Old Testament history as a message from the Lord to his ancient people; but its abiding relevance is also brought out in Professor Mackay's careful application of the material. This will quickly become an indispensable tool for anyone wishing to study and preach from the Book of Jeremiah.

IAIN D. CAMPBELL,
Minister of Point Free Church, Isle of Lewis

...a first class explanation of the prophet... It is certain to become the first 'port of call' in my studies of the book, ...he has the ability to uncover the significance of the original message in such a way as to leave the application (almost) transparent.

STEPHEN DRAY,
Minister, Ferndale Baptist Church, Southend-on-Sea

ISBN 978-1-85792-937-9 (Volume 1)
ISBN 978-1-85792-938-6 (Volume 2)

MENTOR
Lamentations
A MENTOR COMMENTARY
John L. Mackay

Lamentations

A Mentor Commentary

John L. Mackay

The five chapters of Lamentations may be easily overlooked. Not only is it brief, but it is also sandwiched between the two giants of Old Testament prophecy, Jeremiah and Ezekiel. Lamentations also deals with realities which we rather wish were not discussed - consequently the book is little studied. However, although there much here to challenge faith, there is much that builds it up. Lamentations was not written in the first instance to serve as warning to others, or to even keep alive the present memory of past suffering, it is the present that dominates the thought of the book.

And in that present are overiding thoughts - 'has God left us?'; 'Have we blown our chance as God's covenant people?' 'Is there a way forward towards the restoration?'

A popular view today is that Lamentations is a dreary book with nothing to say to today's society. The reality is that it could not be more relevant, nor more authentic.

ISBN 978-1-84550-363-5

FOCUS • ON • THE • BIBLE
HAGGAI, ZECHARIAH & MALACHI
GOD'S RESTORED PEOPLE
'Professor Mackay has done it again! ...this is a fine work.'
John Currid
JOHN L. MACKAY

Haggai, Zechariah & Malachi

God's Restored People

John L. Mackay

The ministry of Haggai, Zechariah and Malachi is a record of how God deals with people he has restored as they try to translate their basic loyalty to him into practical action. Restoring their temple and the physical trappings of their ravaged kingdom was not an end in itself. God was, and is, primarily interested in obedient minds and wills in people who have a heart for God.

The term 'Minor Prophets' may suggest they are unimportant, which is anything but true. This exposition is really first-class. John Mackay focuses on the text's meaning and the books' New Testament fulfilment in Christ. While his Old Testament scholarship is very evident, he avoids technical language. Many of the study questions provide valuable projects for the reader.

GEOFFREY GROGAN (1925-2011),
Late Principal Emeritus of Glasgow Bible College

Professor Mackay has done it again! This is an excellent piece of work on three 'minor' prophets that are not well known in the church today. Mackay's commentary is a must read for pastors and serious Bible students who want to become familiar with what these three prophets have to say to the church today... this is a fine work.

JOHN CURRID,
Carl McMurray Professor of Old Testament,
Reformed Theological Seminary, Charlotte, North Carolina

... eminently readable and soundly evangelical ... aimed at encouraging the reader to think deeply about the message of the text for today... Anyone who buys this book will have a treasure house of good things. It will certainly help any preacher and be valuable for personal devotions, but it could also be used for church Bible study groups.

EVANGELICAL TIMES

ISBN 978-1-84550-618-6

Christian Focus Publications

publishes books for all ages

Our mission statement –

STAYING FAITHFUL

In dependence upon God we seek to impact the world through literature faithful to His infallible Word, the Bible. Our aim is to ensure that the Lord Jesus Christ is presented as the only hope to obtain forgiveness of sin, live a useful life and look forward to heaven with Him.

REACHING OUT

Christ's last command requires us to reach out to our world with His gospel. We seek to help fulfil that by publishing books that point people towards Jesus and help them develop a Christ-like maturity. We aim to equip all levels of readers for life, work, ministry and mission.

Books in our adult range are published in three imprints.

Christian Focus contains popular works including biographies, commentaries, basic doctrine and Christian living. Our children's books are also published in this imprint.

Mentor focuses on books written at a level suitable for Bible College and seminary students, pastors, and other serious readers. The imprint includes commentaries, doctrinal studies, examination of current issues and church history.

Christian Heritage contains classic writings from the past.

Christian Focus Publications Ltd
Geanies House, Fearn,
Ross-shire, IV20 1TW, Scotland, United Kingdom
info@christianfocus.com

www.christianfocus.com